# The Politics of Human Rights

# The Politics of Human Rights

Andrew Vincent

OXFORD
UNIVERSITY PRESS

# OXFORD

UNIVERSITY PRESS

Great Clarendon Street, Oxford OX2 6DP

Oxford University Press is a department of the University of Oxford.
It furthers the University's objective of excellence in research, scholarship,
and education by publishing worldwide in

Oxford New York

Auckland Cape Town Dar es Salaam Hong Kong Karachi
Kuala Lumpur Madrid Melbourne Mexico City Nairobi
New Delhi Shanghai Taipei Toronto

With offices in

Argentina Austria Brazil Chile Czech Republic France Greece
Guatemala Hungary Italy Japan Poland Portugal Singapore
South Korea Switzerland Thailand Turkey Ukraine Vietnam

Oxford is a registered trade mark of Oxford University Press
in the UK and in certain other countries

Published in the United States
by Oxford University Press Inc., New York

© Andrew Vincent 2010

The moral rights of the author have been asserted
Database right Oxford University Press (maker)

First published 2010

British Library Cataloguing in Publication Data

Data available

Library of Congress Cataloging in Publication Data

Data available

Typeset by SPI Publisher Services, Pondicherry, India
Printed in Great Britain
on acid-free paper by
Clays Ltd., St Ives Plc

ISBN 978–0–19–923897–2 (Pbk.)
      978–0–19–923896–5 (Hbk.)

1 3 5 7 9 10 8 6 4 2

# ☐ PREFACE

This book derives from the substance of an MA seminar that I have taught for the last five years on human rights. My thanks go to the many postgraduates who have participated enthusiastically and critically in the course. Enjoyable and creative discussions over the years have allowed me to sharpen my arguments. The book overall has a twofold purpose. Primarily, there is an introductory component to the text which is designed, for the most part, for those who are not that familiar with the domain of human rights. This component focuses on themes such as the language of rights, natural rights, and natural law, and the more recent developments of human rights language in international law and politics. However, the overall discussion of the book is couched in a polemical interpretation of human rights, which situates them in the realm of politics. There is therefore a self-conscious attempt to construct a political theory of human rights. The book has been worked on gradually for a number of years, but it finally began to take shape whilst on a visiting research fellowship in the National Europe Centre and Humanities Research Centre, at the Australian National University in Canberra 2009. My sincere thanks go to these admirable research centres, and more particularly to Simon Bronitt (formerly head of the National Europe Centre) for his immensely enthusiastic hospitality and collegiality. The research centres at the Australian National University have always retained a strong place in my affections. They are the jewels in the crown of the Australian National University. They provide an invaluable, creative, and supportive environment where ideas can flow and be discussed in an open critical manner. Whilst working on the book, I have also benefited from the feedback from a number of university audiences in Sheffield, Nottingham, London Metropolitan, Oxford, Manchester Metropolitan, the London School of Economics, Reading, the National University of Singapore, the Australian National University, Wollongong and Otago. I have also been able to discuss the ideas with numerous political theory colleagues over the years, although I would particularly like to thank David Boucher, Michael Freeden, Rex Martin, Matt Sleat, Vicki Spencer, and, of course, my patient editor Dominic Byatt. However, no one but myself is responsible for the position taken in this text.

The final completion of the manuscript and its first polishing was done in my eldest daughter's house in France in August 2009. My deep gratitude to Lisa, Stephane, and my grandchildren Laura and Luca, for providing such a warm and supportive family environment—and of course for putting up with my writing preoccupations. I would also like to thank my daughter Rachael for many searching conversations on the theme of international politics, and finally my wife Mary and our other children Sara and Jason (and their partners) for vital companionship.

Andrew Vincent
Sheffield University

# ☐ CONTENTS

# ☐ LIST OF ABBREVIATIONS

ASEAN    Association of Southeast Asian Nations
CHR      Commission on Human Rights
ECOSOC   Economic and Social Council
ECHR     European Convention of Human Rights and Fundamental Freedoms
ICC      International Criminal Court
ICCPR    International Covenant on Civil and Political Rights
ICESCR   International Covenant on Economic, Social, and Cultural Rights
ILO      International Labour Organization
OSCE     Organization for Security and Cooperation in Europe
UDHR     Universal Declaration of Human Rights
UN       United Nations

# Introduction

There has been an enormous amount written on human rights in recent years. Studies on the topic have proliferated across a range of disciplinary spheres, such as international normative theory, international law, moral philosophy, and anthropology, to name but a few. The present book is unusual, if not heterodox. Primarily, the central argument runs counter to many of the prevailing currents of thought on the topic. It argues, in effect, that an understanding of human rights must focus primarily on politics and we should try if possible to avoid the overt languages of morality and legality or, at least, try to view such languages circumspectly. As such, the book aims to offer a distinctive interpretation of the way in which human rights function in a political context. However, this latter argument should provide no solace for those who wish to approach human rights via political science. Politics is viewed as a more multifaceted and eclectic idea than in most standard political science manuals.

Further, the notion of political philosophy deployed here is also idiosyncratic. A political philosophy of human rights is not a moral philosophy of human rights. A political philosophy of human rights, in my own usage, is necessarily eclectic. To grasp human rights is to engage seriously with historical, legal, ideological, political, as well as moral phenomena. It is not simply a question of imposing abstracted meta-ethical arguments onto an unsuspecting political or legal world. Politics is nonetheless seen as the neglected dimension of human rights studies. However, if the reader sees political philosophy as simply another way of addressing normative ethics or just the rigorous application of moral argumentation to politics, they will be disappointed by the present work. The book is designed to move away from the moral imperialism of much contemporary political philosophy. It is a mistake to argue that humans, by the mere fact of being human, have rights, and that humans are in some way morally considerable in themselves, regardless of social or political context. My argument is that with the development of human association over the last century particularly, certain standards of civil behaviour have become, for a certain sector of humanity, slowly, painfully, and imperfectly more customary. The political form which most adequately captures this overlapping momentum is the civil state. These standards of civility have though gradually extended to a broader comity of states—that is overlapping civil communities. Standards of civility, particularly during the second half of the twentieth century, have gradually extended. Citizen rights have, in effect, become mentors of human rights. This is not a liberal or constitutional idealism, it is rather a registering of the underlying ethos of human rights. What is important here is that we should try not to isolate human rights from debates about the state tradition. The Universal Declaration of Human Rights (UDHR 1948) arose in a particular historical context and reflects inevitably arguments about the character of the state tradition. It was primarily a political document, not a legal or moral one. It was and still is wholly reliant upon the constitutional self-limitation capacity of the civil state. Human rights, at their best, are an ideal civil state vocabulary. What we observe in late twentieth-century debates about civil and social human rights is the continuous dialectic of the civil state itself. Human rights are thus intimately part of self-imposed struggle at the core of the civil state tradition.

One important misapprehension (as indicated above) which often springs out of the discourse of human rights—and consequently embodies a strong trace of an older natural law argument—concerns the idea of the moral universality of human rights. Human rights are often seen as global in character and external to both the state and politics. Their *modus operandi* is that they are not tied to any particular political regime. They therefore pertain in any situation. The idea of moral universality is also linked to the claim that human rights act as external regulative ideals, which lay down standards for all states, from outside their particular legal cultures. The problem with this claim—which will be returned to on many occasions in the book—is that it gives a far too unrealistic and optimistic a reading of human rights which, although rhetorically uplifting and analytically fascinating, is not particularly illuminating. It is a reading of human rights which is also frequently glossed within philosophical, moral, and religious literature. My argument is focused on the proposition that there are *no* external regulative moral or religious standards for human rights. The more abstracted approaches—utilizing arguments drawn particularly from contemporary moral philosophy—to human rights are thus essentially in error. There are however certain subtle normative political standards which are part of what a state (or state-like entity) is; thus, by definition, they are still not external to the state tradition. The state tradition is thus taken as central to an understanding of politics. Human rights, as integral to the state tradition, must therefore be seen as intrinsically political.

Contrary to intellectual trends on global politics, the fundamental figure in politics is still taken to be the state. However the languages of the state are both immensely complex and potentially ambiguous. Thus, the claim that politics is the key to understanding human rights is also both complex and indefinite and contains a number of possible interpretive permutations.

Further, the idiom of law—particularly in terms of human rights—is taken to follow from the configurations of both politics and therefore the state. It will be argued that politics and statehood come prior, conceptually, to the practice of law, both international and domestic. Law, and particularly the rule of law, follow from an understanding of statehood. The state tradition is envisaged as a comparatively recent historical phenomenon. It has only really been significant for the last 300 years and far more important for the last 150 years, in certain contexts. The practice and idea of the state (and thus politics) is therefore taken to be relatively unique in terms of the diverse forms of human collective association.

A number of critical distinctions are made in the course of the book within the concept of the state. In large part, two perspectives are kept ideally distinct: the organic nation state and the civil state. The former is predominantly taken as the location of the important vernaculars of sovereignty, conceptions of power, nationalism, self-determination, ethnicity, and culture. The latter is taken as the location of sustained consideration of constitutionalism, public law, self-limitation, and ultimately human rights. This distinction between state traditions is more pedagogical than actual. It is not conceptually sharp or decisive in practice. Consequently there are considerable overlaps between the two traditions. This latter distinction is though nonetheless immensely important for comprehending the *mentality* of human rights.

In brief outline, chapter 1 analyses the generic word 'right' and then concentrates on a distinction between objective and subjective ideas of right. This latter distinction carries some historical baggage and will jump a little ahead of the discussion to issues around natural right and natural law. The discussion then hones in on the language of rights. This latter examination entails an assessment of a number of conceptual issues. A distinction is drawn between the *sense* and *type* of right; the *sense* focuses on the word itself and what it is trying to connote, the *type* of right focuses on the various and quite diverse classifications, within rights-based literature. The sense and type discussions do though inevitably overlap. The discussion concludes with my own classification and a brief overview of my own understanding of rights. Chapter 2 sketches the complex debates over the origin of the concept right. Thus, natural rights, by default, become a central focus. Discussing the origin of the concept of natural right inevitably entails an account of the concept of natural law, with which it has a tangled connection. The category of natural law is though more complex and variegated than appears at first glance. A number of distinctions are acknowledged in the course of this discussion between ancient and modern, Catholic and Protestant, and religious and secular senses of natural law. However, certain senses of natural law do unquestionably have links with natural rights argument. My own interpretation of this latter issue is that we should not try to draw too rigid a distinction between natural law and natural right. The relation between these terms has often been contingent upon historical and political circumstances. However, by the seventeenth century, and more particularly by the eighteenth century, there was a definite, if subtle, change in accent which gave much greater significance to subjective natural rights, rather than objective natural law. The discussion then outlines a distinction between two senses of natural right in the seventeenth and eighteenth centuries, that is the maximal and minimal senses. It also tracks, very briefly, through some of the political consequences which flowed from these.

The discussion then turns to the questions: why did natural rights vocabulary all but collapse by the mid-nineteenth century, in Europe particularly, and further, why did human rights discourse arise so forcibly in the post-1945 era? The first answer, pursued in chapter 3, focuses on certain potent changes in the discussion of the concept of 'nature' and further the remorseless rise of the state in the nineteenth century. It is then argued that dynamic changes in the concept of nature affected a wide range of disciplines and academic vocabularies. The full answer to the second question lies in the subtle but unstable conjunction of the power of the modern state with the vocabularies of nationalism, racism, and ethnicity, which had developed significantly from the mid-nineteenth century. This conjunction created the potentiality, in certain specific circumstances, for the very modern phenomenon of genocide—examined in detail in chapter 4. Genocide is viewed as the predominantly state-based, intentional, bureaucratic, industrial-level extermination of a people on racial, ethnic, or national grounds. The reality of genocide, in terms of its intimate links with the nation state, is seen to create the groundwork for a human rights culture in 1948. Pre-1939 states, in general, were not inclined at all towards human rights. Post-1945 many had been softened up for its reception through the knowledge of genocide. Human rights could admittedly also be sold to states on other levels, namely, in terms of their latent advantages for foreign or security policy. This was certainly the case during the cold war period. However, these other levels on their own were not enough to initiate the 1948 Declaration. The grim realities of genocide—so closely tied to the nation state—created a predisposition for action.

Chapter 5 is a housekeeping discussion. It concentrates predominantly on elaborating the conventional structural framework within which human rights thinking has been conducted since 1948, particularly in terms of the oft-labelled 'generational arguments'. These latter arguments provide, on one level, a pedagogical device to outline the conceptual architecture of the concept of human rights. No firm stand is taken, at this stage, on the veracity of the generations issue, although a number of arguments are offered which raise doubts over any inflexible distinctions being made between these categories of right. Chapter 6 then argues that the state tradition stands in a complex and paradoxical relation with human rights during the second half of the twentieth century, to the present day. The baseline argument concerns the paradox of the state being both subject and object of human rights. The state tradition is thus both the key promoter and defender of human rights, however, at the same time it is the most problematic offender, for example, as regards genocide. This paradoxical situation is referred to as the *state reflexivity syndrome*. The state, in one of its modes, is therefore prosecutor and this requires a coherent vocabulary of prosecution. The vocabulary of the defendant is predictable, namely, sovereignty, nationalism, self-determination, state immunity from prosecution, and the like. However, as prosecutor, the state tradition has utilized (in the main) arguments drawn, once again, from its own constitutional vernacular. The civil state tradition, in particular, embodies a complex range of necessary limitations contained within a legal framework. Ultimately the chapter develops a dialectical mediation of this subject–object relation, a mediation which underpins the complex political character of human rights.

Chapter 7 begins to flesh out more concretely the nature of human rights and their relation with the state tradition. The argument centres initially on the conception of rights developed within a multilevel theory of recognition. Rights are not seen as justified moral claims. They are viewed conversely in the context of the complex relational structures of social recognition, a recognition which is tied to the nature of political association. The theme of recognition is then extended into the analysis of the recognition of states in international law. At this point the argument lays stress on the political character of law, constitutionalism, and international law. Finally the discussion moves to an unconventional analysis of the ideas of quasi-states, crimes of state, and the doctrine of *jus cogens*. Finally, chapter 8 analyses the symbiotic relation between human rights and citizenship, both united in a sense of what a state should be in practice. The argument is that we comprehend our own humanity (and thus our human rights) through our recognition relations with other humans, principally via our citizenship of a civil state, or a state which aspires to civil statehood. The crucial right-medium through which this civil state setting functions is citizenship. We thus fully realize basic aspects of our humanity through being recognized as citizens of such a civil state, a state which is intrinsically constitutionally self-limited. In this sense human rights are intrinsically political.

# 1   **Rights**

The book is about human rights; however, it is important to gain a handle on the more general concept of right before moving on to human rights. The first chapter discusses the word 'right', and then concentrates on a distinction, which arises from the word use of right, between objective and subjective right. The discussion then hones in on the language of rights. This latter examination will entail an assessment of a number of issues. A distinction is drawn between the *sense* and *type* of right: the *sense* focuses on the word itself and what it is trying to connote; the *type* of right focuses on the various and quite diverse classifications within rights literature. The sense and type discussions do though overlap. The distinction is more ideal and made only for pedagogic purposes. The chapter concludes with my own preferred classification of rights and then turns to the question: who is the subject of rights?

## The word 'right'

The word right is easier to deal with in English than other European languages, such as French, German, and Italian, or, for that matter, Asian languages such as Chinese (see Anglo 2002). For example, the German term *Recht*—a word with close similarities to the French *droit* or the Italian *diritto*—is not limited to 'right', but encompasses issues concerning civil law, justice, and even morality. In Hegel, the term *Recht* embodied the above ideas, including right, but also a concern for the 'ethical life' (*Sittlichkeit*), the state, and ultimately aspects of world history. Hegel's *Grundlinien der Philosophie des Rechts* is therefore sometimes translated as the philosophy of law, the philosophy of the state, or more usually now the philosophy of right. Right, in this latter sense, has an immediately broader conceptual ambit although at the same time it also has close connection with the state as an ethical institution and process.[1]

In English, the word 'right' has a number of half-acknowledged uses. It can, for example, function as an adverb. There is a more commonsense version, namely, that something will be done 'right away'. Further, when the

Old Testament Psalmist comments that 'Then Israel should be right glad'—this is a slightly more arcane adverbial sense.[2] 'Rightly' is another possible, if again awkward, adverbial usage. There is also a verb sense of right, as 'to right a wrong', or more clumsily, 'to righten' something. The verb sense of 'to right' something is still in common parlance, although it is not the use which immediately springs to mind when considering the word right. The most common uses of right, particularly in moral, legal, political, and lay speech, are the adjectival and noun senses. It is these which will preoccupy the bulk of this text.

The first adjectival sense of right can be purely descriptive, as in 'the right-angled triangle', or, 'she was right-handed', or, he was 'politically right-wing'. However, there is another adjectival use which is more pertinent for my purpose, which can still be relatively innocuous on one level. Thus, to take the verb usage again, to right(en) something—say a capsized boat—means to make something straight, balanced, or true again. Therefore, that which is right is that which is balanced, straight, correct, or true (true in the sense of balanced). Something which is right or true, say, for a carpenter or someone hanging a picture in a gallery, implies straightness, balance, and a correct sense of proportion. A good eye—for say a carpenter—is one which sees right proportion. It thus implies a standard of measurement. This latter adjectival sense of right can be regarded as both descriptive and mundane. The Latin term *rectus* (to make straight)—which is the root to the German word *Recht*—embodies this usage. Yet, there is a third dimension to this adjectival use of right which has important implications for the discussion within this book. Unlike the Latin term *rectus*, the English word 'rectitude' (derived from the late Latin *rectitudo*) can mean the quality of straightness or correct judgement—although this is now a rare usage. The more dominant application, from the 1600s, has usually implied a 'moral' straightness, a capacity for moral judgement, moral integrity, or upstanding conduct. The moral road is thus a straight road. In fact, to be 'straight' with someone implies that one is being honest, upright, and honourable, which is, of course, morally right conduct.

It is this latter adjectival sense of right which is most significant for my purpose, since it keys into one important usage of right in contemporary parlance.[3] Right, in this latter adjectival context, essentially means something which is morally correct. There is though admittedly a continuous conceptual slippage between the various adjectival uses of right—thus, 'he gave the right answer', 'he was right to help the person in need', and 'he was in the right attire for the funeral' are all indicating correctness. However, it is the moral sense which most interests me in the present discussion. Another close etymological root to the word right also contains many of the above subtle inflexions. This is the Latin word *jus* or *ius*. The late Latin term *justus* implies something which is upright, straight, or equitable. *Justitia* implies righteousness or rectitude. *Jus*, as the etymological root suggests, can also be translated as law or right—which would be closer to the usages of the German *Recht* or the French *droit* than to the English word right. The term 'justice' could also be added to the list of law and right; *jus* indeed is the etymological root to the term justice. At this stage, however, I do not want to enter into a full discussion of the origin of the word right (or *ius*), rather to observe that *jus* or *ius* means correct, balanced, or morally right (as say an outcome), which also links into this latter adjectival sense of right. I would hazard that this, in fact, is the oldest sense we have of right. It also has some close connections with our modern understanding of justice. Just, like right, can be used in an adjectival sense—a just outcome—or alternatively in a noun sense.

The noun sense of right brings us to the heart of the modern understandings of right. To acquire a more complete grasp of this modern notion of 'a right', it will be necessary to track minimally through chapters 2 and 3. Thus, this present discussion will only provide a preliminary sketch of the noun sense of right. The first thing is to remind the reader, again, that the two primary uses in which the word right occurs—over the last three centuries particularly—are the noun and adjectival applications. If anything, the adjectival sense, that is, 'right action', is the older sense of the term, although it is still very much our present reality as well. This application coincides largely with a moral comprehension of right, that is, 'she was morally right to do X'. The adjective right carries the moral inflexion more directly. The noun sense of right is a later idea; how late remains a contested issue. There is a great deal of argument over this issue. The noun sense of right stresses that 'she has a right'. One should not though make too rigid a distinction between these noun and adjectival senses. The two can and do quite dynamically overlap. Thus, often what it is *right to do* can be what you have *a right to do*. In other words, the normative dimension of what is right can saturate the noun sense of 'a right'. The two terms can thus overlap.

However, the fact of this overlap should not shield us from the fact that the opposite may also hold. Consequently, it would be equally true that there are things which are not necessarily considered morally right, which one nonetheless has 'a right' to do. In addition, there are actions which might be considered morally right which, nonetheless, one does not have a right to do. Some of these cases may also involve different contested understandings of what is a right, as well as what *is* right. To grasp the different dimensions of this argument, one would need to unpack all the various ways in which 'a right' has been understood. However, a few quick illustrations will have to suffice for the moment. Capital punishment *might* be considered wrong—offending against a basic right to life; however, in some political regimes, there is an accepted right to use capital punishment, that is, accepted both legally and morally. Thus, something can be considered morally wrong, but there is a right to perform the act. This example though might be understood also as a clash of understandings of both right and morality. Further, one may have a right, as a liberty, to engage in painful sadomasochistic acts; however, many would not consider these as right actions, and so forth. In the latter case, there are things which might be considered morally right, the freedom to marry whomsoever one chooses, which is not necessarily always right in certain societies. One lurking issue here is the difference between legal and moral or legal and human rights, which might account for some, although by no means all, of these conundrums.

It is also important to realize that despite the fact that 'a right' and 'right action' may diverge or coincide, that nonetheless something else very fundamental takes place in this understated displacement of the adjective with the noun. The shift from doing something because it is right, to claiming a right to do it is quite fundamental in terms of social ontology. It carries implications about the way a society and human relations in general are conceived. The linguistic inflexions are subtle but definite. If I approach you and say, 'I believe this is the right thing to do', this is modulated very differently in intention, structure, and effect than if I say, 'I believe I have a right to do this'. In many ways, there is also a sense in which the modern noun (of a right) absorbs the adjectival sense. Morality then only becomes possible in the context of rights. All morality then can be conceived as a rights-based morality (see Mackie 1998). Apart from this latter argument, there is also something here that is deeply expressive of late modernity in this rights-based morality claim. Thus, for many contemporary lay activists, regardless of any philosophical arguments concerning a right-based morality, human rights are quite simply morality; or, to put this in stronger terminology, human rights have mutated into our modern idolatry. As Michael Ignatieff notes, human rights have developed into 'the major article of faith of a secular culture that fears it believes in nothing else. It has become the *lingua franca* of global moral thought'. In some cases, it has become virtually a secular creed, which Ignatieff describes as 'humanism worshipping itself' (Ignatieff 2003, 53). Even outside the sphere of human rights, rights in general terms can often be the modern surrogates for morality. Thus, 'rights claims' trip off the tongue now with remarkable ease. This is partly due to the fact that rights are part of a broader series of social changes. We have a deep prejudice for rights—they have become part of our current manner of understanding of ourselves.

The subtle shift from 'rightness' or 'right action' to 'a right' was facilitated by certain larger social changes. However, once this shift had taken place, 'right' became not only a standard, but also a defensible and permissible claim to act in a specific manner. The claim, warrant, or entitlement were the key synonyms for articulating a right. This claim or entitlement itself then became a form of standard for measurement. The progress of a society was then ascertained by examining how far it had endeavoured to instantiate a rigorous regime of rights. This has though varied with different societies.

In summary, the modern usage of the word right is employed conventionally in two senses. These could be called the 'right as rectitude', or moral rightness, and a right as a subjective entitlement, warrant, or claim. Thus, 'she has a right' is, at one level, distinct from 'she is right'. These senses can and do overlap, insofar as 'what it is right to do' may well be 'what you have a right to do'. When we think of rights now, vis-à-vis human rights, it is usually the entitlement or warrant dimension which is uppermost—although the moral rightness dimension often provides a strong and pervasive underpinning, particularly in the case of human rights. Rightness is thus often consolidated within the concept of a human right. The oddity here is that human rights can virtually become a form of morality.

## Objective and subjective right

There is another significant distinction which has characterized a great deal of the literature on rights, particularly concerning the relation between older and more recent understandings. The distinction is between 'objective' and 'subjective' right. There is some match here between this distinction and the conclusion of the previous section, namely, the distinction between 'a right' and 'rightness'. The parallels are not perfect, but they are illuminating. This distinction, made by the French writer Michel Villey, has become a *locus classicus* one for many—although not all—scholars (see Villey 1962). It has also become a central theme within the historical analysis of rights. This historical concern is one which is postponed for later discussion. The present section merely utilizes the distinction as a way of further illuminating the various meanings of right in contemporary discourse.

The conventional manner of articulating this distinction is to argue that objective right implies—paralleling the adjectival use above—something that is a standard of moral rightness or moral correctness. One aspect of this view which will be examined more closely in the next chapter is that moral rightness does not necessarily entail 'a right'. In fact, it has been suggested that the concept of 'duty' might suffice, namely, the fact of moral rightness could entail duties or obligations rather than rights (see Glendon 2001, 189). On the other hand, the subjective right argument contends that a right is, largely, an individual warrant or claim, which usually embodies some form of internal justification. This subjective right entails a form of duty or disability on the part of others. Villey's contention is that objective right is a far older conception. He argues that the older conceptions of right in, for example, the medieval period had no conception of subjective right. The Latin term *ius* is taken to have commonly referred to objective rightness. As one recent commentator notes, 'There was no room...in the Roman consciousness of right and law for a notion of the natural right of an individual that was anything at all like the modern subjective idea of natural right' (Herbert 2002, 49). Objective right had more in common with a more traditional doctrine of natural law, understood as a detailed body of natural duties or obligations.[4]

Villey has something in common with other twentieth-century political theorists, such as Leo Strauss, who also saw a significant distinction between traditional doctrines such as natural law and the later use of subjective natural right, in John Locke and Thomas Hobbes (see Strauss 1953; Ferry and Renaut 1992; Haakonssen 1996).[5] For Villey subjective rights are not derived from natural law. In fact, some scholars have suggested, in extending Villey's point, that writers such as Locke are indirectly quite hostile to natural law (see D'Entrèves 1977, 59).[6] In Locke's idea of subjective self-ownership 'neither natural law nor God's authority are required', consequently 'each self-owning person is out there amongst equally self-owning persons. The evidence that others *are* self-owning beings (persons)...is that we hold them responsible for what they do' (see Herbert 2002, 119–20). Aquinas, for Villey, is the last great representative of the older pure classical tradition of natural jurisprudence. Law is about reason and the origin of reason is God. Aquinas' understanding of right is therefore seen in terms of an obligation or duty rather than the licence of the individual subject.

For both Villey and Strauss subjective right—which Villey traces to nominalist philosophy and the writings of William of Ockham—corrupts the traditional objective right tradition. It is thus not simply a neutral academic distinction in Villey's and Strauss' writings. It carries a specific political and moral message concerning the potential destructiveness of natural right. Strauss, for example, draws a sharp distinction between classical and modern political philosophy—the ancients and the moderns—and shows a distinct anxiety concerning the effects of modern political philosophy and modern liberalism on the ancient traditions of objective right.[7] This change from the ancient to the modern is thus perceived as a crisis. The crisis is that the Western world no longer knows where it is going; it has lost, or is in doubt about its own fundamental values. Modern philosophy contributes to this crisis, by adhering blindly to the relativizing of beliefs. The growth of subjective right claims is seen as one dimension of this decline enhancing an underlying commitment to individualism. For Strauss, however, every society needs universal values to remain 'healthy' (Strauss 1977, 3; Bloom 1980, 113). The central motif of classical political philosophy was therefore universal moral values, paralleling Villey's objective right. It focused on the search for the best life and an objective knowledge of the good. These classical moral solutions will not though provide any contemporary recipes. For Strauss, only we can find solutions to our problems. But classical theory can be the starting point for the serious consideration of our problems.[8]

Similarly, Villey expresses an abhorrence for modern subjective rights theory—within which he includes modern human rights—as potentially nihilistic and sterile. For Tierney, for example, Villey's written work often 'reacts with understandable irony to the value catalogues of more or less worthy aspirations that are nowadays presented as lists of "human rights"'. In fact, Villey sees 'the whole modern attempt to base a system of jurisprudence on an affirmation of individual rights as fundamentally misguided'. He therefore sees it as essentially a barren exercise (see Villey 1961; Tierney 1997, 20–1).

Villey's general approach developed from his early intensive studies of Roman law. In these and many later studies, he developed the argument that what is objectively right is wholly divergent from what is subjectively right. For Villey, subjective right is not part of either traditional Roman or medieval law. Conversely, it arose at a specific moment and location in response to specific conditions. For modern jurisprudential writers, certainly from the seventeenth and eighteenth centuries onwards, a right was a subjective power over something, whereas for classical Roman and medieval jurists it was an 'incorporeal thing'.[9] Villey maintains that this notion of power over a thing or person (*dominium*) was not present in early legal or moral discussion. In fact, Villey thinks of a right, understood as *dominium*, as a distinctly 'vulgar' use of the term. Where *dominium* was used in the medieval period, it was not envisaged as a right in the modern subjective sense. Ownership and use of, say, property were not therefore understood in terms of any subjective *ius*. Use did not entail *dominium*. For Villey *ius* meant a form of objective fairness to which others were liable. He then goes on to argue fiercely that Aquinas did not use the idea of subjective right. He, in fact, viewed it as one of Aquinas' great achievements 'to restore for a time the objective, classical meaning of *ius*' (Tierney 1997, 23).[10] The first real statement for Villey of the idea of subjective power was in Ockham in the fourteenth century. Ockham is thus seen to have started a 'semantic revolution' in our understanding of right. However, not all agree with this assessment.[11]

In summary, Villey's influential and powerful distinction between object-ive and subjective right does for certain commentators overdo and simplify a more complex issue concerning the relation between natural law and natural right. Underlying his use of this distinction is also a distinct intellectual hostility to human rights language and to the culture of subjective right. However, the distinction is nonetheless still pedagogically useful in high-lighting a subtle and pervasive debate, which still exists in studies of rights, between rights as individual claims and rights as moral rectitude or moral correctness. In this sense, it reconfigures the earlier debate between the noun and adjectival sense of 'right'. The issue concerning subjective and objective right will however be touched upon again in the discussion of the origin of right and in the debate over natural law and natural right.

# What is a right?

The discussion now turns to the vexed issue of rights language in a more contemporary setting. My assumption (from the above discussion) is that when we discuss rights we are largely focusing on the noun sense of right, or subjective right, although with the important proviso that the idea of moral correctness is not very far distant from many discussions. In focusing on subjective right, the aim is initially to draw a distinction between the *sense* and *type* of right: the *sense* focuses on the word itself and what it is trying to connote; the *type* of right focuses on the various classifications which have been adopted to talk about subjective right. The categories of sense and type do inevitably overlap. It is not therefore a pristine distinction. In asking about the sense of right, the question can be reformulated to ask 'what is a right?' or 'what does right mean?' These seemingly simple questions are however deeply elusive. In answering the question 'what is a right?' it is very easy to slip immediately into a discussion about types and classifications of right, which is something to initially avoid. Gaining some 'sense' of a right is more about gaining some leverage on the 'formal' minimal sense of the concept. The aim is therefore initially to try to pin down certain synonyms which encapsulate the sense of right. The classification of the 'type' of right indicates the substantive content of right and moves immediately into the various classificatory schemes. This will be examined in the next section.

Before turning to the question 'what is a right?', some brief introductory remarks will be made. Rights in general are clearly parts of a much larger moral, political, and legal vocabulary and they inevitably overlap with the vocabularies of duty and obligation. In fact, these latter vocabularies can, in some arguments, virtually take over from rights-based claims, although this is resisted by others who see a 'rightless' moral or legal world as untenable (see Feinberg 1980). Further, duties can also be used as one of the methods of classifying types of rights. In addition, one of the dangers of discussing rights—and this is a particular problem with regard to human rights—is that they can be regarded as unproblematic things or facts in the legal and moral world. There are two ways in which this latter argument can be understood. Many have regarded rights as just positive legal facts. They are therefore seen as relatively unproblematic in themselves. Thus, for example, many legal commentators who are interested in human rights see them as existing facts of the legal world. The real issues are concerned with litigation and enforcement. In other words, human rights can be seen as 'facts' in the legal world. The important issue for lawyers is to ensure that they are properly codified and enforced. Another way of viewing rights, as established facts, would be in terms of some of the older renderings of natural rights. This latter perspective sees rights as either intrinsic or natural in someway to the world. They are *not* the result of human artifice. They are rather existing or immemorial normative facts which humans and states ought to acknowledge.

My own view would be to consider rights—including human rights—as not so much legal facts as a series of socially recognized and accredited reasons for action or inaction. It is a mistake to think of them as simply self-sufficient positive facts. There might well be both good and bad reasons for rights. Some reasons seem to have more legitimacy or wider endorsement than other reasons. But, in this study, it is the socially recognized and accredited reasons embedded in the right which are taken as crucial, not its simple existence. Rights are not though just any type of reason. The reasons involved are usually open to a much broader normative debate in the process of recognition. Rights in fact usually *require* some form of broader normative recognition. The reason for this wider debate and need for endorsement is that 'rights talk' has a particular strength when it enters the legal, political, or moral domain of debate.[12]

The most direct way of speaking about the 'sense' of a right and the most common synonyms for it are words such as claim, warrant, entitlement, title, or power. These synonyms are partly misleading since, as we will see when the discussion turns to types of right, for some scholars the synonyms themselves give rise to differing types of right. At the moment, all that is indicated is the very basic intuitive sense in which we employ the term. The most common synonym is the word 'claim'. It is a 'claim' which standardly belongs to a person or individual subject, although the issue of state and group rights cuts across this argument. It is not though just a claim, as in say a 'demand'. It is usually envisaged as a *valid* claim; it has some degree of recognition by a wider group, that is to say it has been endorsed by the wider group. This would hold for any substantive kind of right. One has a claim to something. A claim right implies the agent is at liberty in respect of X and that his or her liberty is the ground for other's duties to grant him or her X. Others are therefore prepared to recognize the right and the right itself is seen to be justified or valid. To have a valid claim right, as many theorists have asserted, is to have something that society recognizes that it should protect me in the possession of. Its validity does not necessarily mean that it is intrinsically worthwhile or morally justified. In fact, the notion of intrinsic justification will be seen to be problematic. Validity rather means that a society endorses and recognizes it.[13] This valid right enables the agent to bring about a change in the moral, political, or legal situation of himself or others. To have a right therefore 'enables'.

This leads to another standard claim concerning rights. They imply commonly some form of relation with others, namely, others have some form of duty or disability correlative to the assertion of the right. In the fuller context, others are also necessary for recognition of the right. In this sense, it can further imply at least the potentiality for some form of enforcement, although this would vary considerably with the nature of the right involved—this is a particularly pertinent issue for human rights. Minimally others are liable to your valid claims. The valid claim usually protects or promotes a particular legitimate interest of the individual subject. There is also an aspect of permissibility in a valid claim such that to have a right means that it is not wrong (it is thus permissible) to do X. Permissibility also entails that it is wrong to interfere with the agent in pursuing that right. This might be a right to possess something, to receive something, also for an agent to forbear, or to do something.

Other theorists have suggested that rights would be better analysed as entitlements or titles, rather than claims. Thus, for H. J. McCloskey, rights should be 'explained positively as entitlements to do, have, enjoy, or have done, and not negatively as something against others, or as something one ought to have' (McCloskey 1976, 99; see also Milne 1986, 89). These rights are intrinsic to their holders—that is, they are internal to the nature of humans. They also rest upon objective moral considerations which provide a form of authority (McCloskey 1965, 120). These latter points though remain rather vague; it is not clear what intrinsic means in this context. Further, rights as entitlements are always prior to duties; that is they generate duties, but there is no automatic entailment to specific duties. An entitlement is the normative grounds necessary for the establishment of an eligibility for a good. It is not altogether intuitively obvious here what entitlement adds to the concept of a claim. Entitlement just appears to be another synonym of a right.

## Classifications of right

Rights have been classified in many ways. The substantive debate about types of right is not absolutely central to the discussion of human rights, but it is nevertheless important to get some handle on the debates about the sheer diversity of rights schemas before proceeding. There is though one important additional proviso to add here. There is little conceptual or classificatory settlement in the wide-ranging literature on rights. In fact, the precise opposite, widespread disagreement is as much in evidence. Further, much of the analytical literature on this area, as well as being unresolved, has become deeply precious and highly scholastic, often losing all touch with moral and political realities. As one commentator notes, 'Few debates in modern jurisprudence seem so arid as that concerning the formal analysis of legal rights...there is little agreement about the prizes that may be at stake, or about the wider issues that may turn upon the outcome'. He continues, with a large helping of unpalatable truth,

> Anyone acquainted with the analytical jurisprudence of rights...is likely to
> conclude that our more 'conceptual' intuitions about rights can be regimented
> in a great variety of ways. Each regimentation comes, of course, at a price, and
> protagonists in the controversy sustain a sense of intellectual progress by
> drawing attention to the price that others must pay, while making light of the
> entry fee to their own system.    (Simmonds 1998, 116)

With this warning proviso in mind, the discussion turns to a short examination of *some* of the main schemes for classifying rights. I will briefly examine
the following:

1. Classification by will or choice
2. Classification by function in discourse
3. Classification by what one has a right to do or expect from others
4. Classification by correlatives
5. Classification by the substantive content.

## WILL OR CHOICE

One of the more popular analytical distinctions to appear in the literature on
rights is that between what are often called 'will' and 'interest' conceptions.
'Interest' theories are primarily associated with the utilitarian tradition. Will
theories, on the other hand, are somewhat predictably associated with the
more neo-Kantian approach. Indeed another way of configuring this classification is in terms of dominant forms of ethical justification. Thus, rights
could be classified according to the grounds on which they are justified.
Exactly how much insight such a scheme provides into the nature and types
of rights remains open-ended.

The idea of benefit or interest theory originated largely with Jeremy
Bentham. Assuring a good or an interest for Bentham is to confer a right.
Rights are therefore benefits, and whoever benefits from a duty possesses a
right. Interest-based rights thus protect or promote certain specific interests,
usually (but not always) of individual subjects. Rights therefore essentially
consist of interests. Individuals have rights to those benefits which others, as
a matter of justice, are duty bound to accord them. For some critics, interest
theory envisages such a close relation between duty and right that rights
discourse can become practically unimportant. Another synonym for
interest, which is often employed in the literature, is 'benefit'. People thus
have rights only in terms of what benefits them. Consequently, any entity
which is sentient and has interests (which it can benefit from) can therefore
be said to have rights. For some utilitarians, this includes the human foetus
and non-human animals (see Bentham 1970, 283, note 1). The intended
beneficiary benefits from others duties, correlative to the right, although the

duties have a priority here. Having a right is thus enjoying a benefit or having something addressed to one's interests.[14] Rights are therefore focused on the protection or promotion of individual interests or benefits. The theory still has, in various modified formats, a number of supporters (see Lyons 1969; Kramer 1998).[15]

The will or choice theory, which is rooted in neo-Kantian thought, prioritizes the choice, control, or autonomy of the subject over any corresponding duty. Autonomous choice is the key. The most significant early expression of this argument can be found in Kant's *Metaphysic of Morals*. Kant grounded law ultimately in a theory of autonomous will. The will theory is associated now with much more limited concerns than Kant's. For present exponents of will theory, right is always understood as a form of individual choice. To have a right is thus to have a legally or morally respected choice. Thus, rights can be said to promote autonomy, by conferring and protecting one's choices and control over one's life.[16] Many have seen a weakness in this latter argument since it appears to prioritize choice and ignore the content of the action. Thus, choice alone might legitimate a right to potentially immoral action. Further, the range of rights is more restricted than in the interest theory. Only adult human beings can really have rights, since these are the only beings capable of rationality and choice. Many again have seen this as the key dilemma of the will theory, namely, that it appears to deny rights to many unempowered groups, not least children, and renders their interest unprotected on the grounds that they cannot make adequate choices.

The will theory was neatly formulated by H. L. A. Hart in his 1973 essay 'Bentham on Legal Rights' (see Hart 1983). For Hart, the power to waive or demand a duty is not essential to the existence of a right. Many duties do not necessarily entail rights—thus there can be rightless duties.[17] For example, statutory duties laid upon employers do not necessarily entail rights. In terms of rights though, individuals are invested for Hart with powers of control and choice over others' duties. The subject can waive or demand the performance of a duty. The law thus leaves space for individual choice. The individual is consequently left in control. He is not duty bound to give way. All rights involve some protection, recognition, and respect for individual choice.[18] The choice argument is connected to Hart's other well-known argument concerning 'natural rights' (Hart 1955). Thus, to exercise any rights one must be able to choose. Yet one cannot have *any* right unless one is at liberty to use it (or waive it). Any special rights that we exercise are therefore dependent on the logically prior general right of liberty of choice. It is the essential presupposition to any rights usage. The general right to liberty is thus a *necessary logical inference* from the use of *any* special contextual right. In effect, without the general right to liberty of choice all special rights would be empty. This is, in effect, the nub of Hart's minimal logical case for natural right.

## FUNCTION IN DISCOURSE

Some scholars have suggested that we should not have to choose between the interest and will theories since rights can have more than one distinctive function. Thus, as James Nickel points out, one can combine them and say that 'rights serve to direct behaviour in ways that make available to right-holders freedoms, protections, opportunities, immunities, powers, and benefits' (Nickel 1987, 23). Nickel's formulation raises the spectre of a second classificatory scheme which has been the most influential of all the schemes in the whole literature on rights. This is the work of Wesley N. Hohfeld in his book *Fundamental Legal Conceptions* (1946); the core ideas had been developed in earlier articles dating back to 1913. It is also important to grasp that Hohfeld's classification is not necessarily totally distinct from other schemes. Many theorists frequently try to link Hohfeld's scheme with their own favoured classification of rights (see Flathman 1976; Kramer 1998).[19]

Hohfeld formulated a subtle matrix of four sets of legal relations comprised of eight possible legal positions. The four key relations are claims, liberties, powers, and immunities, although for Hohfeld the most strict or narrower sense of a right is a claim (see Wellman 1999, 7–8). However, Hohfeld also felt that most lawyers still recognized a number of legal advantages which could still be characterized as rights. It is also worth noting here one often-neglected point concerning Hohfeld. He was and remained a committed legal positivist and classical legal formalist, that is to say, minimally he was only interested in legal rights promulgated by states. Similar to Bentham, he was not interested in moral or human rights. Many have however gone on to apply the Hohfeldian scheme, regardless, to discussions of both human and moral rights; there is though something conceptually unsatisfactory in such an approach (see Jones 1994, 47–8; Simmonds 1998, 147; Wellman 1999, 8).

Hohfeld's scheme adopts the following structure. There are four types of right for which Hohfeld also stresses both correlatives and opposites. A correlative outlines the status of the other party. Opposites characterize the contrary position to the specific right. Thus, a *claim right* is a requirement or demand for something from someone for something or to do something. It imposes a strict correlative duty—such that any such duty logically implies a claim right. The jural opposite of a claim right is no-right. A *liberty right* or privilege is a space or opportunity to act which is not burdened by any rules or requirements. Hohfeld suggests that the correlative jural relation to a liberty would not be strictly a duty, but no-right. The opposite of a liberty would be a duty. A liberty is therefore in a sense 'duty-free'. A *right as a power* means that someone is legally liable to the exercise of your right (as a power). A legal power can change a legal relation. It gives the agent an authority to act. One would have the power, for example, in law to leave one's property to whomsoever one wishes. Many of those in public office have rights as powers in this sense. A policeman, for example, has a legal power of arrest in certain defined circumstances. One has the legal power to marry or make a will. The correlative of a power is a liability in terms of those who are subject to the power. The opposite of power for Hohfeld is a disability. A *right as an immunity* is essentially to be protected from the action of others or free from another's power. Thus, a member of the British Parliament has an immunity from prosecution for things said in the House of Commons. One is also immune from a neighbour selling your house without your consent. The correlative of a right as immunity is a disability and the opposite is a liability.

There are a number of ways to view this baseline model of the Hohfeldian scheme. Although Hohfeld demarcates these rights (and ultimately thinks that only claims are rights in the strict sense), they can and do overlap. This has led some critics to try to adapt and extend the Hohfeldian analysis. Thus, a legal claim to own a house might also be described as a liberty to do with it as one pleases, it also implies a power to sell it, or an immunity from others interfering with one's ownership. In this sense, any right might be considered to be a cluster of Hohfeldian positions. This argument has led certain theorists to suggest that all rights (including human and moral rights) can be said to embody clusters of Hohfeldian claims (see Nickel 1987, 23; Wellman 1999, 8–9).²⁰ Many would also see this scheme as having a direct empirical reference to the existing use of rights in contemporary politics. Others see no need to improve, extend, or adapt Hohfeld's work. His work forms a perfectly logical structure for grasping rights. In this case, the 'key to understanding Hohfeld's project is to recognize that it was purificatory (analytically purificatory) and definitional rather than empirical or substantive. Hohfeld put forth a framework of deontic logic, with positions connected by purely logical relations of entailment and negation; he did not attempt to prescribe or recount the substance and the distribution of actual entitlements. His framework is therefore not susceptible to moral objections or empirical refutation' (Kramer 1998, 22).²¹

How far one entertains the value and significance of the Hohfeldian scheme is dependent largely upon how far one swallows the whole move from substantive rights to rights talk. Hohfeld's scheme fits very neatly into a more decisive mutation in the Anglo-American philosophical landscape from the 1930s (see Vincent 2004, ch. 3). Rights are regarded in terms of a multifaceted debate over the linguistic, grammatical, and logical usage of concepts and clarifying meanings. 'Rights talk' has thus largely replaced discussion of rights. A large aspect of that debate has focused on the linguistic and logical character of 'rights talk' and Hohfeld provided a virtually paradigmatic logical framework, which many political and legal theorists over the last fifty years have found irresistible. One can understand on another level why Hohfeld has been so attractive. He combines this logical focus on rights talk with an unstinting commitment to legal positivism, which, until the present moment, has been what Ronald Dworkin refers to as the 'ruling theory of law' in the academy. Hohfeld's aim was therefore logical refinement and conceptual clarification.[22] This indeed has been a key dimension of the explosion of rights-based literature in the same period. The Hohfeldian schema has become for many the 'normal science' of 'rights talk' and has consequently preoccupied many rights theorists. One effect of this is that much of the current focus on rights in the Hohfeldian mode 'has not been so much a debate as it has been a kind of conceptual assembly line on which new usages are continually produced in the name of greater clarification' (Herbert 2002, 303). A sterile conceptual scholasticism can permeate such work. Discussions on rights become focused on micro-level distinctions of usage. Although there is some academic mileage in the Hohfeldian scheme, it is wise to recall again that Hohfeld was not concerned at all with moral, natural, or human rights. Hohfeld's rights were all positive legal rights. Further, he had no interest in the broader significance of rights in political discourse and no concern whatsoever with the history of rights. If one accepts the severe limitations of this perspective then it can have some pedagogic value.

## WHAT ONE HAS A RIGHT TO DO OR EXPECT FROM OTHERS

Another older way of classifying rights, which again overlaps in part with the previous two schemes, is that which examines them in terms of 'what one actually has a right to do' or 'what one has a right to expect from others'. There are a number of ways in which this has been reformulated in the literature on rights, and it does definitely have some immediate impact on the way human rights have been articulated. The most common distinctions which occur here are between rights in an active and passive voice. Similar distinctions appear between positive and negative rights, or rights to act and rights of recipience. Alan Milne, for example, draws a parallel distinction between elective and non-elective rights. An elective right confers choices (every right of action is seen as elective). Non-elective rights normatively exclude choices— they are 'rights of recipience which entitle the right-holder not only to receive something but do not entitle him to decline it' (Milne 1986, 92). Non-elective rights are essentially passive rights or negative in character. There is nothing the right-holder is required to do.[23]

Hohfeldian categories can intersect with many aspects of this active– passive rubric. For example, if one regards a Hohfeldian 'claim right' as fundamental, then claims can mean either that one can passively expect the performance of a duty, or alternatively that one can actively claim a right to act, which implies others have a duty to concede that right. That is to say, a claim can either be read as a negative right to be left alone or passively receive some good (to speak without hindrance or to be paid a debt), or, alternatively it can be read as a positive right to act. This distinction within 'claim rights' is not wholly satisfactory, since a claim to be paid a debt might be seen as a negative or passive right. There is no particularly strong reason to adjudicate either way. This claim right might also be analysed as a right of recipience (or even a passive right) as against a positive duty to act. On the other hand, a right to be paid a debt could also be seen as an active claim which can be asserted against someone who has the negative duty to simply pay the debt. Generally in the literature, positive rights are seen as claims to welfare bene-fits and negative rights would be seen as rights of non-interference. Some have suggested that the distinction here parallels an older distinction, between civil rights (to be left alone, for example, in the pursuit of one's religious conscience) as against positive social rights to welfare.

Another way of analysing this same distinction, in terms of the Hohfeldian structure, would be to suggest that claim rights correspond with positive rights (or rights of action) and liberty rights correspond with negative rights (or passive rights). Yet another way of conceiving this distinction is between rights *in rem* and rights *in personam*. A right *in personam* is held against specific persons, whereas a right *in rem* is held against people in general. The correlative duties would thus be either for specific persons or humanity at large. Again, it is possible to superimpose positive and negative rights over this distinction. Thus, positive claim rights can be seen as *in personam*, whereas negative claim rights are *in rem*. Similarly, negative rights, as rights *in rem*, can be viewed as equivalent to the Hohfeldian notion of a liberty. However, the correlative question remains unclear here, since for Hohfeld the correlative of a liberty is 'no-right' (Hohfeld views the opposite of a 'liberty' as a 'duty'), whereas, for others, the correlative of a negative right, liberty, or right *in rem* is a negative or passive duty (see Jones 1994, 19). Thus, my right to speak or associate freely, understood as a liberty (understood therefore as a space or opportunity to act which is not burdened by any rules or require-ments) could imply that humanity at large (*in rem*) has a passive or negative duty to not interfere with my freedom. The central question here is: do we view the prohibition to interfere with my liberty as a situation where no-right is exercisable (as in Hohfeld), or alternatively does it imply a negative duty not to interfere?

One small additional point to mention is that the *in rem* and *in personam* distinction could theoretically give rise to another classificatory scheme, namely, classifying rights 'by whom or to whom they are addressed'. The 'to whom' acts as a demarcating device. Thus, the *in rem* category is always addressed to humanity at large—which some have seen as the key character-istic of human rights claims—whereas *in personam* rights are addressed in specific situations, or in particular circumstances, to definite persons. The *in personam* category might also be another way of speaking of rights in Hohfeld's strict sense—that is, 'claim rights'—as against rights (in a more generic sense as liberties), which would conform more closely to the idea of moral or human rights (that is in being addressed to humanity at large—*in rem*). Thus, rights in this latter scenario could be classified by the *nature of the audience* to whom they are addressed. Another related way of recasting this classification would be in terms of 'how general' or 'how specific' the right is. A right to life or to liberty, addressed to humanity at large, is clearly a highly general right claim which speaks to us at a macro level. Some have taken this latter form of general right as the only defensible form of human right (see e.g. Cranston 1973). Whereas when one speaks of a specific minority ethnic group's right to cultivate their own language and culture, the right of an individual to a pension, or the right to unemployment benefit, and the like, these are much more micro-focused specialized claims, many of which only really make sense in certain established states.

## CORRELATIVES

Yet another related way of thinking about the general distinction between *positive* and *negative* rights would be to reconfigure the distinction in terms of the correlatives of rights. The focus then becomes predominantly the normative duties to which rights correlatively give rise. Many within the twentieth-century literature on rights saw a close correlation between rights and duties, where rights can virtually be categorized in terms of the types of duty they give rise to (Ross 1930; Bradley 1962). Thus, instead of negative and positive rights (rights of action and rights of recipience or non-interference), one can reconfigure the argument in terms of negative and positive duties correlative to the rights. The central categories differentiating rights thus become the type of duty entailed by the right. This way of thinking (with some marked qualifications) is already present within the Hohfeldian scheme, which is systematic about focusing on the correlatives of the various rights; although as noted above, Hohfeld recasts his responses to liberties, powers, and immunities as no-rights, liabilities, and disabilities. Thus, for Hohfeld duties only figure in terms of strict claim rights. However, this argument ignores the possibility of distinguishing between types of duty, or indeed that duty itself might be a tricky and elusive concept. Consequently, it is quite feasible to distinguish between duties to act and duties of inaction or non-interference. There is nothing insuperable in this distinction; in fact, it appears as straightforward common sense. However, Hohfeld seems to take no cognizance of it, which is odd.

Hohfield's scepticism though can be found in other theorists, prosecuted much more vigorously. Some go out of their way to refute the idea of correlativity (see White 1985, 85ff.). Hohfeld, as indicated, of course had his own unique take on this issue. The strict sense of claim right may indeed correlate with a duty, but that is the end of the matter. Rights understood as liberties, powers, or immunities do not correlate with duties per se. For many though the major flaw in the correlativity thesis is that not all duties give rise to rights (see Feinberg 1980; White 1985, 104–5). These duties have often been called imperfect, as in say the duty of charity, conscience, or a duty to aid. Aiding someone in need, for example, saving them from drowning, although recognized by some as a moral duty, is not necessarily premised on any right the needy might possess. Duty alone can suffice for help to be rendered. Thus, as Feinberg notes, 'When we leave legal contexts to consider moral obligations and other extra-legal duties, a great variety of duties-without-correlative rights present themselves. Duties of charity, requires us to contribute to one or another of a large number of eligible recipients, no one of whom can claim our contributions from us as his due. Charitable contributions are more like gratuitous services, favours, and gifts than like repayments of debts' (Feinberg 1980, 144). Thus, any strong sense that rights can always be classified in terms of their respective correlative duties looks problematic.

## THE SUBSTANTIVE CONTENT OF RIGHT

The final classification focuses on a more traditional categorization, with a fresh twist. This classification avoids the question of rights talk and instead concentrates on the substantive content of rights. In examining ordinary discourse, three central categories predominate: legal, moral, and political rights. This does not mean that there may be other substantive rights; however, these are the main usages in current discourse. Natural rights have predominantly appeared as a subspecies of the moral category. Human rights—in terms of the manner in which they have been discussed in the literature—have appeared under the rubric of all three, although mainly under the legal and moral categories. In fact, a large bulk of literature has been preoccupied particularly with the moral status and justification of human rights. Human rights have rarely been considered under the political category; however, in the key arguments of this book, this is precisely what is done. The terms legal, moral, and political are all open contestable categories. They also overlap with the other classificatory schemes. Thus, some of the earlier classification schemes focused on, for example, will and interest rights, negative and positive rights, *in rem* and *in personam* rights, and so forth, are all still relevant for thinking through the content of the three categories. However, my contention is that we need to take account of the way rights are commonly discussed and although we can learn aspects of usage by focusing on the 'language of rights', it is the substantive usage which needs to be our initial guide.

All of the categories are porous. However, legal rights are a quite distinctive area for rights discussion—although not so clear when it comes to human rights. The legal conception of rights—in the broadest terms—identifies rights as arising from a specific rule-structured institution, such as the sovereign state. They imply certain authoritative institutional arrangements which provide procedural guarantees for claims or entitlements. They presuppose both a pre-existent legal association and membership of that association—in terms of the applicability of the right. Rights, in this context, clearly have remedies and processes of enforcement.[24]

Moral rights are justified claims for the acknowledgment of a particular norm. They are constituted through, or consequent upon, the acceptance of some significant moral values or morally considerable beliefs. Thus, for example, to believe that God created all human beings can fundamentally affect the manner in which the purported natural rights of the human being (their life, liberty, and the like) are viewed.[25] Similarly utilitarian, neo-Kantian, or contractarian moral arguments, all transform the way in which we both think about and justify rights. The justificatory structure and norms are frequently considered to be universal and external to the arrangements of any particular association or social arrangement. The validity of many moral rights therefore relates to these external justificatory norms or beliefs. This does not entail that a moral right cannot be codified in a legal association or constitutional framework. However, the ground on which the right is justified, or held to be valid, is usually considered independent of the historical or juridical fact of human association. The only subtle variation to this latter argument would be those moral beliefs which are linked closely to particular communities or cultures. This latter contention refers to a more communitarian conception of moral rights. Again, it is important to note that we should not make too rigid a distinction between morality and politics or even morality and law. Many of the debates that will be examined in this book do cross over these categories.

The notion of political right can be interpreted in a number of ways. There is a basic, more brutish sense of political right which visualizes all rights—almost from a realpolitik perspective—as rooted in a political association. Thus, whenever a right is asserted, it is premised on the fact that human beings have created and enforced a structure over human relations which manifests hegemonic power and a monopoly of violence. In this sense, legal and moral rights could be seen as facade rights. My own use of politics is different. Very briefly—since a large bulk of this book will be examining this idea—humans are taken to be social creatures by nature. We always exist in relational terms with other humans. Politics occurs within certain types of human relational activity. It is premised on human association and an acknowledgement that plurality and difference are the empirical facts of such relational activity. Humans are thus envisaged as conflicting and competing in terms of their interests, norms, and desires; in effect, they try to utilize resources such as overt power to achieve their interests. Politics is an acceptance of this plurality, but also a way of trying to mediate and attend to it. Rights are viewed as part of a process of mutual recognition within a political association—as part of this process of mediating plurality. They are primarily rights of citizenship. They are both recognized guarantees and enabling devices for human beings to realize themselves (as citizens) in terms of their powers and abilities, in relation to others. Human rights are envisaged in the same scenario. This issue will be expanded in the concluding section of this chapter. Thus, the classification of rights in terms of their substantive content can be structured as follows:

1. *Moral rights*
   (a) Natural rights
   (i) Human vis-à-vis creature of God
   (ii) Human vis-à-vis creature of nature and reason
   (b) Human rights
       Human vis-à-vis moral autonomous agency

2. *Legal rights*
   (a) Strict legal rights
       Humans *as* members of a legal association
   (b) Human rights
       Humans *as* universally possessing equal rights under international law

3. *Political rights*
   (a) Realpolitik political right
       Rights as premised on membership or citizenship of a political association
   (b) Human right
       Humans as citizens of a civil state association

A brief explanation of the classificatory scheme is needed. The major broad distinction is between moral, legal, and political rights. Moral rights are subdivided into natural and human rights. Thus, natural rights (which will be analysed in chapter 2) can be subdivided into two arguments. The first relates very closely to traditional natural law theory and sees the right of the human being premised on an understanding of God or a deity of some kind. This contention tracks back to the origins of natural right argument. The second subdivision relates to a subtle shift of argument in the seventeenth century, which did not abandon God, but placed much more emphasis and weight upon the substantive capacities of humans to reason. Further, although nature is viewed as God's artifice, it also embodies universal rules and immutable reasonable laws which even God will not disobey. Thus, nature and its rule-governed structures gain a partial independence from theological considerations. This is not a secularizing argument, but it unquestionably prepares the ground for such a delicate shift.

In the second moral category of human rights, the secularizing process continues apace—although it is still debatable as to whether human rights have not so much evolved from natural rights, as that they are a different class of right altogether. This point will be examined in chapter 2. It is also worth pointing out that the religious arguments do not totally disappear in the human rights setting. Far from it, they keep reoccurring in human rights debates throughout the second half of the twentieth century, although their effect remains problematic.

The legal category is again subdivided. The first conception relates to seminal arguments within the legal positivist school. The basic contention of legal positivism is that law is law (or rights are rights) regardless of content. This is often called the command theory of law in its earliest manifestation. Most legal positivists consequently keep a fairly rigorous distinction in mind between law and morality. The father figure of this position is often considered to be Thomas Hobbes, although his close linkages to the natural law and natural rights positions makes it more difficult to be precise about his legal positivist credentials. A safer ground for legal positivism is the work of Jeremy Bentham and John Austin in the nineteenth century, or H. L. A. Hart, Hans Kelsen, and indeed Wesley Hohfeld in the twentieth century. By the early twentieth century (as indicated earlier), various forms of legal positivism consolidated their position within the North American and European legal academies and have remained the dominant jurisprudential account of law to the present day. The most basic position of legal positivism on rights is that rights find their substantive foundation in a pre-existing legal association. Rights are the creation of the sovereign executives of particular states. The key issue is membership of a legal association. One should not look for moral validation of rights external to that structure of rules present in a particular legal association. The second subcategory relates to the legal perspective on human rights. This is necessarily reliant on the establishment and acceptance by states of international law, international courts (such as the International Court of Justice or the International Criminal Court), and international enforcement. What interests proponents of this argument is the adoption of international case law and the willingness of states to accept international jurisdiction.

The third political category is subdivided into a cruder realpolitik conception of politics and a richer more focused notion of politics (understood as a unique human practice aiming to deal with plurality and diversity). The latter argument is explored in more detail in later chapters. The basic premise of the argument is that rights unquestionably are premised upon a pre-existing association. However, this association is a very particular kind of association. Membership is seen as crucial to understand rights, but that membership within the state has to be understood through the medium of citizenship. Both the state and citizenship are mutable practices which have changed throughout the nineteenth and twentieth centuries. In fact, there are identifiable patterns in the way both the state and citizenship have developed. Thus, one of the crucial things to ask here is: how and why our understanding of citizenship and the state have developed and changed? This form of enquiry will provide insights into our current conception of human rights.

Minimally, the above wide-ranging scheme allows an immediate, if rough and ready, answer to the question 'what gives X a right to Y?' Basically, the substantive content of rights provides the grounds for understanding the nature of the right in ordinary practice. The various substantive grounds outlined in this scheme give us an immediate insight into the particular rights and why they are being asserted. In the case of the present book on human rights, my own emphasis will be on human rights understood largely as a species of the genus of political rights.

## Human rights as political rights—who is the subject of rights?

Who is the subject of rights? On one level the answer may seem obvious, namely, individual human persons. However, this is not quite as straightforward as it appears. A lot depends here on how one classifies rights and how one understands persons. In terms of legal and political rights, the subject of rights is usually the individual person understood as a citizen, although in law particularly it can also focus on larger groups, such as companies, corporations, or states. If, alternatively, one regards rights as choice or will-based phenomena, then this frequently and predictably leads to an emphasis on the autonomous agent or individual persons. The benefit or interest theory however tends to concentrate on sentient interest, or, the capacity to have experiences and have interests. This widens the category of who is a subject for rights potentially well beyond the sphere of human persons. A foetus, sentient animals in general, trees, or even ecosystems could potentially all have interests (depending upon how one interprets the concept interest). However, unquestionably, the most common domain to attribute rights is the individual human person. Some might formulate this as *agents* possessing autonomy or a capacity to exercise reason and freedom, although again this can limit the applicability vis-à-vis the foetus, demented, and so forth. The focus on the individual person has been particularly central for human rights. One problem is though that some debates about human rights do suggest that groups, states, or cultures can also have human rights. This would be the case particularly with the human right of peoples or groups to self-determination. Many understandably find such ideas challenging. Some of these difficulties will be examined in later chapters. However, what of the case of political rights—particularly human rights understood as political rights?

There is something paradoxical about human rights, which will be returned to again in later chapters, which bears upon the question concerning who is the subject of rights? The present discussion will not be delving directly into the complex debates as on the nature of the person; however, there is one issue which needs to be canvassed which is pertinent to human rights. Human rights do focus conventionally on the human person or agent as the sole or most important subject of human rights. Human rights are not alone in this supposition. They share this belief, to a degree, with many rights-based arguments. Even those who focus on group rights have often tried to articulate the argument for group rights through a direct analogy with the human person—thus, we have arguments for 'group personality'. Individual personality becomes the medium to discuss the group. Questions arise here as to why the person is important and why it should be rendered respect or dignity. These questions often arise in the area of human right justification.

The only point to briefly consider here is an oddity in the human rights argument. When thinking about human rights, we often bring into play the idea of moral rightness. Human rights will thus be seen to apply externally regardless of their political or legal location. They are seen to act as a standard of progressive measurement of the success or otherwise of politics or law. When we ask the question who is the subject of rights—in a human rights scenario—the most direct answer is the human subject or person, who is seen to be worthy of respect and dignity. Another question then comes to the fore: what are the features that make the human person worthy of this respect? One of the crucial features is that a person, in order to be a person, needs to be a capable subject. The capable subject perceives itself as a subject. That is to say, the person minimally needs to be able to think of themselves as author of their own utterances. Only such a person can respond to the question: why is the person worthy of respect? The person needs to be able to be reflexively aware of themselves as author of their own action, since this forms a premise to notions of good or duty. It is only this reflexive person who can be a subject of rights.

Leaving aside, for the moment, my particular rendering of this respect argument, the basic contention is that human rights arguments usually assume that there is something quite special about human persons, which entails basic esteem and respect for the dignity of the person. If this assumption is accepted, my additional contention would be that a person in order to become fully a person requires other persons. The argument is a fairly old one, tied to the concept of recognition (although it has been recovered rather loosely in some multicultural debates). Persons, to become persons, require other persons to recognize their personhood. We actualize and narrate ourselves in relation to other persons. A human person, to be a person, requires an 'other'. This idea of the importance of the human person thus rests on the idea of interpersonal or relational recognition, an interpersonal recognition which enables the individual person or subject to grow and establish themselves as a person.

For some, this is where human rights score very effectively. We need no institutional mediation here to simply recognize the human person as a person. The relation is direct and universal in character. We recognize a person universally. Yet can we then assert that our recognition of a person automatically entails some notion of right *qua* human right? In my own reading, there is something important missing in this latter argument. A face-to-face interpersonal relation of affirming human personality is fine on a dialogical level, as might appear in a family or friendship, but in order to be conceived in terms of human rights, something more is required—something which enables the transition from simply being a capable human person requiring respect, to being a 'subject of right'. The right is, as it were, a third dimension between two or more persons who have recognized each others' personhood. This third dimension constitutes a crucial aspect of the relation between persons which allows us to raise the idea of right. This third dimension is the institutional political mediation which allows a person to become a real subject for human rights.

The logic of the argument is therefore as follows: to be a person requires a sense of oneself, understood reflexively as a capable self-conscious subject. This reflexivity requires though another person(s) to provide recognition of personhood. This recognition by the other is sufficient for interpersonal moral relations on the level of friendship, but to conceive of a person as a subject of right requires another dimension of relatedness. People who interact on the basis of right attain another level of relatedness, to which both parties are in a sense subject. This is not a morally superior level. It is just another level which is necessary in itself. There is, in other words, a third-party aspect to the relation (as implied in the concept of a right). This third-party relation moves beyond intimacy or familiarity, into a realm involving a degree of necessary anonymity. No one appealing to a human right wants it to be subject to, or at the behest of, some relational familiarity. A right, in one sense, renders a person partly anonymous. However, it is a necessary anonymity which is also premised upon a mutual public trust.

To act as a person implies the recognition of others, and to act with right implies the recognition of other persons in a setting which transcends each person in terms of a third-party relation. This third-party relation is something to which the acting persons must have some trust, in order to stress the right. It is a realm of publicity in which all persons are implicated when they invoke rights. We are necessarily bound to others through the normal systems of social interaction, that is to say we *have to* interact with other persons for the everyday aspects of our life. When we interact with other persons—outside familiar face-to-face relations—we summon wittingly or unwittingly the notion of right. It is a medium of such interaction. This is the medium of right, including human rights. The system of interaction, because it is necessarily anonymous, implies a realm of institutional political guarantees which ensure the effectiveness of the third-party relations—institutions being the medium of public anonymity. Human rights are, as much as any right, third-party relations which invoke publicity and institutional settings and guarantees. Such institutions need to be trusted by all parties for the third-party relatedness to function. When a human right is recognized, it is more than a face-to-face recognition by another person, on the basis of personal recognition. It is a relation and recognition which surpasses the familiar or solidaristic relation. It is a relation which involves a wider public trust and discourse such that parties put their reliance upon another more anonymous relation—a right. This public fiduciary relation is not just a legal relation, it is fundamentally political. In fact, it involves a conception of a public relationship—this public relationship is a setting which in large part addresses human plurality. The rights and implied public trust are maintained and respected within an institutional setting. Politics is the medium of that setting, that is, a space for public appearances where humans imaginatively and critically address their differences, but it is a setting which has implications for both ethics and law.

Politics can therefore be viewed *not* as realm of intimacy or familiarity, but conversely as a realm of conditional potentiality within a framework of third-party relatedness. Public political space is the formal precondition for human potentiality to develop through the medium of citizenship. Because this public space of institutional settings contains guarantees, the condition of third-party relatedness can act as the condition and enabler of human potentiality (as well as embodying the mutual public trust of agents). Power will need to be present. This is a power which is necessarily commonly willed by citizens through the understanding of right as third-party relatedness.

In sum, in being a person and needing others' recognition to be and develop as a person, we necessarily invoke third-party relatedness and therefore the notion of right. This third-party relatedness is first and foremost a political relation mediated through citizenship. In certain specific contexts—under the force of circumstances—humans have struggled to formalize extra-familiar or extra-solidaristic relations, outside of basic violence and intimidation, they have used certain formal mediums to establish third-party relatedness. This forms the *root* to political right—although right was not always the only form of such attempts.[26] However, right now has a pragmatic track record which makes it a popular medium. Right is thus, indirectly, rooted in an anthropological facet of humanity—the need for persons to interact and the various orders of recognition implicit in that relation. Right, in turn, is comprised of a trust in a public sphere and an institutional arena which guarantees the conditional setting for right-based interaction. In this book, the state, particularly a conception of the civil state, is taken to embody this public sphere of politics.

The invocation of right is not necessarily always overtly asserted or litigated; it is rather the background presupposition through which humans can interact outside the setting of familiarity. It is a political setting which self-consciously tries to provide a ground for the negative realization of human powers. This entails the regularization of politics in law. This third-party relatedness is also a mode of relating which involves dialogue. Rights can appear, *prima facie*, to be the monologic assertions of individuals. However, in reality, they are always premised on the fact of human sociality. They are relational. Rights are not configured as part of any familiar or intimate dialogue, but conversely on a dialogue which invokes publicity and a degree of anonymity. This is the way we should begin to think about human rights.

The problem of current human rights, in a nutshell, is that when it comes to the question 'who is the subject of rights?', it has tended to stress the moral dimension. It often focuses on a restricted moral sense of the individual person. This is mainly because of the 'objective right' or 'rightness' dimension of human rights arguments—as well as the legacy of the natural rights. Human rights have therefore been viewed, commonly, as a subspecies of moral right, vis-à-vis the relation with objective right. Consequently, the answer to the question 'who is the subject of rights?' stresses a contextless moral personality—a person formed outside of politics or relational activity. Oddly, even within the various human rights declarations and covenants from 1948 onwards, this conception remains in an uneasy relation with many of the actual human rights articles. The frontage of many human rights arguments is the moral agent or person with absolute rights, standing universally over and against politics and social order. The person in this latter human rights perspective, in asserting rights, remains at the level of moral relatedness. There is unquestionably a pervasive and powerful logic within this moral argument, which lays stress upon the necessary 'externality' of human rights to politics (that is human rights *must* be seen as standards of measurement for politics and law).

The central problem with the moral argument is that it pays little heed to the fact that rights—including human rights—arise predominantly in the context of third-party relatedness. This is the anthropological condition in which humans both relate as persons and then invoke rights. Rights also presuppose a form of public dialogue which is constitutive of politics. For many human rights theorists, this latter argument might well produce insuperable obstacles to any genuine human rights regime, unless of course the public setting (referred to) is some form of global or cosmopolitan ethico-political-legal order. As yet, though, little attempt has been made to link seriously human rights with a global *institutional* setting, apart from some utopian theories about cosmopolitan democracy or justice and the like, which have little contact with current realities.

The brief I set myself in this book is to make sense of human rights in the context of third-party relatedness, a situation which invokes a sense of political publicity and a specific institutional setting. In short, human rights are viewed through a political lens. Many of the problems of human rights have been related to this fundamental issue, namely, that they have been misconceived from the beginning as residing wholly in a domain of morality, which is in fact theoretically and practically inappropriate for right, although it may still be an arena for 'objective rightness'. Consequently, human rights have been seen predominantly as external moral phenomena, which must be asserted or supervened over politics. Those who have often dominated writing on human rights have either been moral philosophers, who have played endlessly and erroneously with this abstracted moral domain to little effect, or legal philosophers or lawyers, who are either indifferent or suspicious of human rights (since only legal claims are meaningful as rights), or, alternatively, see rights wholly and completely as legal phenomena, the fundamental task being to see them codified and enforced. Both sides fail to see the real domain of human rights. Human rights tends to fade in this context either into the world of emasculated philosophical dreams or alternatively obsessive attention to legal protocols.

My argument would be therefore that the 'subject of rights' *is* the reflexive individual person, who requires social recognition from other persons in order to become and grow as a person. However, the manner in which that recognition develops, outside of a moral setting, is through the third-party institutional setting. This argument roots humans in an anthropological context, emphasizing human sociality and the need for others. Interaction is therefore regarded as inevitable. Different forms of interaction bring into play different orders of recognition. Rights, although presupposing the growth of the person, relate *only* to the individual in the third-party setting. Humans can and do grow in the recognition of family and friendship, but that in itself is not enough. A person, quite simply, cannot really develop or grow in the absence of the political setting. The person requires subtle institutional mediations. Human rights are an important dimension of this setting. Without these mediations, the development of the person is annulled or stunted. Human rights, in the way they have most frequently been conceived, have rested at the level of isolated universal persons. The task is now to reconceive human rights in a political frame, in terms of individual persons who are socializing, mutating, growing, interacting, imputing, and affirming in relation to others, in specific public institutional political settings. It is these settings in which humans flourish or fail. It is also in these settings in which human rights become significant and meaningful.

# Conclusion

The aim of this first chapter has been first to examine the word right and the important distinction between objective and subjective right. The discussion then shifted to the complex language of rights as it developed particularly in nineteenth- and twentieth-century thought. Another distinction was then drawn between the sense and type of right. Although the distinction is not consummate and there are clearly many overlaps between these two categories, nonetheless it does provide a serviceable tool for thinking about rights usage. There are though a number of schemes for classifying rights; some of the key ones are critically reviewed. The discussion is by no means exhaustive, but it provides the reader with an overview of some of the most influential contributions to the classification of rights. Finally, the classificatory scheme, which will form a backdrop to the present book, is briefly unpacked. This involves a distinction between legal, moral, and political rights. This classification is taken to cover three of the main substantive uses of rights in current discussion. Natural rights are taken to be the subspecies of moral rights. Human rights are seen to appear under all the categories. Much of the examination of legal, moral, and political rights takes the form of reportage of the way the concepts function in contemporary discussion. The final section of the chapter, which focused on the question 'who is the subject of rights?' elaborates on my own view. In effect the political dimension provides the key focus for the book.

## ☐ NOTES

1. The way in which French and German law appear to make some recognizable distinctions is between *le Droit objectif* and *les droit subjectifs*. Similarly, in German law there is a distinction between *das Recht* and *subjectives Rechten*; see Dietal (1983) and Cornu (1996).

2. These uses are preserved in some dialect usage—'I am right glad to see you'—but they are still not common.

3. This also overlaps with the noun dimension of right.

4. 'So long as the *ius naturale* remained an "objective" standard of measurement,...it made no difference whether one thought of it as "natural right" or "natural law". There was no significant difference of meaning, and there would be none until a "subjective" notion of right appeared, one that contained within it the idea of liberty, meaning by that liberty *from* the authority of just such objective standards of measurement' (Herbert 2002, 49). This is though a very Straussian reading of the issues; see Strauss (1953).

5. Villey was a neo-Thomist, that is, a follower of Thomas Aquinas' ideas.

6. As one writer argues, 'the "rights of the human person" of the Thomist are something entirely different from the "rights of man"' (see D'Entrèves 1977, 48).

7. As Strauss commented, 'The kind of political philosophy which was originated by Socrates is called classical political philosophy, until the emergence of modern political philosophy

in the sixteenth and seventeenth centuries. Modern political philosophy came into being through the conscious break with principles established by Socrates' (see Cropsey and Strauss 1987, 2).

8. As Strauss' disciple, Allan Bloom, put it, 'men live more truly and fully in reading Plato and Shakespeare...because then they are participating in essential being and are forgetting their accidental lives' (Bloom 1987, 380). Political philosophy therefore aspires to 'build on the foundation laid by classical political philosophy, a society superior in truth and justice' (Strauss 1977, 9). It aspires to a kind of foundational wisdom.

9. Articulating Villey's position, Brian Tierney comments that 'the Roman Lawyers did not have in mind our modern concept of *ius* as a subjective right. For them *ius* was not a power over something; it was a thing itself, specifically an incorporeal thing' (Tierney 1997, 16).

10. Tierney thinks it is true that Aquinas 'developed no explicit doctrine of subjective rights or natural rights' (Tierney 1997, 23).

11. 'One might...want to challenge the validity of attributing to Ockham a modern, subjective notion of natural right when he has not severed the objective link between God and nature, a link which leaves all natural right subject to Divine authority, making it less than what the modern would comfortably refer to as a natural right' (Herbert 2002, 68). The world for Ockham is totally dependent on God. Before subjective right can really come to the fore, it needs to be taken out from the theological context. However Villey, for Tierney, 'selects a few suitable texts, drapes a whole theory of law around them, and then refuses to take seriously any texts that do not fit' (Tierney 1997, 18). Tierney thinks that Villey's assessment of Ockham is skewed, although he agrees with Villey that some contemporary debates about rights are 'protracted to the point of absurdity' (Tierney 1997, 30). Tierney also sees a peculiar Manicheanism present in Villey, that is, Aristotelian reason and objective right being set against Ockhamite darkness and subjective right. Further, for Tierney, 'Once we realize that the assertion of a rights doctrine is not necessarily dependent on a prior acceptance of a nominalist philosophy and that claims for individual rights have commonly existed in a symbiotic relationship, one might say, with theories of objective natural right and natural moral law rather than in opposition to them, then the whole problem of the origin of Western rights theories can be approached in ways different to Villey's' (Tierney 1997, 34). For further, if different, strong criticism, see Tuck (1979, ch. 1, especially 19ff.).

12. In this general understanding of the 'force' or 'strength' of rights talk, Ronald Dworkin has spoken of rights as 'trumps' (Dworkin 1977). Rights, understood as trumps, embody a categorical priority in debates. Thus, an individual can even (in certain contexts) trump the collective power of state with valid rights. How successful this will be remains open. The reasons implicit in such rights, in this later case, are usually considered to be fairly fundamental ones. Given the strength of rights as trumps, there is a continuous and fluid debate concerning how far rights extend. They might be described as high-priority norms. Given this potential effect, the assertion or promulgation of any right usually entails assessing and weighing the reasons implicit in such claims.

13. This is contentious since it implies that human rights, as in a manner outside society, would also need societal endorsement to be rights. Feinberg, for example, thinks of human rights as 'manifesto rights' in this context.

14. Again others have analysed this interest conception as a permission or a power. The importance of any right—in this context—is largely dependent upon the weight of the interest, benefit, or the strength of the permission or power.

15. When interest theory is applied to human rights, it is worth noting that it tends to stress material benefits quite heavily, that is the satisfaction of vital material interests before liberty (see Nickel 1987, 114).

16. 'The function of a legal rights is to resolve…conflicts by guiding legal priority to the desires and decision of one party over those of the other. A legal right is the allocation of a sphere of freedom and control to the possessor of the right in order that it may be up to him which decisions are effective within that defined sphere' (Wellman 1975, 52).

17. 'In the area of conduct covered by that duty the individual who has the right is a small-scale sovereign to whom the duty is owed. The fullest measure of control comprises three distinguishable elements: (i) the right-holder may waive or extinguish the duty to leave it in existence; (ii) after breach or threatened breach of duty he may leave it "unenforced" or may "enforce" it by suing for compensation or, in certain cases, for an injunction or mandatory order to restrain the continued or further breach of duty; and (iii) he may waive or extinguish the obligation to pay compensation to which the breach gives rise' (Hart 1983, 183–4).

18. Hart admits that many 'immunity rights' simply exclude the exercise of powers in a way that would divest an individual of their rights.

19. Whereas Kramer is immensely keen to link his own rendering of interest theory with Hohfeld, the work of other interest-based legal theorists, such as Joseph Raz, Jeremy Waldron, and Neil McCormick, is relatively indifferent to the Hohfeldian analysis.

20. 'I believe that right is a complex structure of Hohfeldian positions, especially of claims, liberties, powers, and immunities. The "core" of a right defines its essential content, that to which the right-holder has a right…. This constitutes a real right, however, only together with a number of "associated elements", other Hohfeldian positions, that, if respected, confer upon the possessor of the rights, both freedom and control over this core. These elements include the creditor's legal power to waive her claim to repayment and thereby cancel the debtor's duty to repay the amount borrowed, the legal liberty to waive or not waive her claim as she chooses, and a legal immunity against the debtor's extinguishing her core claim simply by saying, "I hereby cancel my debt to you"' (Wellman 1999, 8–9). Wellman adds here that this would also be a way in which one could think about human rights. He notes that 'the defining core of the human rights to free speech is the moral liberty of each individual human being to speak out or remain silent on any subject no matter how controversial….Associated elements in this fundamental human rights include the moral claim against the government that it not attempt to silence the right-holder by coercive measures and the moral immunity against the government's extinguishing her moral liberty of free speech' (Wellman 1999, 9).

21. Although even Kramer admits that Hohfeld's writings 'become quite tiresome in their lengthy highlightings of the harmony between his own usages and the usages favoured by certain judges' (Kramer 1998, 23).

22. Most of the current debate on rights 'is no longer concerned with clarification of the nature of rights in general,…but, rather, with clarifying the specific differences in grammatical usage that have been spun in recent decades' (Herbert 2002, 300).

23. Milne suggests that Hohfeld's idea preserves but amplifies the 'action' and 'recipience' distinction.

24. Nonetheless, at the same time, we neglect at our cost the political context of law. There can be no law which creates a rule of law. Law can tell us much about rights, but the insistent demands for jurisprudential specialization and training, combined with a philosophical jurisprudential scholasticism, can evade the very simple fact that law, in itself, is insufficient to account for rights. Legal rules (and the acceptance of legal processes) always develop in political contexts. Legal rights are directly or indirectly, at root, political rights at one remove. An abstract rationalistic legal science focused on legal language and the logic of legal concepts is of pedagogic value in training law students in precise thinking, but it provides little insight into rights as they function in the political world. In this sense, the substantive legal category only takes us so far in understanding rights—particularly human rights.

25. This form of argument obviously profoundly affects many in the pro-life camp within the protracted abortion debates.

26. Rights being entities which derive loosely from fourteenth-century European thought.

# 2 The Context of Rights

Chapter 1 scrutinized the word 'right', and the distinction between objective and subjective right. It then turned to consider the distinction between the sense and type of right. This latter distinction was seen as more of an imperfect but nonetheless functional pedagogic tool for elucidating certain aspects of rights language. Having discussed the various senses of right, the discussion then turned to an evaluation of some of the key classifications of rights, which have dominated the literature. The most hegemonic of these have been the will and interest theories and the Hohfeldian schemes—although they are not necessarily the most illuminating or helpful. The discussion of typologies concluded with the classificatory scheme which underpins this book and focuses on the substantive content of rights rather than simply the logic of rights talk. The final section examined the question 'who is the subject of rights?' It was argued that the subject of rights is the reflexive human person, who requires social recognition from other persons in order to become and grow as a person. However, the manner in which that recognition develops, outside of an intimate moral setting, is through third-party political institutional setting. A person cannot develop in the absence of this setting. The person therefore requires institutional mediations.

The aim of this chapter is, first, to fill in a number of gaps implicit in chapter 1. This entails concentrating more specifically on the *origin* of the term right, in terms of natural right argumentation—natural right often being seen as the precursor of human rights in the twentieth century. Another reason for following the various senses of natural right is to ascertain the main grounds on which natural rights arguments were deployed and, second, to establish the primary senses in which the term natural right was used, particularly in the seventeenth and eighteenth centuries. Some of these arguments have bearing upon human rights theories of the twentieth century. The primary purpose of this chapter is to set the scene for a discussion of human rights. My own supposition here would be to see more of an intellectual space between natural and human rights, certainly more than others allow. This will be developed more fully in chapter 3. There is therefore an analytical purpose contained within the historical discussion.[1]

The central arguments concerning natural right usage are, first, there is no one pristine sense of natural right, certainly in terms of the 'purported' legacy of natural rights into the twentieth century. There are rather a number of senses of natural right which need to be disentangled; for the sake of clarity, a distinction will be drawn between *minimal* and *maximal* senses of natural right. Despite these different senses of the term natural right, there are still certain underlying themes which are present in all natural rights usage, certainly prior to the nineteenth century. My argument will be that ultimately many of these senses of natural right are partly or totally lost by the early nineteenth and early twentieth centuries.[2] What we have then in the late twentieth century are ghostly echoes of a largely redundant vocabulary or, alternatively, odd transmutations of an older terminology. The term 'natural right' continues to appear into the twentieth century, often in *locus classicus* contributions such as H. L. A. Hart's 'Are there any natural rights?', Margaret MacDonald's 'Natural rights', or within Robert Nozick's *Anarchy, State and Utopia* (1974); caution should make us reflect much more carefully and critically upon such contributions in terms of the accuracy of their conceptual usage. In many ways, the somewhat bland ahistorical analytic presence in this body of argument frequently obfuscates rather than illuminates debates about natural rights.

This chapter glosses the fierce and protracted debates over the origins of natural rights; this is an unwieldy, technical, and unresolved series of debates within rights scholarship. Only the broad outline and general contours will be summarized, since the detailed substance is not wholly germane to my human rights focus. The aim is more to sketch in the general background of rights discourse. Second, the discussion will then turn to the concept of natural law, which is seen by many commentators to be closely connected to the concept of natural right. The initial focus will be on the various senses of natural law, particularly on ancient and modern usages, Catholic and Protestant, and religious and more secular uses. This latter section will also examine some of the more standard justificatory strategies of natural law argument, some of which are relevant for grasping natural rights arguments. The discussion will then turn to the various accounts of the relation between the concepts of natural law and natural right. This will be followed by a summary of my own perspective on natural right in terms of what I call the maximal and minimal senses of the term. The general omnipresence of the concept 'natural' (and the particular ways it is understood) in all these arguments forms the platform for chapter 3.

# The origins of natural right

When examining the idea of natural right, we are directly addressing the origin of the word right itself. This was alluded to in the section of chapter 1 concerned with objective and subjective right. In this sense, the origin of natural right is of interest to scholars of rights, since it also sketches the background to 'right in general'. The debate over the origin of natural rights, and indeed rights in general, will not be resolved here and this book is manifestly not about natural right per se. In one sense, it would however be true that discussion of the origins of rights is coterminous with discussion of the origin of natural rights. However, many have seen a strong conceptual connection between natural rights and human rights. As mentioned above, some have seen the terms as virtually one and the same. This is even affirmed in official documentation, such as the UNESCO symposium *Human Rights: Comments and Interpretations*, which speaks of 'the antiquity and broad acceptance of the conception of the rights of man', relating it back to the beginnings of Western and Eastern thought (UNESCO 1949, 260). Similarly a recent theorist, Carl Wellman, notes that although the idea of human rights is a comparatively recent idea, it nonetheless expresses 'an ancient one, for what we call human rights today are the descendents of the traditional natural rights of man' (Wellman 1999, 13–14). One should add a rider to this insofar as Wellman locates the origin of natural rights largely in the seventeenth-century revolutionary debates in North America and Europe. There are many arguments for this claim; however, it is treated with caution in the main discussion.

The general idea behind the judgement concerning the antiquity of rights, particularly natural rights, is to provide rights with a long and esteemed pedigree. The main point would be that all societies have revered some form of justice and civil order, which entails an implicit or explicit understanding of the concept of right. However, it would not be true that all have thought of civil order in terms of rights. Not all civilizations have perceived order and justice in the same manner. The earliest conventional starting point for this is usually the ancient world of the Hellenistic Greeks. Philosophers such as Plato and Aristotle, and more particularly the later Stoic thinkers, are often spoken of as originators of the concept of right. Some have though pushed this back even further to ancient legal codes such as the Hebrew Torah or the Code of Hammurabi (based on the Amorite Dynasty of ancient Babylon), especially where there are perceived public rules laid down for property ownership (see Dagger 1989, 296). There were clearly a number of early law codes in most civilizations, but the majority laid down commands or imperatives. Thus, Moses, for example, handed down commandments and duties, *not* rights (see also Glendon 2001, 33; Sharma 2005, 145ff.).

A great deal depends here—as in the history of right itself—on whether we are concerned about the fact that the word right, vis-à-vis subjective right, did not exist until arguably either the twelfth or fourteenth centuries. There have been three broad suggestions here. The first indicates that there were a range of other, but closely related, words in both Greek and Roman thought. These embody many of the basic themes of a rights-based language, such as the

Greek words *dikaion* or *dike*, which we might now translate as justice. There were strong implications that participation in Greek public affairs in ancient city states such as Athens could be understood as a right, although it is difficult to think of this in terms of an individual or subjective right (see Gewirth 1978, 100–1). Further, any 'right' that could be enjoyed would obviously not be experienced by slaves, women, or children, even in the most open city states such as Athens. In addition, in the Greek context, rights to participation would be enjoyed largely in terms of status within a clan or similar group. Ancient Greek and Roman societies had definite hierarchical components. Similarly, for some, the Latin words *ius* (*jus*), *auctoritas, potestas, dominium* arguably yield dimensions of the rights concept, although once again, whether it was anything that could be described as a subjective claim is doubtful. Second, some suggest that there are strong indications of the awareness of the presence of certain basic issues in ancient Greek drama, which have a rights focus, as in Sophocles' play *Antigone*. We often tend to think of the drama in this context, but whether that is simply translating the play into our present medium remains an unresolved question.

Third, it can be argued that the presence of a concept does not necessarily require a particular word. Thus, although the *word* right was not available till much later (say the twelfth or fourteenth centuries), nonetheless the *concept* of right was still present in very early societies in embryonic form. This view on the presence of the concept is argued, for example, by Alan Gewirth in a predominantly ahistorical format. Gewirth's argument is based on examining the logical conditions for human action. The novelty of his approach is the attempt to derive, logically, normative principles from what is immanent in the concept of human action. For Gewirth, therefore, every agent, simply on the basis of engaging in purposive action, is 'logically committed' to certain principles; that is to say 'evaluative and deontic judgments on the part of agents are logically implicit in action'. Thus, any 'agent, simply by virtue of being an agent, must admit, on pain of self-contradiction, that he ought to act in certain determinate ways' (Gewirth 1978, 26). Gewirth builds on this conclusion to show how this logically requires every agent to accept certain judgements about fundamental rights—rights to the conditions of action. He therefore sees the presence of the concept of rights as a logical issue derived from the conditions of action. This whole position entails that action, wherever it exists, manifests the same features, regardless of historical circumstance.

The one problem Gewirth has here is that no word exists for rights in Greek and Roman thought. He thus makes a further distinction, namely, between 'having or using a concept and the clear or explicit recognition and elucidation of it.... Thus persons might have and use the concept of a right without explicitly having a single word for it: a more complex phrase might signify or imply the concept'. Gewirth goes on to suggest that this throws doubt on any arguments trying to assert the purely modern nature of right. Gewirth thinks it a fundamental error to restrict rights to the early modern or modern eras. Rights themes can be found even in Plato and Aristotle and indeed many, as Gewirth puts it, 'primitive societies' (see Gewirth 1978, 99–101). Undoubtedly there were equivalents to right and wrong (in Michel Villey's objective sense of right) in ancient Greek and Roman societies. Something could be perceived as right or just by nature, but that is *not* the same as the distinctive notion of subjective right. In fact, Gewirth's argument, lacking as it does any real sound historical apparatus or scholarship, is distinctly shaky and wholly speculative on this whole issue. He also assumes crassly the timelessness of his own understanding of both argument and logic and indeed philosophy.

Roman law is, as indicated, in a similar position to the Hellenistic Greek understanding. Undoubtedly for some scholars the first uses of subjective right can be found in documents such as Justinian's *Institutes* and *Digest*, although for others the writings of Cicero on natural law would be another fertile area.[3] The problem again here is that these various writings and legal codes, although embodying conceptions of natural law, contained no explicit sense of, what we would now understand by, 'a subjective right'. Thus, as indicated earlier, there are strong indications of objective right, just outcomes and just states of affairs, but no real sense of subjective claims being made by individuals (Kamenka and Tay 1978, 78–9; Tuck 1979; Herbert 2002, 42). This bears out Alisdair MacIntyre's argument—directly alluding to Gewirth's arguments above—that 'there is no expression in any ancient or medieval language correctly translated by our expression "a right" until near the close of the Middle Ages: the concept lacks any means of expression in Hebrew, Greek, Latin or Arabic, classical or medieval, before about 1400, let alone in Old English or in Japanese even as late as the mid-nineteenth century' (MacIntyre 1981, 67ff.). Reflecting upon MacIntyre's comments, Brian Tierney complains though that although MacIntyre is absolutely correct in his judgement on Gewirth, he still does not really comprehend the history. MacIntyre, for Tierney, is therefore in error when he argues that no language existed to discuss natural rights (as subjective claims) before the fourteenth century (see Tierney 1997, 3, 44). The qualification is small but important for Tierney.

This brings the discussion onto the three more popular accounts in the literature indicating the origin of subjective right. A great deal of time and effort has been expended on each of these arguments; however, they will only be briefly summarized. The three periods are essentially the twelfth, fourteenth, and seventeenth centuries. The last two tend to be the two most popular periods amongst scholars. Brian Tierney is probably the best-known exponent of the twelfth-century argument. Tierney complains that most historical discussions of rights place its origin in either the late medieval or early modern periods. He contends that there has been a 'welter' of work on rights, particularly on certain early modern areas in the seventeenth century. But there has only been 'a thin trickle' of work on the 'idea of natural rights in the premodern era' (Tierney 1997, 6). Tierney sees natural right as often connected wrongly with nominalist philosophy, the inception of the doctrines of individualism, and modern political economy. Tierney's own position is that 'the humanistic jurisprudence of the 12th century, especially the writing of the medieval Decretists, may provide a better starting point for investigating the origins of natural rights theories than either fourteenth-century nominalism or the nascent capitalism of the early modern period' (Tierney 1997, 43).[4] The key Decretist figures, for Tierney, are commentators such as Rufinus, Ricardus, Hugucio, and Alanus, amongst others.[5] For Tierney, there is no one decisive or single great text amongst these writers on subjective right; nonetheless by the close of the twelfth century, their views on rights were familiar and formed an important background influence on thinkers such as Jean Gerson and William of Ockham (Tierney 1997, 54). He thus complains that scholars such as Michel Villey and Richard Tuck have paid far too little attention to canonists and such Decretists (Tierney 1983, 1997). He suggests that many of the key themes and distinctions that can be found in modern rights theories in the twentieth century can also be found in these very early Decretist writers.[6]

Tuck, in his study of the origin of natural right, also focused on another late twelfth-century grouping, the Glossators.[7] It was in the late twelfth-century Glossators, such as Accursius, that for Tuck we can see the first glimmerings of subjective right, via the assimilation of *ius* with *dominium*. For Tuck, by the early fourteenth century, an agent could be seen as *dominus* (owner of a property) over an area or object and it could thus be perceived as an early form of subjective property right. In fact, all rights came to be viewed in these terms (see Tuck 1979, 3, 13). The only proviso to add here is that these early rights arguments, via the Glossators, were all 'claim rights'; that is, they were understood passively. There were no active rights. They functioned insofar as others had to forbear from interference. Subsequently, therefore, 'there is a direct line linking Accursius with the late medieval rights theorists, and through them with the great seventeenth-century figures' (Tuck 1979, 16). Medieval lawyers, after the likes of Accursius, thus tended to see *ius* in terms of *dominus*—and hence as a subjective property right. Yet for Tuck one should not make the mistake of simply seeing this as a form of early liberal theory.

For Tuck the more complete understanding of subjective right developed in the writings of Jean Gerson (Chancellor of the University of Paris) in the early 1400s. Tuck sees in Gerson the first development of right as an 'active liberty', rather than a passive claim right. Prior to Gerson, the idea of liberty, ability, or faculty had been only part of non-moral discourse. A *liberty*, particularly in Roman and medieval law, could not be a right. *Libertas* in fact contrasted with *ius*. However, Gerson, says Tuck, for the first time was 'able to assimilate *ius* and *libertas*'. *Ius* becomes a power to do something in line with what reason dictates. Further, liberty becomes a form of property right (*dominium*). Tuck comments that 'Gerson left it to his successors to develop it fully. It was in the universities of Tübingen and Paris, both famous in the fifteenth and early sixteenth centuries as centres of Gerson's kind of nominalism, that the work was done'. These successors transformed the twelfth-century 'claim right' into an active right of liberty—which was then seen in terms of a sovereign control over one's world, an active *dominus*. Consequently, for Tuck by the end of the sixteenth century, 'the Gersonian theory of right seemed to reign supreme' (Tuck 1979, 25–8).

Tuck develops the above argument partly against the interpretation of Michel Villey. Villey's general views, which have already been alluded to in chapter 1, are fairly common currency in the rights literature. The general contention is that the first real understanding of subjective right can be found in the writings of the fourteenth-century philosopher William of Ockham, who, for many commentators inspired nominalist philosophy, voluntarist thinking, and the embryonic doctrine of individualism. This is a position that one can, for example, find argued in MacIntyre's *After Virtue*, amongst other writings (MacIntyre 1981, 66–7, see also Wilks 1963; McGrade 1974, 1980). The nominalist attack on universals and metaphysics is seen as working in parallel with similar changes in moral and political life, thus forming a key background to the more modern obsessions with individualism and subjective right (see e.g. Brett 1997, 49ff.). There is thus a metaphysical shift within epistemology and legal and political philosophy. This is where Villey and indeed Leo Strauss place the whole subjective right debate. The conflict between older objective notions of right is set against the modern doctrine of individualism and the subjectivism of rights. Both Villey and Strauss see a profound moral message here, signalling a deep conflict between the ancients and moderns. For Villey, particularly, Aquinas is the characteristic expression of the pure classical tradition of natural law, Thomist understanding of right being an obligation or duty, rather than the liberty of the subject. Both Tierney and Tuck vigorously disagree with this Ockhamite argument. However, Brett suggests, contrary to Tuck and Tierney, that Ockham was innovative in his use of *ius*. He does invoke a distinctive and unique theory of human agency. In this sense, she sees some virtue in Villey's thesis that right in Ockham implies a 'subjective power of action' (Brett 1997, 63).

For Tierney, though, Villey's thesis is far too uncritically accepted by the scholarly community. Villey was influential, for Tierney, but he was neither correct in his academic judgements, nor was he at all innovative (Tierney 1997, 53). Tuck also maintains—against Villey—that it was not Ockham, but rather the late twelfth-century Glossators who were most innovative. The latter are thus seen as critical for understanding subjective right, in terms of the blending of *dominium* and *ius*.[8] For other scholars, Tuck's account is deeply unsatisfactory. Brett, for example, suggests that it is 'anachronistic to talk of the equivalence of *ius* and *dominium* as the beginning of subjective right' in the period of the twelfth century. She also contends that any equivalence 'is far from being the universal outlook in the moral theology of the middle ages—not even among authors who can be said to have had a notion of "subjective right"' (Brett 1997, 11). For Tierney, neither Villey nor Tuck (nor one suspects Brett) presents 'adequate or satisfying' accounts of these origins (see Tierney 1983, 1988, and quote from 1997, 7). Tierney, for example, sees Tuck as doubly wrong—he is seen to mistake active liberty rights for passive claim rights, contending that Tuck's active–passive distinction makes little or no difference anyway. He also vigorously disagrees with Tuck's reading of Gerson, which he describes variously as total 'nonsense' and 'unpersuasive' (Tierney 1997, 216–17).[9] Although Tierney himself has his own favoured origin in the Decretists, nonetheless, his position is more nuanced and slightly more eclectic than it originally appears. He thus comments that 'If we want to seek the origins of a doctrine of natural rights we must learn to understand a medieval religious tradition and medieval society where the values of individualism and of community were equally cherished. Holist and individualist doctrines can be forced to extreme where they seem mutually exclusive. But they do not have to be so forced' (Tierney 1997, 235). Consequently, he echoes a point made at the opening of his book, namely, that the story of natural rights is largely one of the contexts or environments in which they were used (Tierney 1997, 6).

The third and the most popular account of the origins of natural right lies in the seventeenth century, which many scholars have viewed as the great classical period of natural right (see e.g. Ritchie 1952, 5ff.; Melden 1970, 2; D'Entrèves 1977, 51ff.; Jones 1994, 75ff.; Wellman 1999, 14; Baehr 2001, 2; Herbert 2002, 105ff.; Donnelly 2002; Tomuschat 2003, 11ff.). Tierney admits that this view persists, but contests it, complaining that in a book such as Ian Schapiro's *The Evolution of Rights in Liberal Theory* (1986), the author naively 'writes as though the world began in the seventeenth century' (Tierney 1997, 44, n. 4). The classical period covers a wide range of thinkers including Francisco Suárez, Hugo Grotius, Thomas Hobbes, John Locke, and Samuel Pufendorf. The period also overlaps—most decisively for the modern era—with social contract theory, the growth of individualism, modern political economy, and the conception of a more atomized view of society (see D'Entrèves 1977, 51ff.; Jones 1994, 77–8). For some scholars, such as Knud Haakonssen (and Tuck to a lesser degree), the Dutch seventeenth-century writer Hugo Grotius takes on a decisive role here (Tuck 1979, 58ff., 1987; Haakonssen 1985, 1996). For others, such as Leo Strauss and Michael Oakeshott, Hobbes figures as the decisive influence on the modern concept of right (Strauss 1952, 155–7, 1953; Oakeshott 1991, 221ff.). However, for the larger majority of commentators, it is John Locke's work which is the key to grasping modern natural right.[10]

The standard natural rights in this later period were still fairly limited in scope, namely, usually life, liberty, happiness, and often property. They were also largely negative in terms of non-interference. Grotius' *De Jure Belli ac Pacis* (1625) argued, in effect, that instead of something being in accordance with law, *ius* (right) is seen as something that a person actually has or possesses. *Ius* was seen by Grotius though as both the ability of the person to have or do something justly, as well as what is just in itself. The concept becomes more closely linked to the claims of the individual human subject. It thus centres on the individual person and *ius* develops into a moral power (*facultas*) of that person. Further, human life is envisaged as one of the competing individuals. *Ius* is a moral power over people, keeping others apart from one's own *suum* (see Haakonssen 1985, 240). Natural law is then configured as mutual respect for subjective natural rights. Controversially, although this can be overdone, Grotius indicated that a belief in natural law does not necessarily logically require belief in God.

In Thomas Hobbes' *The Leviathan* (1651), natural laws become prudential maxims, which are largely separated from natural rights. Law is viewed as a restraint and rights are powers and liberties. Hobbes' natural rights are thus seen predominantly as subjective *liberties* or *powers*. Hobbes' conception of a natural liberty (*naturalis libertas*) is that of a natural faculty of doing what one wills, initially in terms of preserving oneself. It is a right of nature, as Hobbes sees it, and it is close to what earlier jurists called a *facultas animi*.[11] It is the opportunity of acting upon one's own will, and of using what power one has in accordance with that will. Hobbes' natural liberty can therefore be described as the free faculty of will. It is, in part, surrendered to a commonwealth. In John Locke's *The Two Treatises on Government* (1690), natural rights become the dominant feature of the argument, focused on specific individual claims (life, liberty, and property). A right for Locke is a claim, circumscribed by natural laws. A right is largely a constraint on others, which implies that they must forbear from interfering with my life, liberty, and property. Natural law serves an underlying supportive purpose here to natural right. It gives directives—which are not just prudential guides to action. They are more morally substantive. Natural law, first, directs us not to harm others in 'life, health, liberty or possession'; second, everyone is bound to preserve themselves (i.e. their own lives) and also all other human beings (unless there is good cause not to); third, everyone has the basic right (in preserving themselves and their possessions) to punish transgressors. Natural right thus becomes an individual claim or entitlement.

The seventeenth and eighteenth centuries have frequently been viewed as the age of natural rights. This age drew together conceptions of human autonomy with rights as powers and liberties. Even Tierney acknowledges this, namely, that by 'the seventeenth century...complex rights theories existed in which words like "nature", "reason", "licit", "right", were inter-woven with words like "power", "freedom", "faculty"'. He also suggests that the most able exponent of this rights language was the eighteenth-century philosopher Christian Wolff (Tierney 1997, 51–2). This was the age of the early Bills of Rights in Virginia, North America, France, and so forth. It was also an age of rights, which many see as the precursor to the human rights documents of the twentieth century. Legal, moral, and political legitimacy became increasingly inseparable from subjectivity. This, as indicated, then formed a baseline for contract and consent theories of the government. It had close links, for some scholars, with conceptions of popular sovereignty, namely, where the will and interest of each individual subject had to be repre-sented in some way.

Having reviewed some major accounts of the origin of right—particularly natural rights—and before moving onto my own understanding of natural right and its relation with human rights, I want briefly to discuss the concept of natural law.

## Natural law

The discussion of natural law is necessary—within limits—since it has a tangled relationship with natural right. Indeed, in the same way that some have seen a close relation between natural right and human rights, others have seen some close connections between natural law and twentieth-century human rights—if only via natural rights.

One problem in focusing on natural law is that the terminology sur-rounding 'nature' and 'natural' is complex.[12] The first thing to get a handle on here is the concept of natural law itself. What does it mean? The origin of natural law overlaps with natural right. Some indeed have traced natural law (and right) ideas directly to Greek, particularly Aristotelian thought. The natural law that will be focused on here has roots in Roman law, originating in the fifth-century law codes of Justinian—the *Corpus Iuris Civilis* (AD 534), and then revivified in the twelfth century.[13] Natural law was one of a troika of laws inherited from the Romans: the laws of particular communities *ius civile*, the laws of nations *ius gentium* (which some have seen as an early form of international law, although for the Romans it was more of a functional tool in dealing with new peoples) and the *ius naturale* (which referred loosely to a standard of justice). There is a great variety of opinion on the exact relation-ship between these terms—some see them as separate, others think that natural law is the most authoritative dimension. However, it is clear that the *Corpus Iuris* did not assert the superiority of natural to any other type of law.

The natural law that became familiar from the early medieval period was a blending of Christian thought with Roman law and elements of Greek philosophy, particularly Aristotelianism and Stoicism. The first and most impressive thinker to systematically present and synthesize natural law, one who is mentioned in virtually every discussion of natural law, is Thomas Aquinas. Natural law has a pivotal role in Aquinas' theories, particularly of law, politics, and morality.[14] His work can also be taken as representative of traditional medieval natural law thinking.

Natural law at its simplest indicates that there is a close relation between law and morality, that is to say there are moral reasons for laws and further that individuals require moral reasons as to why laws should be obeyed. Law can therefore only be law when it 'ought' to be, or, alternatively, law ought to live up to certain moral standards. Further natural law theory assumes that humans, universally, have a natural inclination to be rational, and thus natural law is founded on our rational natures. Further, natural law assumes that humanity forms one universal community, and such laws are rooted in a common unchanging universal human nature. Natural law is consequently a body of innate, self-evident, substantive principles implanted in human nature and right reason. It embodies the dignity of humans, above all created things, namely, through our ability to participate intelligently in a rational order of the universe. By using our reason we can perceive both our own duties and the duties of the state. It is therefore the source of positive legislation and the ground on which political and moral relations can be comprehended. To relate this directly to chapter 1, natural law is the most important form of 'objective right'.[15] Law should always mirror what is objectively morally right.[16]

It is important though to make an immediate distinction here between forms of natural law. There is a traditional, usually Christian-based, natural law rooted in medieval thought and there is a later more secularized variant which relies more extensively on reason as an authoritative principle, rather than God or scripture. One should not though exaggerate this distinction, since there are many subtle variations within these arguments.

## RELIGION AND NATURAL LAW

All natural law presupposes a cosmic or transcendent norm or value which is beyond any questioning; this provides the grounds for moral judgement. There is, in other words, a fundamental universal or unchangeable foundation which is completely authoritative over all human beings. In all the early Western forms of natural law, this foundation was God and the imperatives were contained in biblical scriptures (*lex naturalis in corde scripta*). Natural law in Aquinas is one aspect of a series of laws. Ultimately there is eternal law (a rational plan by God for all creation). Natural law is an aspect of divine providence. It is a necessary, but not a sufficient, condition for salvation. One also needs grace, which can arise through revelation, which is a form of divine law (with the same basic content as natural law, but still a different category of law for Aquinas). It is worth noting here that this traditional form of natural law does *not* begin with an individual, or any notion of subjective right, but conversely with God and certain absolute norms. If anything, natural law is a bridge between the individual and God, a way for the individual to identify God's purposes.

Another important dimension of natural law focuses on reason, or more precisely, practical reason. The more traditional natural law argument would go as follows: nature is God's creation. Human nature is therefore God's creation. Reason is a central identifying feature of human nature. It constitutes our uniqueness and the source of our spiritual dignity. Through practical reason we can participate intelligently in the rational order of the universe. Reason is constituted by rules. Natural laws constitute these rules; thus, natural law *is* what is practically reasonable.[17] To follow practical reason is therefore to follow natural law, which is God's law. Natural law is thus embedded in practical reason. All humans, regardless of sex, age, ethnicity, or nationality, can know this substantive content by using their own reason (a reason implicit in their nature as humans). The reasonable contents of natural law always direct us to certain goods, which facilitate the development of our natures as human beings. The most fundamental natural principle is that we should always do good and avoid evil. Aquinas also refers to procreation, knowledge, life, and social existence as additional intrinsic goods. To follow these goods is to make one's actions rational and intelligible. Aquinas thinks therefore that there is a nucleus to all practical knowledge, and all humans can grasp it, even if the connotations of that knowledge can sometimes be difficult to identify.

Practical reason therefore implies that there are choices to be made—between good and bad actions. Action is performed for an end, which can be called a good. There are many partial or limited goods for humans which provide temporary passing satisfaction. Evil though is a lack of good, although it is also parasitic on good. Evil is basically a fundamental absence of reasonable human existence. Good is the only real object of rational human appetite and the real substance to human existence. A completely rational good must satisfy our full human nature; it is identifiable *only* through reason. This is the most complete good for our rational appetites. The complete good is thus tied to the essence of reason and human nature. The essence of practical reason is God (who is perfectly good); reason always directs us to that perfect good, via natural laws. The complete good and happiness can thus only be found in God (*beatitudo*). By using our practical reason, we can perceive both our own personal moral duties and our duties to the state. We can also grasp what a state or civil order ought to do. Natural law is therefore the source of positive legislation and civil laws. It is also the ground on which political and moral relations can be comprehended. This is the standard hegemonic natural law position that moved into the early seventeenth century.

## SECULARITY AND COMPLEXITY IN NATURAL LAW

Yet there is another form of natural law which developed in the seventeenth century which was basically a more secularized conception. In speaking about a more secular conception of natural law, one has to proceed with some caution. The area is far more multifaceted than at first appears. There are three subtle distinctions to observe here: the first is between religious and secular natural law; the second is between Catholic and Protestant versions of natural law; and the third is between older and more recent or modern versions of natural law. All these distinctions have overlapping, occasionally contradictory, aspects. The present discussion can only provide a brief gloss on these intricate scholarly domains.

It is true that 'natural law theories during the seventeenth and eighteenth centuries lost more and more of their theological appearance, and as they increasingly became theories of state law, they instead gained in purely juristic technicality' (Haakonssen 1985, 247). However, as a number of scholars also observe, we should not be too premature is seeing outright secularism here. It is rather an increasing *neglect* of moral theology in favour of the juristic technicalities, rather than any outright rejection. It would, however, also be true that by the later eighteenth century, and even more true in certain mid-twentieth-century attempts to revivify natural law, secular reasoning does take a much more self-conscious role.[18] Rational juristic and moral philosophy were the predominant motifs, usually with God as a background cheering chorus. Thus, in a late twentieth-century natural law philosopher, such as John Finnis, natural law only embodies 'theories of the rational foundations of moral judgment' (Finnis 1980, 25). This is not though a wholly accurate picture, since there are also Catholic philosophers well into the twentieth century, such as Jacques Maritain (who was involved in the official human rights debates in 1948), who see natural law and natural rights in terms of a systematic moral theology and religious philosophy (see e.g. Maritain 1944). Reason *can* though become wholly self-sufficient in making the case for natural law.

It would also be true that some of the late seventeenth- and early eighteenth-century trajectories of reasoning on natural law towards secularity coincide—to a certain degree—with the shifting onus of natural law philosophy from Catholic to Protestant thinkers (see Tuck 1987; Haakonssen 1996, 15ff.; Tierney 1997, 316).[19] One of the major Protestant thinkers to be associated with natural law and natural right, as well as the shift to secularity in modern natural law understanding, was Hugo Grotius (1583–1645). Indeed he is often seen as the father figure of modern natural law theory.[20] Others have doubted as to whether Grotius' most eminent book *De Jure Belli ac Pacis* (1625) was that unique. Grotius borrowed a great deal from late Catholic natural law scholasticism, particularly from the work of the Spanish Catholic Thomist Francisco Suárez.[21] However, there are still unquestionably novel dimensions to Grotius' work, although not many Grotian scholars agree what exactly that novelty actually consists in. Some see him replacing natural law with natural right, others see him combating the scepticism of Michel de Montaigne and Pierre Charron, and others again see him introducing secular reason into natural law discussion. The latter would particularly be the case in his *etiamsi daremus* doctrine, which argues that even if there were no God natural law would still exist. This doctrine has been read as proclaiming the self-sufficiency of secular reason. However, even this can be over exaggerated, since it was a fairly common idea in scholastic writing and was probably borrowed by Grotius from Suárez (see Tierney 1997, 319). It was not really until the writings of the eighteenth-century philosopher David Hume that there began to be serious doubts about the idea that God created the world and was the source of natural law (see Hume 1966).

Grotius, although articulating the idea of the self-sufficiency of reason, was not a secularist. The content of Grotius' natural law was not that novel. It was in fact reliant upon a more traditional natural law scholasticism. The law of nature was still largely seen as implanted in man by God; yet these natural laws needed to carry a conviction for Grotius, in spite of moral theology. Further, there are subtle distinctions in Grotius between natural law and natural right—although this is again also present in Suárez's writings. Natural law and right in Grotius were embodied in human nature, particularly in terms of those actions which do not injure another. Human nature blended requirements for self-preservation, self-interest, and a deep-seated social inclination. All humans naturally wish to preserve themselves. But we also need to be able to live with others in a social frame. For Grotius, God implanted in us the means to achieve these ends. *Ius* is what a person possesses in oneself or has a claim to. Natural law and right refers to those actions which do not harm others' basic natural claims.[22]

Hobbes' work constitutes a more definite change in natural law argument. He also makes a very sharp distinction between natural law and natural right. Natural laws (*lex*) are those things which bind and determine people's actions; rights (*ius*) are those liberties to do or forbear. Natural laws were still seen as divine. Further all humans were bound, to a degree, by them. Like Grotius, Hobbes works within a theistic religious frame. Yet, the way he formulates the natural laws looks much more like prudential maxims for self-interested individuals, rather than religious commandments.[23] Like Grotius (although the idea again is very familiar in scholastic writing), the fundamental human good is self-preservation and natural law tells us prudentially how we can achieve this (Hobbes 1968, 189). Hobbes' natural laws though begin here to look, for some modern commentators, very like secular guidelines for irreligious individuals, although it is doubtful that Hobbes viewed them exactly in this manner.[24] Nonetheless these prudential natural laws constituted what Hobbes thought of as the true moral philosophy (Hobbes 1968, 200ff.). Further, in Hobbes, more so than Grotius, natural law is very much on its way to becoming a theory of natural rights (understood as wholly subjective right claims). Like Grotius, Hobbes works with a tense motif, namely, a natural law argument which assumes the existence of God. He then uses the argument to account for individuals' behaviour, apparently without any clear theistic beliefs. As Haakonssen puts it, despite his theistic beliefs, Hobbes gave 'a complexly subjectivist account of what is good and bad and of moral judgment'. Natural law and right reason might appear to curtail this natural right, but we still have 'no objective standard for recognising when others are or are not doing this'. The only point at which natural law can become effective is when it has become institutionalized in a sovereign's law (see Haakonssen 1996, 35). This latter claim certainly provides effective laws and standards, but at a cost to the whole natural law argument. Consequently, Hobbes, despite his deep roots in natural law, is seen in nineteenth- and twentieth-century legal theory as the father figure of legal positivism.

To grasp the status of natural law in the seventeenth and eighteenth centuries—the growing secularity and the move from a religious doctrine to a modern rationalistic conception—the discussion needs to be placed, in part, within a religious framework, particularly in terms of Protestant theory.[25] To fully appreciate this point one also needs to grasp certain internal divisions within Protestantism itself. This is probably the most revealing aspect of the modern notion of natural law. A central problem in the seventeenth- and eighteenth-century renditions of natural law is an old one relating to the authority of God. The religious view of natural law, synthesized in Aquinas, and dominating much Catholic thinking up to the eighteenth century, was that natural law derived its authority from God. The morally obligatory character of natural law derived therefore from God's will. The problematic issue to arise here in thinkers such as Hobbes and Grotius was 'whether or not there were moral values shared by God and humanity which entailed the moral obligations of natural law independently of our regard for God's willing this to be so. This was closely associated with the question of what powers of moral discernment human beings possessed, and that was in effect a question of the impact of original sin' (Haakonssen 1996, 6).

If we take the latter issue first: one major Protestant position on humanity and the nature of reason focused on the concept of original sin. For many Protestant thinkers, from Luther onwards, faith took priority to reason.[26]

Humans had no way of climbing out of their own sinfulness without God's grace and assistance. Reason and natural law-based morality were thus viewed as essentially false.[27] One would therefore never presume to have any knowledge of God's nature. Luther was not denying that God had laws. However we could only relate to God through faith; we could neither relate to him through our own works nor our knowledge of his laws. In one sense, this was a partial re-enactment of Aquinas' argument that a measure of our sense of God comes through revelation and grace—that is divine law—although in the final analysis, for Aquinas, grace perfects reason.[28] The other dimension of the Lutheran argument was that authority lies in our own conscience (in relation to God), without the need for mediating priests or the church. The important issue here was that it was the *individual's* conscience which became authoritative. Early Lutherans and Calvinists argued, in effect, that human conscience was guided, in faith, by the inner light of God's grace. However, the issue of internal moral discernment and private conscience can be read in different ways. If our private conscience (or even relation with God) is primarily authoritative, then it is a very short step to saying that our 'will' and 'reason' are authoritative. Pure Lutheran Protestantism, like Augustianism, would not have taken this step on theological grounds, but it *was* taken by Grotius, Hobbes, Pufendorf, and Locke. The nub of the case was that it was the individual's self-preservation, private conscience, personal moral judgement, and practical reason, which were primarily authoritative. In fact, this could still be given a religious imprimatur, namely, that God was implicit in our natural reasoning (an idea that was wholly familiar within scholastic writing). Yet it was still true that in these Protestant thinkers God increasingly became more of an adjunct to the arguments—certainly in the manner that we *now* look back at these debates.[29] The crucial point here is that if reason was becoming more self-sufficient, it did not take much effort to abandon or simply evade God's providence. Thus, Adam Smith's 'invisible hand' argument in *The Wealth of Nations,* underpinning political economy and morality, can be interpreted in a wholly secular manner—indeed this would now be the predominant way of reading Smith's position in modern political economy. Whether that is how Smith, or many of his contemporaries, would have read it remains an open question. However, the upshot of this whole argument is that conceptions of God's providence in society gradually mutated into the natural history of civil society, or even more presciently, the natural history of religion (see e.g. Hume 1966, 31ff.).

There are four crucial issues in the process of natural law mutation. First, the foundational premise of natural law was a form of abstract rationalism (which became central to Enlightenment thinking). Reason was present in our nature (which was an old scholastic idea), but it was being used in different ways. Reason was becoming increasingly a self-contained authority. It was something which could subsist even if God did not exist. It was developing into a standard of measurement. Natural law was therefore a self-sufficient coherent body of rules in its own right. This was the manner in which Pufendorf or Leibniz, for example, approached natural law. It began to resemble deductive sciences, such as mathematics or logic. This version of natural law slips imperceptibly into the natural laws of political economy in the eighteenth century. Although natural law in Grotius or Hobbes was not overtly secularist, the argument was nonetheless moving, almost imperceptibly, in this profane direction. Second, natural law was increasingly focusing on the individual subject and his or her reason, self-preservation, conscience, and self-interest. This created further ambiguities in terms of the various versions of social contract theory. Third, the onus of natural law argument was increasingly shifting, particularly in thinkers such as Grotius and Hobbes, into natural rights—that is individual reasoned subjective claims to do or forbear, as against conceptions of objective right. Objective right was thus being transformed, at times virtually indiscernibly, into subjective right. Fourth, there were political consequences which flowed from this whole transformation of natural law, consequences which were linked to concepts of individualism, self-interest, contract, and natural subjective right. These political consequences were potentially radical, but not necessarily liberal and certainly not democratic. It is important to recall that Hobbes' political absolutism was as much a consequence of natural right as Locke's proto-constitutionalism.

What we are seeing here, overall, is a new idea gradually arising. This new doctrine of natural law, with all its ambiguities, was becoming more of a standardized doctrine in eighteenth-century European and North American universities.[30] In political terms, it 'received much of its inspiration from the need to settle confessional and colonial conflicts, and its eighteenth-century successors produced recognisably modern systems of the law of nations in response to European wars' (Haakonssen 1996, 61). It had become, by the mid to late eighteenth century, a hegemonic perspective. Its crowning achievement was to become systematized in the great rights declarations of the latter part of the late eighteenth century in North America and Europe.

## NATURAL LAW GOODS

Unsurprisingly the various accounts of natural law and natural right, including the Catholic and Protestant religious and more secular forms, produced different accounts of fundamental human goods. Aquinas certainly saw the most fundamental natural law as doing good and avoiding evil. Doing good meant looking to scriptural sources, such as the ten commandments (the Decalogue). For Aquinas, life was a fundamental good, also procreation, social existence, knowledge, and rational conduct. In the era of the Protestant ascendancy on natural law—particularly where natural law began to mutate into natural rights—the goods became more restrained and simplified. Self-preservation (thus life), liberty, property, and occasionally happiness were seen as the core goods. In fact, natural law in one sense serviced or provided a platform for the goods of natural rights. As Locke put it, 'The State of nature has Law of nature to govern it, which obliges every one: And Reason, which is that Law, teaches all mankind, who will but consult it, that being all equal and independent, no one ought to harm another in his Life, Health, Liberty or Possessions' (Locke 1965, section 6, 311). Natural law thus exists to direct us to natural rights. This slightly more conservative view of what constitutes both natural law goods and natural rights is though very characteristic of all the early documents on rights.

The Thomist-inspired tradition oddly has been more generous in what it perceives to be human goods, particularly in the twentieth-century writing on natural law. Thus, in a writer such as John Finnis, the list is fairly extensive (Finnis 1980). His argument is that natural rights are justifiable insofar as they embody intrinsic natural law goods. He essentially puts forward a non-religious argument, claiming that it is misrepresentation of natural law argument to base it solely on religious foundations. He thus premises his own position upon an account of intrinsic goods, not on claims about God. Intrinsic goods do not need to be demonstrated. They are self-evident objective goods (moral facts), in that their value stems not from individual's *desiring* or *wanting* them, but rather from there being basic aspects of all human well-being. They are thus desirable because they are good. Goods are consequently not reducible to pleasure or desire. Conversely they are the essential grounds for human flourishing. It follows that if we are rational we ought to support these goods. Finnis identifies seven basic intrinsic goods: life, knowledge, play, aesthetic experience, sociability, practical reasonableness, and religion. These all indicate what we 'ought' to do. Practical reasonableness is crucial for Finnis. It is the good which allows our intelligence to bear effectively upon any problem of choosing.[31] Finnis thus sets out principles of practical reasonableness: we all pursue a coherent plan of life, we must give due significance to each of the basic goods and rationally adjust our pursuit of these to our capacities and circumstances, and we must not treat others arbitrarily.[32] He agrees that there may be some disagreement over goods; other goods may also have a role to play. But, nonetheless, he sees the list he mentions as fundamental universal goods. One major problem here, even with twentieth-century Thomism, is that there is little agreement on the final list of goods (see Grisez 1983; Chappell 1995). Many of the goods themselves also remain somewhat opaque, namely, what kind of aesthetic experience or sociability is being articulated? This whole argument concerning what are core human goods arises again within the human rights debates.

# A change of accent

What though of the relation between natural law and natural right? The question is a difficult one. There are clearly those who see natural rights as deriving directly from natural law (Jones 1994, 75–6). This analytical judgement is exactly the same point made by certain Thomist-inspired writers in the twentieth century, although the argument is by no means simple. Both Finnis and Maritain, for example, see natural rights as extrapolations from natural law, although even their arguments are dissimilar in coming to essentially the same conclusion (Maritain 1944; Finnis 1980).

If we take Maritain as an example, his reading of Aquinas is that a right is a direct correlative of law. If natural law dictates charity to the poor, care of children, keeping promises, and so forth, then it can be argued that rights are implicated correlatively with natural law. Natural law and natural right are thus co-equal terms. In his *The Rights of Man and Natural Law*, Maritain argues that '*natural law* deals with the rights and duties which follow from their first principle: "do good and avoid evil", in a necessary manner' (Maritain 1944, 39). This is pure Thomism. The basic argument goes as follows: the human person 'possess rights because of the very fact that it is a person'; the human person is more than just a parcel of matter (see Maritain 1944, 36). A person implies agency, intelligence, and reason. Persons are not isolated creatures but stand in complex relations with others in society. Society can thus be understood as a conjunction of valued persons. Because persons embody fundamental rights, society must be premised on a common good, namely, dedicated to the achievement of the flourishing of human persons through cultivating and upholding their rights. Natural law thus facilitates the achievement of the common good. To be dedicated to the conditions for the flourishing of human persons entails for Maritain that certain fundamental rights should be respected. These flow directly from natural law. The rights implied are: the right of the human person (rights to exist, personal freedom, pursue a moral life); rights of the civic person (political rights to vote, participate in political life); and the rights of the social person (just wage, trade unions, right to work) (Maritain 1944, 41–60).

A second view suggests that there is separation between natural law and natural right. For many commentators Aquinas never actually used the term right in any subjective sense. His focus was wholly on objective right and on duty.[33] A brutal or tyrannical ruler was not offending against natural rights, rather he was failing to perform his duties under the strictures of objective right. Further, a duty to the poor, care of children, or keeping promises are nothing but duties. They are not rights possessed by children or the poor. It is thus a fundamental error to try to supervene rights over a basic duty-based argument. Consequently, it has been argued that natural law is wholly separate from natural rights. This argument is given a distinctly polemical edge in other commentaries. We have already encountered this in previous sections. Thus, Michel Villey, in his various detailed writings on natural right, argues that it is a fundamental intellectual blunder to try to extrapolate natural rights from natural law. Natural law (as objective right) is a wholly different category to subjective natural rights. The writings of Ockham to Hobbes which focus on subjective natural rights are envisaged essentially as a corruption in the natural law tradition (Villey 1961, 1962). This was seen as part of a more general collapse into individualism, contractualism, and a detached potentially nihilistic rationalism. This is a position argued—in a very different manner—by non-Catholic writers such as Leo Strauss (1952, 1953).

My own view here would not be to make too hard a distinction between natural law and natural right. What is more significant here is the gradualness and subtlety of a change of accent in arguments about law and right. In many ways, this was a gradual change of emphasis from *objective* to *subjective* right. However, the form in which this change of accent appeared was often dependent on circumstances. What we are seeing here overall is a new idea gradually taking shape. Some thinkers appear more conscious that a change is taking place; at other points, others who use natural right arguments do not seem quite aware of their moral and political implications. In this sense, the idea of natural right emerges in an unpredictable and contingent manner, although in my estimation it is something which becomes much more self-consciously developed from the seventeenth century. To try however to find a wholly precise point of origin may be a hopeless task. As Michael Oakeshott put it, 'The appearance of a new intellectual character [such as natural right] is like the appearance of a new architectural style; it emerges almost imperceptibly, under the pressure of a great variety of influences,... all that can be discerned are the slowly mediated changes, the shuffling and reshuffling, the flow and ebb of tides of inspiration, which issue finally in a shape identifiably new' (Oakeshott 1991, 13).

## Maximal and minimal natural right

The discussion now turns to a more simplified summation of the state of natural right argument. It draws a distinction between maximal and minimal senses of natural right. In order to elucidate this distinction, the focus will be on the conceptual usage of the term 'natural', particularly in seventeenth- and eighteenth-century thought—in relation to natural rights. Inevitably this will only provide a crude sketch; however, it forms a baseline from which the argument of the book moves in subsequent chapters.

There were two senses of 'natural'—vis-à-vis natural right—which figured widely in discussions. These are the maximal and minimal senses. The first was a more directly religious sense of the term with deep roots in scholastic medieval philosophy. 'Nature' in this scenario was understood teleologically, as the creation of God, an ordered world created for humanity. This idea had close links with an older Greek sense of nature as a world in which everything was locatable and purposeful.[34] Nature implied a purposeful intelligent teleology and ordering. A design, purpose, or mindfulness was therefore present, as interpreted through myth or theology. As such, nature embodied normative rules and standards to judge human conduct. 'Right'—as objectively right—was established by observing the implicit order of the world and then consulting one's practical reason. Nature was consequently normatively authoritative. Justice and right were rules implicit in the nature. From the Christian perspective, God is the sole author of nature. The 'natural' is thus an aspect of divine providence. Whilst a Christian God remained the reasonable architect of nature, the relation between natural law and natural right, between the fourteenth and sixteenth centuries, remained relatively benign. From the human perspective, nature contained all the necessary principles of practical rationality (which were all universally binding). Human sociability and human reasoning powers were implicit in this natural order.

In summary, 'natural' referred to a rich array of implicit normative rules implicit in human nature and the world humans inhabit. Therefore, natural right, in what I have referred to as a maximal sense, embodied a particular conception of what is natural. This implied a universal normative order, implicit in human nature, practical reasoning, or at least implied in the concept of human action and usually sanctioned by a rational deity. Rights were authoritative insofar as they were premised on this innate rule-governed sense of nature. This notion of natural was very close, conceptually, to the more general understanding of natural law.[35] Right was in many ways bounded by natural law. This would also be the case with the early realization that a right could be considered as a power or liberty. *Dominium*, power, or liberty—as articulations of an earlier form of subjective right—were all still morally circumscribed, before the seventeenth century.[36]

The second sense of natural has an ancestry dating back to Roman legal thought and aspects of scholastic thought—although its later manifestations in the seventeenth century are unexpected. This sense of natural referred not to any sense of moral discernment, but rather to a *facultas animi*, that is, something that might be considered normal in a particular situation for a given being. In the most basic sense, this was something we shared with animals. This notion of natural did not give rise to a rich moral system of rules; conversely, it indicated a *minimal* range of virtually instinctive rules. Thus, natural referred to certain basic needs that we had, particularly for self-preservation and personal survival (or more prosaically a right to life). As indicated this idea originated in scholastic thinking. The important point to note though is that self-preservation still had a divine imprimatur. We had a natural 'right to life'—that is to say, a kind of instinct or *conatus* to self-preservation—which was willed by God. In addition, reason and will took on a stronger role, in the terms of what was 'natural'. Glimmerings of the latter ideas were again implicit in older scholastic arguments, but they came very much more to the fore in the seventeenth- and eighteenth-century usage.[37] Owning and formulating one's own proper will, and using what power one has in accordance with that will, became crucial figures in the 'social contract tradition'. The notion of natural was though very gradually being detached from overt moral constraint. Natural referred more closely to certain minimal conditions of self-preservation.

There were strong indications of this understated change in Hobbesian arguments. Hobbes, for example, saw natural rights being enjoyed in a state of nature where there was no actual civil government. Natural right was the 'liberty each man hath, to use his own power, as he will himselfe, for the preservation of his own Nature; that is to say, of his own Life; and consequently, of doing anything, which in his own Judgment, and Reason, hee shall conceive to be the aptest means thereunto' (Hobbes 1968, 189). The state of nature was a domain where subjective rights, understood as powers and liberties, potentially clashed. This constitutes the 'state of warre' characteristic of the Hobbesian state of nature. Individuals for Hobbes had to forsake these natural rights in order to enter civil society.[38]

A more pointed example of this form of argument can be found in Benedict de Spinoza's political treatises in the 1600s. Spinoza understood natural law as the way in which we 'live and act in a given way', in exactly the same way as 'fishes are naturally conditioned for swimming, and the greater devouring the less'. Natural right, for Spinoza, was thus wholly 'coextensive' with *power*. The power of nature was still though the power of God and it is important to retain this premise in mind. A natural right was simply the power that you naturally had or had been allotted. Thus, as Spinoza put it, the 'rights of an individual extend to the utmost limits of his power as it has been conditioned'. First and foremost an individual will expend this power in trying to preserve oneself 'without regard to anything'. Whatever an individual needs to do to preserve itself, it has a natural right to do. Thus one 'who does not yet know reason, or who has not yet acquired the habit of virtue, acts solely according to the laws of his desire with as sovereign a right as he who orders his life entirely by the laws of reason'. Thus, the individual is at total liberty to do anything with natural right. No one would know what was wrong or right unless they had matured in reason. Spinoza sees a scriptural source for this judgement in St Paul, namely, that 'living under the sway of nature, there is no sin'. Consequently, the 'natural right of the individual man is thus determined, not by sound reason, but by desire and power' (all quotations Spinoza 1951, 200–1). Given for Spinoza that the majority of humans often remain ignorant and without fully developed reason, this was therefore the condition of humanity at large. This meant that to defend one's natural right could entail 'force, cunning, entreaty'. Equally, strife, hatred, anger, and deceit were all acceptable in preserving one's natural rights. Nature *only* prohibited what was not desired. Nature was not bounded by the laws of overt reason to Spinoza.[39] Thus, 'that which reason considers evil, is not evil in respect to the order and laws of nature as a whole, but only in respect to the laws of reason' (Spinoza 1951, 202).

Human beings though try to avoid hatred, fear, and deceit where possible; this in turn for Spinoza leads to the logic behind a social compact or contract, which removes us from many of these uncertainties. Like Hobbes, Spinoza suggests that a compact needs force to maintain it. The individual needs to be 'restrained by the hope of some greater, or the fear of some greater evil' (Spinoza 1951, 204). The result of this process is a sovereign who is also *not* restrained by law. Once a community, with a sovereign dominion and institutional religion, is in existence, we can then grasp the concepts of right and wrong (Spinoza 1951, 210). The oddity of this account of modern subjective natural right is that it often culminated in a form of absolute sovereign power in civil dominion (in Hobbes, for example) which was anything but liberal or benign. Yet this seemed to follow inexorably from the minimal notion of natural right.

In sum, this second sense of 'natural' stresses, especially in writers such as Hobbes and Spinoza, is something equivalent to 'natural instinct' (either that which we are at a complete natural liberty to do, or that which we have a power to do). It is not though an instinct in the nineteenth-century biological sense. This idea does though begin to loosen the earlier religiously inspired teleological dimension of nature. It also lays more stress on individual will and reason. Further, this is a natural right (as a subjective claim) to be at liberty *from* authority and *from* any objective measurement of what is right. Right defines a sphere of action. It was a natural right in the absence of civil dominion. This created a situation from which human beings needed to escape, via contract, into the civil condition. In addition, a natural right, in this minimal sense, did not really confer dignity on a person. It was rather focused on self-preservation alone. Natural law was just about prudence. Natural right was also prior to any reasoned understanding of what was objectively right and wrong. We should not make the mistake therefore of confusing maximal and minimal understandings of 'natural'. Further, we should not confuse early scholastic moves to natural right with the understanding of natural right in Hobbes, Spinoza, or even Locke. We should also exercise care here with the chronology of natural rights arguments, since the scholastic— more maximal sense of natural—still carries on in the Catholic tradition post-1948. In fact, it is still very much alive and well in the academy.

Yet, at the same time, we should not make another mistake of thinking that the more 'minimal' sense of natural right had abandoned theology or religious commitments, or, alternatively that these were wholly secularized rights. Despite its modern appearances, the minimal sense of the word 'natural' in Hobbes or Spinoza still contained strong theological and design motifs. These were shared, to a degree, with the maximal understanding. Thus, God was still the power in nature and the architect of nature. We might find this idea of nature worrying, but for Spinoza this is simply because we do not have the reason to grasp what is taking place. God still desired our self-preservation. He had implanted will and reason within us. God thus embedded natural rights (minimal or maximal) in us. Religious themes were therefore still very much present, but in a more ambiguous or muted sense. Both maximal and minimal readings of 'natural' were also universally binding on humanity. They were pre-social in character, even if they existed in the mind of God, or implicitly in reason or nature; that is, natural rights were not reliant upon political or legal mechanisms to create them. These natural rights—maximal or minimal—which were implicit in nature and perceived via reason, were not subject to change. Humans, wherever they existed, would seek the natural right to life, via self-preservation. There was also a strong sense that some-where along the line God was implicated, even if it was only as a background invisible hand.

## Politics and rights

One germane aspect of 'natural right' argument, in the way that it developed during the eighteenth century, was its increasing politicization. There are though various dimensions to this process. The best-known dimension of the politicization of natural rights language was embedded in the writings of J. J. Rousseau, Thomas Paine, Richard Price, Mary Wollstonecraft, Joseph Priestly, and a host of others, who became associated (to a greater or lesser degree) with more radicalized political movements and revolutionary events during the latter part of the eighteenth century. There were aspects of the way the natural right argument was generally configured which enabled this novel ideological formation. This configuration was not inevitable by any means; however, natural rights (maximal or minimal) were seen to be possessed by individuals. In fact, presciently all individuals possess them *equally*. Civil society was constituted by such individuals. There were no greater or lesser natural rights. Natural rights had no logical room for hierarchies or special privileges—unless one adopted a Hobbesian route to an absolute sovereign. Individuals, their consciences and their practical reason, were authoritative and sovereign. The practical reason of individuals had to be consulted for the sake of legal, moral, and political legitimacy. The embryo of an account of popular sovereignty was implicit in this claim. In other words, consent or agreement was needed. Many of these ideas became central to much social contract writing. The rights we see being codified in North America and Europe during the late 1700s were general protective rights, limiting what states could do, that is, protection of life, liberty, property, happiness, and freedom of conscience. All these ideas—individualism, equality, equal liberty, conscience, consent, contract, popular sovereignty, and legitimacy—became deeply familiar by the nineteenth century. Natural right therefore was connected to a constellation of ideas which provided the backdrop for many of the political ideologies of the nineteenth and early twentieth centuries, such as liberalism, anarchism, and socialism—although many of the familiar *grounds* for natural right all but disappeared in these latter ideologies.

Prior to these eighteenth-century events (previously mentioned), there were pointers to the direction of the natural right arguments. One fascinating and well-researched event took place in Spain in the 1550s (see Pagden 1986; Boucher 2009). It focused on the Spanish colonies of South America. In 1493, Pope Alexander VI had granted Bulls of Donation, which in effect formed a legal title for Spain to explore South America. However, in 1537, Pope Paul III (on the basis of Spanish conquistadors' savage record in South America) issued *Sublimis Deus*, which basically demanded an end to conquest, colonization, and the enslavement of native peoples. The Spanish monarch Charles V had the papal document impounded, the papal messenger was arrested, and critics were threatened.[40] Charles was still uneasy. On 16 April 1550, he called a temporary halt to conquest and gathered a group of jurists and thinkers to determine 'how conquests may be conducted justly and in good conscience'. An official public debate took place in front of Charles in Valladolid between 1550 and 1551. The key protagonists were Juan Ginés de Sepúlveda and Bartolomé de Las Casas. The issues at stake were large: empire, religion, civilization, natural law and rights, and most fundamentally what or who is humanity?

Sepúlveda essentially gave four reasons to justify the conquest: first, the seriousness of the religious offences committed by the Indians, particularly their idolatry; second, the sheer coarseness of Indian intelligence was such as to make them servile and barbarous—equivalent to Aristotle's slaves. Sepúlveda was a scholar of ancient Greece who had translated Aristotle's *Politics*. He used Aristotle's terminology to compare the conquerors with the natives, describing the Spaniards' work in terms of the rightful 'domination of perfection over imperfection, strength over weakness, lofty virtue over vice'. Indian peoples were destined to be ruled by more highly evolved peoples, such as Spaniards. As Sepúlveda says 'Not only are they [Indians] without science, but they do not use or know about any system of writing. They have preserved no historical monuments, except a vague and obscure memory of certain things recorded in a few paintings. Nor have they any written law; only few barbaric rules and customs. They do not even recognize the right to own private property' (quoted in Finkelkraut 2001, sect. 12). Indians were thus regarded as subhuman. Sepúlveda sees them as different to humans as monkeys. The Spaniards, on the other hand, were viewed as pure and full of humanity. The ungodly and impure Indians needed to be colonized for the sake of their own salvation. Third, there were the needs of the Catholic faith. The subjection of Indian people would facilitate their final conversion. Finally, the Indians had sinned against natural law, particularly in terms of sacrificial offerings of human beings. This needed to be corrected by Christians.

Las Casas was Bishop of Chiapas in South America and the official protector of the Indians. His response was that Indians already had well-established customs and disciplined ways of life (see Las Casas 1971, 1992). They were prudent, with an aptitude to govern. They organized themselves in recognizable social units such as families. They were by any measure reasonable and civilized peoples. Further, if they had never had encountered the Christian faith, how could they be punished? In addition, they could not be forced into faith—this would be irrational. Faith is freely accepted. The Indians fulfilled all the conditions that Aristotle considered to be part of a good life. Las Casas thus remarks that the native Indians 'are not ignorant, inhuman, or bestial. Rather, long before they heard the word Spaniard they had lived in properly organized states, wisely ordered by excellent laws, religion, and customs. They cultivated friendship. Lived in populous cities in which they administered the affairs of both peace and war justly and equitably, truly governed by laws that are on very many points superior to our own, and could have won the admiration of the sages of Athens' (quoted in Cornish 1996, 108). Las Casas also questioned the category of 'barbarian': 'We consider a people barbarian when they do not have systems of writing or a scholarly language. But people of the Indies could treat us as barbarian, since we do not understand their language' (quoted Finkelkraut 2001, sect. 16).

The Valladolid debate ended inconclusively. The judges refused to prefer either position.[41] Regardless of the outcome, a number of scholars have seen something quite fundamental taking place here. The fact that the debate took place at all was in itself significant. If one cuts through the structures of the debate, there are certain very fundamental issues at stake. Using the language of natural rights, the crucial question arose: do all humans regardless of race or religion possess natural rights equally? Are some peoples below humanity or reason? Natural law and natural right can swing the argument in different ways—depending on who one considers human. However, the onus of viewing all humans as possessing natural right equally and universally, even minimally for self-preservation, was being taken seriously in this debate. Such rights were seen as inscribed in nature itself. There was in other words a definite potential in these arguments for considering natural rights as linked indissolubly to the human person.[42] The natural rights that arise here are, like those in the later eighteenth-century documents, general and protective in character, and set against the power of the Spanish colonial state. This was one common aspect of natural right argument.

## Conclusion

The present chapter has given an overview of the various disputes about the origins of natural rights. It aimed to provide a sketch map of the background of rights discourse and its final position in the eighteenth-century debates. It then turned to the concept of natural law, which has been identified by many scholars as closely connected to the concept of natural right. The initial discussion concentrated on the various senses of natural law, particularly on the ancient and modern, as well as the religious and secular usages. The argument then turned to the various accounts of the relation between the concepts of natural law and natural right. This was followed by a summary of my own perspective on natural right, in terms of the maximal and minimal senses of the term. Finally, the relation between natural right and certain political implications was briefly outlined. The general idea of rights, which was being prosecuted in both the 1550s, in Valladolid and in the North American (1776) and French Declarations (1789), was viewed as radical by certain contemporaries, but was also quite specific in scope. Rights were general and protective. They did not press, in any systematic manner, for social entitlements to certain conditions of life, but rather sought negatively to protect individuals from the threat of violent incursions against their body, liberties, and property. The rights documents of the eighteenth century developed and systematized these generic protective rights.

There was though a very gradual shift, particularly in the eighteenth-century Protestant and more secularized arguments, from an overt philosophy of natural law to an emphasis of natural rights, understood as subjective protective claims. Natural law began to be seen more as an appetizer for the main course of natural rights. In the final analysis, natural right began to bind natural law. Gradually it was the rights that indicated what was objectively right or wrong (rather than natural law binding natural rights). Natural rights were becoming, potentially, morality. However, religious themes were not absent in this shift to natural right. A rational deity still inhabited the formulations of natural right in the eighteenth century. In addition, the maximal and minimal readings of 'natural' were all seen as universally binding on humanity. Further, rights were legitimate only insofar as they were premised on an intrinsic (maximal or minimal) rule-governed sense of nature. They were also pre-social, in that natural rights were *not* dependent upon any political or legal apparatus to craft or legitimatize them. These natural rights which were implicit in nature and perceived via practical reason were not subject to substantial change. Humans, *wherever* they existed, would seek the natural right to life, minimally via self-preservation. Self-preservation had to be respected. Maximally, the moral person or agent was seen to possess spiritual dignity and should be treated with justice. The maximal sense of natural referred therefore to a rich array of religiously inspired normative rules, implicit in human nature and the world that humans inhabited. However, rights in both the minimal and maximal senses were all general and negative in character. They were essentially aiming at defending or protecting individual life, liberty, powers, and property. The way these arguments were formulated also had major legal and political implications. 'Nature' remained though the core theme in all these writings up to the eighteenth century. Chapter 3 takes up this latter theme, focusing on the increasing intellectual unease with the idea of 'nature' in both the natural law and natural right perspectives.

## ☐ NOTES

1. My contention would be that many of the problems we have with both rights in general and human rights literature in particular are that, on the one hand, a great deal of conceptual legwork on rights has been done in an ahistorical and socially aseptic manner, which often glosses over conceptual history in a thin and unsatisfactory manner, or, on the other hand, focuses almost exclusively on the historical contextual recovery of arguments and meanings. The latter method tends to provide comforting words to show why such detailed historically contextual study of ideas is necessary, namely, that the present use of concepts such as 'rights', needs to be shown in terms of its full historical development in order to avoid any misunderstandings in the present. The 'present' usually puts in a rather paltry appearance as a kind of unseen cheering teleological chorus.

2. This point will be developed in chapter 3.

3. It is through Cicero 'more than any other single channel, that so large a portion of Greek, and above all of Stoic ethics, has become the common heritage of the civilised world' (Ritchie 1952, 36). It is worth noting that Tuck, for one, sees the 'rediscovery' of the Digest in the twelfth century as crucial for the development of subjective right.

4. Decretalism was a twelfth-century doctrine which aimed to elucidate the law of the decretals, that is, responses by the Pope to issues of church and canon law. These responses were collected in works such as the *Decretals of Gregory IX* and the *Decretum Gratiani*. Many of these responses reflected on issues of temporal and spiritual powers.

5. 'By 1200, the canonists had created a language in which natural rights theories could readily be expressed. Their "speech acts" did not merely modify existing language; but they would lead on to the "creation and diffusion of new languages"' (Tierney 1997, 69).

6. 'In discussing modern natural rights language, Hart explained that a right defines an area where the agent is free to act as he chooses, to assert a claim or not assert it. The canonists were making the same point—for them *ius naturale* could mean "to reclaim one's own or not to reclaim it"' (Tierney 1997, 68).

7. 'It is among the men who rediscovered the Digest and created the medieval science of Roman law in the 12th century that we must look to find the first modern rights theory, one built around the notion of a passive right' (Tuck 1979, 13).

8. He thinks Villey takes Ockham completely the wrong way. He comments that Villey 'took the fact that Ockham consistently elucidates the notion of a *ius* in something by using the word *potestas* to be significant; but as we have seen, if we are to look anywhere for evidence that *ius* is being used in an active sense (which is the kind of subjective right which interests Villey), then we must look first for the assimilation of such a *ius* and *dominium*—and that had occurred already in the writings of the post-Accursians' (Tuck 1979, 22–3).

9. Tierney comments that 'It was a great merit of Tuck's work that called attention to the jurisprudence of the twelfth and thirteenth centuries as a possible source of later rights theories; but he misunderstood the relevant texts and so produced only a confused account of the subsequent development' (Tierney 1997, 218). He notes that most of Tuck's use of texts are 'mistranslated or misunderstood being taken out of context' (Tierney 1997, 220).

10. Locke's contribution has been endlessly debated in the literature. However, for many, he is seen to have been influential on the Glorious Revolution (1689) and in the constitutional monarchy settlement, which subsequently formed part of the ideology of the Whig group in England.

11. Natural law is simply about 'self-preservation' (in Aquinas amongst animals). Each species or thing has a natural right.

12. As Brian Tierney comments, 'The simple-looking little phrase, *ius naturale*, is a semantic minefield'. He continues, 'Erik Wolf once observed that the word "natural" had seventeen meanings and the word *ius* fifteen; so, he concluded, there could be two hundred and fifty-five possible meanings for *ius naturale*. But this was too modest a count'; Tierney continues however that Lovejoy also found sixty-six meanings for 'natural' (Tierney 1997, 48).

13. The laws codes of the *Corpus Iuris Civilis* were comprised of three works: *The Institutes* (an educational handbook), *The Digest* (a collection of excerpts from earlier jurists), and the *Codex* (a codification of Imperial constitution). The *Corpus Iurus Civilis* was finished (under Justinian's orders) in AD 534. Interestingly Justinian was given a special place in paradise by Dante (see D'Entrèves 1977, 23).

14. There were two main sources for Aquinas' view of natural law: the Greeks (particularly Aristotle) and a revivified Roman law. Aquinas' most mature statement on natural law is in the *Summa Theologica*, in the first part of Part 2, Questions 90–7.

15. It is also worth noting that Michel Villey was very directly sympathetic to Thomism.

16. Sometimes it was linked, and sometimes it was separated from the law of nations (*ius gentium*) and civil law (*ius civile*).

17. The key areas where Aquinas developed his ideas on natural law were in his *Summa Theologica* (2a2ae, Question 57 'On Right' and Question 58 'On Justice'). Ideas on objective right are taken by Aquinas from Aristotle's *Ethics*, Book V—blended with biblical resources.

18. Natural law works such as Pufendorf's *De Iura Naturae et Gentium* (1672), Burlamaqui's *Principes du Droit Naturel* (1747), or Vattel's *Droit des gens ou principes de la Loi Naturelle* (1758) had little to do with moral theology.

19. 'The idea of natural rights grew up among Catholic jurists and theologians during the medieval era. The further development of the doctrine in the early modern period was

almost entirely the work of Protestant political theorists'. The key figure here was Hugo Grotius (Tierney 1997, 316).

20. A judgement which can be traced to one the great figures of eighteenth-century natural law philosophy Samuel Pufendorf (1623–94).

21. 'Grotius' underlying theory conveyed to Protestant Europe large parts of natural law utilized by the great scholastic thinkers, especially those of sixteenth century Spain' (Haakonssen 1996, 15).

22. Individuals with natural rights are thus the 'units of which all social organization is made. They are people who balance pure self-interest and social inclinations by entering in contractual relations with others about property and about modes of living together, especially about authority' (Haakonssen 1996, 28).

23. This is another way of viewing the Grotian *etiamsi daremus* idea.

24. Behind the modern view of Hobbes lies the anachronistic assumption 'that Hobbes had to find his way among the same concepts of obligation as we do', rather his doctrine is 'situated within a doctrine of natural law and natural rights—and this is neither traditional nor modern' (Haakonssen 1996, 33).

25. My argument here follows the insightful discussions of Haakonssen (1996).

26. 'For Protestant thinkers the starting point was the complete discontinuity between God and man, a discontinuity which made it impossible to give a rational account of human morality by reference to God and his eternal law. Only faith could bridge the gulf' (Haakonssen 1996, 25).

27. The doctrine of justification by faith led to Antinomianism.

28. This debate also has echoes in an older debate within the Catholic church between Augustinians and Thomists. For Augustinians earthly blessings can be enjoyed and should not be scorned, but they are not of the highest good. In fact grace again is needed for humans to achieve salvation, as against the Thomist reliance on reason.

29. Which may of course be our problem rather than theirs.

30. As Haakonssen comments, 'By the early years of the 18th century, natural law was established as the most important form of academic moral philosophy in most of Protestant Europe—Germany, the Netherlands, Switzerland, Scandinavia—and it was fast gaining ground in Scotland, in the academies of the rational Dissenters in England, and, eventually in the North America colleges. As the "core curriculum" in practical philosophy, natural law became the seed-bed for new academic disciplines, notably political economy' (Haakonssen 1996, 61).

31. Practicable reasonableness should govern our conduct in general since it is the good of 'being able to bring one's own intelligence to bear effectively (in practical reasoning that issues in action) on the problems of choosing one's actions and life-styles and shaping one's own character' (Finnis 1980, 88).

32. Sociability is part of our goods. Sociability is the 'other-directed' aspect of 'practicable reasonableness'.

33. 'St. Thomas nowhere committed himself to anything which may be said to approach even remotely the idea of an "original" or "natural" right' (D'Entrèves 1977, 32).

34. As Clarence Glacken commented, in his magisterial study of the history of nature, 'The thinkers of antiquity developed conceptions of the earth as a fit environment for human

life and human cultures whose force was still felt in the nineteenth century. The conception of a designed earth was strongest among the Academic and the Stoic philosophers, but even among the Epicureans there could exist a harmony between man and nature, orderly even if not the product of design'. Glacken continued that geographically this was also an important idea: 'if there were harmonious relationships in nature...of which man was a part, the spatial distribution of plants, animals, and man conformed to and gave evidence of this plan; there was a place for everything and everything was in its place' (Glacken 1967, 147).

35. This would be Maritain's position.

36. 'By around 1200 many canonists were coming to realise that the old language of *ius naturale* could be used to define both faculty or force of the human person and a "neutral sphere of personal choice", a "zone of autonomy". But they did not, like some modern critics of rights theories, expect such language to justify a moral universal in which each individual would ruthlessly pursue his own advantage. Like most of the classical rights theories down to Locke and Wolff they envisaged a sphere of natural rights bounded by natural moral law. The first natural rights theories were not based on an apotheosis of simply greed or self-serving...rather they derived from a view of individual persons as free, endowed with reason, capable of moral discernment, and from a consideration of the ties of justice and charity' (Tierney 1997, 77).

37. 'In medieval thought self-preservation always had been seen in moral terms as a duty enjoined by divine law that implied a corresponding right of self-defence and a right to acquire the necessities of life' (Tierney 1997, 322; Herbert 2002, 49). This also accounts for the continuing ambiguity of Grotius' *etiamsi daremus* doctrine.

38. Hobbes' individual 'remains a natural individual whose natural right to self-preservation is extended and made rational rather than alienated as he enters civil society. The natural desire for domination of others...follows only from the demands of self-preservation' (Herbert 2002, 100).

39. For Spinoza if nature seems cruel and blind then this is largely because we are so remarkably ignorant.

40. One of Charles V's legal advisers was Francisco de Vitoria who also commented on the conquest of Peru and Mexico by Spain. He wrote a work on this issue entitled *De Indis*, which although not questioning the conquest did raise a range of issues. The central question was 'whether barbarians in question were true owners in both private and public law before Spaniards arrived' (see Cornish 1996, 102). Vitoria suggested they exercised both civil *dominium* and natural *dominium*. Critics suggested that Indians were equivalent to Aristotle's conception of a natural slave—that is to say they could not exercise any dominium. Vitoria countered that Indians had lived for generations in peaceable possession before Spaniards conquered them. He also saw common human order encompassing Spaniards and Indians. They both had cities, laws, and religions. Only sinners, unbelievers, simpletons, and irrational beings could be considered incapable. Yet, Indians are not simpletons, irrational, or slaves. Even if dull-witted this would still not provide any title for invasions and conquest. The actions of the Spanish in Peru were contrary to natural law as objective right. Vitoria did however raise the point that it was a law of nations (*jus gentium*) that one ought to be able to travel in a territory and receive its hospitality. Thus, the Indian princes should have

been hospitable. The Spanish therefore had some right to travel in the Americas and to respond to Indian aggression.

41. Charles never in fact endorsed Sepúlveda's position, although the Spanish councils in Mexico rewarded him with gifts. However, words like 'pacification' were later used in documents instead of 'conquest'.

42. 'The debate was based upon the assumption that all human beings possess rights by virtue of their humanity, since such rights were, indeed, inscribed in nature, and the nature of no individual, or even group of individuals, could be modified by their beliefs or their patterns of behaviour unless there was reason to suppose that these were so extreme that they could not be held or practiced by truly human beings. It became, therefore, not a debate over what rights the American Indians did, or did not, have, but how they stood as persons under the law of nature' (Pagden 2003, 178).

# 3 The Twilight of Natural Rights

Chapter 2 noted the omnipresence of the concept 'natural' in all the eighteenth- and early nineteenth-century debates over rights. Although there were different senses in which the concept right was being employed, nonetheless there were also certain *common features* which clustered around the concept 'natural'. It was these common features which gave rise to certain problems, which will be discussed in the present chapter: first, the concepts 'nature' and 'natural' began to go through subtle mutations in the nineteenth and twentieth centuries and the 'common features' looked increasingly dubious, if not superfluous. Second, for those who see a close connection between natural and human rights, this latter judgement, in turn, raises serious issues. If the commentator on human rights wants to continue asserting the connection between natural and human rights, then they are in imminent danger of contaminating human rights with the same potential redundancy as natural right. Third, it is instructive to examine why the concept of natural right became superfluous in the nineteenth century, since many of the arguments are still deeply relevant to the question of human rights post-1948.

The present chapter is therefore a sketch of a conceptual and historical backdrop, against which human rights appeared in 1948. The chapter begins and ends with a different question. The opening question is: why did the vocabulary of natural rights (often seen as the precursor of human rights) drop out of political discussions in the nineteenth century? Natural rights, as argued in chapter 2, was a language which had dominated much European and North American discussion of law, politics, and morality, over the previous two centuries. A cursory answer to my question would go as follows: during the nineteenth century, the discourse of natural rights was gradually but decisively constricted by two dynamic vocabularies focused on the concepts of 'nature' and the 'nation state'. The most important of these changes was a robust vocabulary of nature arising from evolutionary theory. The gradual insertion of this new understanding of nature into legal, moral, and political discussion is not being discussed in a conventional manner, vis-á-vis through 'Social Darwinism', although it has some relevance to Herbert Spencer as well as the later twentieth-century sociobiologists. The argument rather focuses on the incisive intellectual linkages between these two dynamic vocabularies—*nature* and the *nation state*. This conceptual linkage can be observed clearly in many newly forming intellectual disciplines. The specific focus of this chapter will be on ecology and geography, particularly the latter from the 1870s. Essentially geography provided a fundamental bond between the nation state and the vocabulary of nature. In other words, these latter concepts reveal the way certain vocabularies had quite fundamentally mutated. By the beginning of the twentieth century, a powerful matrix of concepts coalesced around the idea of the nation state, which, in effect, undermined the efficacy of the vocabulary of natural right, which was then subsequently viewed as a quaint museum piece or a spooky myth which obsessed some North Americans in their less-reflective moments.

The debates to be discussed were not confined to politics or law, but figure across the whole intellectual spectrum of the nineteenth-century European thought. Further, these debates were not just academic fripperies, but conversely were often related to very immediate and, at points, quite brutal events and institutional processes. In fact, we have not yet moved beyond the vocabulary of these debates. Much of the terminology is still very much alive, although many concepts have often morphed into different, but still familiar, terminology. This in turn explains much of the anguish of human rights in the late twentieth century and early twenty-first century. Put very crudely, many of the vocabularies of the late nineteenth century—as inherited preoccupations—still underpin current debates over human rights. This is particularly the case with the complex conceptual configuration of the 'nation state'.

The chapter begins with a brief reminder of what natural rights denoted at the beginning of the nineteenth century, in terms of an understanding of nature. It then examines the changing conception of nature in evolutionary theory and the manner in which it was developed in the disciplines of ecology and geography. The effect of this geographical work is then tracked in relation to the state. The content and legacy of the nation state is then scrutinized in more detail, concentrating on the concepts of self-determination and state personality theory. The chapter ends with a sketch of a preamble to human rights and poses a core question which sets the agenda for chapter 4.

# The state of natural right

The argument in chapter 2 distinguished the minimal and maximal senses of natural right. The maximal was more directly religious with definite roots in late medieval philosophy. Nature was understood teleologically and overtly as the creation of God. This idea had close links with an older Greek sense of nature as a world in which everything is locatable and purposeful.[1] Nature implied a purposeful ordering. A design, purpose, or mindfulness was therefore present, as interpreted through myth or theology. In summary, *natural* referred to a rich pattern of tacit normative rules implicit in human nature and the world humans inhabited. The second sense of natural also had an ancestry going back to Roman legal thought and some aspects of scholastic philosophy. Natural implied a *facultas animi*; this was something we shared with animals. This notion of natural, *qua* natural right, did not give rise to a rich moral system; conversely, it indicated a minimal range of virtually instinctive rules, powers, and permissions. Thus, natural referred, for example, to certain basic needs that we had for self-preservation and survival. We therefore had a natural 'right to life'—that is to say as a *conatus* to self-preservation. This could be seen as a power or a liberty. Nonetheless, even if minimal, these natural rights were still seen as fundamental and directive on human conduct.

Despite the subtle difference in usage, there were unquestionably certain underlying common features which characterized the use of 'nature' and 'natural' in the seventeenth and eighteenth centuries—in relation to the specific usage of 'natural right'. There were four core components to this background. First, nature implied—analytically—a creator, God. Second, this creator God had assembled nature as a one-off event. It was widely accepted that the authority for such judgements lay in biblical scripture, particularly Genesis. Elements in nature, such as organic species, had not and would not ever change. Nature was thus viewed as largely quiescent and frequently benign. Third, nature—as the creation of a wise designing deity—implied a plan and teleology. In fact, by observing nature carefully we could identify this design. Fourth, human beings had a very special status in this view of nature. They could be distinguished, for example, from all non-human creatures through their possession of a reasoning soul. Humans, in possessing reasoning souls, also exhibited the singular qualities of language, autonomy, and a moral capacity. Humans were therefore quite uniquely spiritually distinct and valuable in this 'natural scenario'. Yet it was their natural telos (end or purpose) to develop—with the assistance of natural law and natural rights—into fully autonomous moral beings living within God's laws or God-inspired reason.

Thus, first, a concept of a rational creator deity underpinned the concept of nature. Atheism was the exception rather than the rule. The deity was viewed as a judicious and benevolent creator. Nature without God made little or no logical sense. Even if nature was viewed as more machine-like (as in much seventeenth- and eighteenth-century science), this still did not undermine the belief in God. For Galileo, for example, what was true in nature was measurable and quantitative; however, God was still the connection between mind and nature. It was God who could, in the final analysis, grasp the connection. Nature was viewed as a relatively unchanging constant. There was no sense of any very dramatic change or alteration in nature itself whether normative or mechanistic.[2] Nature was, and had remained, as it had been created by a wise rational deity. More particularly, the idea, for example, of species change, demise, or transmutation was not something that had any intellectual currency, until minimally the early 1800s in innovatory thinkers such as Jean Baptiste Lamarck, and even then it was not widely accepted till much later in the nineteenth century. Nature was thus a created entity, that is, created by a rational deity. Second, creation had been a once and for all act and nothing had really changed since that point. There was, in fact, a very precise dating for this divine creation. With hindsight it may now seem very odd, but this dating was widely accepted up to the 1840s by the intellectual establishment of the time (and it should be noted that it was also accepted by Charles Darwin as a younger man and by most of his teachers and intellectual colleagues).[3] Thus, Bishop Ussher of Armagh, in the 1650s, had stated quite categorically that 4004 BC was the precise year of God's creation of the whole natural world. Christian scripture was viewed as the authoritative source for this judgement. The Genesis description was taken as the reliable account.[4]

Third, underpinning this divinely created more or less static understanding of nature was a belief in rational teleology, as well as arguments from design. The teleological argument had a long pedigree going back to the Greeks. In fact, Aristotelian categories provided one essential tool for design, namely, that everything in nature had a telos or purpose which explained the nature of the thing.[5] Later Christian thinkers simply supervened Christian purposes over the Aristotelian ideas. If nature embodied a telos, this could easily be reconfigured as God's telos.[6] By the mid-1700s there was a sizeable literature on what was often termed physico-theology or natural theology, whose sole function was to demonstrate that nature was a purposeful and designed entity, where the evidence of God's rational plan was there for all to see. As Glacken commented, 'The teleological view of nature became the philosophical—and theological— support for the conventional natural histories of the eighteenth century' (Glacken 1967, 508). Writers as diverse as John Ray, William Derham, Gottfried Wilhelm Leibniz, Alexander Pope, Carl von Linné, Johann Peter Süssmilch, Johann Gottfied von Herder, and most famously in England, William Paley, in his *Natural Theology or Evidences of the Existence and Attributes of the Deity* (1802), developed the design thesis in different ways. Paley declared, in this latter work, that 'The marks of design are too strong to be gotten over. Design must have a designer. That designer must have been a person. That person is God' (quoted in Rachels 1991, 10).[7] For Paley, for example, the human eye is a prime example of such design. It is so well suited for human functioning that it must be evidence of a divine purpose. In the same way that humans designed the telescope, God must have designed the eye (see Rachels 1991, 117–18).[8]

Of course there were eighteenth-century detractors from such views, such as the Comte de Buffon in *Des Epoques de la Nature*, Hume in his *Dialogues Concerning Natural Religion*, Voltaire in his *Philosophical Dictionary*, and

Baron D'Holbach in various writings. Hume and Voltaire particularly ridiculed the optimistic idea of natural design. One of the major natural events which encouraged this criticism was the disastrous Lisbon earthquake, and subsequent tsunami, on 1 November 1755.[9] Voltaire used this event to mock design arguments in popular writings such as *Candide*. However, the critical arguments of the likes of Hume and Voltaire were simply not widely accepted by the majority in the eighteenth century, although with hindsight we might find that peculiar.[10]

The fourth major component of the concept of nature was a powerful argument concerning the unique position of humanity in creation. Humans had souls (manifest through their capacity for practical reason) and thus stood out from all creation. Humans were essentially made in the image of God (*Imagio Dei*), as uniquely rational beings.[11] Another way of configuring this is that human beings were moral persons. The concept person has had a complex and tangled history. The present focus is on the religious and moral significance of the person in the context of the eighteenth-century natural right argument. My argument is that this sense of value in the person forms one of the most powerful and enduring legacies of the Christianized conception of nature. The religious and moral sense of the person has deep roots in Judaeo-Christian thought. What mattered to Christian thinkers, by and large, was what happened after death. Whereas groups like the Stoics were relatively agnostic over the immortality of the soul, Platonism (and neo-Platonism) and Pythagoreanism were relatively unusual in Greek thought in sharing, with later Christianity, this interest in immortality. The soul was an immaterial entity which was seen to survive the material body.[12] The *soul* and the *person* become synonymous. Personality becomes the essence of the individual human being and the source of their moral dignity. In the Christian mind, to lose one's personality is literally to be non-existent. The personality attains this central status since it is identified with the soul, which cannot be dissolved or destroyed, except by God. The whole significance of the resurrection, for example, in Christianity is the retaining or regaining of the personality (or soul) after death. The person or soul thus constitutes the very identity and essence of the individual.[13]

Twentieth-century scholars, such as Marcel Mauss, see this moral person glimmering within Stoic thought, but, 'it is the Christians who have made the metaphysical entity of the "moral person"'. For Mauss, even our contemporary notion of the person (e.g. the typical Kantian understanding) 'is still basically the Christian one'.[14] In Christianity, we see a definite change from ' "a man clad in a condition", to the notion of man, quite simply, that of the human "person" (*personne*)' (Mauss 1985, 19). This notion of the person essentially underpins many modern conceptions of the self. This idea, for Mauss, was being built slowly 'almost right up to our own time'.[15] Seventeenth- and eighteenth-century European thought gave, what appeared to be, a slightly more secularist understanding to the Christian sense of moral person-ality. However, the idea of the individual person—specifically as a bearer of natural duties and rights—was still the product of a constellation of reli-giously inspired ideas. The rational person, even in more secular-sounding arguments, was still a surrogate for the immaterial soul. A manifold of ideas attaches to this latter moral and religious sense of the person. In the twentieth century, the person was usually identified by the possession of a capacity for self-determination and rational thought processes. Only persons make intel-ligent choices and act responsibly. Persons are self-conscious, aware of their own mental processes, and have a sense of past, present, and future. They can consciously articulate values, interests, preferences, and purposes and can direct their actions through such values and cite intelligible reasons for their conduct—a being capable of guilt, blame, and accountability. Many would also link this conception of the person with a capacity for conceptual thought and language.[16] Despite the apparent secularity of this theme, it was origin-ally, particularly in the context of natural right arguments, configured in a predominantly Christian framework.

Given this constellation of ideas which underpins the eighteenth-century idea of nature, it was hardly surprising that a rational deity was still seen to inhabit most of the formulations of 'natural right'. In addition, both the maximal and minimal readings of 'natural' were viewed as universally binding on humanity. Further, rights were legitimate only insofar as they were premised on an intrinsic rule-governed sense of nature. In addition, natural rights were not dependent upon any political or legal apparatus to craft or legitimatize them. These natural rights, which were implicit in nature and perceived via practical reason, were not subject to substantial change. Humans, wherever they existed, would seek the natural right to life, min-imally via self-preservation. Such self-preservation had to be respected. Max-imally, the person was seen to possess spiritual dignity and should be treated with justice.

## Conventional explanations of natural rights decline

The central underlying question of the chapter still remains: why did this powerful vocabulary of natural rights, with its deep-rooted assumptions about nature, drop out of political discussions in the nineteenth century? There have been some standard answers to this question in the literature, vis-à-vis the critiques within historical theory, particularly Marxism, Benthamite utilitarianism, legal positivism, and classical conservative thought.

The first argument is historical and has a wide ambit. It focuses on the core claim that all human life is subject to the contingency of sociological and historical circumstance. In many ways this is integral to work of Karl Marx, Max Weber, Ferdinand Tönnies, Émile Durkheim, or Leon Duguit. Every human being is thus seen as a child of their own time and society. They cannot escape from this historical and sociological destiny. Human nature is therefore contingent, mutable, and with no fixed essence. Humans do not have universal interests. Ethics is dependent upon the communal circumstances of individuals. Moral rules can be rich and determinative, but often at the cost of any universality. However, a great deal depends in this tradition as to whether a teleology of emancipation, or the like, is attached to historical contingency. In writers such as Burke, Hegel, or Marx an underlying teleology can make overall sense of historical changes in terms of a sequence of events with an underlying purpose. However, if one abstracts the teleology, then history becomes more a matter of random chance, with no aim, purpose, or sense. This is largely the position of many late twentieth-century postmodern writers.[17] It should not surprise us that the large majority of historical and sociological theorists either ignored or repudiated natural right theory.

The most well-known example of the historical argument, vis-à-vis natural rights, is Marx's historical materialism. It is neatly expressed in his early essay, 'On the Jewish Question', where he argues that the rights of man are nothing but the rights of a member of bourgeois civil society (see Marx 1972, 106–7). Such rights may provide a temporary contingent historical liberation from feudalism, but in the end they only liberate bourgeois acquisitiveness, the gain of the few and the enslavement of the many. Rights are not autonomous from economic interests. The historically mutating economic base is always primary and exists prior to rights. Rights cannot, therefore, ever be explained in themselves. They are part of the ideology of bourgeois society and must be grasped through the historically changing economic interests of the bourgeoisie. Thus, natural rights, in themselves, tell us virtually nothing substantive about a society or about the nature of rights per se. The real meaning of rights lies, for Marx, in the relation between class, ownership, power, and material interest. They are, in effect, a condensation of the economic interests of the dominant class which controls the coercive state apparatus.

The second form of argument is juristic and still permeates contemporary jurisprudence. This is the legal positivist argument, which again has a number of dimensions. The present sketch—which takes no account of any of the subtle nuances of forms of legal positivism—only outlines the most obvious of these. Part of the initial philosophical ground for the legal positivist movement lies in the work of Bentham and some would suggest an earlier formulation in Hobbes. The basic contention of legal positivism—which was founded as an oppositional movement to natural law and natural right theory—is that *law is law regardless of its content*. The strongest statement of this is that law arises from established legal associations with sovereign executives and legislatures. A sovereign cannot, by definition, be bound by any rule other than those it chooses for itself.[18] This is what it *means* conceptually to be a sovereign. A right must therefore be understood as a command of a sovereign backed up by coercive power. Since there are no international sovereigns, and natural rights claim to be universal rules which stand above states, as such, they are either just good-natured moralizing or hot air and consequently conceptually mistaken about what it means to possess a right. In summary, a right implies a command, this implies a duty to obey, this in turn implies a sovereign who makes the command; the command is then backed up by the threat of coercive penalties. A right therefore must entail a legal sovereign, that is, the essential logical presupposition. Without this logic, a right is a meaningless clatter. In this context, the idea of natural right becomes futile.

The third argument is moral, and again has a number of faces. One obvious dimension of the moral intersects with the historical above—an early manifestation of the sociological and the anthropological. Broadly the moral claims which underpin natural rights are historically, sociologically, and anthropologically contingent. This inevitably undermines the argument for the universality of natural rights. However, one does not have to move onto this relativist path. Early utilitarians, such as Bentham, also objected to natural rights. However, the Benthamite objection is not focused on the historical or sociological contingency. Rather, Bentham's objection is that such rights misunderstand the use of moral words. The best expression of this is Bentham's comment, in his work *Anarchical Fallacies*, on the *French Declaration on the Rights of Man*, that natural rights 'is simple nonsense: natural and imprescriptible rights, rhetorical nonsense,—nonsense upon stilts' (Bentham 2002, 53).

For Bentham, all human action is under two sovereign masters—pleasure and pain. Humans essentially try to maximize pleasure and minimize pain. We calculate this in any action. The good maximizes our pleasure or interest. The maximum good is the maximization of the interests and pleasure of the greatest possible number. Maximizing pleasure or interests is to our utility. The greatest happiness is thus the greatest utility. Thus, rights cannot be self-justifying entities. The root to our rejection or acceptance of rights is whether it has the *consequence* of maximizing utility. All rights are governed by consequential considerations. It is still possible to make out a case for natural rights on the basis of utilitarianism, if it could be shown that such rights are conducive to maximizing interests or welfare, but such rights are *not* necessarily universal. They depend on human utility, preferences, and interests. In fact, even for quite reasonable liberal-minded utilitarians, human or natural rights can be viewed as arbitrary constraints on policy making. Policy making should be seen as a more empirical balanced practice which would be looking to maximize the public good and not being arbitrarily constrained by natural rights.

The fourth argument is the classical conservative argument, which also has strong elements of the historical approach. The basic contention here, which can be found in many formulations of the more traditional conservative perspective from Edmund Burke onwards, is that rights can only be grasped via the conventions and customs of a community. Reason is not the crowning faculty of human beings. We are rather more complex creatures embedded in tradition—often guided by sentiment, habit, and passion, as much as reason. In this context, natural rights would therefore be viewed as arbitrary fictions which are not rooted in any tradition. Burke's own deeply critical views on natural rights saturate his writings on France during the revolutionary period.

In summary, first, natural rights are historically, anthropologically, or sociologically relative to circumstances, or, in Marx relative to the economic base and ideological hegemony of ruling groups. Second, rights are dependent upon pre-existent legal systems and sovereign entities, yet given there are no universal sovereign entities, it follows that there are no universal natural rights. Third, rights can only be justified consequentially and relate to human interests, preferences, and choices. It follows that they cannot be seen as either automatically universal or self-validating. Fourth, rights relate to the historical circumstances of tradition, conventions, and customs of particular long-standing communities. It follows that there could be no rights which transcend communities. It follows therefore that there are no natural rights.

All the above theories are conventionally discussed in the literature as having an explanatory role in critically undermining the discourse of natural rights. However, ironically Marx's essay attacking natural rights ('On the Jewish Question') was not known until the 1920s, when his early writings were rediscovered and printed. In fact, it was the 1960s which saw any widespread interest in these early writings. Further, Marx himself was not really widely appreciated in the English-speaking world until the early twentieth century. Further, historical and Hegelian argumentation did not really begin to take effect in Britain until the 1860s, at the earliest. Benthamite utilitarianism had a role to play in changing legal and moral language, but the extent of its impact is disputed by many scholars. How many people knew of Bentham's attack on natural rights at the time? Not that many one suspects. The Burkean conservative argument was probably better known and more broadly appreciated, but Burke and many similar conservative thinkers in attacking natural right were certainly not abandoning a traditional Judaeo-Christian natural law language. In Burke, for example, traditional natural law was largely retained and used *against* natural right. If anything, Burke's arguments were using objective right against subjective right. In summary, none of these more conventional explanations are adequate to provide a satisfactory account of why the language of natural right all but collapsed in the nineteenth century. To grasp why natural right declined, it is important to understand why the constellation of ideas surrounding the concepts of 'nature' and 'natural' collapsed.

## A change in nature

In the mid to late nineteenth century, the most decisive idea to affect the conception of nature was evolutionary theory. It dominated biological studies, specifically in the last decades of the nineteenth century. Prior to Darwin, evolutionary ideas were being entertained by many eminent scholars.[19] However, Darwin's concept of evolution was one of the first scientific theories to really capture the imagination of the educated public and provide solid evidence for its central claims. In this sense, in 1859, the publication of *On the Origin of Species* was one of those rare moments when a decisive change of human consciousness was clearly enunciated.[20] By the 1860s Darwin was one of the most talked about writers and scientists in Britain and Europe.[21] The *Origin* was translated, in a comparatively short period, into many world languages. The central ideas enabled humanity to envisage itself in a totally different way. Evolution theory offered an intellectually convincing explanation across the whole field of the natural and social sciences. The allure of such an all-encompassing way of understanding was irresistible. It found expression not only in biology, geology, paleontology, and anthropology, but also in history, philosophy, poetry, politics, and religion.[22] Many writers and scholars immediately began to see strong and quite specific parallels between the natural world and the world of human affairs.[23] In my reading it became a 'framework-making' idea, which enabled many different disciplines to reconfigure their core concepts.

For the purpose of argument it is also necessary to note how it affected the constellation of ideas underpinning 'nature' from the eighteenth century (and consequently natural right arguments). Darwinism admittedly was not necessarily a consistent or wholly unified doctrine. Certainly this would be the case for post-Darwinist theory. Darwinism has clearly meant different things to different scholars. However, there were certain immediate effects deriving from the central arguments of the *Origin* which should be noted.[24] First, evolution—together with extensive fossil evidence from geology and palaeontology—demonstrated that the natural world was somewhere in the region of 15 billion years old, and had not been created in any 'one-off' event. Rather it had changed over time, often through catastrophic events. Second, species in nature were neither separate nor wholly distinct (as created by God), but had all derived from a common descent. In fact, many species had died out and new forms had evolved. There was no essence to any species, including humanity. All species evolved and transformed. Others, such as

Buffon and Lamarck, had toyed with this idea of common descent, but none had developed it so systematically with such a strong evidential base as Darwin. For Darwin there was an enormous variety of species, some of which had been lost, and others which had evolved from older species in new geographical and physical conditions. The sheer variety of species was simply due to the same species (by descent) adapting to different physical or geographical circumstances and thus evolving in different ways. The mechanism of change here was natural selection; those species which successfully adapted to an environment survived and reproduced and passed on their inheritance, those which did not became extinct.

There were obvious implications flowing from this argument. Nature no longer appeared benign, but was rather capricious and seemingly wasteful. No species had any essence and none had any *right* to exist. All species change gradually and many become extinct in the process of trying to survive. Descent theory had also shown—even though Darwin was wary of the idea— that the descent of man was an equally plausible idea. Humans had not been created in any 'one-off' creation. Rather they had evolved very gradually from ape-like ancestors. Humans were just another dimension of the phylogenetic tree of organic life. There was *nothing* special about us. Darwin realized of course that this decisively undermined the argument from natural design. As he stated in his *Autobiography* (1887),

> The old argument of design in nature, as given by Paley, which formerly seemed to me so conclusive, fails, now that the law of natural selection has been discovered. We can no longer argue that, for instance, the beautiful hinge of a bivalve shell must have been made by an a intelligent being, like the hinge of a door by man. There seems to be no more design in the variability of organic beings and in the action of natural selection, than in the course which the wind blows.
> (Darwin 1958, 87)

By the mid-1850s, it appears, Darwin had wholly abandoned the ideas of both natural teleology and design. Many were to follow in his footsteps. Karl Marx saw clearly that this total abandonment of natural teleology and rational design was the central nerve of the *Origin* argument. Marx referred to this Darwinian argument as dealing a 'death blow' to all such claims to natural teleology (quoted in Clark 1984, 212). In addition, what we think of as a rational morality was for Darwin merely a complex extension of the same functional evolutionary instinct. Morality can—through encouraging cooperation in certain circumstances—contribute to survival. There is nothing more to it than that. The moral instinct is a social instinct, which is in turn a survival instinct. Good conduct is a naturally functional conduct. Morality, for Darwin, therefore had pre-human ancestry and an evolutionary basis. The evolutionary reading of morality was taken up much more forcefully in the work of Herbert Spencer, for example, *The Data of Ethics* (1879), and in the writings of twentieth-century sociobiologists, such as Conrad Lorenz's *On Aggression* (1966), Desmond Morris's *The Naked Ape* (1967), or E. O. Wilson's *Sociobiology: The New Synthesis* (1975).

The final decisive effect of the *Origin* theory was to undermine the whole concept of the centrality of humanity in nature. Moral anthropocentrism became unfeasible.[25] Humans were clearly not made in the image of God. Humans were not uniquely rational. Many other animals showed precisely the qualities which the older natural theology arguments considered to be essentially human. The difference between humans and animals in general was not one of a kind, but rather one of degree. Darwin, in his private notebooks, ridiculed the idea that human souls (and reason) could be distinguished somehow from their bodies. Thought and consciousness were just material things, merely a 'secretion of the brain' (Darwin quoted in Rachels 1991, 30). Mind and reason were therefore simply natural characteristics of the human biological organism as it evolved.

Another consequence of this denial of anthropocentrism was to undermine an idea implicit in all natural law and the bulk of natural right argument, namely, that humans, as uniquely intellectual creatures, were not only superior to other creatures, but were more morally significant. In thinkers from Aquinas up to Kant, and beyond, one can find the idea that human beings are worthy of a special kind of moral esteem and dignity, as distinct from all other non-human creatures. Darwin was admittedly careful in print as to exactly what he had to say on this issue, as on religious issues in general. But the upshot of his *Origin* argument is clear enough: human dignity, human centrality in nature (moral anthropocentrism), human uniqueness, and moral inviolability are all the illusions of a bankrupt set of arguments about nature. Darwin's *Origin* basically systematically removed all the supports from this eighteenth-century notion of nature. God was therefore extraneous to any argument about nature. The authority of the Bible and religion were bankrupt. Nature had evolved over billions of years, it had not been created. No species was immutable, including humanity. The only laws in nature related to the mechanisms underpinning evolution, namely, natural selection and descent. These laws led to unpredictable results, since circumstances and natural selection gave rise to both chance and probability, rather than any fixity of species. There was no teleology in either nature or history. There was no rational design, no perfectibility of humanity, and no natural progress. There was no compassionate benign natural world, but rather a natural world characterized by struggle, risk, and infinite probabilities.

It was this background understanding of nature which dominated intellectual discussion from the 1860s. It was a background theme which knocked away all the intellectual supports from natural right, as a particular understanding of 'nature'.[26] One crucial facet of this new language, which arose from the constellation of ideas introduced by Darwin, was the application of natural selection criteria to social selection. Politics increasingly became biologically naturalized. Purportedly scientific reasons were therefore provided for revitalizing our understanding of politics on evolutionary grounds.


# Ecology

Evolution theory therefore provided a powerful—in my terminology—*framework-making vocabulary* for a wide range of new intellectual disciplines. The two to be discussed here are ecology and geography. Both were focused on the integral relation of humanity with nature—nature being understood in an evolutionary framework. Evolution also linked both disciplines to the concept of the modern nation-state—something that will be explored in a later section.

There is little contention concerning the first usage of the neologism 'ecology' in European thought, as a term indicating a new disciplinary idea. It was employed by the German zoologist and philosopher Ernst Haeckel (1834–1919), who was at the time professor of Zoology at Jena University and later a professor of comparative anatomy.[27] Haeckel's use of the term ecology (*Oekologie*—an economy of nature) in his *Generelle Morphologie der Organismen* (1866) and *Natürliche Schöpfungsgeschichte* (1868) denoted 'the science of relations between organisms and their environment' (quoted in Bramwell 1989, 40). Haeckel was a prominent figure for a time in German and British thought. He was a key popularizer of Darwinian ideas.[28] Haeckel saw Darwin as not only transforming our understanding of nature, but also as the founder of the new disciplines of ecology and indeed a new understanding of anthropology (see Haeckel 1917, 146ff., 1929, 64ff.). Further Haeckel was not shy of identifying strong political and historical implications in the evolutionary perspective. For example, he developed his own account of the way nations develop through evolutionary conflict. He linked this to his more general conception of 'biogenetic theory'. It led him to some comments on the need for 'mature races' to supervise the 'immature' ones.[29] Unlike Darwin, Haeckel adopted a more Lamarckian perspective on humans—for which he enlisted the support of palaeontology—to show that humans had progressed and ascended from a lower to a higher biological level. The political consequences of this were directly aristocratic. The winners in evolutionary struggle were in a sense the natural aristocrats.

Haeckel's influence passed rapidly into a number of disciplines. For example, one of the greatest German jurists of the period Rudolf von Jhering (1818–1922) entitled his major jurisprudential work *Der Kampf ums Recht* (1872). The title was modelled on Jhering's admiration for Haeckel's terminology '*Der Kampf ums Dasein*' ('the struggle for existence'). For Jhering, 'The life of law is a struggle—a struggle of nations, of the state power, of classes, of individuals' (Jhering 1915, 15). This was a sentiment that corresponded directly to Haeckel's own biogenic theory. For Jhering, struggle, directed by a strong sense of what is right, was a far more important idea for explaining the nature of law than any fine-grained conceptual analysis. Human inner drives or instincts, national struggle, and historical development provided deeper insights into the nature of law. Another pupil of Haeckel's was Ludwig Gumplowicz (1838–1909), a professor of sociology and politics in Graz. In books such as *Rasse und Staat* (1875), *Der Rassenkampf* (1883), and *Grundriss der Soziologie* (1885), he directly reiterated the theme of struggle, in this case between races. He saw a biological concept of race as underpinning all politics. The state and legal structures had therefore to be grasped via this naturalistic evolutionary logic of struggle and natural selection. A state for Gumplowicz was simply the 'natural' institutional structure of a 'settled folk' or settled racial group. Humans were always identified naturally with racial groups. Identity was therefore always racial. There was no distinction in Gumplowicz between nation and race. Gumplowicz's ideas were deeply influential, amongst others, on the ideas of the early American sociologist Lewis H. Morgan in his *Ancient Society: Researches in the Lines of Human Progress from Savagery through Barbarism to Civilization* (1877) and the German theorist Albrecht Wirth in *Rasse und Volk* (1914).

Haeckel's influence spread not only in scientific, political, and legal circles, but also within the literary and religious establishments. He was a prime mover in a wave of evolutionary naturalism in Germany and Britain in the last decades of the nineteenth century which was deeply indebted to both Darwinism and Lamarckianism.[30] In serious academic works and more popular texts, such as *The Riddle of the Universe*, Haeckel went on to develop a philosophical monism which would act ultimately as a proxy religion. Nature was envisaged as being of fundamental spiritual importance.[31] Denying atheism, he referred to his view as 'pantheism'. God, for Haeckel, was completely immanent in nature, or as he put it, 'God, as an *intramundane* being, is everywhere identical with nature itself' (Haeckel 1929, 236).[32] With the death of god, Haeckel proclaimed optimistically that 'the new sun of our realistic monism...reveals to us the wonderful temple of nature in all its beauty'. A nature religion thus replaced 'the anthropistic ideals of "God, freedom, and immortality"' (Haeckel 1929, 311). Haeckel thus saw nature as a unified balanced organism of which humans were an important part. This monistic, natural, and harmonious organism also had lessons to teach us in terms of the organization of society, as well as our relations with nature.[33]

Given the assumptions underpinning natural right, outlined earlier, it is worth pausing for a brief moment to reflect on a passage in Haeckel's valedictory book, *The Riddle of the Universe*, when he is outlining the problems that his monistic evolutionary philosophy is designed to counter. The central problem relates to the 'anthropistic ideals', or more briefly, 'anthropism'.

This latter term denotes for Haeckel a 'world-wide group of erroneous opinion which opposes the human organism to the whole of the rest of nature, and represents it be the preordained end of organic creation'. Anthropism is made up of three false dogmas: the *anthropocentric* dogma 'cultivates the idea that man is the preordained centre and aim of all terrestrial life', which Haeckel sees as arising from the religions of Judaism, Christianity, and Islam. The *anthropomorphic* dogma likens 'the creation and control of the world by God to the artificial creation of a skilful engineer or mechanic'. Humans are conceived as being made in the image of God. Third, the *anthropolatric* dogma results from the analogy being drawn between humans and God. It stresses the personal immortality of the human 'soul', as distinct from the body; in other words, it adheres to a pervasive dualistic dogma. All of these dangerous errors are rejected by Haeckel on evolutionary grounds (Haeckel 1929, 10–12). In effect, on strict evolutionary grounds, we can see in these arguments the rejection of the idea of a creator God, teleology and rational design, and of the moral centrality of humanity.

From Haeckel onwards, ecology has often had a moral and spiritual import for humanity. The manner in which we interact with the environment, organize our societies, economies, and personal lives has direct bearing on the same naturalistic evolutionary logic. One other aspect worth mentioning is that the ecology, from its early inception in the 1860s and 1870s, had strong links with nationalist movements across Europe. The key point to stress here is that this ecological conception had powerful implications for politics—nature and politics were essentially *linked phenomena*. Politics was literally 'naturalized', in an evolutionary sense. This thesis was more subtly and overtly explored in geography.

# Geography

One of the key intellectual events which took place, after Darwin's voyage in the *Beagle* to the Galapagos, was his realization that what looked on the surface like different species of finches (on different islands in the Galapagos chain), were all in fact traceable to one remote ancestor, probably from South America. Common 'descent theory' became, as indicated earlier, a backbone of evolutionary theory (see Darwin 1985). The idea of common descent had been mooted in Buffon and Lamarck, but in Darwin's *Origin* it took on a central role. The crucial determining factor here was geography or biogeography. The geographical location of species played a crucial role in understanding their variation and descent. Two chapters of Darwin's *Origin* were consequently devoted to geography. In this sense, geographical distribution of species was crucial.

Of course one can trace geographical speculation back to early Greek or Roman writers. A more common strategy though is to see its development in the late eighteenth and early nineteenth century.[34] In the first few decades of the 1800s, two of the most famous geographers were Germans, Karl Ritter and Alexander von Humboldt. Humboldt was, for example, closely linked to the development of measurement and mapping. For Humboldt each region of the world had its own distinctive qualities and life forms which geography carefully charted. Despite the considerable reputation of Humboldt and Ritter, by the 1860s, both geographers were seen to be far too bogged down in late-eighteenth-century, quasi-romantic philosophical speculation and teleology.[35] Fortuitously, both the latter geographers died in 1859, the year of the publication of Darwin's *Origin*. Neither Ritter's nor Humboldt's work were seen, at the time, to be in tune with this new conception of nature.

Within a decade of the publication of Darwin's *Origin*, one of the most significant founding figures of European and North American geography Friedrich Ratzel (1844–1904) was publishing his first book.[36] At the time, Ratzel was a keen aspiring young zoologist. He had attended enthusiastically Haeckel's lectures at Jena University in 1869 and was for a time wholly absorbed with Haeckel's use of evolutionary theory.[37] However, his interest in the question of the relation between humanity and the environment took a new turn by 1875, this time to geography, or as he called it later *Anthropogeographie*. Unsurprisingly Ratzel also saw his own work as making major contributions to both anthropology and ethnography (see Dickinson 1969, 63ff.).[38] Ratzel turned against not only the geography of Humboldt and Ritter, but also against the shortcomings of Haeckel's ecology, especially in terms of giving a completely satisfactory account of the relation between humans and nature.[39] For Ratzel, the way forward was a radical new science of geography which would integrate all that was best from the evolutionary arguments into a much broader theory. Ratzel's scholarly output was enormous. His most famous work was the *Völkerkunde* (*History of Mankind*) in three volumes published in 1885, 1886, and 1888, the two volume *Anthropogeographie* (1882 and 1891), and *Politische Geographie* (1897). One of his fervent disciples, Ellen Churchill Semple, subsequently became a founding figure in North American geography. Her key text *Influences of Geographic Environment: On the Basis of Ratzel's System of Anthropo-Geography* was published in 1911.

## Ratzel's thesis

Ratzel's basic premise is that nature and humanity are ontologically linked. The being of humanity is *within* a place, a particular land. This point had already been partly argued in Haeckel's science of ecology. As Ellen Semple put it, 'Man is a product of the earth's surface. This means not merely that he is a child of the earth, dust of her dust; but that the earth has mothered him, fed him, set him tasks, directed his thoughts, confronted him with difficulties.... She has entered his bone and tissue, into his mind and soul' (Semple 1911, 1–2). The definition of humanity is thus integral to nature. To comprehend human beings one needs to understand the land within which they exist.

However, the relations between humans and the land 'are infinitely more numerous and complex than those of the most highly organized plant or animal. So complex are they that they constitute a legitimate and necessary object of special study'. For Ratzel and his disciplines, geography was the science for studying this ontology. This crucial dimension of understanding humanity receives only 'piecemeal' explanation in anthropology, ethnology, sociology, and history.[40] For Semple, for example, 'all these sciences, together with history so far as history undertakes to explain the causes of events, fail to reach a satisfactory solution of their problems largely because the geographic factor which enters into them all has not been thoroughly analyzed' (quotations from Semple 1911, 1–2). In essence, geography is the real basis for grasping human history and politics.[41]

A brief additional side issue to note here is that Ratzel's conception of geography does alternate between two tendencies, which still characterize modern geography, namely, between *Naturlandschaft* and *Kulturlandschaft*.[42] In fact, he never settled fully on either aspect. Ratzel retained strong interests in the more positivistic, empiricistic, and deterministic aspect of *Naturlandschaft* (which still has a strong following in physical geography). However, he was also clearly inspirational in the development of *Kulturlandschaft*, which became more popular in the twentieth century. This was the idea that land does not wholly determine human nature, but that there is conversely a reciprocal shaping process. In the twentieth century, this latter concern has developed its own niche in terms of human and cultural geography. One of the key early theorists to take up this *Kulturlandschaft* theme was Otto Schlüter (1872–1959). He emphasized particularly the human aspect of geography and formulated quite precisely the notion of a 'cultural landscape'. Land, in other words, becomes as much a human artefact. A similar theme was taken up in the founder of French geography, Vidal de La Bache, and in American geography in Carl Sauer's work in the early twentieth century. In some ways, cultural geography was taken up with the intellectual theme of German *Geisteswissenschaften* (cultural and human sciences), contra the positivistic understanding.[43] Sauer subsequently inspired a wide-ranging group of early twentieth-century geographers, such as Fred Kniffen, David Lowenthal, Wilbur Zilensky, and Peirce Morgan amongst others. In fact, this cultural geographical approach developed considerably in the later twentieth century (see e.g. Meinig 1979; Lowenthal 1985; Baker and Biger 1992; Craig 1998).[44]

## Geography and the state

For geographers such as Ratzel, humans live naturally in groups and each group needs a physical space which it will naturally try to exploit and then, through demographic pressures, expand.[45] The most dynamic and significant group for Ratzel is the modern 'state', or more precisely what he calls the 'organic state'—as subsisting in relation to land.[46] As Ratzel puts it, 'a state is a living organism', that is to say, states should be regarded, quite simply, as 'living bodies'.[47] The form, character, and actions of that body will be dependent on both the physical conditions and what Ratzel calls the 'greatness on its inhabitants' (quotes from Ratzel 1996, 526). Greatness, in this context, for Ratzel relates to the fact that certain 'races' appear much more adaptive and successful in the evolutionary stakes. Geography also explained the type of state and the manner in which they are internally organized.[48] The idea of the organic state had been used before this period, particularly in romantic political thought; however, in Ratzel the direct link with the evolutionary account of nature and ontological naturalism gave it a unique intellectual gravitas at the time.

In addition, Ratzel's organic state was—as importantly—a 'nation state'. In fact, Ratzel's use of, and interest in, the nation was closely linked to his interest in race (see Hannaford 1996, 332). Nationality and race were both seen as connected evolutionary phenomena.[49] For Ratzel, nationality evolves with an intellectually and culturally mature people, within a substantial resource-rich territory (Ratzel 1996, 529). The growth of national consciousness, national languages, and national literature are wholly dependent on the territory, soil, land, in sum, the geographical location of a people. Immature, less-civilized nations, with their own language or dialect do not usually possess large territories, and they will commonly be absorbed by larger nations. All the significant states, for Ratzel, therefore have a strong sense of themselves as unified nationalities. The greater the land mass occupied and the more intense the focus on it, the more politically significant the state becomes.[50] It is these states to which, for Ratzel, one can attach the concept 'civilization', and significantly such great nation states 'are situated in Europe and the European colonial territories'. The only exception to this for Ratzel is China (Ratzel 1996, 526).

This evolutionary conception of the organic nation state immediately explains a range of phenomena. The territorial unity and expansionist policies of mature states are biologically *natural*. The nation state needs to grow in order to survive and remain biologically healthy; the unhealthy state will eventually be absorbed by the healthy one. This idea is wholly dictated by the evolutionary process of natural selection. The rule is the same for both peaceful competition and war, namely, 'that the aggressor must advance on the ground occupied by his opponent, and in overcoming him he must assimilate...him' (Ratzel 1996, 535). This argument has enormous implications for conceptions of war, colonialism, international law, and international migration, as Ratzel was very much aware. The organic nation state, he contended, in its natural growth, always 'selects the geographically advantageous positions, occupying the good lands before the bad, and if its growth is accompanied by encroachment on the territory of another state, it takes possession of the important points, and then advances towards the less valuable parts' (Ratzel 1996, 532). This explains, for Ratzel, what might be termed, the *natural history* of European colonial expansion.

An organic nation state thus resembles an organic 'fluid mass slowly ebbing and flowing', and such an ebb and flow is rarely over 'unoccupied areas'.[51] Movement, 'as a rule', takes the form of an 'encroachment and usurpation,...small territories, with their inhabitants, are annexed to larger ones. Similarly these larger states fall to pieces, and this union and disintegration, expansion and contraction, constitute a great part of those historical movements which geographically are represented by a division of the surface into greater or smaller portions' (Ratzel 1996, 526). As Semple puts it, quite neatly, a legal border must always be viewed as the 'periphery of the growing or declining race' (Semple 1911, 210). Yet Ratzel notes that 'growth which never goes beyond mere annexation creates only loose, easily dismembered conglomerations' (Ratzel 1996, 529). Annexation therefore has to be complete, a process of fully absorbing and nationalizing a territory.

## Land and identity

The crucial anthropogeographical assumption is that humans are 'a product of the earth's surface'. For Ratzel, there is no such thing as 'complete severance from the soil' (Ratzel 1996, 530). Humans are shaped and, in turn, continuously shape and reshape a land (what Ratzel called *Kulturlandschaft*).[52] This is the dimension of Ratzel's work which was taken up much more thoroughly in geographers such as Schlüter and Sauer. For Ratzel, a nation state always has roots deep in a land. He thus remarks that it is no metaphor to speak of a nation state 'taking root'. A nation state is an 'organic body which in the course of its history is fixed more and more firmly in the soil on which it lives. As the individual contends with the virgin soil until he has converted it into cultivated land, so a people struggles with its territory and makes it ever more and more its own by shedding its sweat and blood on its behalf'. He continues that 'We cannot think of the French apart from France, or the Germans apart from Germany' (Ratzel 1996, 529–30). A land is thus integral to a nation state, both are part of the same organic body. A land is stretched out in time, shaped and reshaped, and written and rewritten by the organic 'nation state'. As one would expect, this land and human symbiosis never stands still; as Ratzel comments, in a 'stationary condition weakness and decay creep in, whereas aggression demands organization' (Ratzel 1996, 534).[53]

It became, in the last few decades of the twentieth century, a relative commonplace to think of a person's identity as tied in certain fundamental ways, or at least inflected by their ethnicity, nationality, culture, gender, religion, and so forth. Admittedly this modern focus on identity was not so closely (or ontologically) tied to land. Identity arguments from the 1980s were usually configured in normative terms. This was, in part, a return to a pre-evolutionary romantic conception. However, the identity arguments between 1860 and 1940 were fundamentally marked by evolutionary language. Identity, in the most general terms, implies some form of recognition. One of the most powerful of these 'identity vocabularies' in the late nineteenth and twentieth centuries has undoubtedly been nationalism. Ratzel, for example, sees the organic nation state as the most evolutionary mature of all identity-based social groupings. Further, national culture is explicitly linked with a place and a land. To be part of the land one has to be a *member* of the national culture. Human identity, for Ratzel, is naturalized via this evolutionary concept of the nation, which is in turn linked indissolubly to a physical land.[54] As Semple notes, a land 'is fully comprehended only when studied in the light of its influence upon its people' (Semple 1911, 51). For Ratzel's geography, state, nation, land, and identity are all therefore mutually supportive concepts. They are embedded in the same naturalistic ontology. Land and national identity are two sides of the same coin. They provide the key for understanding modern politics.

One additional point to mention here with regard to Ratzel's view of nationalism concerns the terminology of the *Volk*—as in his substantial *Völkerkunde* work. Ratzel clearly saw a close connection between his understanding of nation and race. The word *Volk* is etymologically fairly open on this question, although there is a separate German term for race—*Rasse*.[55] However, Ratzel saw himself advancing his more general theory in helping to establish the *Archiv für Rassen* in Germany, whose function was to study and publish the findings of race biology and psychology. This society was later linked to the German Society for Race Hygiene and the British Eugenics Education Society before the First World War. In other words, Ratzel's understanding of a nation and *Volk* were intimately linked to the concept of race. At the time though, in the 1880s and 1890s, such a study seemed perfectly in accord with scientific evolutionary biology. Ratzel's and others' interest in the biological question of race was therefore not out of kilter with the general intellectual interests of the time.[56]

# The organic nation state

The rise of new disciplines, such as ecology and geography, is significant for two reasons. First, both disciplines integrate a powerful new discourse about nature and evolutionary theory into mainstream academic study. This new discourse integrates humanity and nature in a dynamic and complex symbiosis, in the form of a naturalistic ontology. Human identity is defined *in terms of* natural environments and land. Second, these ideas provide a very powerful imprimatur to the organic conception of the nation state and its role in terms of land, territory, identity, and, in turn, war, conquest, and colonial expansion. The argument now turns to explore this issue of the organic nation state more closely by focusing on three more questions: first, *when* and *why* were these debates about the organic nation state taking place; second, *where* were these debates taking place; and third, what have been the longer-term effects of this organic nation-state language?

## WHEN AND WHY THE NATION STATE?

The era in which evolution came to dominate discussion of nature (and the moment when geographical and ecological ideas were beginning to develop) was also a period of accelerated nation-state formation—including, for example, Greece (1830), Belgium (1831), Italy (1861), and Germany (1871). The United States had also just gone through the trauma of civil war in the 1860s and was searching for some path towards a unifying national identity.[57] In France and Britain, it was not so much state formation as identity and empire consolidation. Another related point is that the inception of these intense debates about geography, ecology, evolution, and the state occurred during a decade when Germany was itself unifying as a nation state. For Ratzel's generation this was a deeply emotive experience. It was in the last stage of this push for national unity that the Franco-Prussian war erupted (1870–1). We should note that this was a war which Chancellor Otto von Bismarck described in ethnological terms as illustrating the superiority of the energetic Aryan race over and against the spent Latin race (see Hannaford 1996, 287–8). Ratzel volunteered in 1871 for military service in the Baden Infantry and was wounded in action. The war made a deeply positive impression on him.[58]

Ratzel was not alone in this nationalistic stance. National unity—prospective or retrospective—was arousing many in Europe and elsewhere during the nineteenth and twentieth centuries. The arguments were also frequently carried on in terms of the concept of race.[59] Significantly, national groups claimed that they needed some form of political autonomy; characteristically they sought for some form of statehood. They also needed land. Land was usually seen as tied irrevocably to the identity of a national group. This was *not* a romantic longing for land; it was seen by many as a collective natural right—natural in this case being understood in biological terms.

With hindsight one of Ratzel's most tarnished neologisms arose in this context, namely, *Lebensraum* (living space or living room). The concept follows logically from the central doctrines of anthropogeography.[60] The idea purports to show a clear scientific evolutionary reason as to why land was so central to a nation state and also why states expand or contract. Each nation state naturally needs *Lebensraum*. The organic state, as a spatial biological organism, necessarily expands up to its natural limits. If opposition is not mounted by strong neighbours, or by physical geographic barriers, a state will 'naturally' overflow into its neighbours. Ratzel thus saw *Lebensraum* as a 'biogeographical' scientific concept. By the 1930s, however, the concept had become part of the verbal arsenal of national socialism, which has subsequently coloured our perception of it till the present day. However, the concept of *Lebensraum* has carried on as a central part of the unspoken subtext of 'identity-in-land' politics, to the present day. It is perhaps no longer necessary for a group, culture, or state to 'spill over' into another group—although it still happens and is justified in very familiar terms. This is what might now be considered the negative pole of *Lebensraum*. But, the idea that a 'nation' and its 'identity' are linked indissolubly to a place and land (which might be described as the more positive pole of *Lebensraum*) is still very much alive and well. Contemporary identity politics is in many ways our modern version of *Lebensraum*.

## DISCIPLINARY MOMENTS: UNIVERSITIES AND THE NATION STATE

As well as being an epoch of accelerated nation-state formation, the mid- to late nineteenth century was also a period of the development of a number of disciplines within universities—universities which had an expanded role within developing nation states. In the early nineteenth century, psychology, economics, anthropology, geography, sociology, and political science did not exist as independent academic disciplines. Despite their recognition, to some degree, as traditions of thought, they were not researched or taught independently as autonomous subjects. Significantly, it was not until the 1860s and 1870s that they began to take on institutional form.[61] All of these academic disciplines developed in the context of nation-state-sanctioned universities.

Many of these early disciplines, when set up, had a strong focus on the nation state. There were obvious reasons for this. There was a symbiosis between, on the one hand, the growth of states and nationalism in the nineteenth and early twentieth centuries, and, on the other hand, the concentration on the concept of the nation state within many academic studies. The fact, for example, that the discipline of politics grew within the universities of most modern European states during the very late nineteenth and early twentieth centuries and that the primary focus of the discipline was the nation state, is not at all fortuitous.[62]

The 'state focus' was also closely tied to educational imperatives. To concentrate on the nation state was not only to learn about the history of institutions, but was more importantly to be inculcated with national sentiment. This inculcation was embodied in the idea of civic education, and the various elaborate celebrations and ceremonies of citizenship—a perennial theme in many states throughout the twentieth century to the present day. Citizenship education was a way of encouraging civic awareness, civic virtue, and civic identity. Further, with the considerable growth of the public state sector in the late nineteenth and early twentieth century, there was a strong perception of the need for trained personnel to fulfil the growing requirements of the specialized public services within nation states. The same logic applied to academic history. It grew, as a self-conscious discipline, during the nineteenth century.[63] What united the discipline of history, from the 1860s, and in fact well into the 1940s, was the view that it was focused on *national* education and the grooming of national character. A similar process took place in all North American, European, and colonial universities.[64] History was made by national historians for national ends.[65] Events and texts were 'frozen with meanings for national ends' (Soffer 1994, 33–6).

Further, much of the literary output in the same period is unsurprisingly deeply interwoven with the idea of the nation. The idea of the nation was and is an extraordinarily malleable tool for historians, poets, journalists, lexicographers, etymologists, and novelists. In interpreting the nation to itself, academics and writers perform a nationalizing function. One result is national poetry, national art, national literature, national film, national histories, national language dictionaries, dictionaries of national biography, national museums, national monuments, and so on, in an endless liturgy to the nation. Yet, writings on, or portrayals of, the nation—no matter how scholarly— cannot be treated as if they were abstracted neutral commentaries on some external social object. These commentators are the imaginative architects and ideological propagators of the nation. They invent, sustain, and massage it. The development of academic disciplines was quite directly related to self-conscious policies of nation states in the nineteenth and twentieth centuries. There is therefore a close relation between, on the one hand, the rise of universities—and the development of historical, literary, legal, geographic, and political curricula—and, on the other hand, the rise and consolidation of nation states during the late nineteenth and early twentieth centuries. In this sense, neither geography nor ecology is alone in giving profound intellectual succour to the nation state.

## THE LEGACY OF THE ORGANIC NATION STATE

What were the immediate effects of these discourses in the early twentieth century? One obvious effect was that organic nation-state discourse provided a much more powerful rendering of state sovereignty than that provided by, say, the rather obtuse and abstract doctrines of legal positivism. Legal positivism could therefore find a supportive intellectual ally in organic state theory. There were forceful evolutionary reasons as to why nation states expanded, grew in legal competence, and indeed dominated over certain lands and colonies. It also showed why the integrity of a particular land was so significant. This argument was legal positivism with naturalistic or biological *esprit*. Second, the sovereign nation state, of course, became the crucial actor in twentieth-century politics—something that the *League of Nations* and the *United Nations* both bore witness to in their very titles, and yet also tried desperately to control through their structures. This nation-state dominance was particularly important in the realm of law and rights cultures. Further, international politics was largely about the interaction of nation-state actors—an assumption which from the late 1920s was and remains the key premise of the novel twentieth-century discipline of international relations.

Third, international law, up to the 1940s, was focused largely on the relation between state actors. International law had tended, up to the early nineteenth century, to be linked with the older normative 'law of nations' (vis-à-vis *jus gentium*) discourse. By the end of the nineteenth century, as one would expect from the above argument, it became closely linked to the public or constitutional law of nation states. In fact, most European legal theories during this period became completely focused on 'the power of the state'— especially in relation to colonialism. In one sense 'the whole of Europe was caught up in the wave of expansionism' (see Hueck 2001, 204; Koskenniemi 2001). In other words, international law became positive state law.[66] Fourth, because of the direct link with the organic nation-state argument, the vocabularies concerning identity and land acquired immense moral, political, and legal gravitas. Although the evolutionary and organicist terminology gradually dropped into the background after the 1940s—apart from socio-biological theories—nonetheless it did not disappear. Conversely, it morphed subtly into other terminology, such as the 'self-determination' of states.

Thus, the most popular terminology for discussing the nation-state discussion in twentieth-century politics and law was (and remains) self-determination. It also appears in the context of secession *from* nation states. Self-determination is though a comparatively recent neologism, although its origins for some lie in certain Enlightenment conceptions of individual autonomy, implicit in thinkers such as Kant. Most scholars agree that it first appeared—in legal and political argument—in the 1920s, after the Versailles

Treaty. President Wilson is often mentioned in relation to its first usage, although this remains uncertain. Others see V. I. Lenin as the first to coin the term in 1917. Minimally, self-determination, since the 1920s, has become a conventional claim by nation states, so much so that it has now ironically become a codified human right.[67] We are overly familiar with the analytical implications of this argument, namely, that each homogeneous (*natural*) people has an exclusive right to autonomy; that if such a people controls a state and land of its own, it has a collective absolute right to both exclude and subordinate members; that the state has a right to make its own policy without external interference; that if there is no state then that people has the right to struggle for one (and the land that is implicated with the state); and that other peoples have a duty to leave them alone or assist them in their struggle. Those who have the right to self-determination are those who are capable of building and maintaining an independent sovereign nation state.

My surmise would be that it should not surprise us that self-determination arose in the 1920s. It was already imminent in the language of the 'organic nation state'. Self-determination was regarded as valuable because it corresponded directly with the idea of nations as active collective unitary organic entities. Self-determination therefore followed straightforwardly from the identity argument concerning the nation state. If a people (group, community, culture) shared substantive beliefs, language, ethnicity, or a common history, then the nation could then be said to act and determine itself. How exactly one establishes the reality of this 'sharing' remains an open issue—plebiscites and referenda are historically notorious for being easily manipulated. The basic logic of the self-determination argument would be this: to have an embodied *self* (legal, moral, or natural) which can be *self-determining*, there needs to be a *self* or *identity* in the first place. Therefore, the nation state needs to be regarded as a unitary self, rooted in a particular land. Self-determination has of course always been a two-edged sword. In Versailles, it was used by the Allies to break up the Hapsburg Empire and thus to contain Germany. But in 1935, a plebiscite in the Saar region saw a move back to Germany. This was followed by the *Anschluss* in Austria. The same self-determination logic was then used on the German sections of Czechoslovakia by the Nazi regime. What had been introduced at Versailles was now beginning to reveal rather alien fruits. Self-determination is not an anodyne, new, or positive democratic device, conversely (minus any overt evolutionary trappings), it is rather the modern, somewhat thinner, reincarnation of the organic state argument.

Another argument—which adds brio to the self-determination argument—is that of personality theory, vis-à-vis the state. If a nation state has an identity which can self-determine, then one needs a vocabulary to speak of 'state persons' (or group selves). This vocabulary exists, although it is not to everyone's taste. It does not even necessarily require one to speak of a state as an organic entity.[68] In the mid- to late nineteenth-century state personality theory was a commonplace in many European legal and political theories—although its origins can be found in Roman, late medieval, and early modern jurisprudence. The personality of states (or corporations) became a fairly standard jurisprudential device (see Vincent 1989). As one late nineteenth-century *Staatslehre* text put (a text which was used in Oxford University legal and historical curricula during the 1890s and 1900s):

> A person in the juridical sense is a being to whom we can ascribe a legal will, who can acquire, claim and possess rights. In the realm of public law this conception is as significant as in the realm of private law. A State is *par excellence* a person in the sense of public law. The purpose of the whole constitution is to enable the person of the state to express and realise its will, which is different to the individual wills of all individuals, and different from the sum of them. (Bluntschli 1895, 27–8)

In European political theory, personality theory did roughly the same work as self-determination.

Although dropping out of usage in the 1930s in political theory and political science, the use of the term personality—to account for the nation state—has now been partly resurrected by certain writers in the discipline of international relations and international law.[69] In this context, the state has been described as an *actual* person with a will and full-blown intentionality. States apparently can get angry, jealous, or sad, can strike out at neighbours, and make peace or war. They have all the attributes (rationality, interests, beliefs, etc.) you would normally consider as relevant to organic human persons.[70] Thus, the American international relations theorist Alexander Wendt suggests that we should now reconsider the state as a non-metaphorical, real 'super-organism', which has a bonafide physical and intellectual existence in the realm of international politics (see Wendt 2004; see also Wight 2004). However, this is a thesis which is unlikely to attract much support.

## Preamble to human rights: reading a rights culture

The arguments given above are illustrative of a powerful intellectual legacy concerning the centrality of the sovereign nation state in twentieth-century political and legal vernaculars. How does this link with the failure of natural rights language? My answer to this core question has focused on deep-seated changes in our understanding of nature, combined with the profound historical significance of the rise of the state, nationalism, and race theory in the late nineteenth century. Consequently, by the early twentieth century, it was difficult to make any kind of secure case for rights as being rooted in human nature, unless it was an evolutionary grasp of nature. Basically, the marriage of the discourse of nature with that of the nation state gave rise to a new and powerful vocabulary for speaking of law, rights, and indeed morality. The *natural* importance of land and identity flowed from this same premise. The main spin-off from this in the twentieth century—certainly up to the 1940s—was the crucial dominant figure of the nation state.

Another dimension of the problem faced by human rights arguments in the late twentieth century can be observed in debates concerning self-determination. The irony here is that self-determination—because of its intricate connections with the identity of individual persons—has literally become a human right. The figure of the human self predominates, even for collective entities such as nation states. Yet, self-determination has no simple or exclusive connection with individual human agency; in fact, self-determination can actually crush human agency, via the self-determination of state or group. In a nutshell, the promotion of ethnic or national self-determination, as a human right, is actually promoting something which can potentially undermine human rights. The reason for its presence in current discourse though relates, once again, to the central figure of the nation state. Another way of reformulating the dilemma here is that the human right to self-determination problematizes the whole understanding of what it is to be human. When national, cultural, racial, or ethnic claims are stirred into this unholy concoction, it becomes even more difficult to know where the argument will go. Self-determination and nationalism are both unpredictable double-edged swords as far as human rights are concerned.

## Conclusion

My central question has been: why did the language of natural rights decline in the nineteenth century? My answer was that the language of natural right embodied a particular conception of what is 'natural', which implied some form of either maximal or minimal pre-social, universal, normative order, implicit in human nature, human reasoning, or at least, implied in the concept of human action, and frequently sanctioned by a rational deity (somewhere along the line). Rights were authoritative insofar as they were premised on this pre-social or innate rule-governed sense of nature. This argument came under extreme pressure in the mid-nineteenth century. In fact, it would not be too picturesque to say that it was squeezed by two initially independent forces. First, the concept of nature changed markedly in evolutionary theory, away from any notion of either a God-designed order, or even an inert mechanistic structure to be measured or quantified. Nature became a *process* of adaptation and change through competition, struggle, and natural selection.

Humans were integral to this process. Humans were in fact merely protrusions from a natural environment. Every human action related to survival, selection, and reproductive success, including social existence. Given that humans naturally subsisted in groups and such groups needed land resources to survive, it followed that the issue of land was seen through evolutionary eyes. This legacy reinforced the connection of land with the organic nation state.

The second pressure on natural rights came from the accelerated growth and profound historical, political, and legal significance of nation states. The growing power of states was given added zest by the linkage of the state with the vocabulary of nationalism and identity. This focus on the nation state was again furnished with additional intellectual support via the consolidating academic disciplines within European and North American universities. Nationalism was an academic brief for most of these new disciplines. There was therefore a peculiar self-fulfilling prophecy in academic writing, since those who serviced the national agenda were the very academic disciplines which were largely dependent upon its existence. The *pièce de résistance* of this whole process was the marriage between the first and second pressures in the 'organic state tradition', which received a fulsome and rapturous academic imprimatur in disciplines such as geography and ecology (amongst others), often figuring importantly in anthropology, sociology, history, law, and politics. Geography though, as the *Ur*-science, illustrated the natural necessity of the state for the whole conception of politics. It helped connect identity, nationality, land, and statehood (ultimately also self-determination) in an immensely robust matrix of concepts. This was—and partly still is—the conceptual matrix faced by human rights in 1945.

In conclusion another crucial question arises from this whole argument, which will be addressed in chapter 4. In some ways, this chapter has been a convoluted way of broaching this question. There seemed little or no prospect of any revival of the redundant antiquated discourse of natural rights. The arguments rejecting it had been authoritative and influential. The question then arises: why did the idea of human rights arise so forcefully in the post-1945 era, and further, why has it grown so pervasively to the present day?

## ☐ NOTES

1. As Glacken commented, 'The thinkers of antiquity developed conceptions of the earth as a fit environment for human life and human cultures whose force was still felt in the nineteenth century. The conception of a designed earth was strongest among the Academic and the Stoic philosophers, but even among the Epicureans there could exist a harmony between man and nature, orderly even if not the product of design.' Glacken continued that geographically this was also an important idea: 'if there were harmonious relationships in

nature...of which man was a part, the spatial distribution of plants, animals, and man conformed to and gave evidence of this plan; there was a place for everything and everything was in its place' (Glacken 1967, 147).

2. For Ernest Mayr all the major philosophies of the eighteenth century saw species of organisms with essentialist eyes. Each species, in other words, had a specific unchanging essence. For essentialists there could therefore be no evolution, only sudden specific creation (Mayr 1991, 41).

3. For one noted scholar on evolution theory the design argument 'continued to be strong in England, and all of Darwin's teachers and peers,...were confirmed natural theologians' (Mayr 1991, 55).

4. Bishop Ussher's judgement was added as an explanatory note to the Authorized King James Version of the English Bible and remained a popular accepted account until the mid-nineteenth century.

5. As Glacken commented, 'The thinkers of antiquity developed conceptions of the earth as a fit environment for human life and human cultures whose force was still felt in the nineteenth century' (Glacken 1967, 147).

6. Glacken saw this teleological conception as immensely significant (Glacken 1967, 147).

7. Darwin was, for a time, impressed with his idea whilst a student.

8. However, designing a telescope can be done and observed, but not so the eye. Paley, however, was required reading for university students in the early 1800s.

9. There were also difficulties with many of the arguments on other levels, particularly in relation to fossils in rocks (and particularly fossils of sea shells, such as ammonites, found on mountains). Eighteenth-century geology was certainly increasingly aware of the immense age of the earth comparative to the ideas of creationists. They also discovered evidence of abundant extinctions. The French scholar Cuvier specifically worked out certain extinctions and their age. However, such geological ideas did not have a widespread effect until the nineteenth century.

10. In addition even though design was rejected in many thinkers, biology remained teleological. Kant's views on biology, for example, remained teleological (see Lenoir 1980).

11. James Rachels argues that the core of a traditional understanding of morality was based on humans as unique in creation and consequently possessing a fundamental spiritual dignity. Morality was thus 'conceived to be, primarily, the protection of human beings and their rights'. For Rachels, by the mid-nineteenth century, 'The idea of human dignity turns out, therefore, to be the moral effluvium of a discredited metaphysics' (Rachels 1991, 4–5).

12. Thus, as has been remarked, 'Only in the dialogues of Plato and the contemporary teachers of Platonists, and of the adherents of a revived Pythagoreanism much influenced by Plato and hardly distinguishable from Platonism, could Christians find a doctrine of the survival of man's self, of his intellectual and moral personality' (Armstrong and Markus 1964, 44).

13. Needless to say this idea does not appear in all religions and cultures. Buddhism and Hinduism, in fact, tend to see the person as a spiritual hindrance.

14. The Kantian self becomes the necessary transcendental presupposition for any unified understanding or reasoning about the world. In this sense, the self 'proper', in Kant's

thought, remains an 'unknown', that is, the transcendental presupposition to experience—including moral experience. In his *Introduction to the Metaphysics of Morals*, Kant remarked that 'A *person* is the subject whose actions are susceptible to imputation. Accordingly, moral personality is nothing but the freedom of a rational being under moral laws.' For Kant, the person is understood as a self-determining ethical being with a capacity for responsible conduct. The possession of personhood is also seen as the ground for universal moral respect (Kant 1965, 24).

15. 'Up to the seventeenth century and even up to the end of the eighteenth century, the mentality of our ancestors is obsessed with the question of knowing whether the individual soul is a substance, or supported by a substance' (Mauss 1985, 20).

16. To a large extent, many of the central moral beliefs of Western civilization over the last 300 years have tended to revolve around this sense of the moral person. For writers from Locke and Kant up to Rawls, this has been a primary locus of moral attention.

17. Genealogy, in Foucault, for example, can be considered as a form of analysis utilizing strong accounts of historical mutation and sociological reduction without any teleology.

18. This argument can be given a more sophisticated reading. Thus, one could argue that there are universal 'minimal' elements necessary for any legal system in the world which need to be fulfilled. All humans are profoundly vulnerable, all are approximately equal, all have limited altruism, and so forth. Any system of law or rights needs to take cognizance of this. So one could argue that human rights provide the minimal good sense for any legal order and act as a measure or standard, although crucially they still have to be enacted by a legal sovereign to become meaningful.

19. For example, Jean-Baptiste Lamarck had argued in his *Philosophie Zoologique* (1809) that natural species developed and transmuted and that human beings had descended in some manner from ape primates. Darwin added a historical sketch of his precursors to the third edition of *On the Origin of Species* (1862). He expanded upon the sketch in subsequent editions. As Lovejoy notes, 'It is less commonly remembered, but perhaps not universally forgotten that among English-speaking naturalists the theory [of evolution] was a commonplace topic of discussion for two or three decades before 1859, and especially after the publication and immense circulation of the successive editions of Robert Chambers *Vestiges*, of which the first appeared in 1844' (Lovejoy 1968, 357). However Lovejoy adds that it also would be true that before 1859 hardly any naturalists espoused descent theory, after 1859 they all did.

20. 'The worldview formed by any thinking person in the Western world after 1859, when *On the Origin of Species* was published, was by necessity quite different from a worldview formed prior to 1859' (Mayr 1991, 1).

21. In its first year the book sold 3,800 copies and in Darwin's lifetime, overall, 27,000 copies.

22. The success of Darwin's theory was, of course, possible because of the great strides made in geology and palaeontology in establishing that the Christian view that the earth was created a little over 4,000 years ago was a gross underestimation.

23. Some of this interest in evolution found an immediate congenial home in the idea of historical change, which was developed in writers such as Herder, Hegel, and Turgot. Historical change could easily be transposed into natural change.

24. Darwin himself, at the time of his voyage on the *Beagle*, was obviously not fully aware of what he was about to unleash. His favourite reading on the voyage was Milton's *Paradise Lost*, which exemplified all that he was about to overthrow.

25. He introduced the idea that 'humans were not the special products of creation but evolved according to principles that operate everywhere else in the living world' (Rachels 1991, 1).

26. This did not mean that design and teleology were abandoned; both arguments carried on into the twentieth-century discussion. Even many evolutionary theories from Bergson to Teilhard de Chardin have had strong teleological components. As Clarence Glacken remarked, 'teleology will be with us for a long time because it is an expression in ever-recurring form of the quest for meaning in man, in nature, and in the relationship between the two' (Glacken 1967, 550).

27. In fact he was also the popularizer of other neologisms, such as 'phylum', 'phylogeny', and 'ontogeny', which have now become more standardized biological terms.

28. Although his own interest in evolution (within the area of natural selection) was more Lamarckian rather than Darwinian.

29. This matched perfectly many of the debates of the time concerning Germany's imperial state ambitions.

30. In Britain, some of the key figures were Herbert Spencer and Benjamin Kidd.

31. Sciences could uncover underlying patterns and structures which, whether consciously or not, took on a sanctified aura. Like Herbert Spencer (whom he deeply admired), Haeckel posited an evolving force within nature, governed by a basic law which he called the 'law of substance' (Haeckel 1929, 224, 310).

32. Haeckel's views have strong parallels with Spinoza's monistic philosophy. It is therefore not completely fortuitous that late twentieth-century ecophilosophers, such as Arne Naess and Warwick Fox, were clearly fascinated with Spinoza's philosophy.

33. From its inception in the 1870s, the evolutionary aspects of ecology were often meshed into a subtle pantheistic doctrine. Nature itself was seen to have spiritual standing and was tied integrally to our destiny as animals. Nature also embodied a dynamic teleology which we ignored at our cost. Those now studying ecology, who try to maintain the purity of the scientific motif, unsullied by religious input, need to stop for a few moments to study the history of their own discipline.

34. For example, all the major European geographical societies were set up in the early 1800s and most university teaching posts developed during this same period. For example, in France the first geographical society was founded in 1821, the Berlin Geographical Society in 1828, and the Royal Geographical Society in Britain in 1831 (although it was not till 1887 that the first university teaching post came up in Oxford). The American Geographical and Statistical Society was founded in 1851. In developing geography as a systematic discipline, Germany was in many ways in advance of most other countries at the time. The first university department in geography was set up in 1874 in Germany, followed later by France, Britain, and the United States.

35. Ritter, for example, was seen by many in Germany as too caught up in a 'serene, pious teleology' [which was] 'no longer in keeping with the times' (Wanklyn 1961, 17). It should be noted though that Darwin remained a deep admirer of Humboldt.

36. The book was entitled *Sein und Werden der Organishcen Welt* (1869), although it was not on geography, but rather on Darwinian-based zoology.

37. 'Ratzel had indeed taken his views on evolution largely from Haeckel's earlier writing and made no secret at the time of his unqualified admiration for the work of the Jena zoology professor' (Wanklyn 1961, 7).

38. The introduction to the English edition of Ratzel's *History of Mankind* (1896) was by the famous English anthropologist E. B. Tyler.

39. For Ratzel, Humboldt was too concerned 'with the interdependence rather than the origins and spread of things and ideas over the earth' (Dickinson 1969, 66).

40. 'Most systems of sociology treat man as if he were in some way detached from the earth's surface; they ignore the land basis of society' (Semple 1911, 53).

41. This conception of the relation of humans to land is very broadly conceived. Some brief quirky examples will have to suffice here to illustrate the general argument. First, the shape of the human body is created by land. As Semple comments 'on the mountains [a land] has given him leg muscles of iron to climb the slope; along the coast she has left these weak and flabby, but given him instead vigorous development of chest and arm to handle his paddle'. Second, land bears directly upon the way humans conceive of religion. Semple notes that 'Up on the wind-swept plateaus... where the watching of grazing herds gives him leisure for contemplation,... his ideas take on a certain gigantic simplicity; religion becomes monotheism, God becomes one' (all quotations from Semple 1911, 1–2). Third, all human art and literature develop in certain kinds of land. Towering mountains apparently paralyse literary and artistic expression. Higher altitude, it seems, discourages 'the budding of genius because they are areas of isolation, confinement, remote from the great currents of men and ideas that move along the river valleys'. Mountains also require considerable labour and lead to 'toil-dulled brains'. However, 'by contrast, the lower mountains and hill country of Swabia, Franconia, and Thuringia, where nature is gentler, stimulating, appealing, and not overpowering, have produced many poets and artists. The facts are incontestable. They reappear in France in the geographical distribution of the awards made by the Paris *Salon* of 1896. Judged by these awards, the rough highlands of Savoy, Alpine Provinces, the massive eastern Pyrenees, and the Auvergne Plateau, together with the barren peninsula of Brittany, are singularly lacking in artistic instinct, while art flourishes in all the river lowlands of France. Moreover, French men of letters, by the distribution of their birthplaces, are essentially products of fluvial valleys and plains, rarely of upland and mountain' (Semple 1911, 19–20). Fourth, climate—in direct relation to land—explains the location of key cities, states, and urban or cultural centres. For Ratzel, the majority of civilized cities and states exist in temperate climatic zones.

42. This echoes the broader debate taking place in German thought from the 1870s between *Geisteswissneschaft* and *Naturwissenschaft*.

43. For Sauer, 'The cultural landscape is fashioned out of a natural landscape by a cultural group. Culture is the agent, the natural area is the medium, the cultural landscape is the result' (Sauer 1929, 46).

44. For the substance of this additional note I am grateful to the geographer Ken Taylor (University of Canberra); he drew my attention to this broader debate in geography in discussion and also gave me a copy of his interesting paper, see Taylor (1998). His paper provides an excellent summary of these subsequent developments in geography.

45. The three central issues of geography are therefore the distribution of human societies, the relation between these distributions, and the physical environment and the effects produced by this physical environment of societies.

46. 'A simple political body, if left to itself, renews and multiplies this body continually.... The family is renewed in this offspring and creates new families, From the family tribe or the race another family tribe branches off and so on. All these corporations become states through connection with the soil' (Ratzel 1996, 533). 'Just as the embryo state found in the primitive Saxon tribe has passed through many phases in attaining the political character of the present British Empire, so every stage in this maturing growth has been accompanied or even preceded by a steady evolution of the geographic relations of the English people' (Semple 1911, 12).

47. One other small point here is that it would be unfair to say that this geographical organic politics is simply the preserve of German thinkers such as Ratzel. I have no space to discuss him, but the key founder of British geography—Halford Mackinder—is of course well known for his own distinctive ideas on political geography and the fundamental role of the organic nation state. His most famous, if not notorious contribution, was his distinctive reading of geopolitics—focused on the potential strategic effects of any nation state dominating the Eurasian land mass. This was an idea which remained popular with military strategists and politicians well into the twentieth century (see Gray 1996). Ratzel's obsession with the centrality of geography, the deep integral relation of humans with land, the crucial role of the nation state in relation to land, and so forth, all figure in Mackinder's approach. For Mackinder's contribution to geography see Blouet (1987).

48. 'In democratic or representative forms of government permitting free expression of popular opinion, history shows that division into political parties tends to follow geographical lines of cleavage' (Semple 1911, 23).

49. As Semple comments, 'Every country forms an independent whole, and as such finds its national history influenced by its local climate, soil, relief, its location whether inland or maritime, its river highways, and its boundaries of mountains, sea or desert' (Semple 1911, 12).

50. As Ratzel comments, 'As the appreciation of the political value of land becomes greater, territory becomes to a greater degree the measure of political strength and the prize towards which the efforts of a state are directed' (Ratzel 1996, 534).

51. For Semple, nature 'abhors fixed boundary lines'; thus, 'everywhere she keeps her borders melting, wavering, advancing, retreating' (Semple 1911, 204).

52. When a state has taken full advantage of its natural conditions 'the land becomes a constituent part of the state, modifying the people which inhabit it, modified by them in turn, till the connection between the two becomes so strung by reciprocal interaction that the people cannot be understood apart from the land. Any attempt to divide them theoretically reduces the social or political body to a cadaver' (Semple 1911, 60).

53. Although critical of Ratzel and Semple, the American geographer Carl Sauer summarizes the point about land in a very Ratzelian manner. He noted that, 'We cannot form an idea of landscape except in terms of its time relations as well as its space relations. It is in a continuous process of development or of dissolution and replacement' (Sauer 1962, 333).

54. A variant of this argument has become a central aspect of cultural geography to the present day. Thus 'landscape implies above all a collective shaping of the earth over time.

Landscapes are not individual property; they reflect a society's—a culture's—beliefs, practices and technologies. Landscapes reflect the coming together of all these elements just as cultures do, since cultures are not individual property and can only exist socially' (Craig 1998, 15).

55. The *Concise German Dictionary* records the synonyms of *Volk* as people, nation, or race (*Rasse*) (see Sawyers 1982, 569).

56. In Britain, a number of writers such as Francis Galton, Karl Pearson, and F. R. Weldon— outside of geography—nonetheless had the same race interests premised on evolutionary biology.

57. This was an era of nation-state formation. The list is fairly extensive: 1878 Romania, Serbia, and Montenegro; 1905 Norway; 1908 Bulgaria; 1913 Albania; 1917 Finland; 1918 Poland, Czechoslovakia, Estonia, Latvia, and Lithuania; 1922 Ireland, and 1944 Iceland. This process continued post-1945 with post-colonial state-nationalisms in Africa and Asia, as well as the break-up of the Soviet Union and Yugoslavia in the 1990s.

58. He was wounded at Neudorf and Auxonne. He later wrote an essay on these war years entitled *Gewittersschwüle* (Thunder Heat). Ratzel dwelt upon the experience of the war for the rest of his life and was proud of his Iron Cross and Karl Friedrich military medal. Anti-war sentiment or pacifism expressed by students or colleagues always infuriated him.

59. In fact, national and racial identity went on making people emotional throughout the twentieth century.

60. The term *Lebensraum* though is said to have been first coined by Wolfgang Goethe.

61. In the United States, for example, economics was the first to form a professional organiza- tion, in 1885, followed by psychology in 1892, political science in 1903, and sociology 1905. In Germany particularly, the state idea had already taken a firm shape in academic terms during the early nineteenth century, although this became more feverish by the 1870s. It was to these traditions, particularly the German, that early American scholars of politics, law, philosophy, literature, and history commonly turned to for intellectual sustenance.

62. Some scholars have also argued that political studies, as they developed in the late nine- teenth and twentieth centuries, were remarkable for being so closely linked to the char- acter of their own nation-state traditions (see Castiglione and Hampsher-Monk 2001).

63. It first became an honours degree in Britain in Oxford in 1872 and Cambridge in 1873. The first chair of history—although set up in 1724, was first filled by a committed historian in 1866. The Chichele Chair of Modern History in Oxford was created in 1862.

64. 'The satisfaction of national pride and culture, and the rendezvous with destiny that it often implied, whether in England, Germany, or America, reflected the distinctive meaning of government education, and history in each country' (Soffer 1994, 6).

65. As Soffer comments on the development of the discipline in Britain: 'The acceptance or rejection of new disciplines was part of a larger debate about the relative merits of con- tinuity and change within an expanding society.... Among these contending fields, history provided the most consistent moral panorama able to satisfy a variety of intellectual, emo- tional, and aesthetic needs' (see Soffer 1994, 3).

66. In Germany 'With the foundation of the German Reich in 1870–1, a change of perspective in several respects can be detected. There was a certain move away from the international

perspective and from the citing of political motivations and ethical problems. At any rate the emphasis on the individual state was increased and the focus switched to a concept of sovereignty based on the idea of the nation-state' (Hueck 2001, 204).

67. Thus, the ICESCR (1966)—in identical wording to the ICCPR (1966)—states in Article 1 that 'All peoples have the right of self-determination. By virtue of that right they freely determine their political status and freely pursue their economic, social and cultural development'. Article 3 continues that 'The States parties to the present Covenant, including those having responsibility for the administration of Non-Self-Governing and Trust Territories, shall promote the realization of the right of self-determination, and shall respect that right, in conformity with the provisions of the Charter of the United Nations.'

68. Many legal personality theories, such as those of Johann Bluntschli, are quite explicit about keeping organicism distinct from personality. Although much depends here on precisely what one means by the term organic.

69. It has remained a standard conceptual tool of international law.

70. 'In both academic and lay discourse we often refer casually to states "as if" they have emotions and are therefore conscious. States are routinely characterized as angry, greedy, guilty, humiliated, and so on—all conditions that, in individuals at least, are associated with subjective experience' (Wendt 2004, 313).

# 4  From Genocide to Human Rights

Chapter 3 focused on one key question: why did the language of natural rights decline in the nineteenth century? My argument was that an older more static understanding of nature was steadily compressed by two fresh vocabularies during the nineteenth century, focused on the concepts of 'nature' and the 'nation state'. The more significant of these was a new vocabulary of nature which was embodied in evolutionary theory. Nature was viewed as a process of often random variation and alteration through competition and natural selection. Humans were integral to this haphazard process. Human group activity was also explicable through the same vocabulary. Further, given that humans *naturally* subsisted in social groups, and such groups needed land resources to survive, it followed that the issue of land was seen necessarily through evolutionary eyes. This connection between land, nature, and politics was given a more concrete and influential intellectual format in certain burgeoning disciplines in European and North American universities such as ecology and geography. One central motif in these disciplines, particularly geography, was the nation state. The nation state was viewed as a natural phenomenon—*natural* being understood in largely evolutionary terms. Since the dominance of land resources was essential to the natural survival of the state, this, in turn, reinforced and gave an evolutionary gloss to the connection of land and territory with the organic nation state. The vocabulary and practices of the nation state accelerated massively during the nineteenth century. In fact, it became the leitmotif of many growing disciplines in universities. This vocabulary was enhanced specifically by the conceptual association of the state with the nation, and the further linkage with the evolutionary language of nature. The *pièce de résistance* therefore of this whole process was the marriage between the two vocabularies (that of nature and the nation state) in the 'organic state tradition'. My argument therefore concentrated on the strong intellectual associations between these two vocabularies—*nature* and the *nation state*—and the powerful effects of that conjunction. This was largely an intellectual and practical scenario which faced human rights discourse in the late 1940s.

The train of the arguments in this present chapter can be stated straightforwardly. The central doctrines utilizing the terminology of 'nature' in political argument in the early to mid-twentieth century were nationalism and race theory. In fact, the ideas of nation and race slipped together with remarkable ease up to the 1940s. The concept of race, prior to the 1940 period, did not have the serious problems that were subsequently attached to it post-1945. Further, this notion of the nation state (and for a time race vis-à-vis imperialism and colonialism), acquired fundamental importance in terms of the theories and practices of international law and politics. By the later nineteenth-century nature *qua* natural rights was seen as arcane and utterly naive. The most important figure for modern politics was the self-determining nation state.

The question arose at the end of chapter 3—given the irrelevance of natural rights in this period, why did human rights acquire such a strong presence in the post-1945 era? My thumbnail sketch of an answer to this question is that race was closely linked to the dominance of the nation state. One of the most advanced nation states from the nineteenth century—where the language of statism had developed in richness and substantive content—was Germany. Yet by the 1930s, the German conception of the nation state was, in effect, the most succinct exemplar of a racial state. This racial state (or nation state, the two terms were largely coterminous in National Socialist thinking) then initiated in the 1940s particularly, with full intent, the most bureaucratically organized state-orchestrated extermination in recorded history, largely on race grounds. There had been massacres, war crimes, and slaughters aplenty in recorded history. The appalling Turkish massacre of the Armenians in 1915 was in many ways a precursor to later events in the early 1940s, but there had been nothing comparative to the industrial and bureaucratic level and scale of killing in the German case. It was this case which gave rise to a wholly new word in 1940—*genocide* (see Weitz 2003*a*, 1–7).

Admittedly, even in 1945, it still took a great deal to shock extant nation states. The majority of nation states—even the apparently more liberal and constitutional ones—were all historically well blooded with petty wars and vicious colonial oppressions. However, genocide is something qualitatively different. My contention is that genocide is the key that opens the door to human rights. It is not though just genocide alone (in terms of a moral or spiritual horror); conversely, it is genocide as an *integral dimension* of the more advanced nation state—a nation state understood as purportedly the very epitome of human civilization. This genocidal activity of Nazi Germany was a jolt to even some of the more jaded palates of the governments and intelligentsia of many existing nation states post-1945, even those intellectually well attuned to eugenic ideas. Not that there was a general clamour for human rights. Many state executives at the time would clearly have been more than happy to have left all talk of human rights behind at the Nuremberg or Tokyo Tribunals and that includes many in Europe and North America. Yet genocide, vis-à-vis the nation state, gave rise to a demand, a demand which sought a voice. It found that voice in human rights. However, the various 'state parties' to human rights advocacy did not so much strive for human rights, as they were morally, politically, and legally 'softened up' by the knowledge of the scale and organization of the genocidal horror revealed within the German nation state. The argument that states needed in future to have some form of guaranteed control and limitation was hard to counter in 1945, although many nation states would still have liked to deny it and have gone on denying it until the present day, usually on the ground of their right to self-determination or sovereignty. In fact, paradoxically, many of the subsequent human rights conventions and covenants have continued to embody a profound internal tension over the role of nation states. It is this internal tension that is ultimately addressed in the ensuing arguments.

One real dilemma faces all those who promulgate and support the move to human rights from 1948 to the present day. The dilemma embodies *two* overlapping issues. First, the language of universal human rights is problematic. By the twentieth century, natural rights, as argued, were seen as largely bankrupt. Claims about a common human nature, universal values, and inalienable rights look deeply shaky in a world of very different nations, cultures, and races. A related point concerns the inexorable rise and power of the modern nation state. This had taken over the ground of law and right. We should also be alert to the fact that the nation state is still largely the key player in international politics. The second main problem that human rights faced in 1948 was therefore the nation state itself. It had been seen—in respect of genocide—where the logic of the modern nation state could potentially lead. This was the catalyst for the human rights movement. Yet, paradoxically, if human rights were to be successful then it still required states to bring them into practice and enforce them. This whole scenario was and remains the core paradoxical dilemma of human rights. This chapter first examines the issue of genocide in relation to the state and human rights and then turns to a brief outline history of human rights from 1948 to the present day.

## Genocide and the state

The neologism 'genocide' was first coined by the Polish jurist Raphaël Lemkin in 1940. It derived from the Greek word for people or tribe (*genos*) and the Latin suffix for murder or killing (*cide* from the Latin *caedare*) (see Lemkin 1944, 2002). Lemkin had searched desperately for a way of conceptualizing what was happening to the Jews (and others) in Germany. For a time he became a virtual one person crusade for the criminalization of this extermination practice. That aside, the word genocide was first employed officially in the post-war Nuremberg trials. It was used in the wording of the indictment, but it did not figure in the trials.[1] The Nazi war criminals were convicted on three counts of crimes against peace, war crimes, and crimes against humanity.[2] The Nuremberg Charter also cited some precedents for its actions; for example, in 1827, England, France, and Russia had intervened in the atrocities of the Greco-Turkish war. There had also been condemnation of the Turkish massacre of the Armenians in 1915, by states such as Britain and France, as 'crimes against humanity and civilization'. It was not though until after the cessation of hostilities in 1945 that the UN devoted significant attention to a UN Convention on Genocide. On 11 December 1946, the UN General Assembly passed a resolution calling for legislation to outlaw genocide, which it defined as the 'denial of the right of existence of entire human groups... when racial, religious, political, and other groups have been destroyed, entirely or in part'. It is worth noting that the full Genocide Convention was eventually signed on 9 December 1948, preceding the Universal Declaration of Human Rights (UDHR) signing by one day. In this sense, it is worth reading both documents in tandem.

Genocide, in its first usage, was very specific in terms of location and substance, namely, it focused on Germany in the 1940s. Further, we should not forget one very simple but nonetheless irresistible fact that is oddly easy to miss. Genocide was indissolubly *internally* linked to the concept and practice of the nation state. This may sound, on one level, strange, but my argument is that this is fundamental. The nation state was the vessel which carried the hopes and expectations of so many groups in the world from the late nineteenth century. It had been *naturalized* (in evolutionary terms) in the later nineteenth century and had subsequently absorbed all the language of law, history, politics, and even morality. For many it was also the fundamental unit of social evolutionary struggle; it was also self-determining (in fact, it had a *right* to be so). In sum, this deeply valued model of political organization had self-generated, from within its own institutional logic, the practice of genocide. Genocide, in its completeness, was quite simply impossible without the resources and policy commitments of the modern nation state.[3] The logic of genocide is thus part of the inherent logic of the nation state *given certain circumstances*. However, the German genocide (particularly the killing of the Jews) has with good reason remained the archetype. Many other mass killings have come very close; in fact, many see these as genocide, as in Stalin's Russia, Pol Pot's Cambodia, or even Milosovic's Serbia, but the German example stands out in terms of the specific nature of the race/nation ideology, the clear intent, and the sheer mechanistic scale and bureaucratization of the killing (see Smith 2003, 213).

This does not mean that all nation states are teetering on genocide. This would be a rash thesis. Rather the argument is that the concept of the nation state contains the consistent potential for genocide. The logic is simple but devastating: to affirm a unified nation, and particularly to dress it up as a racial issue, and then to link that unitary nation with the immense power and resources of the modern state, creates an immediate dilemma as to what to do with non-nationals, aliens, or foreigners. The non-nationals, as long as they pose no threat, might well be ignored. However, any more profound strain, fear, or insecurity that arises in the life of the nation state creates a problem; this is a problem which can be massively amplified through racial language. In fact in some cases, such as Germany, there does not have to be any overt anxiety or verifiable threat attached to the group who are subject to genocide. The ideology suffices. Thus, the nation state embodies a *potential* legitimation for focusing on non-nationals as a source of anxiety. Thus, as we can see from many examples in the twentieth century, 'the simplest solution to the perceived problems of ethnic groups in a State is to remove them' (Smith 2003, 213). That removal can of course take many forms. However, if that anxiety contains a biological or racial imprimatur, the legitimation for state action against the group looks that much stronger. How one configures both nation and race, and whether one has a strong sense of the superiority and inferiority of races, then become the key aspects of public policy making.

## Defining genocide

In Article 2 of the Genocide Convention, genocide is defined as 'acts committed with intent to destroy, in whole or in part, a national, ethnical, racial or religious groups as such'. It takes genocide therefore to cover: '(a) Killing members of the group; (b) Causing serious bodily or mental harm to members of a group; (c) Deliberately inflicting on the group conditions of life calculated to bring about its physical destruction in whole or in part; (d) Imposing measures intended to prevent births within the group; (e) Forcibly transferring children of the group to another group'. This definition was carried through directly to Article 6 of the 1998 Charter of the International Criminal Court (ICC). Article 7 of the ICC Charter also links genocide directly with crimes against humanity. This, in part, corresponds to Lemkin's own original aims and definition, namely, genocide was viewed, by him, as the 'destruction of a nation or of an ethnic group'; he continued that 'It is intended... to signify a co-ordinated plan of different actions aiming at the destruction of the essential foundations of the life of national groups, with the aim of the annihilating of these groups themselves. The objectives of such a plan would be disintegration of the political and social institutions, of culture, language, national feelings, religion, and the economic existence of national groups, and the destruction of the personal security, liberty, health, dignity, and even the lives of the individuals belonging to such groups. Geno-cide is directed against the national group as an entity, and the actions involved are directed against individuals, not in their individual capacity, but as members of the national group' (Lemkin 2002, 27). Despite these definitions, it would be true to say that nearly every scholar is uneasy with the above definitions of genocide.[4] There have been a number of seminal studies of genocide, since the late 1970s, but as yet little overall final agreement on exactly what it denotes (see e.g. Kuper 1981; Chalk and Jonassohn 1990; Kiernan 1996; Charney 1999; Fein 2002). A minority have been satisfied by the UN definition, most have not. Some have wanted to widen the definition. Some have tried to fit genocide onto a comparative and ascending scale, with other types of killing (see Uekert 1995; Hinton 2002, 79; Semelin 2003).[5] Others see genocide as a unique issue; without this uniqueness the relation between genocide and other types of killing can become blurred.

It is worth noting though that the preparatory debates over the Genocide Convention were far from smooth. The minutes of the initial Economic and Social Council of the UN make somewhat gloomy reading. Controversies raged over the wording; articles were reformulated many times. Most states— particularly the four major post-war powers—examined and constructed the Convention largely in terms of their own self-interest. Questions were raised as to what groups were covered. Racial, ethnic, and national criteria predominated. The Russian delegation, though, insisted that political groups could not be included, since any such inclusion would not correspond with the 'scientific definition of genocide', vis-à-vis to ethnicity or race. Other representatives argued that if political groups were excluded then governments, which were usually complicit in genocide, could always use political criteria as a concealment. Rwanda would be a more current example of such attempted duplicity. At the time of the Convention debates, the Russian delegation feared that their own policies could be scrutinized on such political grounds. Later this led to oddities, namely, in Cambodia where the mass political murder of Cambodians by the Khmer Rouge (as distinct from the racially motivated murder of Vietnamese or Muslim minorities) did not legally qualify as genocide under the Convention. Consequently, much of the Cambodian 'killing field' activity was not officially at the time regarded as genocide. Similarly, the state-based killing of around 500,000 in Indonesia in 1965 was not genocide, because the victims were said to be communists (thus political groups) and were legally excluded—even though the large majority of these just happened to be Chinese. During the Genocide Convention debates on this question, the French representative argued that although in the past race and religious issues had come to the fore, in the future, it was likely to be political grounds, which proved to be a prescient point. However, the upshot was that political groups were excluded from the convention.

There were also debates over the issue of cultural genocide, that is, the complete and intended destruction of a culture. Russia pressed for its insertion, whereas Britain, amongst others (with anxieties over their colonial record), vigorously opposed it. Cultural genocide was thus eventually excluded. There were also debates on the Convention as to whether any sense could be made of the idea of a collective intent to commit genocide. In other words *who* was to be made responsible for a collective intent? Further, intention is not quite straightforward in state terms; in many genocides, it is not altogether clear who has given orders or where the chain of command lies. The issue of enforcement and punishment also raised considerable disagreement. The United States particularly objected to this idea. In 1948, Article 6 of the Convention predictably left enforcement and prosecution up to the states themselves. All states were worried over the loss of their sovereignty and their capacity for self-determination. The US Congress, for example, took forty years to ratify the Genocide Convention. However, on the same day as the Genocide Convention was passed, the General Assembly did ask the International Law Commission to examine the idea of an international court to deal directly with genocide and similar crimes, although it took many years to bear fruit and the institution still raises considerable misgivings amongst nation states. In Rome, in July 1998, the UN finally established the International Criminal Court (ICC). However, again, at the time, the United States joined Iraq, China, Libya, Algeria, and Sudan in opposition to it. President Clinton eventually signed on the eve of his departure from presidential office; however, Senate confirmation still remains in doubt.[6] Many states have also clung tightly to their derogations and reservations from the Court.[7] The ICC now resides permanently in the Hague. In addition, the continuing inability of non-state parties to invoke the Convention has been considered by many to be a real weakness. Another area of disagreement and critical unease focused on the issue of at what point does mass murder, ethnic cleansing, or massacre become genocide. How much murder is genocide? Again this remains unresolved.[8]

Genocide is also sometimes seen to occur against the backdrop of warfare, threat of war, or some perceived social or political crisis. This would certainly cover the cases of Cambodia, Rwanda, and Yugoslavia. However, it does not quite fit the prime example of Nazi Germany where genocidal ideas and even practices were being developed in the early 1930s.[9] Genocide can thus be an issue of both war and peace. Some scholars have also seen issues such as a general breakdown of moral restraints, socio-economic upheaval, discriminatory political changes, and an apathetic international response as additional factors. These might be seen as 'genocide primers' which could, in some situations, generate the killing (see Kuper 2002, 14–15). Some scholars have also noted that there is often a ritualistic dimension to genocide, in terms of the process of purification of a land from alien elements. Further genocide appears to ritualize the total domination of its victims. Finally, although there is still a dispute on this point, the process of genocidal killing requires the mobilization, active participation, or willing compliance of the dominant national population. However, the questions still remain what gives substance to this ritual and what facilitates the mobilization of populations?

## Two central themes of genocide

All the above points have cogency; however, my argument develops *two* central themes of genocide. Although each genocide has its own unique tag (given that we accept that there are other examples of genocidal acts), there are nonetheless certain identifiable similarities, and in order to understand the movement and energy behind human rights, it is crucial to understand these two themes.[10] Genocide in the UN Convention is first and foremost correlated to race, nationality, and ethnicity. Although religion is significant in many of the prime examples of genocide, it is usually linked with racial or nationalist criteria. A victim population is thus most often particularized through national or racial criteria. This theme is embodied in the articles of the Genocide Convention. In this context, genocide—particularly in the archetypal German National Socialist case—is directly correlated to racial and/or nationalist beliefs. In fact, it often indicates the hegemony of this manner of thinking about human beings. Genocide is the means, but beliefs about race, nation, and ethnicity are the key underlying factors. This race/nation theme also underpins all the language focused on ritual, purification, and cleansing. It is worth recalling here that this understanding of race and nation in the 1930s and 1940s was still widely articulated in evolutionary terms.

Second, the idea of a 'collective intent' to destroy a whole racial or national group (as distinct from mass deportation, flouting the Hague Conventions or basic massacre), and the necessarily high level of resources required to achieve that end, implies one necessary institution—the state or more accurately the nation state. Genocide is identifiable, particularly in the German case, by the sheer bureaucratic industrial scale and impersonality of the killing. In other words, achievable genocide requires the state. Outside of this, it becomes massacre or some other form of atrocity. It follows that the more powerful and well organized the nation state, and the more unified that state feels nationally, the more substantially effective the genocide will be.[11] However, the crucial issue is still that genocide correlates directly with the state. In each case of genocide, it is a nation state which has a vision of a unified population which needs to be purified. This requires the state to address the problem of the alien and the different.

It is in these two interlinked themes of a biological-orientated understanding of race and nation and the institutional structure of the nation state which were initially generated by the case of Nazi Germany. The UN Genocide

Convention, for example, found its source material for the definition of genocide in the German case. In effect, as Leo Kuper notes, events in Germany were clearly 'the historical point of departure in the conception of genocide as a crime against racial and national groups.... Genocide was essentially bound up with fascist and Nazi ideologies, and other similar racial theories' (Kuper 2002, 57).[12]

These two themes will now be explored in a little more detail. First, in terms of the link between genocide and nationalism, race, and ethnicity: the period 1860 to the 1940s saw an intense focus on racial and nationalist argument.[13] It is still odd that UDHR (1948) and other human rights covenants, up to the 1960s and 1970s, contain a number of references to nationality (and to race), even to the right of nationality, but little or no attempt is made to clarify the concepts. It is strange given the problems that these terms have thrown up for human rights argument. Yet neither race, ethnicity, nor nation should be taken as self-evident. These concepts all have protracted and complex histories. All three concepts precede the nineteenth-century evolution debates (although historically by not a great deal of time); however, as argued in chapter 3, it was in the mid-nineteenth century that we can begin to see a strong focus on these terms under the rubric of 'nature' and 'science'. With hindsight, we might now view all these terms as having a socially constructed or artificial character; however, at the time, this was far from the case. That is to say the concepts of nation, ethnicity, and race were viewed as *biologically naturalized*.[14] As already argued, the crucial dividing line arose from Darwin's work and the transformation of our understanding of the concept of nature.[15]

Further, if one examines the voluminous literature on these concepts in the late nineteenth and early twentieth centuries, it becomes quickly clear that there were no sharp demarcations between them.[16] It was only after the post-1945 knowledge of the holocaust that scholars, en masse, became highly sensitized to this overlap. Race, nation, and ethnicity, although having different etymological trajectories, nonetheless blend and merge together in late nineteenth- and early twentieth-century debates. Thus, this slippage of meaning 'from the nation as a political community to the nation as a racial community became more prevalent when culture, not political rights, was made the defining element in the formation of the nation—an intellectual move accomplished largely by German theorists' (Weitz 2003a, 31).[17] For those who doubt the slippage of meaning between nation and race, they need look no further than the articles of the Genocide Convention (1948). Its framers were clearly of the opinion that these terms were largely coeval.[18]

This slippage was further assisted by the change in meaning of nature (as argued earlier). It was so much easier in this scenario to speak, with a scientific pastiche, of purifying or cleansing a race or nation. In fact, two additional areas began to merge with the discourse of race, nation, and ethnicity during this period—medicine and eugenics. Purity of race or nationality entailed careful bureaucratized attention to racial health, weeding out the unfit, protecting the healthy, and discouraging the breeding of the unhealthy, handicapped, or mentally feeble. This theme contained the core idea of the eugenics movement, which had an immensely popular following in Britain, Europe, North America, and elsewhere during this same period. Thus, when one of the key National Socialist designers of race purity legislation, a Dr Wilhelm Frick, was criticized in a 1930s international congress for German policies on sterilization, he replied coolly by pointing to the popular eugenics movement in England and North America and the decisive role of British figures such as Francis Galton or Karl Pearson (see Hannaford 1996, 365–7).[19] One should also note that fairly early on in the life of the National Socialist regime, in December 1935, medicine was officially declared a state function and the medical profession was placed fully at the disposal of race hygiene. This was part of the logic of the racial (or nation) state. In fact, eugenic ideas permeated virtually all the ideologies of the early twentieth-century period. Liberalism (particularly liberal imperialism), socialism, conservatism, and so forth were *all* taken up with ideas of race, health, and eugenics. In Britain, for example, there was a vigorous early twentieth-century campaign for 'national efficiency' which had wide cross-party political support and was basically tied into eugenic concerns.[20] The only concept which inhibited the development of this eugenic language in socialism and Marxism was class. Class rather than race, and internationalism rather than nationalism, tended to characterize much socialist thinking. This of course was not much of a restraint upon Joseph Stalin, although of course he could claim that his lethal actions were 'political' rather than 'racial'.[21]

The final point is large and controversial and can only be sketched in the barest outline. It is also a point made by a number of scholars. In effect, the concepts race, nation, and ethnicity are all phenomena of modernity.[22] There are, of course, many commentators who still try to make the case for the longevity of nations or ethnicity, now that race has dropped out of fashion. However, it still remains a suspect view.[23] Exactly the same form of argument as is now made for the longevity of nationality was made extensively for the prolonged existence of race. This argument figured strongly up to the 1930s. Race, like nationality, was therefore seen to have a remote antiquity, characterizing the real difference between peoples.[24] In the same way as the fascination with racial skull types was still preoccupying many anthropologists, amongst other disciplines, well into the 1930s (including many extant museum skull collections), many political theory commentators in 2010 are still obsessed with the antiquity of nationality and ethnicity. Many will no doubt reflect back in 2100 on our own generation of nationalists in the same manner as we now look back at those in 1900 with their race and skull obsessions. Our contemporary nationalist obsessions will no doubt in this future be regarded as weird, disturbing, and deservedly antediluvian. As for now, we simply have to live with these quirks of academic and practical fate.

In speaking of the modernity of race, nation, and ethnicity, the argument is keying into a thesis that has been expounded by other writers. Basically, if race, nationality, and ethnicity are creatures of modernity and they constitute the substance of genocide, then genocide itself is also a feature of modernity.[25] This is not to say that mass killing and atrocity are modern phenomena. These phenomena are part of recorded human history. However, genocide implies a qualitatively different form of action. It is the highly organized, state-based, mass killing of a whole people on the grounds of their ethnicity, race, or nationality. In this sense, genocide is neither a regress into an ancient barbarism nor a stunted or warped development of a state. It is conversely a potentiality within the modern nation state.[26] As Zygmunt Bauman comments, 'Modern civilization was not the Holocaust's sufficient condition; it was, however, most certainly its necessary condition. Without it, the Holocaust would be unthinkable. It was the rational world of modern civilization that made the Holocaust thinkable' (Bauman 2002, 111).

For Baumann particularly genocide is the result of the tragic coalescence of several aspects of modernity. His argument relates to the ideas of critical theory on both the Enlightenment and modernity. The Enlightenment is largely equated with modernity and the enthronement of a particular understanding of reason and natural science—which had immense benefits but also unexpected costs. One of the prevailing themes was the view that the compound of instrumental reason, positivism, and natural science-based explanatory theory had begun to dominate all areas of human knowledge. In effect, this conceptual compound, which had been used painstakingly for the examination of the inanimate world, had been turned (quite illegitimately for critical theorists) to the analysis of human action in the social, moral, political, and economic spheres. As the critical theorist Max Horkheimer commented, 'the manipulation of physical nature and of specific economic and social mechanisms demand alike the amassing of a body of knowledge such as is supplied in an ordered set of hypotheses. On the other hand, it made facts fruitful for the kind of scientific knowledge that would have practical application in the circumstances, and, on the other, it made possible the application of knowledge already possessed' (Horkheimer 1972, 194). The analysis of this compound—in critical theory—also owed a great deal to the work of Max Weber and his rich sociological account of the rationalization of society. For Weber, in modernity, both capitalism and bureaucracy embodied this one-sided instrumental positivist sense of rationality—a rationality which contained no normative ends. Rationalization, for Weber, was seen in terms of an 'iron cage', constricting substantive human reasoning. As Habermas noted, summarizing what he took to be the critical theory position: Enlightenment reason ultimately 'destroys the humanity it first made possible', consequently from its outset 'the process of enlightenment is the result of a drive to self-preservation that mutilates reason, because it lays claim to it only in the form of a purposive-rational mastery of nature' (Habermas 1998, 110–14).[27] Reason had thus become overly focused on an instrumental format, and this, in turn, was seen to suffer from a deep affliction. Such a concept of reason provided increased technical expertise and control; however, this control moved in tandem with 'deepening impotence against the concentrated power of the society'. The technological advances of bourgeois thought and practice were inseparably connected to this function, in the pursuit of science and instrumental reason. Consequently, 'a technical civilization has emerged from precisely that undaunted Reason which it now is liquidating' (Horkheimer 1996, 360). Humans had become shallower and societies more subtly and technically oppressive.

In sum, critical theorists rejected this domination by positivist-inspired 'instrumental reason'—a dominance which for them was imminent in the whole enterprise of the European Enlightenment. For Bauman this idea forms the background to genocide. Genocide is a modern phenomenon linked to instrumental reason, positivism, and technological sophistication. For Bauman, for example, the fact that the SS department dealing with the Jewish question was called the *Section on Administration and Economy*, 'faithfully reflected the organisational meaning of [its] activity'. It also fits the Weberian conception of rational bureaucracy and reminds us 'just how formal and ethically blind is the bureaucratic pursuit of efficiency' (Bauman 2002, 111–12). This argument is *not* suggesting that instrumental reason and bureaucracy *cause* genocide, rather that they are the necessary accompaniments to genocide. Further, instrumental reason and rational bureaucracy are incapable of preventing genocide. Racial cleansing is just another bureaucratic problem to resolve as efficiently as possible. Consequently, much of the killing that took place in Germany, Ukraine, Poland, and elsewhere had an impersonal, regimented, dull, and uniform aspect to it.[28] Those participating often had a small-minded bureaucratic mentality. Genocide thus became an aspect of state-based social engineering, in this case an engineering structured through nationality and race. Bauman links this idea to what he calls 'the gardening vision of the state', that is, a process of designing and weeding out. As he comments, 'The Holocaust is a by-product of the modern drive to a fully designed, fully controlled world' (Bauman 2002, 122). Genocide consequently is reliant upon a complex division of labour, well-developed efficient bureaucratic skills, and a certain dominant type of instrumental reasoning.

The discussion of the modernity of genocide, race, and nationality leads to the second major concept which is also the key linking component, that is, the state. In many ways, this second concept answers, in large part, the question put at the close of chapter 3, namely, why did the culture of human rights arise in the post-1945 era? My argument is that it is impossible to think about the idea of the state in the period 1860–1940 without conjuring in someway with the idea of the nation. In Britain, the compound term 'nation state' was given its most well-known nineteenth-century explicit rendering by J. S. Mill. In the early twentieth century it became more or less a commonplace in political speech across Europe and elsewhere. Ernest Barker, for example (a very benignly liberal-minded thinker), in a number of popular writings, such as *National Character* (1927), summarized the idea quite concisely: 'The history of the century since 1915...will teach us that in some form a nation must be a State, and a State a nation....A democratic State which is multi-national will fall asunder into as many democracies as there are nationalities' (Barker 1927, 17). Despite some critics, the compound term 'nation state' still endures in political speech to the present day. In fact, as Anthony Smith has remarked, 'The nation state [now] is the norm of modern political organization and it is as ubiquitous as it is recent. The nation state is the almost undisputed foundation of world order, the main object of individual loyalties' (Smith 1971, 2; Kohn 1945, 17).[29] It even appears as a norm amongst many modern political thinkers. Thus, as one recent theorist notes, 'like it or not, most states are nation states and...nationalism both as a generalized sentiment of attachment to one's national identity and as a form of organized political activity, is a salient feature of the contemporary world' (Archard 2000, 156).[30]

We thus have the regular use of the compound term nation state, predominating in the legal and political literature, as well as political practice. Further, the concept nation was, prior to 1940, used virtually synonymously with race. In addition, both terms had biological or quasi-biological sense to them. Both were seen to have longevity; however, race tended to dominate until 1940. Thus, 'race as an organizing idea claimed precedence over all previous formulations of nation and state' (Hannaford 1996, 326–7). Even in the post-1945, post-holocaust period, the odd synonymity of terms still prevailed. The doyen of early British political studies, Ernest Barker, could still remark in a new footnote to the post-1945 fourth edition of his book *National Character* (1947), that 'the facts of race remain what they were' (see Barker 1927, 12). This very odd lack of sensitivity, even post-1945, can be observed during the early UN debates on human rights in 1947.

A brief example will have to suffice: when the British Foreign Office was looking for delegates for the new human rights commission (to discuss and formulate the UDHR) a number of names came up, for example, J. B. Priestly and R. H. Tawney. Tawney was regarded as too old and Priestly too difficult. One important name which made considerable mileage was Hersch Lauterpacht, who had already written the well-received *An International Bill of Rights of Man*. Lauterpacht was a noted scholar of international law who had the support of the US delegation. However, the British Foreign Office declined his appointment. Its legal advisor, Eric Beckett, thought his appointment would be a disaster and penned the following advice to the Foreign Office: 'Professor Lauterpacht, although a distinguished and industrious international lawyer, is, when all is said and done, a Jew fairly recently come from Vienna. Emphatically, I think that the representative of HMG on human rights must be a very English Englishman imbued throughout his life and hereditary to the real meaning of human rights as we understand them in this country' (quoted in Sellars 2002, 12). Britain's very English Englishman turned out to be the unprepossessing, unwell, and unwilling Charles Dukes. Beckett's advice though, apart from contradicting the essence of what human rights were actually being designed for, nonetheless still unwittingly speaks volumes about the deeply rooted race assumptions of the time in government circles.

Understandably many scholars now find the race and nation literature of this period (1860–1940) intellectually bankrupt, but it is important to realize that at the time it engaged an enormous audience and was often taken for granted in academic and everyday discourse.[31] Given that both nation and race were in many ways conceptually synonymous and that the idea and practices of the state were also closely linked during this period with the nation and race, it follows that the 'race state' was as valid a description as the 'nation state'. There was little to choose between them in intellectual substance. It is important for my argument here to realize that this race state is not the state per se, but rather the practices of the state tradition infused with both nationalism and racism.[32] This is the real issue for twentieth-century (and indeed some twenty-first-century) politics. Further, most nation states up to the 1940s used the language of race, and often spoke with interest and concern about eugenic and similar race-based policies. Not all followed it through rigorously or with any great commitment, but it was still part of the political and moral vernacular. Further, what was regarded at the time as one of the most advanced nation states from the late nineteenth and early twentieth century—where the political and legal language of statism had developed—was Germany. By the 1930s, the German conception of the nation state was, in effect, the most comprehensive example of the racial state in theory and practice. The German nation state also became preoccupied with the ideology of racial purity.[33] It then initiated, with full intent, the first and most comprehensive example of genocide. Genocide was thus focused on race, but it was a focus which required the modern state to achieve its end. It is no wonder in this context that Helen Fein comments on the burgeoning scholarship on genocide from the 1970s, that 'virtually everyone acknowledges that genocide is primarily a crime of state' (Fein 2002, 79).[34] Yet, race was not an add-on to the European state tradition. It was, with nationality and ethnicity, one central and hegemonic way of defining the state in the period 1860–1940. It was certainly not, as indicated, the only way the state could be defined. In fact, even in this period, there were other competing conceptions of the state. However, the nation state or racial state was still dominant. What Germany did was efficiently to take the race state idea to its apogee. Although this extreme example of the race state was bankrupted by 1945, nonetheless, the conception of the state, as linked to nationality and ethnicity (and in our present era to culture), still infects our current discourse and thinking about state organization.

Thus, one fundamental reason why human rights appeared so forcibly in the post-1945 period was, at the time, a palpable sense of disbelief and profound unease amongst established states, particularly the United States, France, and Britain, that the most advanced political organ—the nation state—on which so many human expectations and aspirations had been built since the nineteenth century had been so integrally linked with the phenomenon of genocide. As indicated, states at the time were not so much directly engaged with human rights as they were politically pushed into an engagement. Further human rights did not mean the end of the state or the nation state, far from it. Many states (initially the United States) saw human rights as useful foreign policy tools; this certainly became an important aspect of their existence in the cold-war era. As one can see, time and time again over the last half century, permeating through the UDHR, Genocide Convention, and later human rights covenants, the nation state is the ever-present spectre haunting all human rights debates. The nation state is always both the subject *and* the object of human rights.[35]

## Modernity and human rights

The above conclusion does not deny that speculation about human rights existed prior to the full knowledge of the holocaust. Jurists and philosophers such as Hersch Lauterpacht (United Kingdom), Quincy Wright (United States), and Jacques Maritain (France) had put forward earlier rights-based schemes. In the early 1940s, the novelist H. G. Wells had published an idiosyncratic bill of rights which would form the basis for what he called a 'The New World Order'. A *Déclaration des droit internationaux de l'homme* had been adopted by the Institute of International Law in New York on 12 October 1929. Various rights charters were also submitted by organizations such as the Movement for Federal Union (1940), the Catholic Association for International Peace (1941), the New Educational Fellowship (1942), the Commission to Study the Organization of Peace (1943), the American Law Institute (1944), and the American Anthropological Association (1947). In other words there was no shortage of schemes.

Human rights literature is also replete with claims to ancient lineage. A 1978 US State Department pamphlet thus saw human rights as 'old as its ancient enemy, despotism', and mentions anachronistically in this context the themes of the ancient Greek play *Antigone*. Magna Carta (1215), the various constitutional documents of the English Civil War, and the 1689 Bill of Rights have all been fingered by scholars as points of origin. The more popular account usually traces the origins of human rights to the various codifications of natural rights in the eighteenth and early nineteenth centuries, for example, the Virginia Declaration (12 June 1776); the Declaration of Independence of the United States (4 July 1776), which incorporated a bill of rights; the 1789 French Declaration of the Rights of Man and the Citizen (prefixed to the French constitutions of 1791, 1793, and 1795); and the 1809 Constitution of Sweden and of Holland in 1815. The fundamental problem with all these claims is that (as previously argued) human rights are *not* simply a modern way of speaking about natural rights or the rights of man. Some scholars undoubtedly have been misled into the view that the two are the same (see Jones 1994, 72). But this idea involves certain fundamental confusions both in terms of historical contexts and substantive content (see Herbert 2002, 293–4).[36] There are some family resemblances, but the human rights movement from 1948 had little or no point of contact with the concept of 'natural' embodied by the older and earlier sense of right. Further, during its first fifty years, human rights had little sense of any overt religious content or context. In many ways, from its inception the human rights movement has tended to try to avoid such substantive content with good reason. The more secularized concept of the human person comes very much to the fore in human rights; but this is not the case in natural rights. The range and extent of human rights claims is extensive, whereas natural rights, comparatively, are really quite thin and simple in basic content. Human rights were fundamentally derived from a confrontation with the powers, resources, and long reach of the modern nation state, something that was largely historically extraneous to the motivations of the natural right tradition.

Even in the context of the twentieth century, it is difficult to find very direct antecedents for human rights, certainly before the 1930s and early 1940s. There were though a number of precursors for the human rights perspective which created a latent groundwork. For example, the concept and practice of international law itself had developed in embryo from the seventeenth and eighteenth centuries. It is arguable that the notion of customary international law, in particular, created a body of expectations about how states ought to act. However, the really significant shift in outlook from the pre- to the post-1945 conception of international law was that previously international law had largely regulated the relation of states; whereas post-1945 both state *and* human individuals were significant international legal actors. The key general issue here was that there was, implicit in international law, a conception of a body of norms, rules, and expectations that states 'ought' to live up to.

Comparable normative themes had been embedded in certain nineteenth-century movements, such as that against slavery which had been first internationally condemned in a Treaty of Paris in 1814. The League of Nations adopted a Convention to Suppress the Slave Trade in 1926 and the structures were carried through to the United Nations. Other organizations, such as the Red Cross—founded in 1863—were also concerned about international standards of treatment of prisoners and civilians.[37] The Versailles Treaty (1919) and the subsequent League of Nations Covenant further initiated a number of moves to widen international standards and humanitarian objectives—although there was *no* explicit assertion or reference to human rights. The Versailles Treaty, for example, contained a number of legal protections for minorities—with continuing legal supervisory functions taken up by the League of Nations (see Tomuschat 2003, 19ff.).[38] The Covenant of the League of Nations was further committed to protections against the trafficking of women, children, and the maltreatment of colonial peoples, and further protections against racial and religious abuse. One important institution, sponsored by the League, was the International Labour Organization (ILO) founded in 1919. It later became a specialized agency of the United Nations in 1946. Its activities in the 1920s and 1930s were in some ways a precursor to the push for economic and social human rights in the 1960s and 1970s. The ILO was concerned largely with humane labour laws, factory health and safety, child and womens' labour, social security, issues of discrimination, and trade union rights.[39]

Despite the above developments, the period between 1918 and 1945 still remained in many ways embedded in more conventional ways of thinking about politics, law, and international relations, although there were certain initiatives, as mentioned above, which undoubtedly prepared the ground for the human rights movement. The really significant transitional point for human rights was the full knowledge of the holocaust in Nazi Germany, which entailed a complete, if still grudging, realization that the nation state could become a bureaucratic killing machine on an unprecedented scale, via its own nationalist ideology.[40] The Charter of the International Military Tribunal at Nuremberg, although it did not use systematically the words genocide or human rights, nonetheless focused attention on the idea of 'crimes against humanity' as crimes of international law. It established the point that how a state and its leadership treats its citizens is a matter of international concern.[41] One primary component of the Nuremberg trials was therefore genocide. There were a number of other more pragmatic and foreign-policy-related arguments which gave succour to those who still retained anxieties about human rights developments. However, any account of the origin of human rights needs to be read against the background of genocide and the constellation of concepts including race, nationalism, and the state tradition.

# Human right and history

Despite the UDHR being an enormously significant document, there is nothing triumphalist about it. As Michael Ignatieff put it, its construction was trying in effect to create 'fire walls against barbarism' (Ignatieff 2003, 5).[42] This was a unique barbarism—one implicit in the racial/nation state. It was therefore, in simple terms, 'a warning by Europeans that the rest of the world should not seek to reproduce its mistakes' (Ignatieff 2003, 65). The human rights culture was trying, in another sense, to extricate the more positive dimensions of the Enlightenment from the more negative technical and instrumentalist dimensions, in full awareness of the horrific genocide that had just taken place. Resolutions against aggressive war, the Genocide Convention (1948), the Geneva Conventions (1949), and the Convention on Asylum (1951), all partook of the same general ethos. In essence, the UDHR aimed to prevent a recurrence of genocide.

The working draft for the 1948 Declaration was assigned to the Commission on Human Rights (CHR), a subsidiary of the Economic and Social Council (ECOSOC). They decided it should be a declaration—not a legally binding document.[43] Eleanor Roosevelt, chair of the CHR, saw the Declaration as a universal benchmark of achievement for all peoples and all nations. Legal enforcement was vaguely hoped for, but never came to fruition. Eighty-one meetings were held of the CHR. The General Assembly Committee on Social, Humanitarian, and Cultural Affairs held another 100 meetings. The General Assembly of the UN adopted the Declaration in December 1948, just after the Genocide Convention, with eight abstentions: Saudi Arabia, Czechoslovakia, Poland, Ukraine, South Africa, USSR, Yugoslavia, and Belorussia.[44]

The conventional history of the human rights movement has been told on many occasions (see e.g. Morsink 2000; Glendon 2001; Hunt 2007). Thus, only the briefest of historical surveys will be given. After the UDHR, there were two key further extensions and elaborations of the Declaration: the International Covenant on Civil and Political Rights (ICCPR 1966) and the International Covenant on Economic, Social, and Cultural Rights (ICESCR 1966). These latter treaties only received enough ratifications to become operative in 1976. The ICCPR largely contains and elaborates on the civil and political rights found in the UDHR.[45] The ICESCR elucidates and develops the economic and social rights found in the second half of the UDHR. Subsequently, there have been a enormously wide range of conventions which developed and further extended the reach and detail of human rights, for example, the International Convention on the Elimination of All Forms of Racial Discrimination (1966), the Convention on the Elimination of All Forms of Discrimination Against Women (1979), the Convention on the Rights of the

Child (1989), and the Convention against Torture and Other Cruel, Inhuman or Degrading Treatment or Punishment (1984). As indicated earlier, in the discussion of genocide, an International Criminal Court was established in the Rome Statute of 1998.

The development of an international human rights culture led to the creation of a number of regional initiatives, some of which have been remarkably successful in terms of ratification, implementation, and in one case enforcement. For example, the European Convention of Human Rights and Fundamental Freedoms (ECHR), which was passed in 1950 and came into force in 1953, covers standard civil and political rights. The European Convention was designed to strengthen democracy and rule of law and act as a bulwark against any incipient totalitarianism in Europe. Its basic rights are very similar to the first twenty-one articles of the UDHR. In fact, it was consciously modelled upon them. Economic and social rights were dealt with in a separate document, The European Social Charter. The participants in the ECHR were originally the countries of Western Europe, but with the end of the cold war in the early 1990s and European enlargement, many countries in the Eastern European domain have subsequently joined. In many ways, the European Convention is the most effective human rights regime at present.[46]

Two further regional initiatives have been established: the first is the Inter-American system operating under the auspices of the Organization of American States. The American Declaration of the Rights and Duties of Man was set out by the Organization of American States in 1948. The second element was the American Convention on Human Rights (The Pact of San José), passed in 1969. It was moulded on the European Convention, and was concerned almost exclusively with civil and political rights. A further Protocol from 1989, the Protocol of San Salvador, added social and economic and cultural rights. Its major institutional organs are the Inter-American Commission on Human Rights (established 1960) and the Inter-American Court of Human Rights (established 1979). The second regional initiative is the African system, sponsored by the African Union. This was established in the Banjul Charter (named after the Gambian Capital where it was drafted). The treaty created by the African Union was the African Charter on Human and People's Rights (1981). The African Commission on Human and People's Rights was created in 1986. African countries are required to give regular reports to the Commission on their human rights problems and efforts to tackle them. The African Court on Human and People's Rights was established in 1998. There has also been an Islamic-based charter the Cairo Declaration on Human Rights in Islam (1990) and an ASEAN Inter-Parliamentary Human Rights Declaration in Bangkok (1997).

The period between 1948 and 1970 was marked not only by the extension of human rights conventions but by two other key issues: decolonization and the advent of the cold war. Decolonizing countries frequently used human rights language largely to pursue their own national agendas for self-determination, via a sustained critique of the colonial powers. The other major issue was the cold war. Both the United States and the Soviet Union, during this period, often used human rights largely as instruments of foreign policy. The cold war basically reinforced the reluctance of many states to submit to the international regulations of human rights. The cold war did though have one more moderately constructive outcome, namely, the Conference on Security and Cooperation in Europe, which later became Organization for Security and Cooperation in Europe (OSCE). The OSCE debates led to the Helsinki Final Act (1975) in which [then] communist states largely symbolically accepted certain human rights commitments in return for border agreements. The final act of the conference was though non-binding. However, with the gradual fading of the colonial debates and the end of the cold war in the 1990s, the discourse of human rights has changed markedly again, in some cases leading to a resurrection of older cultural and nationalist arguments.

## Conclusion

My central question in this chapter has been: why did the culture of human rights arise in the post-1945 era? My response to this question, which briefly invokes again the arguments from chapter 3, is as follows: the concept nature, as argued, changed dynamically in informed public discourse during the mid- to late nineteenth century. This change focused primarily on the concept of evolution. This became the background ethos through which a range of concepts were discussed in the social and natural sciences. It was, as suggested, a framework-making theory. This concept of nature was consequently embodied in discourses concerning nationality, ethnicity, and race, which became crucial ways of articulating ideas of human difference. The concepts nation and race, particularly, overlapped in discussion during the period 1860–1940, within the evolutionary setting. In fact, at points, the two concepts became, by the early twentieth century, virtually synonymous. It must also be noted that before 1945 the concept of race was regarded as largely unproblematic. It also had close links with popular eugenics movements in many developed states. In addition, the concepts of race and nation were tied closely to the theory and practice of the modern state. The sovereign state was not only the crucial vessel for grasping and understanding politics, it was also an institutional phenomenon which had massively expanded in significance in the nineteenth and early twentieth centuries. The vocabulary and practice of the state has no necessary connection with race or nationality; however, during the later nineteenth century the terminology clearly began to overlap, such that the compound term 'nation state' entered the everyday political vernacular of the twentieth century. States were thus seen to imply nations (or races) and vice versa.[47]

Given that the sovereign nation state was the primary political player in international politics, and given that nationality and race were virtual synonyms in this period, it was therefore as feasible in political deliberation to speak of the racial state as of the nation state. Both compounds promulgated a specific vision of a 'naturally' (or ethnically) unified and occasionally eugenically purified community—if only in aspiration. This nation state or racial state was, and in some accounts remains, the central aspect of the political vocabulary of the twentieth and twenty-first centuries. It was not—as emphasized earlier—the only conception of the state, but it was nonetheless the most significant during this period. It underpinned both liberal democratic and non-liberal states. For many, the sovereign nation state represented the apex of political achievement. It was the central political aspiration for communities.

One of the most advanced of these nation states from the late nineteenth century, widely admired across the world—where the vocabulary of statism had developed in a very rich format—was Germany. However, by the 1930s Germany was also the clearest instance of the racial state. It represented in many ways the climax of this particular vision of the state. It then instigated in the 1940s, with full intent, a bureaucratically organized and industrial-level killing of certain groups on ethnic and racial grounds. This, in turn, gave rise rapidly to the neologism *genocide*. Thus, a profoundly advanced nation state had become intimately associated with the new practice of genocide. As many noted, the constellation of concepts surrounding and underpinning genocide were all comparatively modern and not related to Germany as such. Genocide itself was rather a distinctly modern phenomenon. It was a misdemeanour of the modern nation state—*given certain circumstances*. Even more significantly, it was a transgression directly linked to racial or national criteria. In sum, genocide is (and remains) a potentiality of the theory and practice of the modern nation state. This is not an argument which focuses on the state per se, but rather on the nation state or racial state. The potentiality for the modern crime of genocide is implicit in the conception of the nation state, that is, a state fixated with national or racial ideologies. Further, the 'nation state' remains the key player of modern politics to the present day. All the twentieth-century attempts to integrate or control states acknowledge this basal point.[48]

The overall culture of human rights is still in large part designed with political and security motives in mind. It aims to contain the worst excesses of nation-state activity. The idea of human rights was thus generated initially from this negative political setting. The central paradox of this negative setting is that the state persists both as the subject and the object of human rights. The nation state cannot actually be fully curtailed by human rights for the very basic reason that it is the critical actor in both ratifying and acting upon human rights. It is potentially both judge and defendant.

## ☐ NOTES

1. Defendants were charged with having 'conducted deliberate and systematic genocide, viz the extermination of racial and national groups, against the civilian populations of certain occupied territories in order to destroy particular races and classes of people and national, racial or religious groups, particularly Jews, Poles and Gypsies, and others' (quoted in Kuper 2002, 55).

2. In Moscow in 1945, there was a Four Power Agreement (England, France, Russia, and the United States) which established a Charter for dealing with Germany. Article 6 of the Charter indicated three types of crime: crimes against peace, war crimes, and crimes against humanity.

3. Given that it is often groups within a state who often (but not always) experience genocide, genocide is a potentiality from within the logic of the 'nation state'.

4. Helen Fein defines genocide as 'sustained purposeful action by a perpetrator to physically destroy a collectivity directly or indirectly, through interdiction of the biological and social reproduction of group members, sustained regardless of the surrender or lack of threat offered by the victim' (Fein 2002, 82). Bartov suggests that 'The simplest definition of modern genocide is that it is mass murder conceived and perpetrated by modern states.... This in turn depends on our definition of the modern period and modern states and organizations. Conversely, the nature of genocidal actions is also a measure of the modernity of the perpetrator organizations. In this sense, bureaucratic, industrial, systematic genocide may actually serve as a signifier of modernity' (Bartov 2003, 76).

5. 'Researchers go from a sweeping approach—such as that favoured by the *Encyclopaedia of Genocide*—to a more restricted one based on the United Nations 1948 Convention on the Prevention and Punishment of the Crime of Genocide, favoured by Ben Kiernen, the founder of the Genocide Studies Program at Yale University' (Semelin 2003, 353).

6. The Bush administration was wholly negative and the recent Obama administration has remained politely distant.

7. The International Criminal Court stated 'The origins of the [Genocide] Convention show that it was the intention of the United Nations to condemn and punish genocide as a "crime under international law."'...The first consequence arising from this conception is that principles underlying the Convention are principles which are recognised by civilized Nations as binding on States, even without any conventional obligation' (quoted in Smith 2003, 215–16). The instruments creating the International Criminal Tribunals for Yugoslavia and Rwanda largely confirm this view.

8. It is said that one of the Serbian generals, noting this contentious point, coined a catchphrase for his troops: 'a village a day keeps the UN away'.

9. Euthanasia, compulsory sterilization, and systematic killing were already being exercised on the insane, mentally feeble, and handicapped in the early 1930s. As Bauman comments 'well before they built the gas chambers, the Nazis, on Hitler's orders, attempted to exterminate their own mentally insane or bodily impaired compatriots' (Bauman 2002, 120).

10. With regard to the UDHR and the Genocide Convention, 'There is thus a temporal link and, perhaps, an understanding that the two documents may be read together' (Smith 2003, 213).

11. It may also require additional facilitating elements, such as a particular type of military culture within a state (see Hull 2003).

12. The majority of scholarly studies of genocide consequently take the case of Nazi Germany as the archetype of genocide. The beginning of this whole process goes back to 1935. Between, for example, 1935 and 1937, some 225,000 people were sterilized in Germany for various forms of disability, handicap, or the like. Racial cleansing legislation was passed in the same period. For example, marriage was forbidden between German nationals and other races; there was a positive attempt to decrease the birth rate of other races in German territory and a state-based encouragement to increase the birth rate of the German *Volk*.

13. For some commentators national and racial language also had an important role in colonial and imperial debates. Arendt maintains in *The Origins of Totalitarianism* that European imperialism (along with anti-Semitism) was at the heart of a constellation of ideas that focused European states on mass violence, legitimized by ideologies of expansion and superiority. Imperialism was particularly closely linked in Arendt's mind to totalitarianism. Imperialism denoted a form of limitless expansion. Originally this expansion was economic, in terms of capitalistic motifs. However, as imperial policy developed it abandoned any limits on its expansion. Imperial state policy also mutated into a racial policy. Destructive violence was then engaged in for the sake of power alone (see Arendt 1966, 137).

14. As one scholar notes, 'Biology provided the pseudo-scientific underpinnings for race thinking in its heyday, roughly 1850–1945' (Weitz 2003*a*, 22).

15. 'The Darwinian era marked a profound departure from all that had gone before in the science of man. The principles of political philosophy that had once guided human affairs were now replaced by the principles of natural selection and the processes of social evolution set in an ideological frame of reference' (Hannaford 1996, 325).

16. This is of course not to argue that nationalism is always necessarily linked to racism. However, there were in this period a series of quite fundamental overlaps.

17. All these terms—particularly nation and race—also contain deep internal tensions and complexities which have never really been seriously addressed in human rights codification work post-1948.

18. The only problem being that there was no real attempt to clarify the terminology.

19. Wilhelm Frick's racial cleansing legislation—Preservation from Hereditarily Diseased Posterity—was passed in Germany on 14 July 1935. Basically all the people institutionalized or not who suffered from feeble-mindedness, epilepsy, blindness, drug or alcohol problems, deformity, or who were physiognomically offensive were to be sterilized. At the time, this was regarded by many in Britain's and America's eugenics movements as a courageous act.

20. Galton had a very strong following. In 1911 the Galton Eugenics Professorship was established in University College London and a new Department of Applied Statistics was created (initially focused on the idea of eugenics). In the same year in the United States, the Eugenic Records Office was set up in Cold Harbor on Long Island. The work of the US academic Charles B. Davenport (1866–1944) was significant here. Davenport was

focused on the issue of US immigration policy in relation to eugenics. He advocated state licenses to control marriage, sterilization policies for certain groups, and overall race hygiene in US immigration policy (see Hannaford 1996, 333–4).

21. 'The Soviet Union under Stalin did not become a "genocidal regime"...The absence of a fully developed racial ideology, and the belief—though intermittently applied—in the malleability of human beings, acted as a brake on the Soviet regime's population politics, preventing the unfolding of a full-scale genocidal program along the lines of Nazi Germany' (Weitz 2003a, 101).

22. Although the intellectual themes of modernity are traced to the Enlightenment, my own use (which might be described as a period of high modernity) covers the later nineteenth and twentieth centuries.

23. '[E]thnicity is a product of modern politics. Although people have had identities...for as long as humans have had culture, they have begun to see themselves as members of vast ethnic groups, only during the modern period of colonization and state-building' (Bowen 2002, 334). Hannaford also comments that 'ethnicity is essentially an idea introduced in modern times, and that it has prospered in proportion to the decline in political ideas concerning the disposition of civil affairs' (Hannaford 1996, 398).

24. As a long-term Balkans observer, Misha Glenny, observes: 'the roots of the current Balkan violence lie not in primordial ethnic and religious differences but rather in modern attempts to rally people around nationalist ideas. "Ethnicity" becomes "nationalism" when it includes aspirations to gain a monopoly of land, resources, and power. But nationalism, too, is a learned and frequently manipulated set of ideas, and not a primordial sentiment' (quoted in Bowen 2002, 335). Bowen also notes that 'ethnic thinking in political life is a product of modern conflicts over power and resources, and not an ancient impediment to political modernity' (Bowen 2002, 336).

25. 'Racism comes into its own only in the context of a design of the perfect society and intention to implement the design through planned and consistent effort' (Bauman 2002, 117).

26. This is not to say that religion could not again become a dominant motif in identifying and killing peoples. Genocide would then be based upon apostasy.

27. Or, as Horkheimer put it, 'progress has a tendency to destroy the very ideas it is supposed to realise and unfold' (Horkheimer 1996, 359).

28. This is linked to what Arendt called (in relation to the trial of Eichmann) the 'banality of evil' (see Arendt 1992).

29. However, as Smith remarks, the state 'refers exclusively to public institutions, differentiated from, and autonomous of, other social institutions and exercising a monopoly of coercion....The nation, on the other hand, signifies a cultural and political bond, united in a single political community' (see Smith 1991, 14–15).

30. In the same volume Paul Hirst also sees the nation state, with some qualifications, as 'pivotal' (see Hirst 2000, 178).

31. Hitler obtained all his racial ideas from the widespread European literature of the pre-1914 period.

32. '[T]he fictitious unities of race and nation whipped up by the philologists, anthropologists, historians, and social scientists of the nineteenth century as alternatives to the antique political state led them to forget a very important past and to invent in its place

novel ideological forms of governance that were pursued with vengeance and arrogance.' The nemesis of this form of racial governance was Dachau and Auschwitz (see Hannford 1996, 399).

33. As one scholar remarks: 'When the powers of modern states were hinged to the revolutionary impulse and an ideology of purity, the results could be deadly' (Weitz 2003*b*, 73).

34. '[T]he modern state, when linked to the ideologies of nation and race, has been the source of the genocides...and many other cases of massive human rights violations' (Weitz 2003*a*, 254); further, 'Massacre and mass killing become genocide only when an entire ethnic group is targeted by the state' (Bartov 2003, 94).

35. As one genocide scholar notes, 'the international law against genocide protects "individuals" against the violation of their "human rights", while paradoxically guarding the sovereignty of the nation-state' (Fein 2002, 6).

36. 'The widespread acceptance of this claim has become so entrenched in contemporary rights theory, and has become so responsible for the out-of-focus understanding we have of the history of rights today, that it needs to be brought up once again. The concept of *human* rights is not only *not* descended from the concept of *natural* rights; it is a repudiation of the concept of natural rights, both ancient and modern' (Herbert 2002, 293).

37. The Hague Conventions of 1899 and 1907 had also been focused on rules of warfare.

38. There was some sense that minorities in new states might not be treated fairly. Five states concluded specific agreements with the Allied Powers (Greece, Czechoslovakia, Poland, Romania, and Yugoslavia). Other states were also covered: Austria, Bulgaria, Hungary, and Turkey. Germany and Poland concluded a convention on the Upper Silesia. Instruments were designed in all of these for minorities. The articles advocated educational equality (in one's own tongue), non-discrimination, and guarantees in respect of cultural identity.

39. Significantly the United States refused to join or have anything to do with the ILO in the 1920s. Germany and Japan withdrew from it in 1933 and the USSR was excluded in 1939 after the Nazi–Soviet pact.

40. Many states initially regarded human rights as pious clichés. What they could not foresee was that 'once articulated as international norms, rights language ignited both the colonial revolutions...and the civil rights revolution at home' (Igatieff 2003, 6). Human rights, in one sense, came like a thief in the night to international politics.

41. Nuremberg was a 'landmark, establishing the world's first international criminal trials' (Orend 2002, 220).

42. 'A consciousness of European barbarism is built into the very language of the Declarations' (Ignatieff 2003, 65).

43. The Canadian lawyer John Humphrey produced the first draft of the UDHR based on a survey of national constitutions.

44. A number of organs both within and outside the UN are involved with human rights; thus, the UN High-Commissioner for Human Rights, the UN General Assembly and the Security Council, the Commission on Human Rights, the Economic and Social Council, the Sub-Commission for Prevention of Discrimination and Protection of Minorities, the Commission on the Status of Women and Committee on the Elimination of Discrimination Against Women, UNESCO, and the ILO. These organs amongst others can be involved

directly or indirectly in human rights. In addition there are a large number of non-governmental agencies (NGOs), for example, Amnesty International, Human Rights Watch, the International Commission of Jurists, Doctors without Borders, and Oxfam. NGOs are seen everywhere in the international human rights system. They attend and participate in UN human rights bodies, provide information, shape agendas, and provide links between the international human rights system and domestic politics.

45. The ICCPR illustrates the standard UN system for implementing an international bill of rights. The Covenant created an agency, the Human Rights Committee, to promote compliance with its norms. The eighteen members of the Human Rights Committee serve in their personal capacity as experts rather than as state representatives, which gives them some freedom to express their own perspectives as experts rather than those of their country. Unlike the ECHR, the ICCPR did not create a human rights court to give authoritative interpretations of its norms. The Human Rights Committee can express its views as to whether a particular practice is a human rights violation, but it is not authorized to issue legally binding reports. The ICCPR requires participating states to report periodically on their compliance with the treaty. The Human Rights Committee has the job of receiving, studying, and commenting critically on these reports. The reporting procedure is useful in encouraging countries to identify their major human rights problems and to devise methods of dealing with them over time. But the reporting system has few teeth when dealing with countries that stonewall or fail to report.

46. Three bodies were initially given the role of upholding the rights regime: the European Commission of Human Rights (set up in 1954), the European Court of Human Rights (set up in 1959), and the Committee of Ministers of the Council of Europe. This latter body was comprised of the Ministers of Foreign Affairs of the member states or their representatives. Most European states usually always concur with the judgment of the court. However, the work of the court has increased massively. A lot depends here also as to whether human rights have been integrated into existing member states legal systems.

47. The vocabulary also entered debates about colonialism and empire, usually in the context of evolutionary, advanced, or inferior races.

48. Thus the titles of the League of Nations and the United Nations.

# 5 Structures of Human Rights

The previous chapter focused on one question: why did human rights discourse arise in the post-1945 era? The response to this question rested upon the conclusions of chapter 3, namely, that there had been significant changes in the manner in which nature was viewed in the later nineteenth century, which had wide-ranging if subtle ramifications for both the natural and social sciences. The evolutionary understanding of nature was a framework-making theory which reconfigured subtly many key concepts and disciplinary ways of thinking. One of the significant effects of this subtle change in the discourses of politics, sociology, geography, and anthropology was to provide a vocabulary which naturalized key terminology. Words like ethnicity, nationality, and race—although preceding etymologically the rise of this new understanding of nature—fell gradually under the spell of evolutionary terminology from the 1860s. Further, race and nation were often used synonymously in many writings of the period. In addition, one should note that between 1860 and 1940 the word race did not embody the opprobrium that was subsequently associated with it post-1945. The term race, in fact, is still commonly used in a more descriptive innocuous sense—as in the term 'race relations'—although it remains vague and there is little consensus on its precise meaning. In more contemporary usage, race still drifts in and out of synonymity with the concept of nationality, although some of the strong biological dimensions have now dropped into the background. If anything there has been some resurrection, in the 2000s, of a pre-Darwinian more romanticized notion of nationality.

The key European political concept in the period 1860–1940—a concept and practice which continues to be a central problematic of contemporary politics—is the nation state. Despite the existence of international institutions and established practices, such as the UN, nonetheless, the key issue for the UN and its continued existence is still the state tradition.[1] At the same time, the large majority of theorists and politicians over this latter period were not satisfied with the state per se. It was usually linked with the nation or the racial group. This meant, in turn, that the state concept and practice were indirectly naturalized via nationality and race. Consequently, the idea of the 'organic nation state' had a new lease of life. Its earlier manifestation in the nineteenth century had been in a different format in the writings of political romantics. Organic ideas in these latter theories reflected pantheistic and panpsychist understandings of nature. However, the late-nineteenth-century development of the organic state was linked closely to the new discourse on 'biological nature'—the understanding of the word 'organic' being mediated through evolutionary discourse. It is important to emphasize here again that the vocabulary of the state has no *necessary* connection with nationality and race. Yet, in the period under discussion (and still so for many), the compound artifice of the nation state remained a norm for legal, economic, and political discussion.

By the 1920s, post-Versailles, the 'self-determining' nation state was seen as the archetypal building block of modern politics. Further, one of the most advanced of such states from the 1880s was Germany. By the mid-1930s Germany had also become the most voluble exemplar of the racially unified nation state. This particular nation state then became the key architect and working premise behind the very modern twentieth-century practice of genocide. Despite Germany being an original exemplar, genocide, more broadly, was still linked intimately to the idea and practice of the nation state. Quite literally, genocide, as distinct from other forms of mass killing, could not have existed without the nation state and, as importantly, it was directly related to the *conjunction* of nationality and race with the state. Genocide was thus an integral aspect of both modernity and the phenomenon of the nation state. The fact of genocide softened up many of the key states who had defeated the Axis powers, not only to the idea of both global institutions (for the sake of future security), but also to the concept of human rights. The central problem of this situation was that the nation state was both *subject* and *object* of human rights, that is, both judge and defendant.

Given the importance of the nation state in terms of the historical and normative roots of human rights culture, the question arises as to what effect this state focus has had on human rights thinking? This chapter will initially fill in more of the detail of the way human rights developed in the post-1948 period, to the present day, and examine critically the more predominant ways in which human rights have been analysed. It will then begin to scrutinize human rights development within the framework of the state idea, namely, to unpack the significance of the state for human rights developments. This latter argument will be examined much more closely in subsequent chapters.

# Generations of rights

In order to get some handle on the diverse debates concerning human rights over the last fifty years, it is useful to take up a distinction, which appears and reappears in the literature, that is, between first-, second-, and third-generation human rights. At this stage nothing is said about either the truth or falsity of this distinction. It is clearly immensely significant for many and intensely irritating for others. The design and adoption of certain human right covenants appears to confirm, for some commentators, that there is a fundamental difference between these generational categories. However, in other large practical human rights forums, such as the Vienna conference in June 1993, there was a strong affirmation of the overall unity of human rights. My own adoption of the distinction is for two reasons. First, it has some utility as a pedagogic or explanatory device. It enables various debates in human rights and over specific covenants to be more easily explicated. As to whether it is correct about the nature of the rights involved remains an unresolved question.

The second reason to utilize this distinction is less conventional. It is something which will become much more apparent in subsequent chapters. My argument will be that the generational debate parasitizes upon legal, political, and ideological debates concerning the nature and development of citizenship in the nineteenth and twentieth centuries. This is, in essence, part of a debate about the character of the state. It would be easy at this point to misinterpret the essentials of my argument, that is, viewing my argument as some form of realist contention, in current international relations terminology. This is far from the case. My contention is that the generational debate in human rights literature, wittingly or unwittingly, maps onto debates about the changing nature of citizenship. In consequence, these debates also map onto arguments concerning the form of political organization that we are most familiar with, namely, the state. In fact, 'map onto' might not be strong enough at points. In essence, we are often looking at the same argument transubstantiated.[2]

## FIRST-GENERATION HUMAN RIGHTS

In much of the literature on human rights, these rights are often seen as the *classic* human rights. They are though relatively few in number. In fact, some commentators have considered that they can be summed up in virtually one right—although there are differences as to what that right is, for example, respect for human agency or liberty (see Hart 1955; Ignatieff 2003). These classic rights are commonly seen to be embedded initially in the first twenty-one articles of the Universal Declaration of Human Rights (UDHR) (1948); they are then largely repeated in the initial articles of a range of other human rights documentation: that is, the European Convention of Human Rights and Fundamental Freedoms (ECHR) (1950), International Covenant on Civil and Political Rights (ICCPR) (1966), International Covenant on Economic, Social, and Cultural Rights (ICESCR) (1966), the American Convention on Human Rights (1948), the African Convention on Human Rights (1981), and in the preamble to the ASEAN Bangkok Declaration (1997). They are often viewed as having a more fundamental aspect to them than other forms of human right. In fact, for some commentators, they form the top rung of a hierarchy of human rights—although this idea of hierarchy is vigorously contested by other commentators.

The reason these classic human rights are viewed as more fundamental is due to two factors. First, more generally, they appear to reflect the limited but general claims of earlier natural rights documentation, which have historically carried a moral weight. An article, such as Article 1, of the UDHR reads: 'All human beings are born free and equal in dignity and rights. They are endowed with reason and conscience and should act towards one another in a spirit of brotherhood.' Article 3 states: 'Everyone has the right to life, liberty and security of person.' These kind of general claims have echoes from the familiar historic bills of rights such as the French or American declarations. Thus, the initial opening of the US constitutional document famously reads,

> We hold these truths to be self-evident, that all men are created equal, that they are endowed by their creator with certain unalienable rights, that among these are life, liberty, and the pursuit of happiness. That to secure these rights, Governments are instituted among men, deriving their just power from the consent of the governed. That whenever any form of Government becomes destructive of these ends, it is the Right of the people to alter or to abolish it.[3]

For some scholars, if one deletes the religious language, then the sentiments are pretty much still the same as the opening articles of the 1948 declaration. The rights are basically respect for life and the fundamental equal dignity of the human person, individual liberty of movement, peaceful association or assembly, thought, and expression.[4] These are often seen as having a primary moral status. Thus, for some, this is perceived to be a historical legacy (which some even have the temerity to trace back to Magna Carta in 1215), concerning certain basic classic rights claims which then carry down into the 'basic' human rights.[5] This apparent legacy is in large part mythical, partly because the *grounds* on which those earlier claims were made were largely defunct by the early twentieth century.

The second reason for their fundamental status for many commentators relates directly and more pertinently to the issue of genocide, as discussed in chapter 4. The fact of genocide and the weight it carried at the time, in 1948, led directly to certain imperatives. Put very simply, humans should not be subject to arbitrary killing or execution, torture, enslavement, or unjust cruel punishment. The basic equal dignity and freedom of the human person had to be accorded respect. The nation state in both cases was assumed to be the key offender. The importance of this explains the fact that the Genocide Convention predated, if only minutely, the UDHR. These classic rights were seen to be firewalls against the possible barbarity of the nation state. Other rights, as we will see, do not appear to fit so easily into this more earthy logic.

The classic rights are also usually seen to have a strong *civil* and *political* character. As one commentator puts it, they are therefore 'possessed by every citizen, or in a wider and more relevant sense, by every inhabitant of some state or society' (Wellman 1999, 15). The civil and political aspect focuses primarily on very basic general demands or imperatives. The UDHR proclaims that it is a 'common standard of achievement' and many commentators have consequently seen the classic rights of the UDHR as part of an 'emerging consensus' in most states about certain core values. This consensus grounds itself in the basic requirements for a state to function as a state, which can be recognized by the international community of states and international law. In this sense, first generation rights indicate certain general responsibilities and norms for any and all states. These rights are consequently frequently seen as basic, minimalist, and general.[6]

## SECOND-GENERATION HUMAN RIGHTS

One of the issues, which was certainly touched upon in the later articles of the Universal Declaration of Human Rights, but is oddly *not* primarily associated with it, is another more general category of human rights concerned with the welfare and social security of individuals. In fact, there are clearly such rights within the UDHR (Articles 22–7); however, the additional point that there are later Covenants in 1966 which focus principally on such social and economic rights is often taken as an indication that they were inadequately covered in the 1948 document. These latter rights are commonly labelled economic and social human rights and they embody the basic content of what we commonly understand as second-generation human rights. A more general way of categorizing them is as welfare rights—understood in the same sense that welfare state rights have developed in the twentieth century. More generally these entail a right to education, basic equality and non-discrimination, access to employment opportunities, fair pay, safe and healthy working conditions, free choice of employment, reasonable working hours, basic wages, social security, an adequate standard of living (that is adequate food, clothing, and housing), basic health provisions, and so forth.[7]

An additional slightly confusing aspect of these is that 'cultural rights'—and even rights to nationality and communal self-determination—are commonly, and in appearance innocuously, tacked onto, for example, the ICESCR (1966). The slightly confusing aspect here is that economic and social rights, vis-à-vis welfare rights, are not necessarily in the same category as cultural rights. In many ways—to jump forward in the argument for a moment—cultural rights seem more appropriate to the category of third-generation rights. Third-generation rights are usually seen as collective, group, or minority-orientated rights—although minority rights and indigenous rights are sometimes separated out. Consequently, as soon as one tries to unpack group or collective rights then the category of culture frequently arises. That is to say, in much modern legal and political parlance culture is often standardly used to elucidate, validate, or legitimize the idea of a group or collective rights (see Kymlicka 1991, 1995; Vincent 2002). A lot depends upon how one approaches such rights. If, for example, one thinks of cultural rights under a more general negative rubric of non-discrimination or equality, then economic, social, and cultural rights can all potentially be linked; that is to say, they can all be viewed under a more formal heading of equality or equal treatment. In this sense, equality might then lead to a concern for social justice and equal treatment, vis-à-vis the equal treatment of gender, children, the economically deprived, and cultural groups. The key normative categories are then equality and non-discrimination. Culture only arises by default as one case, among many others, of possible unequal or discriminatory treatment. However, if one focuses not on equality and non-discrimination, but rather on the categories themselves, that is taking group cultures as ontologically significant, then culture becomes more knotty and it is not so easy to think simply in economic or social terms. This issue is discussed later, but it is worth noting this conceptual anomaly within the second-generation category. The present focus will largely be on the more dominant view of the second-generation category of social and economic rights.

Social and economic rights have been both conceptually and historically separated out from first-generation civil and political rights. Historically, none of the early historic bills of natural rights in North America or Europe focused systematically on an explicit category of social and economic natural rights. Further, none of the early constitutional documents of the nineteenth century, for example, Holland 1811, Belgium 1831, Prussia 1850, and so forth, mentions such rights.[8] Very broadly, the same can be said of the kinds of rights concern of the League of Nations and the more general perception of key initial articles of the UDHR.[9] It was largely the civil and political dimensions of the first-generation rights which were seen as crucial. One obvious reason for this in 1945 was that if genocide was the key to unlocking the human rights mentality, why would one want to associate this overriding concern in any way with the more contingent aspects of social or economic welfare rights? Consequently, whereas there was little open defiance over the convention against genocide or the 1984 convention against torture and cruel, inhuman, or degrading treatment, however the same cannot be said for the ICESCR (1966), which was and remains contested. Social and economic rights were therefore, for many, either another dimension to 'add' to the more *basic* civil and political human rights, or alternatively they were bogus. The sense of adding to, or supplementing, the more basic civil and political rights was partly canvassed in the temporal sequence of Covenants, that is, the

ICESCR was seen as a later supplement to the more basic rights of the UDHR, that is Articles 1–21. The temporal sequence appears to give priority to civil and political rights. A similar temporal sequencing appears in other theatres of human rights. Thus, the ECHR was created by the Council of Europe in 1950, and it was again focused on civil and political rights. The social and economic rights were a later somewhat contentious addition in the European Social Charter (1961).[10] Later again a more balanced policy was sought in the Charter of Fundamental Rights of the European Union adopted by the European Council in Nice in December 2000. Similarly the American Declaration of the Rights and Duties of Man adopted in 1948 and the American Convention on Human Rights (Pact of San José) (1969) were also civil and political in character. The later social and economic dimensions developed from a protocol in 1989 (the Protocol of San Salvador).

One additional historical and ideological reason why there was a tension here between first- and second-generation rights, and further the reason why many insist on prioritizing certain human rights over others, is that the advent of the UDHR (1948) was also the inception of the cold war. In this context the fact that the old Soviet Union (pre-1989) promulgated the importance of social and economic rights was significant. In fact, the Soviet Union reversed the priority with civil and political rights. However, the United States largely held (and still does hold to a degree) the opposite view. This had the effect of ideologizing the whole debate. It became an issue of foreign policy. This continued well in the 1990s, in effect until the collapse of major communist regimes. The ideological character of many of these debates about human rights has also pervaded the internal discourses of Western liberal-minded states. Clarification of human rights therefore has to be seen in the period 1948–89, against the backdrop of cold war rivalries and intense debates concerning the viability and desirability of welfare states, as against more market-orientated regimes. Arguments about various notions of democracy also cross-cut these debates. Furthermore, particular conceptions of human rights were, and remain, for certain states, useful tools of foreign policy, often used as ideological weapons to strike out at ideological, economic, or security rivals.

The conceptual separation of classic first-generation human rights and second-generation social and economic rights, focuses on the issue that civil and political rights have a more general, more obviously universal and basic character than social and economic rights. Consequently, some have suggested that social and economic rights cannot conceptually be considered as human rights at all (see Cranston 1973; Wellman 1999, 22).

The roots of the social and economic dimension of human rights lie in the early twentieth century. The basic argument for them focuses on the point that the welfare of an individual is heavily dependent upon certain social and economic conditions being met. The argument asserts that simply to have one's life protected by civil or political rights against murder, torture, or the like, or having the ability to freely express one's ideas or associate freely, are not enough in themselves to guarantee the real welfare or adequate functioning of the individual. To understand this point it is necessary to understand something about the conceptions of welfare in the twentieth century. A number of states, for example, Germany, New Zealand, Australia, Britain, and the old Soviet Union had already, by the first few decades of the twentieth century, begun to develop social and economic welfare-based policies, in various formats. Embryonic welfare states were thus being formed in the early twentieth century. In this sense, there was a marked trend within a number of developed states towards some form of welfare rights perspective. This gradually accelerated through the twentieth century, particularly in the post-1945 era. Human rights thus became indirectly enmeshed in the more general 'social question' of modern states, states which in the 1950s were prime movers in the human rights debates. A particular view began to dominate discussion, namely, 'that it is not enough for a state to abstain from interfering with individual entitlements' (Tomuschat 2003, 28). States were therefore seen to have a broader social and economic remit for their citizens.

As it is well known, such welfare rights-orientated ideas came under increasing pressure again from the 1980s to the present day. In this context, it should hardly surprise us that the status and nature of social and economic human rights have also come under equal pressure in certain quarters—for example, the continuous critical rumbling debates about welfare rights in Europe and the United States' insistence that poverty and social deprivation are not really human rights issues.[11] Another development from the late 1980s concerns the rise of the idea of the multicultural state. This, once again, coincides with the growth of interest and ardent proselytizing for 'cultural human rights', and indeed, both group and minority rights claims. The focus on such cultural groups, combined with the post-1989 diasporas of groups from economically poorer to richer states, throws some light again on the human rights concern over refugees and immigration. Again these developments are not at all fortuitous, if one examines them in the round.

Returning to the theme of social and economic rights: related developments took place in the social and economic sphere. Post-1918 there were strong intimations of a second-generation rights perspective. For example, as part of the Versaille peace settlement, the International Labour Organization (ILO) was formed in 1919. Its focus was primarily on a social and economic agenda, that is, workers' rights, conditions of employment, women's and child labour. In the broadest terms, the ILO was concerned with social welfare rights. ILO work can indeed be viewed as another direct precursor of second-generation human rights emphasis, although its focus was always on labour-related issues. The general social and economic framework of the ILO was restated in the Declaration of Philadelphia (1944). It later became a specialized agency of the UN in 1946. The ILO now largely makes recommendations to, and coordinates with, the UN's Economic and Social Council. It has subsequently sponsored hundreds of instruments and conventions on working conditions, child and women's labour, holidays, social security, discrimination, and trade union rights.

In summary, second-generation rights are associated with the growth of a panoply of welfare rights that in turn coincide quite directly with the development of the ideas and practices of welfare states. Such rights can therefore be seen in the light of the development of the 'social question' as it evolved, in all its complexity, in domestic state theories during the twentieth century. Disputes over these second-generation claims contain a number of 'flashpoints'. One is the idea that there is radical conceptual difference between 'right claims'—first-generation rights being universal and second-generation being particular and contingent, and further, that it is a fundamental error of public policy to confuse them. A second flashpoint concerns the deep ideologizing of such debates and the manner in which different understandings of human rights have been situated in the context of broader state conflicts over foreign policy objectives. Third, the debates over social and economic rights were not confined to the international arena. In fact, the argument concerning first- and second-generation human rights pervaded the whole domestic arena of a number of states in the period 1945 to the present day. Many developed states in the twentieth century have cautiously meandered around the 'social question', mainly for fear of the economic costs involved. Thus, anguish over the future of the welfare or social state has characterized much British, German, and French policy debates to the present day, especially in times of economic crisis.

This debate over welfare reignited ferociously in the 1980s with the advent of the 'new right' critiques of welfare.[12] It is important to emphasize this latter point, since there is a deeply misleading issue, which arises via certain comparatively recent third-generation human rights debates (and so-called Asian values debates in the 1990s). This argument refers to the contention that social and economic rights were somehow always downplayed by many Western states, particularly by the United States, and that Asian states, echoing one aspect of the old Soviet Union cold war policy stance, have continuously re-emphasized them, although for different reasons. In the Asian values case—so the argument goes—it was because they were more concerned with social cohesion, community, and solidarist cultural values. Further, Asian states have seen the need for social and economic development before any civil or political rights can be established. This latter Asian values critique is mythical and full of contradictions. Social and economic rights have undoubtedly been an issue of ongoing public debate in most Western states throughout the 1980s and 1990s; however, if one compares, for example, even US welfare provision since the 1960s with that of, say, mainland China,

Hong Kong, Vietnam, or Singapore, then one can see immediately how odd the critique is (see Donnelly 2002, 65). Even the United States, which shows the most overt suspicion of the social and economic category, has nonetheless definite communitarian, solidarist, and welfare traditions. Both communitarian and welfare arguments are thus as much part of Western states as any Asian states, even if they are contested.[13] Social and economic rights were not and have not been rejected by Western states; in fact, in many they still have an extensive role. Thus, the idea that Western states are too individualistic and lack communitarian and welfare rights is quite simply false. Further, to emphasize social and economic development (as many Asian states do) is *not* necessarily to emphasize either social and economic rights or communitarian traditions. In fact, such economic development themes, in one reading, can undermine the latter rights and traditions. In addition, economic and social developments can, in turn, undermine cultural and group-based rights.

## THIRD-GENERATION HUMAN RIGHTS

Third-generation rights are the most recently debated domain of human rights. They have a significant prehistory; however, they only really appeared on the international scene in a popular format during the late 1980s and early 1990s. Such rights can be loosely defined as claims, warrants, or entitlements which enable or allow for the protection or promotion of a group or minority interest. Some would identify a more optimistic role for such cultural and group rights, namely, that they are rights which affirm and protect the solidarity, mutual support, and cohesiveness of minority or indigenous groups. In general terms, such rights are usually held against states. They are prima facie frequently regarded as *collective* or *group-orientated* rights. Consequently, they can be—but logically do not have to be—coupled with a critique of first- and second-generation human rights, as too individualistic and too culturally insensitive.

Third-generation rights are plagued with terminological problems. These begin in trying to identify what such rights actually apply to—race, language, religion, kinship, ethnicity, and culture have all been projected as distinct group interests with attached right-based claims. These categories do however cover two overlapping domains, focusing on both minorities and indigenous groups. There is no settled agreement or agreed consensual definitions of either term. Minorities are usually loosely taken to refer to 'groups' within majority populations of nation states, who might be subject to violence, intimidation, discrimination, or forced absorption in a majority. Third-generation rights are thus designed to secure, protect, or promote minority interests. They do not really figure, except by default, in the earlier 1948 document. There were debates, in 1947–8, over a clause on ethnic, religious, and linguistic minority groups; however, there was little agreement and it was dropped.[14] The debate over minorities, as noted, did grow in significance during the 1990s particularly. There were though minimal and maximal readings of this debate. Minimally, minority groups could be negatively tolerated or minimally protected. However, for the majority of minority group activists it was not enough to be protected or to just have a right freedom of speech or association. Different groups had to be more *positively* enabled or promoted, not just *negatively* protected. This positive process demanded a minority policy, often with accompanying funding, for example, for education or language policy.

Debates over *indigenous* groups usually figure in the context of formerly colonized states, with a pre-existing population (that is to say states such as Australia, New Zealand, North America, or Canada). It can also be seen to cover the Catalans, Scottish, Welsh, or Basques. Of course such indigenous groups often form significant minorities. A lot of the discussion in states, such as Australia or New Zealand, focused on claims to traditional land rights, the preservation of culture, financial compensation, and in some cases the exercise of some degree of self-government within those traditional territories. A legal doctrine which figured strongly as a critical background to indigenous claims and colonial doctrine was *terra nullius*, for example, in Australia where land had been considered by the early colonizers as an 'empty territory' with no traditional claimants upon it. In many cases, this doctrine was premised upon a complete misunderstanding of land, property, and ownership amongst, for example, Australian aboriginals. Finally the issue of legal treaties—such as Waitangi in New Zealand—were also made under questionable conditions between colonizers and colonized. This figures as another area for extensive negotiation (see Ivison et al. 2000).

It is important to realize here that much of this debate over minority and indigenous rights drifts in and out of human rights discussion. Not all groups or collective claims (outlined above) are necessarily transmitted in the form of human rights. Far from it, in fact if one examines the history of minority and indigenous group claims, it is only comparatively recently (post-1980) that it has been seriously formulated in terms of human rights. The argument over groups is contentious and there is little settled opinion. The debate usually breaks down into two rather different forms of group category—'self-collecting' and 'other-collecting' groups—only one of which conventionally appears in third-generation human rights debates. Thus, not all collective entities necessarily conform to debates over group rights, let alone human rights. Thus, for example, minimally, crowds or aggregates do not come into the picture. Associations which are formed by states, or through institutional processes (that is *other-collecting* groups), are not seen as relevant to third-generation rights discussion. It is rather groups which, as it were, form themselves (*self-collecting*) on the basis of common ethnicity, culture, or a linguistic basis, which are seen as truly relevant. It is never wholly clear why precisely this is the case, but that is how the debate has been configured (see Vincent 2002, ch. 7)

The debate over collective cultural rights has much wider ramifications in terms of modern understandings of the multicultural conception of the state. However, there is one further crucial distinction here which marks out and, at the same time, raises serious problems about third-generation human rights. The idea of minority or indigenous group rights—whether seen as ethnic, racial, or cultural—can be seen from two very different philosophical perspectives: that of the individual or the collective group. This point has become vital in human rights debate. Most human rights covenants and documentation, which refer to collective group claims, word them in terms of the individual.[15] That is to say, the right is focused on the claim of the *individual as a member of a culture or ethnicity*. This emphasis, for many, accords with the 'individualistic spirit' of the human rights tradition from 1948 and brings third-generation rights more happily into the fold with first- and second-generation claims. The priority always lies therefore with the individual, not the group (see e.g. Wellman 1999; Donnelly 2002).[16] The group or collective interest—say language or culture—thus acquires significance *through* the agency of the individual person.

The alternative formulation—which often saturates the language of certain minority and indigenous group activists on the ground—is that the group interest (tribe, ethnicity, or culture) must take priority to the individual interests.[17] More to the point, the individual is defined *through* the group or collectivity itself. The group is therefore not simply reducible to its membership, it is rather perceived to act in concert. This concerted action is distinct from the actions of the individuals that constitute it. There is, in other words, a recognition of some form of group identity which transcends the individual membership and embodies an internal principle of action. This theme has become more prevalent in the context of the rise of identity politics in the 1990s. In the most extreme example of this argument, groups are seen to have a purpose, intentionality, and even distinct will. This whole debate however throws up an enormous and potentially irresolvable ontological issue, which, in turn, pushes a massive fault line through the whole third-generation debate. Despite the fact that many group rights activists hold something approximating to this latter thesis, the majority of human rights covenants and legal proponents hold the opposite view, which is individualistically based. Many proponents of third-generation rights refuse to face up to this difficult issue.

One additional problem here, which is invoked by this philosophical debate, concerns the precise role of group rights in legal and moral discussion. Again, discussion of third-generation human rights, within existing covenants and documents, sees such rights largely in terms of an *external* protection, and possibly at points where there is external promotion of the individual's group-based interests. The aim is therefore to mainly protect (and occasionally to promote) the individual, in relation to the group, in the context of potential discriminatory actions by majorities within states. However, many ethnic or minority group activists, on the ground, often perceive an additional role for such rights, that is, *internal* control, protection, and promotion of group purposes. The aim then is to utilize such rights to maintain the coherence and unity of the group. This latter activity can involve disciplining, controlling, threatening, or manipulating members of groups to conform to such unified aims. For many more traditional human rights claimants, this latter argument goes totally against the whole spirit of human rights as perceived in 1948, and yet it is nonetheless a powerful dimension of much group right argument.

Group rights have a peculiar chequered history in European thought.[18] Group-based political ideas go back to late-nineteenth-century debates over syndicalism, anarchism, guild socialism, and legal pluralism, although most of these earlier debates over groups, oddly, were not caste in the form of 'cultural' or 'ethnic' groups (see Vincent 1987, ch. 6, 1989). Admittedly group minorities were present in certain contexts, such as the Habsburg Empire or Ottoman Empire, but they did not dominate group discussion at the time. For some, the whole issue of minorities and internal groups (within states or empires) could largely be solved by integrating them into larger political units, such as established nation states. This was a common theme in many writers in the nineteenth and early twentieth century, including most committed liberals. Minorities, in certain political contexts, such as the Hapsburg Empire and Ottoman Empire, were recognized to a degree and their interests were balanced with the institutional framework; however, this was more of an exception to the unifying and assimilation trends of states in the late eighteenth and nineteenth century. Minorities were also occasionally used as a pretext for intervention by states. This was the unusual nineteenth-century beginning of humanitarian intervention. More notoriously, in the twentieth century, this humanitarian claim to help a minority through external intervention can be seen in the German intervention in Czechoslovakia in the 1930s.

Post-1918, minorities became a subject for the League of Nations, which aimed to give protective guarantees to certain minority interests in, for example, Poland, Czechoslovakia, Romania, Greece, and Austria. The League also established supervisory functions and procedures for minorities to register complaints. The ILO also looked at the indigenous and minority issue, although primarily in terms of labour rights. Aspects of the role of the ILO were taken over later by the Human Rights Commission. Post-1945, minority concerns did see terminological changes. The term 'ethnic' was commonly substituted for race and to a degree for nationality. However,

European human rights discussion still used the word 'national', for example, the Framework Convention for the Protection of National Minorities (1994). The word culture seems also to have a 'covering' facility for European human rights drafters. It appears as a convenient ersatz substitute for ethnic, religious, and sub-national issues. As indicated earlier though, the 1948 Universal Declaration was chary of group rights and minority claims. The idea does appear very tentatively in Article 27, which states that, 'Everyone has the right to participate in the cultural life of the community', although one could hardly call it a fulsome commitment to cultural or group rights. It is more of a basic commitment to non-discrimination and equality *for the individual agent*. It is also difficult to know which community is being referred to, vis-à-vis it could be simply referring to the majority national community, which for many is the only viable community. Despite this, a sub-committee of minorities—the Sub-Commission on Prevention of Discrimination and Protection of Minorities—was established by the UN Economic and Social Council in 1947. Some scholars have also suggested that recognition of cultural group rights is implicit in some early covenants, particularly the Genocide Convention (1948). The prevention of genocide can appear to subscribe indirectly to group rights, insofar as it tries to prevent harm to groups within states. Yet, it is largely a negative and protective measure, requiring states to abstain from such action. It also aims to protect, primarily individuals—who are members of stigmatized groups—from genocide. It is also clear that the notion of group rights has no connection whatsoever with the original intentions of the framers of the Genocide Convention.

The idea of cultural rights is mentioned in later human rights documents, for example, in the 1989 Protocol (the Protocol of San Salvador), and added to the Inter-American Convention on Human Rights (1969). The African Charter also has a section on cultural rights. However, the most explicit, widely referred to, and most extensively quoted human rights article on this issue is Article 27 of the ICCPR (1966), which states that, 'In those States in which ethnic, religious or linguistic minorities exist, persons belonging to such minorities shall not be denied the right, in community with the other members of their group, to enjoy their own culture, to profess and practise their own religion, or to use their own language.' This is now more commonly seen as an overt attempt to give some protections to cultural groupings in international law. Although, it is important to remind ourselves, once again, of the wording: it is still for the sake of 'persons belonging to such minorities'.[19] The wording may look innocuous, but it is not. The clause exists for the sake of *individual persons*, not *groups*. Further, as the article indicates, it is states which can still determine (to a significant degree) whether such minority or indigenous groups actually exist.[20] This, in itself, is enormously significant. In sum, this is basically the only human rights clause, between 1945 and 1989, which explicitly mentions minorities in human rights vocabulary, although as indicated the clause still remains cryptic, focused on persons and implying state recognition of groups.

One other fortuitous coincidence here is the coalescence of group rights ideas with those of self-determination. The coalescence occurs in the ICCPR (where Article 27 appears). However, both the ICCPR (1966) and the ICESCR (1966) begin with an identical assertion: 'All peoples have the right of self-determination. By virtue of that right they freely determine their political status and freely pursue their economic, social and cultural development' (that is Article 1 in both covenants). The historical and international context for this at the time was decolonization and suspicion over the legacy of European imperialism in Africa and Asia. The above clause, in respect of decolonizing associations, reflected the intellectual and political mood of that moment, where decolonizing peoples were seen to be articulating the right of self-determination. Putting aside any overt debate of self-determination, it was the serial ambiguity of words such as 'peoples' and 'self-determination', combined with the cryptic quality of the ICCPR's Article 27, which allowed, by the 1990s, a subtle slippage and transference of the older 1960s anti-colonial language of self-determination and ethnic autonomy into 'internal' arguments about groups and minorities 'within' existing states. This slippage is of course as worrying (if not more worrying) to the decolonized states, as it is to the older ex-colonial states. Self-determination, cultural autonomy, and group rights language are promiscuous discourses which show little discrimination for their partners. In many decolonized states, it raised this issue of further rupture and secession with regard to indigenous and sub-national groups.

If one were to try to summarize the impact of third-generation debates, then a convenient way of thinking about them would be in terms of two *waves*. The first wave was between 1948 and 1976. It was the period of decolonization and the end of empires. African and Asian nations, many recently freed from colonial rule, entered the UN. They supported the human rights enterprise, but modified to reflect their own concerns, that is finishing off colonialism, criticizing apartheid in South Africa, and condemning all forms of racial discrimination. The 1966/1976 Covenants, to an extent, reflect some of these concerns. Both have articles asserting rights of peoples to self-determination and to control their own natural resources. Rights against discrimination were also given prominence. This first wave was though only half committed to the notion of group rights per se. If anything it simply prepared the ground for future developments.

The second wave, from the late 1980s to the present day, has seen cultural- and group-focused arguments come to the fore. In 1984, for example, the Islamic Republic of Iran announced that it would not recognize any human rights principles which were contrary to the principles of Islam. This trend became more widespread after the World Conference on Human Rights in

Vienna in 1993. The conference, although affirming the universality of human rights, nonetheless conceded that 'norm-setting' often had a more particularist and cultural background (see Freeman 2002, 48). This period has largely seen a celebration of cultural difference, a proliferation of anti-universalist argument and attempts to modify and adapt human rights to local cultural concerns. However, this second wave of culturalist debates subsequently quickly broke down into three separate lines of argument which are often confused: first, there was the claim that that all minorities, indigenous, and culture groups should be accorded a human rights status as groups. This argument is one which underpins much discussion of third-generation rights, although it often fails to really take on board what is actually meant by this claim. Second, there is an overwhelmingly more negative argument that human rights are really only cultural expressions. The outcome of this assertion is unpredictable as regards human rights discourse. The third, more subtle and positive line of argument claims that human rights ought to find the bulk of their value resource within cultures. This latter argument is still compatible with a universalist argument for human rights.

Third-generation rights are the least well-articulated and least well-explained dimension of contemporary human rights. Some suggest that they should simply be seen in the context of basic equality and non-discrimination; thus, they are an uncomplicated and understandable extension of first-generation rights. In this sense, the language of separate generations might be viewed as both spurious and unhelpful. There is *no* succession of generations. This later judgement could mean though two things. First, it might imply optimistically that all such rights should be integrated into one singular rich conception (see Shue 1980). The second meaning is that there is absolutely no need for third-generation collective rights. It is an unhelpful 'non-category' which spoils a useful concept of human rights and is an example of the obstructive post-1945 proliferation of rights-talk. Indeed, such third-generation rights potentially undermine the good offices of first-generation, and possibly even second-generation, rights by prioritizing the group over the individual.[21] There is clearly a large difference of opinion between third-generation proponents and the legal framers of human rights covenants, particularly over the issue of to whom such rights benefit and apply. Further, there is a continuing puzzle and lack of agreement as to what a 'group', 'culture', or 'people' actually mean as collective entities, and whether such entities can logically be said to have rights in the first place, and, even if they do claim rights, whether collective human rights are simply a category mistake.[22] It is also not clear what the precise criteria for a group are, that is to say, is it something that one is 'thrown' into, or is it something one could intend to join? Further, it is also not clear what these collective rights imply; namely, are they negative or positive in nature and what are the duties which might be said to correlate with such rights? Collective third-generation rights in this case remain both indistinct and deeply contested and yet oddly they continue creating high expectations well into the 2000s.[23] The fashion now is for the particularity of cultures and identity politics and woe betide anyone who disagrees.[24]

## FURTHER GENERATIONS?

Before moving to debates over the relation between generations, it is prudent to indicate that the generational rights arguments do not necessarily stop at the third-generation level. There are prospective fourth or even fifth generations lurking in the wings. Whether they will ever appear is extremely doubtful. The arguments here centre on forms of moral extensionism. The optimistic reading of this issue focuses on a progressive extension of the application of moral terms. Thus, the argument is that there has been an evolution within our ethical and legal sensibilities, over the last 300–400 years, which has seen the gradual widening of the circle of things that can be included. Initially rights would only be conferred on adult male property owners in, say, the seventeenth century. This was then extended to those without property, then to former slaves, women, non-Europeans, and children. The argument contends that there is no overriding reason as to why our moral sensibilities and our application of rights could not be extended or evolve therefore to animals or even to the environment.

There are many arguments here that have been widely discussed on the question of animals. If, for example, one asks a very basic question: why do we value human life, such as to attribute fundamental rights to it, then a number of possible answers arise which have ramification stretching beyond human beings. Thus, the argument is that if we examine arguments about value carefully then it is not humans, in themselves, as say a particular genetic or biological species, which give rise to value, rather it is certain attributes or capacities they possess which form the ground of value. Thus, if one uses *sentience* as the criterion of value, that is to say, the capability of having sensuous experience, and therefore possibly the capacity to have interests and preferences, then there is no obvious reason (on this particular sentience criterion) why animals would not be included. Thus, if sentience is the criterion of value and the premise for the attribution of right, then animals have rights. A similar argument can be pushed from a more deontic angle. If the capacity to make choices, exercise autonomy, possess self-consciousness and language ability are the criteria for identifying the value of agents or persons, and that such personhood and agency are the grounds for the attribution of rights, then it follows, again, that not only are there many humans who do not qualify for personhood or agency (the very young or old, severely handicapped, and so forth), but that many animals, that is higher primates or dolphins, seem to qualify for personhood and agency. In this case, animals also possess rights from a different core of value argument focusing on agency. There could therefore be non-human persons with rights. Of course, if we insist that to have a right means to be able to perform a duty, then this in turn rules out an enormous number of human beings from the rights sphere. In this context there is a body of argument which might suggest that the fourth generation of human rights—although we would have to recast the nomenclature of 'human' rights—concerns the universal rights of animals and that we might look forward to future covenants on this issue.

The arguments do not stop here. Another sphere of rights discussion flows from the recognized importance of human rights. Thus, the UN inspired Brundtland Report linked sustainable development and human rights with the environment. The authors comment: 'All human beings have the fundamental right to an environment adequate for their health and well-being' (Brundtland 1987, 348).[25] More substantial arguments have been made for this latter development. Thus, it is clear that humans are not only embedded in communities, but they are also ecologically embedded. In fact, the latter embeddedness is a crucial criterion of human well-being. Thus, 'we cannot wholly conceptualize what a person is in abstraction from their social belonging and spatio-temporal location and physical being' (Benton 1993, 184). Humans are simply part of the natural order of the world, they are not morally prior to it. We have organic needs which rest ultimately upon a clean and sustainable environment. Like any species we are embodied and we subsist in a particular ecological space or habitat. This argument also has direct implications for animals in general. All species including humans have such habitat requirements. In sum, if the human has value and we wish to discuss the issue of human rights, we are faced with the argument that humans, like all animals, are always embodied in a particular organic habitat and that human well-being is irrevocably and organically tied to the flourishing of this ecological habitat. If humans possess a fundamental value, then we have, derivatively, fundamental rights to uncontaminated food, air, water, and soil. The right to the environmental conditions of organic well-being is therefore crucial. These are of equal importance to any first-generation civil and political rights. Indeed they can be seen as a logical extension of earlier commitments to rights. As civil and political rights have been supplemented and developed in social and economic rights, and these again by cultural group rights, then in future, animals and ultimately the environment (the ecology of our habitat) could be part of our human rights culture. In this context the rights of a sustainable environment could theoretically be seen as the fifth generation of human rights, although it looks highly unlikely.

# Substantive arguments over generational rights

Although there are a wide range of arguments over extending our moral and legal sensibilities, as yet they have not figured in any really substantive debates over human rights. Indeed, many of the more substantive arguments—as to what particularly might be ratified as a legitimate human right—have not really been settled in the first-, second-, or third-generation categories. This would particularly be the case in the debates between first- and second-generation rights. There are still some who think that only first-generation rights can qualify as genuine universalizable human rights and that social and economic human rights are a travesty (see Cranston 1973, 65). Some have conceptualized this shift as one from general universal human rights (usually understood as civil and political liberties and powers) to special or highly contextual social and economic welfare-based rights. The more recent interest in third-generation rights could be classified merely as an extension of such 'special' contextual rights.

The earlier debates from the 1950s and 1960s over differences between first- and second-generations claims, although frequently set against the background of cold war conflicts between the United States and Soviet Union, nonetheless, as indicated earlier, have wider implications for internal policy debates within North America and European states. The debates focus largely on the nature and ends of the state and public policy. Such debates have a distinctively ideological character. The arguments break down fairly crudely into two positions, one which asserts that there has been a radical shift of human rights argument from general defensible political and civil rights towards a regime of contextual special rights which are ideologically suspect. The other argues that there is no radical shift at all, but rather a process of enrichment of a singular but compound concept of human right.

The radical shift argument found considerable ideological sustenance from those who opposed welfare arguments in general. In this sense, the 1980s were a fertile area for interpreting human rights in a very specific way. The phenomenon of the new right during this period (although in itself internally complex), nonetheless often configured rights in this very particular manner. Theorists, such as Robert Nozick, Hillel Steiner, Friedrich Hayek, Tibor Machan, amongst many others, have thought of rights largely in terms of general negative constraints which protect individuals and their property from the redistributive policies of welfare states and social justice regimes.[26] As Steiner comments, for example, the 'job of rights,...is to demarcate domains—spheres of practical choice within which the choices made by designated individuals (and groups) must not be subjected to interference'. Rights therefore 'reserve parts of the world to their owners' discretion' (Steiner 1998, 238). These general rights are also linked conceptually to ideas on negative freedom. A general right is thus envisaged as a personal space surrounding the individual agent which ought to remain sacrosanct, unless they intentionally harm others. The duty characterizing others is usually one of forbearance. In many ways this latter argument has become a 'stock-in-trade' feature of the ideological 'new right' and the large bulk of neo-liberal theorizing.

In the domain of human rights discussion the 'radical shift' argument was usually formulated in terms of an alteration from *general* rights (understood as civil and political liberties and powers) to *special* social and economic human rights. Later examples of special rights would be the cultural rights of minorities. This would be the case unless one interpreted such third-generation rights as simply 'negative entitlements' which implied protection of freedom of choice. In this latter context, a cultural right would be interpreted as an extension of a first-generation civil right to basic liberty. One has a basic right in this sense to enjoy one's group culture as long as one is not harming others. However, any implication that such a right carries any positive connotations to, for example, financial assistance or even legal self-determination would tend to drive it out of this general domain.

In summary, a *general* right is held intrinsically by an individual human agent. Such rights are comparatively few if fundamental. Such rights are asserted when an 'unjustified interference' is intended by another. It is general in terms of applying to all humans *qua* humans (thus, it can be seen as constitutive of being human). It is negative and protective and held against others. Such general human rights are brought with the human agent into social, economic, or cultural practices, but they are not dependent on those practices. They are ontologically independent and pristine. The next stage of this radical shift argument is to indicate that there have been subtle but definite modifications in human rights language. Human rights have mutated illegitimately into *special* rights, which are wholly dependent on established practices. In other words, they are dependent upon social, economic, or cultural contexts for meaning, reference, and application. *Special rights* are thus rights which presuppose, for example, that certain social and economic resources exist. Such rights are therefore unique, promotional, positive in character, and wholly dependent upon certain kinds of social collectivities for their realization. Those who hold to the radical shift argument have frequently illustrated the argument by reference to differences between the various articles from rights declarations. Some indeed see particular continuities between the original eighteenth-century natural rights declarations and the UDHR.[27]

One of the common critical arguments one finds here is that a failure to distinguish *general* and *special* rights has potentially regrettable consequences. The argument that validates special rights as human rights signifies that, for example, developing societies which maintain courageously a regime of general human rights (and a general rule of law structure) could still potentially be vilified for being unable to meet the costs of, say, universal medical services or pensions. Thus, the failure to uphold special rights leads to a more wholesale condemnation of that regime. However, more developed economies, with politically autocratic regimes, who ignore the general rights (such as the general liberty of the person), could nonetheless still provide well-funded medical services, holidays, or unemployment insurance and could thus claim to be fulfilling special human right demands, certainly as much as any developing societies in the 'general' domain. Some see this scenario as profoundly obtuse. It appears to give a human rights imprimatur to political autocracy and fails to show any sensitivity in its handling of developing regimes who are struggling towards human rights and the rule of law.

The key point of this argument is that it is only the general first-generation claims which are genuine human rights. In a nutshell—and corresponding to a large degree with aspects of the ideological turn of the 1980s—economic and social rights do not conform to fundamental human interests. Further, special rights are not feasible empirically in many developing states and to try to realize them would be too burdensome and unrealistic for many governments and taxpayers. In addition, proponents of the radical shift argument have suggested that there are certain conceptual tests which differentiate between general and special claims. These tests would enable us therefore to differentiate, in essence, between genuine human rights and other kinds of right category. These would be the practicability, paramount importance, and universalizability tests. The practicability test argues that it must be possible for all human beings to be guaranteed the right in question. The paramount importance test argues that the right must be such that no one could be deprived of it without a grave affront to basic justice and human dignity. The universalizability test argues that the right in question must be possessed by all human beings, universally, simply by virtue of being human.

As regards the practicability test: the critics of special rights argue that it is technically impossible for everyone to have social security, pensions, and the like. These special rights require a certain level of gross national product (GNP). This is not therefore a practical policy option in many states. However, one must ask another related question here: is the maintenance of general human rights (life, liberty, speech, fair trial, security of person) really inexpensive? Surely it is a basic fact that such general rights require legal structures, legislatures, courts, judges, advocates, policing frameworks, military forces, and a massive array of training and regulatory mechanisms, all implied by the latter processes. It hardly needs stating here that all these processes are phenomenally expensive. Thus, why is it practicable to spend exceptional resources on general rights, but not on special rights to, say, basic medical, social security, or educational services? There seems to be no reasonable answer to this question other than the ideological preferences of policy-makers.[28] It is not therefore a question of actual practicability, but conversely a basic unwillingness rooted in alternative value priorities. The reasons are not therefore economic or technical, but normative. Moving to the second paramount importance test. Again, the question needs to be broadened. The suggestion of the radical shift proponent is that it is a much more serious issue to deprive someone of their liberty or freedom of speech, than to allow them to remain in poverty. The crucial question to be asked here is therefore: is social and economic deprivation not a grave affront to justice and human dignity? It is not at all clear why the radical shift proponent would argue that an infringement of general rights is more of an affront to human dignity, than for someone, say, to be condemned to lifelong poverty and deprivation. This is not though a claim for either one or the other. It is rather a contention that both are of importance. Why therefore should welfare rights not be accorded paramount importance equally with the general rights to life or liberty?

Finally, what of the issue of universalizability? In a similar vein to the above discussion, some would argue that unemployment benefit or medical services are dependent on the basic ability of a society to pay. If developing societies do not have this ability, then such special rights cannot pass the universalizability test. Yet, once again, surely not everyone can, hypothetically, afford fair trials, guarantees of free speech, protection of property, and the diverse services involved in such practices. These are not necessarily any more universalizable than medical or suchlike services. In this context, general human rights do not necessarily pass the universalizability test any more than special human rights.

In summary, it is very questionable as to whether the conceptual tests make any secure case for drawing clear distinctions between general and special rights. The effect of the tests is highly unpredictable. Thus, the radical shift argument looks unstable. The tests certainly do not allow us to weed out genuine human rights from more special welfare-orientated social and economic rights. If anything the conclusion would be that all human rights have political, economic, and social implications for states.

Another important critical response to the 'radical shift' argument takes up an underlying intuition which frequently intrudes into the above discussions. The intuition focuses on the key question as to whether the distinction between general and special rights actually makes any sense. A number of comparatively recent theorists have therefore argued that the distinctions between separate generations of human rights, and those between special and general human rights, are all basically deeply misleading if not false. The basic issue is that in the same way that we might be said to need rights to liberty and fair trial, we also equally need basic guarantees of material and economic subsistence (see Shue 1980, 178; Davidson 1993; Freeman 2002, 71; Orend 2002, 111ff.; Tomuschat 2003, 46; Donnelly 2002, 65).

The gist of the above view is that human rights are justified insofar as they protect everyone's access to a set of objects which are seen as necessary for being fully human. Humans are always finite and needy creatures. Human rights protect those things which are vital for human existence. To live requires certain necessary conditions to be met. Some conditions are necessary for enjoying any right; therefore, every human being has a right to these 'other things' which are necessary for enjoying a right. This argument constitutes the essence of Henry Shue's distinction between basic and non-basic rights. Basic rights allow us to exercise non-basic rights (see Shue 1980, 9, 34–6). Liberty alone—contra Herbert Hart's argument—is not enough (see Hart 1955). Liberty requires not just opportunities and forbearance from others, but also basic sustenance, security, health, and moderate physical well-being. Someone who is physically famished will not be capable of realizing or appreciating free speech. In other words, even if one acknowledged some distinction between special and general rights, nonetheless special rights are only fleshing out or giving a more concrete substance to general rights. All three generations of rights are therefore seen to be entailed by a basic respect for life and human dignity. As Shue indicates, this would then imply a range of negative and positive duties, consequent upon holding the enriched notion of human rights: that is, negative duties to refrain, positive duties to protect, and positive duties to aid (see Shue 1980, 54ff.). Minimally, one could still acknowledge that general civil rights might imply more abstentions than anything else (although even this is questionable), and that second-generation special rights imply more positive actions. However, this still does not mean that both categories cannot still fruitfully be seen as part of the same basic human right. For those who deny the terms of the 'radical shift' argument, there is then a general acceptance that each of the generations of human rights is required for an acceptable concept of human rights.

# Conclusion

In all the above-mentioned argumentation on the generations issue a great deal depends on how one conceives the concept of right itself. There is a tendency for many to view rights as simply highly general, negative side-constraints. The function of a right is primarily passive or protective. This has been particularly characteristic of forms of classical liberalism over the last fifty years. This notion of right also fits fairly precisely with one reading of the concept of the rule of law. The origin of this sense of right has family resemblances to earlier constitutional declarations of natural right in the eighteenth century. There is undoubtedly a focus on life, liberty, free elections, trial by jury, respect for property, free speech and press, and so forth, in these earlier declarations. This is reflected again in the UDHR.[29] However, there is no explicit or developed discussion in the eighteenth-century declarations of the material welfare or economic security of individuals, except in a negative protective sense. Basically property and the person are protected. This rendering of first-generation rights arises from the development of constitutional and later liberal-constitutional understandings of the state and citizenship in the eighteenth and early nineteenth century. In many ways this concept of civil right is the most basic position on right developed in the majority of Western states.

This fairly long-standing tradition of first-generation civil-orientated rights encouraged certain mid- to late twentieth-century liberal critics to disparage more *positively* orientated second-generation social and economic rights. This disparagement was, as argued, rooted in the ideological structure of constitutionalism and classical liberalism. The fundamental correlative issue for such first-generation rights proponents concerns duties of forbearance in others, that is, correlated to negative general protective rights. In essence, respecting human rights and human dignity implies leaving the individual alone. Given then that many second-generation rights tend to be more overtly positive and potentially interventionary, this immediately creates conceptual and practical problems for classical liberal critics. Second-generation human rights, focused positively on the social and economic welfare of the individual, are very much a product of the early to mid-twentieth-century commitment to the concept of the welfare state. As indicated in the previous section—on the question as to whether one should separate out the various generations of rights—there is no necessity (as argued by Shue 1980; Donnelly 2002) to divide the more constitutionally orientated civil rights from social and economic welfare rights. Although certain liberal writers have striven to keep them apart, there are grounds for seeing them as symbiotically contributing to the same enriched human rights end. Whatever the conclusion is to this debate, it is still undeniable that there is a frequently suppressed ideological dimension to much human rights arguments. Thus, a debate over first- and second-generation human rights is often—by other means and in a different setting—a debate between classical liberal and social democratic ideological theories.

A resonant argument has arisen over third-generation rights, although to some extent these latter arguments have become bogged down in recent internal wrangling over culture wars. Some conceptualize third-generation rights in protective negative terms. These claims then become re-assimilated into first-generation rights. The decisive issue becomes the individual's civil freedom to choose—the culture or group interest is just the choice an individual makes. Rights then remain indifferent to culture. Others have implied that third-generation rights are linked to second-generation economic and social rights, insofar as they are conditional aspects of a meaningful human life. Like material welfare—vis-à-vis the work of Shue—cultural well-being is seen to be a crucial feature of human functioning. It is thus a necessary prerequisite of being human. Others again see group, cultural, and minority rights as a unique conception of human rights. In this context such third-generation rights are differentiated conceptually from first- and second-generation rights. This argument usually then moves third-generation deliberations into the sphere of multicultural and difference-based arguments—characteristic of a number of debates over the 1990s and 2000s. All the above renderings of these theories have subtle links with arguments concerning the character of the state and citizenship. This latter point will be explored in chapter 8.

In conclusion, the aim of this chapter has been to fill in certain gaps in the discussion of human rights by discussing the more popular format of human rights debate in terms of the three generations. No firm stand has been initially taken on this debate. However, the discussion has raised doubts about any complete separation of rights generations, and about the fundamental veracity of any one particular generational conception. The argument has though acknowledged that there are different ways in which rights can and do function in legal and political discourse. Further, no claims are made about philosophical priorities, or about any hierarchy amongst these rights. There are, and inevitably will be, continuous conflicts and jockeying between these various generational arguments. This is not something to be overly concerned about. All such rights are part of political life and such political life within civil states is always characterized by disagreement.[30] Human rights, at all levels, provide the conditions and often substance for such public debates. One key underlying supposition in the present chapter is that each of the generational arguments is rooted in slightly different conceptions of the substance of the state. This argument reinforces the point that there are no external regulative moral standards which characterize human rights. There are conversely normative standards which are part of what a state (or statelike entity) ought to be. They may have universal significance, but they are still not outside the state tradition per se.

## ☐ NOTES

1. Although at the same time states were the key upholders of the UN.

2. The attentive reader will immediately note an oddity in my argument, concerning what has already been argued about the state in respect of nation and race. However, it has been argued at a number of key points that the state is not the same category as the nation state or race state. The self-determining nation state is the root of the problem for human rights. The state conversely is the core to the possibility of human rights.

3. The 1776 Virginia Declaration of Rights states, 'That all men are by nature equally free and independent, and have certain inherent rights, of which, when they enter into a state of

society, they cannot by any compact deprive or divest their posterity; namely, the enjoyment of life and liberty, with the means of acquiring and possessing property, and pursuing and obtaining happiness and safety.'

4. Some of the issues which spin off from these rights to liberty are free elections, free speech, and a free press.

5. There is of course an enormous debate about what is basic. The classic study of basic rights is Shue (1980). The Magna Carta point can be found in a number of sources (see Davidson 1993, 5ff.; Wellman 1999, 16).

6. Although even many of these can be set aside in situations of emergency; see, for example, Article 4 of the ICCPR.

7. The ICESCR's list of rights includes non-discrimination and equality for women in the economic and social area (Articles 2 and 3), freedom to work and opportunities to work (Article 4), fair pay and decent conditions of work (Article 7), the right to form trade unions and to strike (Article 8), social security (Article 9), special protections for mothers and children (Article 10), the right to adequate food, clothing, and housing (Article 11), the right to basic health services (Article 12), the right to education (Article 13), and the right to participate in cultural life and scientific progress (Article 15).

8. It was not incorporated in France into the Constitution of the Fourth Republic. It was rather relegated to the Preamble.

9. In fact the UDHR does mention social and economic rights. The UN Charter (1945) also committed signatories to promote a 'higher standard of living, full employment, and conditions of economic and social progress and development'.

10. Apparently still contentious for the British Conservative Party in 2010.

11. The United States is the state which most 'resolutely rejects economic and social benefits as constitutional entitlements' (Tomuschat 2003, 28).

12. In the older Federal Republic of Germany the social question was kept apart from the Basic Law, although the social state was nonetheless still affirmed. In France the social dimension was only integrated constitutionally in 1971 (see Tomuschat 2003, n. 6, 27).

13. '[T]he common claim is that Asian societies are communitarian and consensual and Western societies are individualistic and competitive. What exactly is this supposed to explain... Dutch or Norwegian politics is at least as consensual as Thai politics. The Dutch welfare state is in its own way as caring and paternalistic as the most traditional of Japanese employers. Such examples are easily multiplied' (see Donnelly 2002, 97).

14. There was a proposal relating to minorities, yet 'as the draft proposal went from one committee to the next, it was edited and finally removed altogether... recognizing diversity was construed as inviting instability' (see Jackson-Preece 2003, 57).

15. As one commentator notes, 'both liberal philosophy and international practice directed at human rights have been historically ill disposed to minority problems' (Jackson-Preece 2003, 50).

16. For Carl Wellman, for example, only individual moral agents possess moral rights: 'every right includes liberties and powers, and one exercises a liberty or power by acting in the appropriate manner.... Because I believe that groups, including peoples, are incapable of acting collectively, I deny that a people as such could have any moral rights' (Wellman 1999, 35).

17. A moral philosopher such as Peter French holds that it is possible to make the strong case for group rights, where groups would be understood as moral persons (see French 1984). For discussion of the broad debates around this issue, see Vincent (1989).

18. These can be traced back to sixteenth- and seventeenth-century debates over religious minorities.

19. One can see this emphasis throughout the ICCPR document. Thus, Article 2 notes that (my italics): 'Each State Party to the present Covenant undertakes to respect and to ensure to all *individuals* within its territory and subject to its jurisdiction the rights recognized in the present Covenant, without distinction of any kind, such as race, colour, sex, language, religion, political or other opinion, national or social origin, property, birth or other status.'

20. Even in Europe there was a tendency between 1945 and 1989 to play down minority rights 'due to the widespread fear that this might rekindle old ethnic conflicts' (Jackson-Preece 2003, 58).

21. Standard individual rights can be especially significant for ethnic and religious minorities, particularly rights to freedom of association, freedom of assembly, freedom of religion, and freedom from discrimination, although once again, most human rights documents phrase this in terms of the individual's right (as a member group).

22. One possible way around part of this dilemma is to see rights in terms of 'interests' or 'benefits'. This links in with what was discussed in chapter 1 in terms of the benefit or interest theory of rights. An interest can be seen as part of an individual's good. A right can therefore be seen as an interest or benefit-based reason. This, in turn, can imply duties in others to protect or promote that interest. Some of these interests might *only* be enjoyed in common with others (in groups). Therefore, there can be collective goods for individuals which imply collective rights (see Waldron 1993). I am not convinced though that this really encompasses the ontological *spirit* of group rights. Once again, the latter argument views rights largely through the lens of individual interests. The group is not a prior interest to the individual.

23. In fact a number of academics, most prominently Will Kymlicka, have made a career of promoting such cultural rights. Others have made an equally strong reputation for opposing them (see Barry 2001).

24. The fashion though is more of an intellectual stance than a political reality.

25. A 1972 UN Conference on the Human Environment in Stockholm also affirmed that a right to an adequate sustainable environment must appear firmly on the agenda of future human rights debates. The issue of global warming has recently focused more attention on this domain.

26. Such negative rights theories were often formulated in terms of 'choice-based theory' of rights (see chapter 1).

27. Thus, the UDHR opens with the rousing words: 'All human beings are born free and equal in dignity and rights. They are endowed with reason and conscience and should act towards one another in a spirit of brotherhood.' It continues, in Article 3, 'Everyone has the right to life, liberty and security of person.' These *general* civil rights to freedom, dignity, life, and security of person are also seen to be present in earlier declarations. For example, the Virginia Declaration of 1776 begins with the statement: 'That all men are by nature equally free and independent, and have certain inherent rights, of which,

when they enter into a state of society, they cannot by any compact deprive or divest their posterity; namely, the enjoyment of life and liberty, with the means of acquiring and possessing property, and pursuing and obtaining happiness and safety.' The same point holds for the American Declaration of 1776. However, for critics, the UDHR, particularly from Article 22 onward, initiates another category of *special* right which has no precedent in the earlier charters. Thus, Article 22 of the UDHR declares that 'Everyone, as a member of society, has a right to social security.' Article 23 focuses on the 'right to work'. Article 24 embodies the favourite bugbear for 'radical shift' critics—the human right to leisure and holidays. Article 26 opines on the right to education. Many of these latter rights are given a more thorough rendering in the ICESCR. For critics, these latter human rights instigate a new category of right. It is a notion of right which is wholly dependent on particular social, economic, and institutional practices for its realization.

28. Unless one argued that civil order and the rule of law must precede any other kind of rights regime.

29. Although whether the reasons for these rights declarations are the same is open to scholarly debate.

30. 'At best, rights create a common framework, a common set of reference points, that can assist parties in conflict to deliberate together' (Ignatieff 2003, 20).

# 6 The Political Dialectic of Human Rights

The argument expounded in this chapter takes up the theme that the state tradition stands in a paradoxical relation with the human rights tradition during the twentieth and twenty-first centuries. Politics is the key to this relation. If we focus simply on the moral or legal dimensions of the state tradition, we miss the point. The state is primarily a political entity—although the notion of politics itself carries moral and legal implications. My baseline argument focuses on the paradox of the state being both subject and object of human right. The civil state tradition, in particular, embodies a complex range of limitations contained within a legal framework. My argument is that human rights are part of the configuration of the civil state—understood politically. However, as discussed, there is another powerful aspect of the state tradition in the nineteenth and twentieth centuries which overlaps with the civil tradition, that is, the organic nation-state theory. What characterizes this latter theory is a constellation of interests focusing on issues such as nationalism, culture, identity, and race, which have often claimed to be a 'natural' language of the state. Both of these dimensions of the state tradition configure understandings of citizenship, rights, and law. These latter two dimensions should also be kept distinct from the wide range of groupings and organizations which appear and would like to be considered as states (and are often treated as such in both UN practices and in much international relations vocabulary), but are, in point, not-yet-states or quasi-states. They are agglomerations of various kinds of autocracies, tyrannies, military dictatorships, juntas, and the like. We should not expect any serious rights or coherent legal processes (domestic or international) to arise from these associations. In fact, it is doubtful whether we could say that politics genuinely exists in these settings.

As argued in chapter 4, genocide has had a very intimate relation with the practice of the state. Genocide is largely an activity of a *form of state*. There is no reason though that genocide might not arise from those groupings or institutions, referred to above, which are attempting to approximate to statehood, that is, autocracies and the like. In the latter case, though, because of the frequent disorganization and chaos of the quasi-state apparatus, genocide is never as systematic or wholesale as one finds in developed nation states. My argument would be that genocide is an issue largely of the developed organic nation state—a state manifest particularly through its interest in nationality, culture, identity, or race. It is the national, cultural, identity-based or racialized practice of the state, which is the primary carrier of geno-cide. The fragile solution, in part, to genocide—and the major carrier of the human rights argument—lies in the civil state tradition. The focus therefore falls on the state and, more significantly, the civil state tradition. The civil state is not simply a legalistic notion. It is rather a political idea which, by default, raises serious questions about the role of practices such as culture, religion, and nationalism in relation to both the state and human rights.

## Politics and modernity

Politics has had a complex career as a concept. The genealogy of the concept will not be traced here; rather the focus will be on aspects of its usage in the nineteenth and twentieth centuries. From the nineteenth century, in the Anglo-European context, until the mid-twentieth century, the idea and prac-tice of politics have been predominantly associated with the state or the nation state.[1] To learn about politics therefore was to learn about the state (or the relation of states if one were examining international law or international politics), and the state meant not only to account for its various empirical and constitutional forms, but also to study the conceptions of right embodied within it. This state idea became a mainstay of disciplines such as political science, history, law, and sociology from the mid-nineteenth century well into the twentieth century. As Max Weber, for example, noted, 'politics' for modernity was something which was therefore focused primarily on the 'state' (Weber 1970, 77–8). Politics, for Weber, could be associated either with *government*, as a specialized sphere (as distinct from other spheres, such as the economy), or it could be seen as transcending government, namely, some-thing that forms the continuity of a public authority, which is then invoked *by* governments. For Weber, the state could not be understood through any end or telos, since, as he suggests, 'there is scarcely any task that...[it] has not taken in hand' (Weber 1970, 77). Weber thus preferred to define it in terms of the 'means' specific to it, that is, its monopoly of physical force or domination. This was not an arbitrary force for Weber. Rather, the state 'is considered the sole source of the "right" to use violence. Hence, "politics" for us means striving to share power or striving to influence the distribution of power, either among states or among groups within a state'. A state is thus a 'relation of men dominating men, a relation supported by means of legitimate vio-lence' (Weber 1970, 78). The key point to be underscored here is that politics, particularly since the nineteenth century, and indeed prior to that, has been associated with the state or the nation state (see Vincent 1987, 2002, ch. 2).

One key assumption of this study is that politics, although linked closely with the state, also focuses on certain crucial aspects of human association. Politics, in effect, anticipates that all human association involves latent conflict, divisiveness, indeterminacy, and uncertainty. This is envisaged as the character of human coexistence. Politics is thus premised on the variables of collective human coexistence; more importantly, politics, per se, is a way of addressing this plural coexistence. Politics, in this sense, is a way of mobilizing or withholding support, distributing significance, maintaining stability, establishing competences, constructing patterns of order, and utilizing collective power.[2] Politics embodies, therefore, *both* the fact of conflict and plural uncertainty *and* its possible mediation. Politics, in itself, is not a means to something else, some moral value, although certain types of institutional arrangement, facilitated by politics in liberal democracies, can and do merge contingently with aspects of such value.[3] Politics in its everyday manifestation can be crude, apparently amoral at times, frustratingly ineffective, and it regularly invokes a range of skills which can indeed look, at times, morally disquieting. As Stuart Hampshire comments, as human beings 'we are not masterpieces in our lives, and the lives of communities are not master classes. We look for some relaxation of tension, but, until death, we do not expect the neat disappearance of conflict and of tension, whether in the soul or in society' (Hampshire 1999, 40). Conflict, indeterminacy, and uncertainty, in themselves, are not a sign of any deep problem. This does not entail a Hobbesian war or threat of war, it simply implies—what all notions of justice imply—that there will always be scarcity, moderate selfishness, and limited altruism in all human coexistence, which needs to be mediated. What is also distinctive about politics, as a mode of coexistence, is that it is the modus operandi through which pluralism is also mediated. Politics constitutes a public setting in which conflicts, competences, mobilization, power, and distributional allocations can be negotiated and deliberated, maybe not solved, but certainly addressed. Politics thus denotes a specific approach to public affairs and collective coexistence. Predominantly over the last two centuries (and possibly longer), this approach has been embedded in the state tradition.

Prima facie there is an initial deep scholarly unease concerning any overly direct connection of politics with human rights. Given the close conceptual links between the vocabulary of nationalism, patriotism, the state, and politics—as highly 'particularist' vocabularies—it is no surprise to see an underlying tension with the moral universalism or cosmopolitanism implicit in much human right argument. Politics, as a by-product of its intimate connection with plurality and conflict, can indicate faction, partiality, expediency, and even amorality. This can lead to a form of anti-political politics, one which values impartiality and neutrality, particularly with regard to institutions such as the state. This argument frequently uses the language of morality to address politics. This impartiality can also masquerade as the ethos of human rights. Thus, human rights can wear an anti-political moral badge with pride. For some, therefore, human rights ought to be anti-political or non-political. Many theorists and practitioners would therefore want to envisage human rights as universal moral entities, by definition, that is, the possession of humanity and not of any particular regime, culture, state, or ideology. That for many is the point of human rights. The idea that human rights are potentially political therefore raises awkward questions: for example, surely this entails that human rights are at the beck and call of the arbitrariness of states, political executives, or ideologies?

My argument is that we face an important binary tension in the argument concerning human rights and the state. A convenient way of viewing this binary is via, what I call, three permutations. The terms *subject* and *object* are employed here in formulating these permutations. These terms are simply strategic or pedagogic devices to render the arguments. *Subject* implies the key initiator or key theme which enables an explanation or account of the *object*. In the first permutation, the state is the object of human rights, human rights are the subject. Human rights in this scenario have an independent status; they embody morally prior universal claims, set over and against the secondary significance of the state. In other words, the state is the institutional object to which they are systematically applied. The central intuition here concerns what might be termed the moral independence and universalism of human rights. The second permutation takes the converse position, viewing the state as the primary legal and possibly moral subject and human rights as the object. This latter argument tends to resist both the category of universalism and claims to independence made by human rights exponents. The broad movement of ideas behind this second permutation can be loosely termed 'particularism'. The central intuition underpinning this argument concerns the largely local character of our legal, moral, and political knowledge. The third permutation focuses on the proposition that the state can be viewed as both subject and object. This relation is complex and dialectically nuanced. The central intuition here is that the essential problem of the human rights culture has always been the institution of the state; post-1945, the state has been both the key promoter of human rights, as well as the key offender against such rights. It is this latter permutation which most accurately captures the odd status of human rights in modernity.

## THE STATE AS OBJECT

Beginning with the first permutation concerning the state as object: properly speaking, for many, human rights are considered to be intrinsic to the human person or agent—in essence, they constitute the basis of human dignity (see e.g. Griffin 2008). They are pre-social, or even asocial, in character, in the sense that the individual person carries them *into* society. A legal order is not something which constructs such rights, conversely, rather it needs to affirm the moral validity of such rights. Such rights are possessed equally by all human beings regardless of age, gender, ethnicity, and the like. They are not related to status or position in any society. They are considered to be universal in the sense that they apply regardless of social or political context. They also are inalienable, in the sense that no one can simply abandon them or give them up. They are usually linked with some form of moral justification, which refers to a morally considerable belief, standard, or objective norm.[4] In this permutation, therefore, human rights are the primary subject. The object is, largely, the state to which they are rigorously applied. This is the more conventional understanding of human rights.

A little further elucidation is required here: briefly, the specific sense of 'right' envisaged here is that of a *claim* or, more specifically, a valid claim or entitlement. A valid claim is implicitly or explicitly affirmed as valid by a wider group. This would hold for any substantive kind of right (see Feinberg 1980). One has a valid claim to something. This implies that the agent is, for example, at liberty (as a valid claim) in respect of X and that her liberty right is the ground for other's duties to grant her X. This connects to another standard argument: human rights imply some form of correlative relation with others, namely, others have a duty or disability correlative to the assertion of the valid claim. Minimally, therefore, others are liable to your valid claims. The valid claim is usually seen to protect or promote a particular legitimate interest.[5] One further, more palpable point to mention here is that human rights are conventionally thought of, in this permutation, as at root moral rights. Moral rights are constituted through, or consequent upon, the acceptance of some significant moral value or morally considerable belief. Thus, for example, utilitarian, Kantian, or contractarian norms transform the way in which we both think about and justify rights. The justificatory structure and norms are considered to be universal and largely external to the arrangements of any particular association, institutional structure, or social arrangement. This does not mean that a moral right cannot be codified in a legal framework. However, the solid ground on which the right is justified or held to be valid is, in itself, independent, ostensibly of the historical, political, or juridical fact of association.

## THE STATE AS SUBJECT

The second permutation presents a profoundly critical alternative to the more standard conception of human rights outlined above. The discussion of this second permutation could have focused on a wide range of nineteenth- and twentieth-century theorists; however, for brevity's sake, the discussion concentrates on two examples, which present the counter-arguments neatly and polemically.

For the twentieth-century theorist Carl Schmitt, the state forms the central theme of politics. The state indeed 'presupposed the concept of the political'. The state itself is 'the political status of an organized people in an enclosed territorial unit'. The real issue here for Schmitt is: what characterizes the political? What defines politics as distinct from other domains, such as the economic? This leads to Schmitt's account of the friends–enemies dichotomy, as the essential mark of the political—as embedded in the state. Thus, the 'political is the most intense and extreme antagonism'; the enemy is neither a person (or collectivity) who is personally hated nor anything that could be considered a competitor. Rather, 'The enemy is solely the public enemy, because everything that has a relation to such a collectively of men, particularly to a whole nation, becomes public simply by virtue of such a relationship'. For Schmitt, therefore, 'it cannot be denied that nations continue to group themselves according to the friend and enemy antithesis, that the distinction remains actual today, and that this is an ever-present possibility for every people existing in the political sphere' (all quotations from Schmitt 1996, 28–9).

The state is thus wholly configured in this friend–enemy context. As Schmitt comments, any understanding of the state 'is incomprehensible if one does not know exactly who is to be affected, combated, refuted, or negated by such a term' (Schmitt 1996, 31). Conflict does not though automatically entail open war between states; however, it is an ever-present possibility and it thus remains the 'leading presupposition which determines in a characteristic way human action and thinking and thereby creates specifically political behaviour' (Schmitt 1996, 34). It follows from this that to have a universal order, consensual international law, or a pacified globe, would essentially entail no friends, no enemies, no states, and the end of politics. In this context, Schmitt remarks disparagingly on the Kellogg–Briand Pact (1928), which effectively condemned war as a way of settling international disputes. He notes that 'as long as a sovereign state exists, this state decides for itself, by virtue of its independence, whether or not such a reservation (self-defence, enemy aggression, violation of existing treaties, including the Kellogg Pact, and so on) is or is not given in the concrete case' (Schmitt 1996, 51). War cannot be outlawed as long as politics exists and politics resides in states.[6]

If a particular state exists, there will inevitably be other states. There is no universal order, only a pluriverse of antagonisms. The state, by the logic of the case, cannot be universal and politics, per se, cannot embrace humanity. The concept humanity (as in universal human rights claims) for Schmitt is a self-consciously mystifying tool used by particular states for their own self-interested policy ends. As he notes, the concept of humanity is a 'useful ideological instrument of imperialist expansion, and in its ethical-humanitarian form it is a specific vehicle of economic imperialism'. He continues, 'Here one is reminded of a somewhat modified expression of Proudhon's: whoever invokes humanity wants to cheat' (quotations from Schmitt 1996, 54).[7] Its early usage, particularly in eighteenth-century rights documents, is again, for Schmitt, a directly conflict-based usage, reflecting an antagonistic relation to aristocratic and monarchical states. Universal human rights, in this scenario, for Schmitt are viewed as simply the ideological weapons of particular states. In a similar vein, he quipped (in somewhat bad taste) during the Nuremberg trials, that Germany committed 'crimes against humanity', whereas America committed 'crimes for humanity' (see Salter 1999).[8] Strictly speaking, if the moral thesis of universal human rights were correct for Schmitt, it would mean the end of both politics and states.

Another, more current example of a similar argument is Raymond Geuss's book *History and Illusion in Politics* (2001). The central political figure again is the state, which, for Geuss, if anything has grown in significance and power since the nineteenth century. Realistically, for Geuss, we must grasp that it is the positivistic source of all law and rights.[9] However, ironically for Geuss, human rights are usually invoked as 'prior to the given positive legal code' (Geuss 2001, 139–40). This is the key moral assumption of human rights as justified valid claims—as outlined earlier. For Geuss, the major question for human rights can be stated quite bluntly and it circumvents the empty philosophizing:

> either there is or there is not a mechanism for enforcing human rights. If there is not, it would seem that calling them 'rights' simply means that we think it would (morally) be a good idea if they were enforced.... A human right is an inherently vacuous conception, and to speak of 'human rights' is a kind of puffery or white magic. Perhaps if we repeat claims about natural rights long enough and loudly enough, and pass enough resolutions, people will stop doing various horrible things to each other. (Geuss 2001, 144)

This has echoes of MacIntyre's comments on belief in human rights as equivalent to those of a belief in unicorns (MacIntyre 1981, 67). Geuss continues, on this same theme,

> *even if* (and it is a cyclopean 'if') it *were* to be or come to be the case that such Declarations [as the UDHR 1948] had more than rhetorical effect, they would constitute not so much a vindication of the doctrine of human rights as a transformation of individual components of someone's moral belief into a system of *positive* rights. We would merely have begun to invent and impose on the nations of the world a new layer of positive (international) law. (Geuss 2001, 144)

For Geuss, such a system is potentially realizable but it would require states to do it with force and military interventions. Human rights would exist because they had been forced on groups, yet for Geuss this runs against the standard logic of human rights themselves.

For Geuss, therefore, there are *no* meaningful human rights; they are illusions. We can institute them, but they then need overt enforcement. This transforms them into positive state rights. In times of peace and stability, human rights can *appear* to work for short periods, in certain types of state. We thus get the passing impression that these particular moralistic claims have some stability and universality. They are, though, simply the luxuries of stable affluent industrialized societies and it is likely that they will never move beyond this. In general, Geuss therefore sees them as 'otiose and pointless'. Further, like a wide range of predecessors, Geuss is clear that virtually all states have the means to override any such rights at any point, whether in times of crisis or simply for their own immediate utility. Geuss comments, 'Rights discourse might...be a tempting general way to think about society if one had a fantastically optimistic view about God, the world, natural resources, and the avoidability of conflict.' In fact, in a world of scarce resources, it is more likely that the inflation of human rights covenants will in the end intensify conflicts between states. The reality of the political world for Geuss, as for a large contingent of current international relations theorists, is 'competing states'. The intrinsic conflict of nation states is endemic and irresolvable by any appeals to human rights. Human rights are thus neither well-formed nor morally grounded. Their flimsy existence is always set against the taken-for-granted contingent background of moderately stable affluent states. Human rights discourse is simply 'a way of trying to immobilize society, to freeze it in an idealized version of its present form' (all quotations Geuss 2001, 149, 154).[10]

## THE STATE AS SUBJECT AND OBJECT

The discussion now turns to the third permutation. This allows a potential mediation out of the stalemate of the previous arguments. However, it also raises a range of new issues with regard to human rights and indeed states. The permutation is explored through two arguments, which draw upon the work of other writers. The first argument relates rights directly, if uneasily, to the state, but affirms a moderately positive dimension to the state tradition, namely, the right to have rights. The second argument focuses on certain characteristics of the state tradition linked to constitutional self-limitation. In the final analysis, the two arguments are blended.

The first argument is embedded in Hannah Arendt's work, particularly in studies such as *On Revolution* and *The Origins of Totalitarianism*. These latter works form part of a much larger project on totalitarianism and revolution, which will not be dwelt on. One root to the Arendtian argument is the historical contention that the sovereign nation state reached a recognizable modern form on the back of political revolutions in particularly America and France.

One of the key dimensions of this state form was that it embodied a perplexing legacy premised on the universal 'rights of man', the 'sovereignty of the nation', and the 'consent of the governed'. As Arendt notes,

> Man had hardly appeared as a completely emancipated, completely isolated being who carried his dignity within himself without reference to some larger encompassing order, when he disappeared again into a member of a people. From the beginning the paradox involved in the Declaration of the inalienable human right was that it reckoned with an 'abstract' human being who seemed to exist nowhere.... The whole question of human rights, therefore, was quickly and inextricably blended with the question of national emancipation; only the emancipated sovereignty of the people, of one's own people, seemed to be able to insure them.   (Arendt 1966, 291)[11]

The basis of the paradox here was that universal human rights could only be achieved—insofar as they could be achieved—within modern forms of sovereign nation states. Yet nation states were, at the same time, the key offenders against human rights. Outside of the framework of states human rights were largely otiose. Further, it followed for Arendt that there were no universal moral foundations for human rights. There was nothing inevitable about any such order. There was neither any universal order of nature nor any objective good to be discovered. There was rather the historical contingency of certain nation states, which embodied, constitutively, the rights of man and notions of consent. The historical fact was that humans were not born equal; conversely humans were constituted as equal (as citizens) in specific conditions within certain modern states.

The basic point is that human rights are fragile abstractions and any attempt to justify them is largely fruitless, since what is basic to human development is not individual rights as such but nation states. The fact that human rights exist at all is due to the complex artifice of certain states. Without a state, humans become vulnerable and no human rights rhetoric or philosophizing will save them. Arendt affirms here the critical vulnerability of human rights.

Her critique of human rights has though a number of interesting facets which make her argument into a transitional notion (away from the second permutation argument). First, she sidesteps part of the paradoxical relation of human rights, vis-à-vis states, by affirming that human rights *do* exist for citizens of certain states. The universalist baggage of moral justification which accompanies them may be heavily inflated, but they still do exist concretely. Second, she accepts the importance of post-1945 debates over human rights, indicating that the Nuremberg trials had opened the possibility of formalized agreements on what was permissible for nation states. She sensed here that there was a desperate need to respond to the Nazi genocide. The idea of a comity of nations deeply attracted her, as did the idea of

European federation. Third, the Universal Declaration of Human Rights (UDHR) was significant for her insofar as it initiated a widespread public dialogue and formed a background for debate about rights both within and between states. Fourth, she indicated that a certain type of state form was more conducive to the development of human rights; she considered this as republican.[12] For Arendt, republicanism could form a more solid bulwark against totalitarianism.

Finally, although deeply sceptical about making any hard and fast case for human rights, Arendt nonetheless suggests, tantalizingly, that there is one potentially universalizable right. This fundamental right—which ties in with her notion of the prerequisite for the state—is 'the right to have a rights' (see Arendt 1966, 296, 298). There are clearly multiple philosophical issues here, however, put rather crudely, this is taken to indicate that the most basic right is to membership of a community, or more succinctly the right to live in a political framework. For one commentator, this might be seen as one way in which Arendt directs our attention to the 'irreparable groundlessness of rights, affirming our own precarious, existential, collective self-care when it comes to creating and maintaining in this world the conditions of civility and humanity' (Michelman 1996, 207). Ironically, at the same time, this minimal right can appear as a normative expectation which 'ought' to be embodied in political membership. If it is a normative expectation it looks, to all intents and purposes, like a minimal universal which is *external* to political member-ship. However, in terms of the latter argument, it remains a deeply elusive universal since, as Arendt argues on a number of occasions, human rights cannot be premised on external notions of universal reason, history, nature, or God. I therefore take Arendt to be indicating that human rights are in some manner *constitutive* components of a conception of the state. This is the elusive core of the right to have rights.

The discussion now turns to a second argument, drawing attention to important facets of the state tradition with regard to rights. Georg Jellinek's *Declaration of the Rights of Man and the Citizen* still makes intriguing reading for those interested in rights argument.[13] His thesis is complex and multilay-ered, but a few quick points can be made. He examines the *French Declaration of the Rights of Man and of the Citizen* in an idiosyncratic manner, basically viewing it in terms of the history of public law, contending that 'it is under the influence of this document that the conception of the public rights of the individual has been developed in the positive law of the states of the Euro-pean continent' (Jellinek 1901, 2).[14] Jellinek, overall, was impressed with the development of a rights culture in North America, France, Britain, and else-where; however, contrary to the standard logic of natural rights, he sees such rights *not* as pre-social, natural, or external entities; conversely he views them consistently in the context of public law, that is to say, in terms of a theory of law which is constitutive of an understanding of the civil state and which governs the relationship between individual citizens and the state. Such rights always have to be 'vitalized' in the 'process of detailed legislation' (Jellinek 1901, 6). What interests Jellinek here is the argument that rights are protected by general principles of law, such that 'any restraint of the person can only come about through legal authorization' (Jellinek 1901, 53). The right to liberty, for example, is thus interpreted by Jellinek as resting on the supremacy of law itself. Put in a more succinct way, human rights are the implicit duties and functions of the civil state. As Jellinek (1901, 88) comments, 'declarations of rights did nothing else than express the existing condition of rights in definite universal formulas' (Jellinek 1901, 88).

The crucial issue question here—which parallels Arendt's arguments—is what guarantees such rights? A critic might argue that this argument appears to deliver human rights up to the none-too-tender mercies of states. However, this critical anxiety moves the discussion to the most fertile argument in Jellinek's jurisprudential work. Jellinek deploys a neo-Kantian argument, invoked in this case for the concept of state personality.[15] He conceives of the state as a form of 'subjective will'. The state as a subjective will is an autonomous legal personality. The autonomous state legislates to itself. The will of the state appears, prima facie, to come prior to law and rights.[16] In this argument, international law could look immensely fragile. However, in terms of will, Jellinek did not mean pure voluntarism. The will is not heteronomous but autonomous. The character of the autonomous will comprises internal constitutive limitations upon itself. The state's duty is therefore to be true to its autonomous legal personality.

This latter argument may sound somewhat legally abstract. However, the core of this autonomy thesis is exemplified in Jellinek's concept of 'auto-limitation'. It is also sometimes described as the self-binding argument (*Selbstbindung*). There is a paradox here, which many commentators have found tricky in interpreting Jellinek, namely, that something conditions the nature of law, implying what it ought to be, but this 'ought' is at the same time conditioned by the law. This is emphatically not natural law. Thus, rights are concessions from a state that is constituted via self-binding or auto-limitation. Autonomy, in this sense, necessarily implies self-limitation. The state as a legal personality, acting autonomously, limits itself in the *process of willing*.[17] Only the state—as a juristic person—could limit its own power internally and externally, but that limitation is implicit in autonomous willing, such as to give rise to individual rights, as embedded constitutively in public law.[18]

This argument did not imply that there were fixed limitations on the state. A reasonable or non-arbitrary change of will in international affairs was acceptable.[19] A right, whether domestic or international, consists in the fact that it forms part of the substance of the state. It is the means by which the state shows itself and implicitly through which the state limits itself.[20] For Jellinek, this whole conception of the auto-limited state (as legally self-bound by its own character and historical circumstance) was a distinct development in human self-organization and civil existence.

Jellinek's general conception of the state tries, in effect, to embody the inner dynamic of the French and American Declarations of Rights, namely as contributions to public law and international law. Whereas natural right argument had been seen as the moral basis for public right (as in the logic of valid claims), for Jellinek the reverse was the case. Public right forms the basis for subjective right. To make any sense of natural (or human) rights, it is necessary to reconfigure them as elements of public rights. This is what Jellinek meant when he analysed the French and American Declarations as contributing to the development of 'the modern state and in understanding the position which this state assures to the individual' (Jellinek 1901, 6).[21]

Jellinek offers a way of configuring certain arguments which contain resonant correspondences with elements of Arendt's arguments. Like Arendt, Jellinek (insofar as one can use the vocabulary of human rights) suggests that human rights do exist for citizens. Like Arendt, he is not concerned with any overt universalist justification of rights as external valid claims. Second, Jellinek, without the benefit of the Nuremberg trials and Nuremberg Charter, was still committed to the idea of a comity of civil states, which could be formalized in treaties and international law. Third, the 1776 and 1789 Declarations (like the UDHR for Arendt) were significant for Jellinek insofar they contributed to a civilizing process within particularly European states and thus initiated a public dialogue both within and between states about international law. Fourth, like Arendt, Jellinek implies that a certain type of state form was more conducive to the development of such rights (the *Rechtstaat*). In Jellinek it was a limited constitutional monarchy, which he hoped would develop in Germany. However, one can extrapolate from this an underlying commitment, in both Arendt and Jellinek, to a conception of a civil state. Fifth, Arendt's 'the right to have a rights' is an elusive argument, but it appears to entail that humans ought to be able to live in political communities and that the law of such communities is constituted imperfectly by the substance of what can be called human rights. This argument is developed by Jellinek in the auto-limitation thesis, namely, when we speak of the actions of the autonomous civil state, it is a self-limited action which embodies an implicit commitment to human rights and international law. Human rights are thus embedded, imperfectly, within the very concept of the civil state. Finally, as in Arendt, Jellinek also stresses—less forcefully—the historical contingency and fragility of civil states and the structural historical forces within them which often militate against civil statehood. Jellinek was clearly aware that political life in Germany between 1860 and 1911 did not look very much like his own legal theories. Similarly, Arendt in focusing on both European and other states in the late 1940s and early 1950s was painfully aware of the vulnerability and fragility of civil statehood. However, if there are to be human rights and successful international law, they have to arise from within a specific state tradition—warts and all.


# The civil state

A core working assumption in the present argument is that politics (as argued earlier) entails both plurality and conflict; it also embodies the potential means to mediate that conflict. As argued, one of the ways in which politics has addressed such plurality is via the state. A particular dimension of that state tradition has been the civil state. In terms of the twentieth century, the most resonant way of institutionalizing this mediating role of politics has been via civil statehood. Civil statehood, embodying politics, invokes constitutionality, which entails a capacity for self-limitation. This capacity is implicit, imperfectly, in the practices of all civil states. Human rights can thus be conceptualized as embedded claims, derived from a constitutional culture, that is to say they are a systematization of core elements of civil statehood, civility, and politics.

Some more needs to be said here though concerning the civil state. Broadly a civil state equates with a concern for a rule of law, an independent judiciary, a structured elaborate system of accountability for those who exercise power, and an acceptance of human plurality. In the civil conception, cultural consensus, moral solidarity, a common doctrine, ideological agreement, loyalty to a nation, patriotism, and so forth, are quite clearly different forms of ordering, but they are *not* defining features of civil statehood. A civil state therefore is not necessarily a community with any immediate consensus or common moral purpose. A civil state is not alien to a sense of community, but it is not in itself a community. It does though qualify the actions of communities via the rule of law. Civil order is not about designing human experience. It also recognizes implicitly the unruliness of human individuality. It is rather an order sanctioning continuous experimentation in the manner authority is structured. It provides inevitably plentiful opportunities for policy blunders.

Active solidaristic principles can clearly be part of political order, but they do not comprise political order in a civil state. In this sense, we should neither elide the civil conception with any minimal conception of the state nor necessarily with liberalism as an ideological doctrine. The civil state has no necessary hard and fast understanding (as in classical liberal thought) of discrete and identifiable public and private spheres. These are envisaged as shifting boundaries. Further, the civil state has no necessary relation with any particular form of economic order. It is only focused on the manner in which power, in general, is exercised, not on the content of economic activity. Again though economic activity would be qualified by the rule of law. The civil state qualifies actions, whether they are the actions of parties, interests, religions, economic groups, governments, or individual leaders. It does not act itself. Further, a civil state is not necessarily a democratic state, it may be a necessary prerequisite for democracy, but it is not absolutely identical with it.[22] In addition, the civil state is not determined by absolute sovereignty and power. Unqualified sovereign power per se undermines civil statehood. Thus, the rule of law should not be seen as a coercive power structure, it is rather the intrinsic condition of civil existence. There is nothing beyond or over and above this idea. There is no ultimate foundation of which it rests, except a form of public dialogue in which civil existence is imbricated.

Civil statehood is intimately linked with politics. This does not entail any notion of international anarchy or disorder, except insofar as other forms of organizations such as organic nation states, and the like, foster it. Authoritative issues of civility actually do cross jurisdictions without effort. The extensive discussions of a European constitution, for example, exemplify this. This constitutional debate does not undermine the civil state, but rather exemplifies—extending way beyond the artificial boundaries of its territoriality—its civil and political character.

A state's authority is thus premised on the verve of its *civil* public dialogues, not its cultural exclusivity, nationality, absolute sovereignty, or weaponry. Civil statehood must also be continuously rehabilitated via public dialogues. The actual boundaries of civil states are not external, but largely internal to the dispositions of individual citizens. This issue links with an understanding of rights. A right is a relation and form of recognition which is distinct from any solidaristic relation. It is a relation which invokes a wider public trust and discourse, such that parties put their reliance upon another more anonymous relation, that is, a right. This public fiduciary relation is not just a legal relation, it is also very fundamentally political, since it links directly with the character of the civil state. In point, rights involve a conception of a public relationship, which is a politico-juridical relation. The rights and implied public trust are maintained and respected within an institutional setting. Politics is the medium of that setting. The public setting self-consciously provides rights as a negative realization of human powers. Rights are not configured as part of any familiar or intimate dialogue, but summon conversely a dialogue which invokes publicity and a degree of anonymity. This is the manner in which we should begin to think about human rights. The aim therefore is to reconceive human rights in a political frame, in terms of individual citizens who are socializing, mutating, and acting in relation to others, in specific public institutional settings. It is these settings in which humans flourish or fail. It is also in these settings in which human rights become significant and indeed extend beyond artificial territorial boundaries.

## The organic nation state

In articulating a sense of politics within the practice of the civil state, two further issues need to be noted. The first is a distinction between the civil state and the nation state. Both are crucial and important facets of a European state tradition and they do clearly overlap in significant ways. The basic difference between them can be stated quite bluntly. In the organic understanding of the state, there has been an overwhelmingly strong emphasis upon a common or shared culture or identity, something which makes the state unique.[23] The link between nationalism and the state is thus strong in this organic conception.

In fact, it has been a deep-rooted practice during the nineteenth and twentieth centuries to consider the state and nation as virtually coterminous. This is, in fact, still the stock-in-trade vocabulary of politicians, international relations theorists, many political theorists, and historians. From historically recent debates on the unified currency in Europe, the rights of ex-colonial states, or UN Security Council debates about humanitarian intervention, and so forth, the compound term—'nation state'—is the dominant assumed background category for discussion. Nationalism was not just an episode in state development, but was the linchpin of the state.

In historical terms, up to the present day, the nation state has unquestionably been the more popular form of political organization to aspire towards for developing or seceding groups. The compound also has a close conceptual resonance with concepts such as self-determination. This popularity in fact accelerated exponentially in the twentieth century. In many ways, the concept of national self-determination is a comparatively recent idea, arising after the Versailles Treaty (1918). It then became enshrined in UN documents. Terms like League of Nations or United Nations, and the like, all largely presuppose the pervasive terminology of the self-determining nation state.[24] With the growing enthusiasm for this particular 'political form' over the mid-nineteenth and twentieth centuries, the older multinational states were seen increasingly as anachronisms—'prisons of peoples' to use the Mazzinian phrase—which had to be broken open for emancipation. This was the particular fate of the Hapsburg, Tsarist, Ottoman, and British Empires. More recently, the same logic has been applied to the old Soviet Union and even to Yugoslavia during the 1990s. Not only was the nation state envisaged, over the nineteenth century, as the precondition to genuine independence, self-determination, and political freedom, but also the ground for functional modernization and economic development. Some commentators have therefore seen a definite empirically identifiable pattern to this gradual evolution of the nation state.

In summary, it has become a conceptual commonplace to link the state with the nation. This does not have to be a point of high-minded principle. Even on the most mundane level, the state is seen to provide a framework for nations—although whether nations provide the groundwork to states or vice versa is still a contested question. The conventional view here is that the state provides the forum or shell within which national identity can be articulated, represented, and legitimated. This may be partly fortuitous, simply because of the context of a particularly strong European statist culture, which not only developed on a practical political level, but was also given a powerful academic imprimatur by a large and growing band of lawyers, historians, philosophers, and political theorists writing in the gradually expanding European universities of the late nineteenth and early twentieth centuries. Academic national history in universities and the 'nation state' itself have had an immensely close and symbiotic relation since the mid-nineteenth century. For some, this process has continued, with minor interruptions, to the present day.

## Limitations on the subject–object argument

The first limitation relates to certain inferences from the Arendtian argument. First, nation states demonstrate an unreliable capacity to defend human rights, even within their own polities. More significantly, if human rights are dependent on being a citizen of a state, then what happens to stateless persons? Without a state, the human rights of refugees and migrants simply do not exist—unless a state or states are committed to defending them. As Arendt comments, 'The fundamental deprivation of human rights is manifested first and above all in the deprivation of a place in the world which makes opinions significant, and actions effective . . . loss of a polity expels him from humanity' (Arendt 1966, 296). This argument carried further problematic insights for Arendt into imperialism and colonialism. The basic point is that the appalling abuses of peoples, carried out in many colonial theatres over the last few centuries, were largely due to the fact that colonial powers perceived no states in these locations (*terra nullius* in some cases), therefore it followed that there were no established rights (civil or human). If the colonized did not possess citizenship, then imperial authorities could happily dissociate power from consent and rights. *De facto* force predominated over *de jure* right. Another implication was that post-1918 treaties, such as Versailles, which marked the European political landscape so significantly in the twentieth century, worked on the same reasoning, namely that it was only in national sovereign states that rights could be protected. This critical scenario creates a disturbing sense of the fragility of human rights. This is a profoundly sombre issue, but it is surely one which has to be addressed in the context of the development of the civil state tradition. It will not be solved outside of it. There is no cosmopolitan imperative to aid refugees other than the continuing pressures of civil societies on their own states and the agreements amongst states. At present, it is surely the only feasible strategy.

A second issue concerns the question: what particular conception of human rights is invoked by the statist reading in Arendt and Jellinek? This is where the arguments hit another conceptual and practical obstacle. The nucleus of this obstacle is embodied in the distinction between the social and the political. The key issue is that the political has a close bearing on the state (or at least a certain type of state) and that this state should not be confused with the social realm. The basic argument in Arendt and Jellinek is that if human rights are to be generated out of the political realm of the state, then the rights must be seen as civil and political and *not* social in character. The social implies in this context society—that is, society denotes individual and private concerns.

For Arendt, in particular, politics is understood as a unique form of public action distinct from social issues such as labour or work. It is about thinking and conducting public affairs in the polity, in common with others. It implies what Arendt referred to as an 'enlarged mentality' or broader vision in which self-interest is merged into the freedom of a public focus and political judgement. For Arendt, the political sphere had a unique dignity. However, one of the problems of modernity, for Arendt, was the expansion of what she thought of as the social realm (a realm of necessity) *into* the political realm. The social is *not* a realm of action and judgement. The origins of the social for Arendt lie in the Greek notion of the household. The social focuses on the basic necessities of living and then pulls them into the political realm—in terms of a glorified national housekeeping. Economics, for example, is allowed to dominate the public realm. The social for Arendt consequently becomes a pseudo-public realm. The social focuses largely on 'necessary' issues such as production, consumption, and distribution. What really characterizes the social is a herd-like conformity, settled around material interests. Put very simply, when the social seriously penetrates the political we are on the cusp of the mass society and then ultimately a form of totalitarianism. The realm of the political (freedom) then becomes distorted into the realm of the social (necessity).

The social, for Arendt, was developed in the French and Russian revolutions. In both cases, something distinctive characterizes the social. Those who drive the concern for the social (e.g. the *sans culottes* in the French Revolution) were focused on poverty (see Arendt 1963, 54ff.). In Arendt's mind, this drew the French and Russian revolutions as distinct from the American, which she saw as primarily political. Subsequently, poverty became the key motif of the social. What was a private issue became in effect political. As she remarked,

> In this stream of the poor, the element of irresistibility, which was found so intimately connected with the original meaning of the word 'revolution' was embodied....Nothing we might say could be more obsolete than the attempt to liberate mankind from poverty by political means; nothing could be more futile and more dangerous....The result was that necessity invaded the political realm, the only realm where men can be truly free.
> (Arendt 1963, 110; see also Oakeshott 1975, 287, 304)

A number of critics have suggested that Arendt is simply wrong here. Social questions (economics, wages, housing, pensions, welfare, and poverty) are in the end always political. My own answer to the question—concerning the social and political relation—focuses on the dialectic of internal struggle within the self-limitation process of the civil state, a struggle which remains unresolved. Thus, what we see in the domestic and international debate over social and civil rights is one focused on the character and purpose of both the state and politics itself. Thus, the real nature of the debate over social rights is, in fact, a debate between civil and social conceptions of the state. The civil principles underlying the Genocide Convention are *prima facie* those which are generally recognized by any civil state. These more basic civil rights can more easily be integrated into the current scenario of human rights, that is, those rights which shield the individual from unjust interference, cruelty, torture, or the like. However, can the same be said for the attempt to eradicate hunger and extreme poverty? Do these second generational positive rights warrant consideration as human rights? The answer one gives to this question is largely dependent on one's civil state philosophy and the role of politics.

## Registering the state

Basically the argument of this book begins with the fact that human rights, from the UDHR onwards, were based initially upon a survey of established state structures and constitutions. This should still be a starting point for thinking about human rights. However, there are a number of deep ambiguities in this contention. The state is in an uncertain position here. First, it is both the source and ground of human rights. As such it forms the primary prosecutor of human rights, however, at the same time it is the key defendant.[25] We might see this as the *state reflexivity syndrome*, that is, in dealing with human rights the civil state is always in a reflexive situation. My argument would be that this scenario breaks down between conflicting (but overlapping) senses of the state, that is, between the organic nation state and the civil state.

Second, there is an ongoing tension between these dimensions of the state. Human rights can therefore be seen as continuously reconciling 'the effectiveness of state power with the protection against the same state power' (Tomuschat 2003, 7).[26] Thus, the purported international characteristic of human rights cannot be separated historically, conceptually, or legally from the internal domestic activity of human rights within certain forms of state. Human rights can be viewed as a countervailing protection against the state, but at the same time this protection is generated *by* the vernaculars of the state. The sources for human rights therefore lie in public law and constitutional law. Post-1945, we see these human rights emerging from the state level to the international.[27] This argument, in my reading, ties in closely with the theories of both Arendt and Jellinek. In fact, the idea of the 'state-reflexivity syndrome' catches the gist of Jellinek's auto-limitation thesis.

Third, there is the issue of the social and political distinction which appears in many theorists. As argued earlier, for many theorists politics is bound to the state; further, politics should not be confused with the social. If the state is the ground of human rights, then human rights are essentially political. It then follows that the social (vis-à-vis social rights) is a corruption of both politics and therefore human rights. Is there any way of reconciling the conflict? This whole argument would appear to limit human rights to certain basic civil minima. My own argument is that this latter statement gives, paradoxically, too much substance to the civil state. The civil state, although political, is not committed to any particular substantive enterprise. It is possible that the realm of the social can be configured as an experiment or exploration of the conditions for one's humanity, that is what enables the human being to flourish. In this sense, the auto-limitation process is potentially compatible with social rights.

## Conclusion

In this chapter, the first two permutations concerning the state as object and subject have been put aside in favour of a more nuanced dialectical relation. What is important therefore in the third permutation is that we should try not to isolate human rights from broader debates about the state tradition. What we see in the debates about civil and social human rights is *not* just a reflection of a domestic state-based debate about constitutional, social, and civil rights. On the contrary, it is rather the continuous dialectic of the idea and practice of the state itself.[28] The UDHR arose in a particular historico-political context and reflects arguments about the character of the state tradition at that time.[29] The UDHR was primarily a political document, not a legal or moral document. It was and still is wholly reliant on the idiosyncratic reflexive character of the civil state. What we see in human rights, in one reading, therefore is an ideal civil state vocabulary; they are part of self-imposed struggle at the core of the state tradition itself.[30] In addition, the real achievement of human rights, in whatever format, is something that can be enhanced by a comity of states. Enjoyment of human rights can only be the result of *concerted* efforts by civil states and their own civil societies. However, any such comity is wholly dependent upon the character of each state and the implied civil society involved.[31]

## ☐ NOTES

1. For political ideologies which oppose this vision, such as anarchy, still see it as the key enemy to be overcome.

2. I have derived this particular terminology from the work of Michael Freeden.

3. However, many have and still try wrongly to subsume politics under morality, philosophy, law, or religion.

4. Some have even suggested that such rights are self-justifying, that is, they are completely morally self-evident.

5. There is also a permissibility in a valid claim, such that to have a right means that it is not wrong (it is thus permissible) to do X. Permissibility also entails that it is wrong (morally) to interfere with the agent in asserting that right. This might be a right to possess something, to receive something, also for an agent to forbear, or do something.

6. Schmitt comments, in similar terms, on the League of Nations; such a body could exist (as a league of states), as long as it had an enemy, when this no longer existed the league became redundant.

7. Schmitt later argues, 'War is condemned but executions, sanctions, punitive expeditions, pacification, protection of treaties, international police, and measures to assure peace remain. The adversary is no longer called an enemy but a disturber of the peace' (Schmitt 1996, 79).

8. In this reading the Nuremberg trials would be seen as nonsensical.

9. For Geuss, the state is an 'abstract structure of authority located in a socially separate and distinct institutional sphere which had certain coercive powers at its disposal. In the modern period its powers seemed to increase so dramatically that it became an object of fear' (Geuss 2001, 128).

10. Taking the negative appraisal one step further—even the idea of the liberal democratic state can be viewed as a *contradictio in adjecto*. The state is, at root, a structure of power and coercion. It can never be viewed as a voluntaristic entity. This, by default, puts it into a continuous tense relation with the values of liberalism and indeed democracy. Liberalism tries to cope with this paradox with sophisms about individual freedom and

human rights, and so forth. The same point holds for indirect democracy. Indirect democracy cannot contain or tame the state. In the end, the mechanism that liberalism invokes to force its values cannot actually hold the mechanism itself. Geuss's position here is neither uncommon nor rare in the fields of politics and law—certainly if one looks back at the nineteenth and early twentieth centuries.

11. There are further dimensions to this paradox which I will not pursue. For example, Arendt notes in the case of, say, Israel, a democratically elected government and the restoration of basic human rights being achieved through national rights and the liquidation of another people (the Palestinians).

12. Although it is different from the more recent rush of interest in republicanism.

13. Georg Jellinek's (1851–1911) most famous work was his *Allgemeines Staatslehre* (1900); however, I refer to his work *The Declaration of the Rights of Man and of Citizens: A Contribution to Modern Constitutional History* (1901). To fully understand these works, it would be necessary to analyse the political and intellectual context of Germany in the period 1860 to 1900 and the multifaceted academic traditions characterizing this period. My own task is much more limited. I want in effect to annex certain aspects of Jellinek's arguments in order to throw some different light on the state–human right relationship.

14. For Jellinek, prior to the Declaration public law literature recognized the rights of heads of state, class, and privileges of individuals or special corporations, 'but the general rights of subjects were to be found essentially only in the form of duties on the part of the state, not in the form of definite legal claims of the individual' (Jellinek 1901, 3). Public law constitutes the existence of the state.

15. The Kantian dimension of Jellinek's work may well have been influenced by his university colleague at Heidelberg, Wilhelm Windelband (1848–1915).

16. For Jellinek, this would be equivalent to viewing the state as *legibus solutus*.

17. Sovereignty is thus described by Jellinek as the 'quality of a State to be obligated only through its own will' (quoted in Koskenniemi 2001, 204).

18. Jellinek also applied this auto-limitation argument to international law. Self-legislation was not, by definition, in conflict with international laws, but was rather the guarantor of its legal force. It reconciled autonomy and authority. International law was thus understood as part and parcel of the auto-limitation of the state. This explained 'not only the State's being bound by constitutional and administrative law but the very possibility of there being subjective rights against the State' (see Koskenniemi 2001, 201). This argument also facilitated the explanation of treaties, international agreements, international law, and ultimately (in my reading) human rights.

19. This was always accepted in the legal doctrine of *rebus sic stantibus*, allowing treaties to become inapplicable under certain conditions or changes of circumstances.

20. This is also for Jellinek implicit in sovereignty. Sovereignty is seen as the *capacity for self-limitation*. It implies sovereignty in terms of free persons, recognizing their autonomy as an implicit auto-limitation within the practice of sovereignty. It would contradict the inner character of the civil state and sovereignty to simply just dominate the individual.

21. This might also be conceptualized as a juristic liberalism, which has abandoned any strict sense of legal positivism and legal formalism in favour of a system of law which is considered in a historical and sociological framework.

22. In Britain, for example, forms of civil association long predated the development of democracy.

23. This theme is particularly strong where the people are regarded as taking part in government is some manner.

24. Among the nations created over the nineteenth and early twentieth centuries: 1830 Greece; 1831 Belgium; 1861 Italy; 1871 Germany; 1878 Romania, Serbia, and Montenegro; 1905 Norway; 1908 Bulgaria; 1913 Albania; 1917 Finland; 1918 Poland, Czechoslovakia, Estonia, Latvia, and Lithuania; and 1922 Ireland. The League of Nations, founded in 1920, had forty-two members, the United Nations, founded in 1945, had fifty-one, by 1969 eighty-two, by 1973 135, and by 1988 159, and the list will no doubt keep growing into the new century.

25. As one of the first systematic commentators and advocates of human rights in the late 1930s, Hersch Lauterpacht, succinctly put it, 'The challenge of human rights is inextricably bound up with the history of the modern state: on the one hand, the state has been accepted as an organization well-suited to promote the interests of its members in the never ending fight for resources among different communities; on the other hand, it has also been identified as a lethal threat to the life and well-being of its members' (Lauterpacht 1950, 73).

26. As one recent commentator remarks 'On the one hand, the state is the guarantor of human rights, the institutional framework called upon to safeguard the existence, the freedom, and the property of the individual citizen; at the same time, however, historical experience tells the observer that time and again persons or authorities vested with sovereign powers have infringed the rights of the citizen' (Tomuschat 2003, 7).

27. Thus, it is 'at a second stage that the idea emerged to establish mechanisms at the international level in order to accommodate instances where a national system has broken down' (Tomuschat 2003, 9).

28. 'No more is suggested than the simple truth that the intellectual frame of society conditions its practices in the field of human rights' (Tomuschat 2003, 320).

29. As one commentator notes: if one examines say an article of the UDHR, such as Article 28, which states that 'everyone is entitled to a social and international order in which rights and freedoms set forth in this Declaration can be fully realized', then 'As a lawyer, one cannot appreciate such a provision which promises just anything'. However, Tomuschat continues, 'Before blaming the drafters...one should remind oneself of the political character of the UDHR' (Tomuschat 2003, 29).

30. International protection of human rights is a 'chapter of legal history that has begun at a relatively late stage in the history of mankind' (Tomuschat 2003, 7).

31. 'In order to satisfy the needs of a population, governmental institutions and society have to cooperate with one another. The state is never an almighty institution with unlimited resources. Against widespread resistance on the ground, its authorities are hardly able to discharge their functions in an effective way. This applies to a great extent also to rights of the first generation. In order to attain this goal, citizens must share together with all the holders of public office the lofty objectives encapsulated in the lists of human rights as they are laid down in the UDHR or in the two Covenants of 1966' (Tomuschat 2003, 320).

# 7 The Human Rights of Politics

Chapter 6 argued that the state tradition has subsisted in a fruitful but paradoxical relation with the human rights tradition during the twentieth and early twenty-first centuries. Politics was seen as the key to this relation, politics implying conflict and uncertainty as well as the means to mediate this. The institutional means for such mediation was identified with a particular aspect of the state tradition, namely the civil state, which is drawn as distinct from the concept and practice of the nation state. The civil state is marked out by many features, not least its intrinsic adherence to constitutional auto-limitation and its relative indifference to issues of identity, nationality, or culture. Human rights are thus understood in the context of a conceptual matrix within the civil state conception. In consequence, the development of a human rights culture from 1948 is situated within an internal dialectic contained by the civil state tradition. The argument thus emphasizes the historical and political setting in which the stress on human rights has been developed post-1948.

One immediate concern was identified in the work of Arendt, amongst others, that is, the criticism of any attempt to extend the understanding of both the state and rights beyond the civil conception. My answer to the issue—concerning the civil and social aspect of right—is to see them contained within an internal dialectic of struggle, which is within the self-limitation processes of the civil state, a struggle which remains still substantively unresolved. Thus, what we see in both the domestic and international struggle over social and civil human rights is a debate focused on the character and purpose of both the state and politics. Consequently, the real character of the dispute over social and civil rights is, as such, an argument between civil and social conceptions of the state and the degree to which auto-limitation extends. In this chapter, the dialectical tension within the tradition of both human rights and the state tradition is explored more fully. The argument focuses initially on the grounding of rights within an account of recognition. The nature of the state is then explored in terms of the recognition conditions of statehood, particularly in the context of international law. The stress of the argument then falls on the subtle political character of law, constitutionalism, and international law. This then moves the argument to an analysis of the ideas of quasi-states, crimes of state, and the doctrine of *jus cogens*.

# Recognition of persons

The conception of rights developed in this book sees them in the context of a particular set of institutional arrangements. The theory which explains this context is recognition based. In this sense, the individual acquires rights insofar as she is granted normative status by others within an institutional relational setting. The idea of recognition itself has a complex genealogy in European thought and the theory itself is both multilevel and complex. The theory of rights, as premised on recognition is, in other words, rooted in a more general theory of recognition. Space will limit what can be discussed here; however, it is important to indicate something of this broader intellectual frame, before proceeding to rights theory.

Most commentators have identified the writings of Hegel as one key philosophical root to the recognition argument. Hegel's arguments on recognition appear most presciently in his early writings, particularly the *Jena Realphilosophie*. Hegel's basic idea is premised on an account of human identity, that is to say, human identity exists via the recognition of others. It follows that the concept of an isolated discrete human individual—considered as separate from all social ties—make little or no sense. Individual identity only arises in the context of mutual social recognition. To place this in a more contemporary parlance—the human person is formed relationally within the context of existing society.[1] Hegel uses this argument in his account of both individual and state personality.[2] Consequently, the identity of the state and individual persons presupposes the existence of other states and persons, who recognize them.[3]

The subtle dimension of this argument in Hegel is that one cannot *be* conscious of one's self as a person, unless one is aware of and mutually recognized by other persons. This awareness enables the individual to recognize what it is to *be* an individual agent. Analogously a state cannot be aware of itself as a state without the recognition of other states. Recognition implies being mutually acknowledged as independent agents. Consequently denying recognition is a denial of both personality and autonomy and consequently a form of oppression, humiliation, or disrespect. Given that non-recognition implies a form of oppression or disrespect, it follows that recognition itself suggests a certain type of social, political, and legal arrangements, which invokes, enables, and guarantees mutual recognition. To be an agent, under these arrangements, is to be granted a specific normative status by others. This implies a political vision of institutional arrangements focused on the state.[4]

One recent political thinker who has utilized these ideas is Axel Honneth.[5] The argument on recognition is viewed as an attempt to connect human flourishing with a specific social and institutional structure, embodying three basic levels of recognition.[6] For Honneth, ordinary human self-realization and identity are premised on a basic sense of love, legal and right-based relations, and networks of solidarity. A just society involves therefore complex layers of recognition from the family, through friendships, up to the state. Such recognition is something which has to be struggled for over long historical periods. Lack of recognition is the root to all injustice, inequality, unfreedom, and oppression. Consequently, a just society is one in which individuals have the possibility for self-realization through complex processes of mutual recognition.[7] It is worth immediately underlining the importance of rights in Honneth's argument.[8] Rights, in effect, facilitate and enable self-esteem, self-respect, and ultimately self-realization.[9]

Accordingly, a core theme in Honneth's work—derived from Hegel—is that relating to oneself and developing self-esteem are intersubjective relational processes of mutual recognition. One's attitude to oneself develops through one's encounter with others in a process of mutual recognition. This relation to self is thus reliant upon the recognition of others, with a similar sense of self-esteem. As Honneth notes, 'The individual learns to grasp his or her self as both a full and a particular member of the social community by being gradually assured of the specific abilities and needs constituting his or her personality through the approving patterns of reaction by generalized interaction partners' (Honneth 2004, 354). As in Hegel, this implies both a comprehensive vision of a form of society and a specific social understanding of morality.[10] As Honneth notes, the reason why 'acts of recognition must be moral acts is that they are determined by the value or worth of other persons; acts of recognition are orientated not towards one's own aims but rather towards the evaluative qualities of others' (Honneth 2002, 513).

This particular account of recognition does change the character of political theory. It moves it from themes of equality and distribution to one based on recognition and social struggle. Justice, in this latter context, is not about distribution, but rather about addressing humiliation and a lack of respect and recognition. In this context, the justice of a society is determined by its level of well-being in terms of 'societally guaranteed recognition relations' (Honneth 2004, 354). For Honneth, one can therefore speak of valid moral progress in society.[11]

# Right and recognition

Having indicated very briefly the broader intellectual frame within which recognition argument has functioned, the argument now focuses on the concept of rights and recognition. Rights, in my interpretation, are not germane to spheres such as the family or friendship. Rights do not signify a realm of intimacy. It is nonetheless true that the individual still only acquires rights insofar as she is granted normative status by others through a process of recognition (and often a struggle for recognition). Adopting a felicitous phrase of Derrick Darby's, all rights are thereby unnatural (see Darby 2009). Admittedly, there is considerable normative force in the idea that rights are pre-social moral claims, which inhere in some manner in individuals. Yet this latter claim stands or falls on the argument that a right can only be comprehended as a valid universally justified claim. This argument contends that a right exists *before* it has been recognized. The right appears out of nowhere. The justification of the right is always external to the practices and ties of society. Thus, a right 'would be recognized *as a right* (as something that was fully justified) and would not simply *become* a right in being recognized' (Martin 2003, 180). The real legwork for such an argument lies with these externalized moral sources. Further, what precise features actually endow rights with this externalized foundational justification? The most cursory glance at the diverse moral literature of the last half a century reveals quickly that there is neither any consensus on what this feature is nor how one might adequately justify it.

An accurate assessment of rights is that they are not externalized valid claims, but rather, as Rex Martin argues, 'established' or 'accredited' ways of acting within an institutional or collective setting. As beneficial to the right-holder, they only become valid when 'recognised in law and maintained by governmental action' (Martin 1993, 87). Rights are thus always norms articulated within a moral or political setting. As such they require to be formulated and harmonized in a systematic manner. Government (or more broadly the state) is the institutional agency which systematizes rights—in my reading under the aegis of an impulsion implicit in the civil state tradition. Rights are thus always social in the sense that 'it is unlikely that a right could ever exist except in a social setting' (Martin 1993, 27). For Martin, the most effective manner of dealing with this process of systematizing and harmonizing rights is via the democratic state.[12]

Martin equates human rights quite directly with civil and political rights.[13] Human rights documents are therefore seen to be directed primarily not to individuals—although individuals are the beneficiaries—but to states. He argues, 'human rights claims are addressed to government in particular, we have to regard practices of governmental recognition and promotion as being the appropriate form that such recognition and maintenance must take. To that degree, governmental practices are included within the notion of human right' (Martin 1993, 87). Thus, there is deep link between human rights and the state. Consequently, as Martin notes, 'The right to life or the right to be free from torture is, insofar as it is claimed against individual persons, ultimately also a claim against government for backup promotion and maintenance.' It follows that 'government practices (of recognition and maintenance) are necessarily involved even in such cases' (Martin 1993, 89).

This, for Martin, is both a historical and a conceptual issue, thus 'those institutions and agencies which are central to organized society are necessarily relevant to the status of human rights claims in all societies. In any given society it is these institutions that count.' It follows that 'Human rights *laws*, then, are civil rights laws with a certain kind of moral backing' (Martin 1993, 91–2).

In summary, human rights are not externally justified claims; they are conversely relational social practices which involve recognition within a state. This is distinct from any solidarist, moral, or love-based recognition argument. All rights require recognition, including human rights. Without recognition, such rights do not exist. Having a political or legal right (as distinct from a moral right) is a relation which invokes a wider public trust, such that parties put their reliance upon a more anonymous institutional relation. This public fiduciary relation is not just a legal relation, it is also fundamentally political, since it links directly with the role of the state tradition. In fact, rights involve a specific conception of political relationships. The rights, and implied public trust, are maintained and respected within the institutional setting of the civil state. Politics, within the civil state, is viewed as the deliberative medium of that setting. Rights—including human rights—are therefore neither configured as externally morally valid claims nor as part of any private moral dialogue, but conversely they are integral to a civil and political dialogue which invokes a high degree of anonymity within the public realm of a civil state. We should therefore reconceive human rights in a political frame, that is within a civil state setting.

## The civil state and recognition

Politics as a practice which negotiates and deliberates conflict and plurality, has developed, specifically over the last two centuries, through the institutions and constraining structures of the nation state (as the most hegemonic form) and the civil state (in rarer cases). These two dimensions of the state tradition have overlapped considerably in practice. However, it is particularly out of the internal character of the civil state tradition that considerations of human rights—understood via recognition—have been brought fully into play in the post-1945 world. There is no perfected formula here for political life, since in large part, as argued, the most usual addressee of human rights is also the state; in my own terms, this is more particularly the powerful tradition of the organic nation state. However, it is still worth reminding ourselves that all developed states are still only 'aspirant' civil states.[14] In this sense, the achievements of what might be expected from civil states are always fallible and fragile.[15]

The state, in more general terms, is an unusual artefact, constructed gradually in Europe during the sixteenth and seventeenth centuries.[16] It developed significantly during the nineteenth and twentieth centuries and was rapidly emulated elsewhere thereafter, to the present day (see Vincent 1987, 2002, chs. 1 and 2). However, the state is not something that can be easily copied. In Europe and elsewhere, it was more the result of irregular and protracted struggle. Notions of national identity coincided fortuitously with the state, predominantly during the nineteenth and twentieth centuries, but, as previously argued, the compounded relation between the state and the nation is a historical artifice of comparatively recent vintage.[17] Loyalty in all states is mixed. Very few communities are all-inclusive, and hardly any now correspond to any ancient ethnic communities—except in daydreams. Boundaries of states remain relatively open and mutable. Further, the state as such is not identical with a government, a people, or indeed sovereignty. The reality of the state is a peculiarly intangible thing. There are naive views of the state understood as power or as an agent of some economic force or class. These all tend to miss the point. The idea and practice of the state, as an association of human beings, has a forceful if oddly subtle presence. It can be identified with many ends, although not many appear essential. As such there has never been a settled theory of the state. In many ways, it is a profoundly authoritative fiction, although fictions should not be seen as lacking in concrete presence. Many fictions can be overwhelmingly forceful and widely accepted presences which are heavily relied upon for human interaction.[18]

One unresolved aspect of the presence of the state concerns its recognition in international law. This is a related, but nonetheless distinct level of recognition. The issue of recognition, for one international law scholar, 'touches the life of States in its most vital aspects'. Yet, recognition of states still remains 'one of the weakest links in international law'; despite this it is crucial, particularly in times of civil disruption or war. The immediate post-1945 period was one particularly decisive moment where this idea of state validity and recognition arose with force. But recognition theory remains a 'glaring gap in the effective validity of international law' (all quotations from Lauterpacht 1947, 3–4).

Recognition, in a nutshell, provides a decisive steer on what might be considered, at a basal level, a state in international legal terms. In early international law writing, around the period of the Treaty of Westphalia, the formation and identification of states were not seen as a noteworthy issues, although certain puzzles arose when secessions occurred. Consequently, the idea of mutual state recognition had little overt place in international law discussion until the later eighteenth century.[19] There was though little unanimity on the question of recognition, even during the nineteenth century. International law remained the basic norms that existed *between* independent sovereign, usually European, states. Recognition implied, approximately, that one had become a member of the society of 'civilized' associations. The notion of civilization here—as in much nineteenth-century international law, political science, sociology, and anthropology—was conventionally distinguished from barbarism or at least lack of civilized norms. In this sense, 'The binding force of international law derived from this process of seeking to be recognized.' Associations calling themselves states were not denied statehood; however, until recognition was granted no notice was taken of them internationally. Thus, through recognition, a 'state becomes an international person and a subject of international law' and is thus admitted to civilized international society. James Crawford refers to this process neatly as a 'juristic baptism' (quotations from Crawford 2006, 15).[20]

Recognition, as indicated, has remained a contested issue in international law. Very briefly there have been two dominant theories concerning the recognition of states: declaratory and constitutive theories. The former see recognition as largely *ex post facto*; in this case, a 'State exists as a subject of international law, i.e. as a subject of international rights and duties—as soon as it "exists" as fact, i.e. as soon as it fulfils the conditions of statehood as laid down in international law. Recognition merely declares the existence of that fact' (Lauterpacht 1947, 41). For some international lawyers, the declaratory theory has far more credence, that is to say, if a state has declared its existence, in practice it will not be ignored by other states (see Crawford 2006, 26). In general terms, if an association is regarded as effective, has a defined territory, a relatively permanent population, some degree of durability, and appears relatively independent, then it can be considered a state, regardless of what any other state might think or hope.

The constitutive theory concentrates on the idea of recognition *by* other states (or an international comity of states), as actually constituting the legal and political existence of a state. Thus, the rights and duties of statehood originate in the recognition of other states, in effect making an association part of a wider judicial and political community. For Lauterpacht, this theory focuses on two key assertions: first that prior to recognition a community has neither the rights nor obligations of a state. It follows that the unrecognized association is not actually a state. Second, recognition appears to be more of an act of discretion than a legal duty. The origin of this latter theory is often seen to lie in the writings of Hegel and his account of will and recognition. The theory is then often seen to be developed, in its classical format, in Georg Jellinek's writings. Another important implication of this constitutive theory is that it assumes that the rules of international law have everything to do with the customary vernaculars of the existing society of states.

The general critique of declaratory theory is that it asserts a legal right where no such right exists. In other words, it is not clear to the critic how the empirical fact of existence entails any legal significance. For some the answer to this query is straightforward, namely, the factual assertion is a political, as distinct from a legal act.[21] However, the latter argument still does not account for how a political fact necessarily entails a legal status.[22] Although associations can assert their state-like existence, the implication is conventionally that such associations must fulfil normative and juridical expectations of what a state is and should be.[23] Despite such criticism, the declaratory theory is still widely admired amongst international law theorists (see Brownlie 1973, 94). Its appeal, unexpectedly, is that it appears to undermine the role of sovereign states in *determining* the actual status of a state, which is considered a virtue. For some supporters, this has an anti-positivist bearing.

The general critique of constitutive theory is that it places too much emphasis on states having the right to grant, or not, recognition. In this context, it is seen as tied too closely to a legal positivist and sovereignty-premised perspective. The recognition and existence of states is then too dependent upon the potentially arbitrary will of other states. Some have found this idea disturbing. The state which is to be recognized, in this context, can be viewed as a second-class association, overly reliant upon the capricious will and interest of other states.[24] Further, on a more sober logical note, how can an entity—which is not a state—nonetheless enter into any treaty or agreement which thereby renders it a state when it is not actually a state at the time of the agreement?[25] Another serious charge which is levelled here is that 'the constitutive act creative of statehood is an act of unfettered political will divorced from binding considerations of legal principle' (Lauterpacht 1947, 41). This 'political' criticism in fact arises in both the declaratory and constitutive theories.

Lauterpacht's solution to the declaratory and constitutive dichotomy tries to blend both theories. Recognition is seen as 'declaratory of an existing fact, such declaration, made in the impartial fulfilment of a legal duty, is constitutive, as between the recognizing State and the community so recognized, of international rights and duties associated with full statehood' (Lauterpacht 1947, 6).[26] Consequently, a state may 'exist as a physical fact, but it is a physical fact which has no relevance for the commencement of particular international rights and duties until by recognition...it has been lifted into the sphere of law' (Lauterpacht 1947, 75). The term constitutive is thus understood not as an arbitrary act, but rather one which is juridically circumscribed. If a state does not recognize an entity—which appears legally to have the basic requirements of statehood—for Lauterpacht this is not the fault of constitutive theory itself, but rather the fault of the 'recognizing state'. However, for Lauterpacht, the 'blended recognition theory' only functions successfully in terms of a comity of states. Such a comity would render recognition more successfully and consistently. He also notes that such recognition is a crucial precondition for the full development of the potentialities of humanity within states (Lauterpacht 1947, 78).[27] Lauterpacht's solution does not meet with much approval in international law circles; however, I leave this to the side for the moment.[28]

# The politics of recognition

A key problem with the recognition of states, identified by a number of writers, concerns the 'political' dimension. For Lauterpacht, for example, in recognition theory there is no other 'field of international relations in which law and politics appear to be more closely woven' (Lauterpacht 1947, v). If recognition is crucial, in some manner, to the existence of states, and linked to the decisions of states, this implies for critics that politics is at the core of international recognition. Politics not only implies the state, but it also indicates national self-interest, national policy, and potential arbitrariness. This makes recognition theory subject potentially to the whims of other nation states.[29] Thus when, for example, Italy and Germany recognized Franco's Spain in 1936 or the old Soviet Union recognized the Finnish government after a Soviet invasion of the country in December 1939, these have been widely regarded as premature or tortious recognitions. Both non-recognition and actual recognition are thus subject to the dangers of the potentially capricious qualities of politics.

The core question for both recognition theories is whether they are focused on a legal or political decision. Lauterpacht wants to confine the recognition of states to the legal dimension. As he argues, 'The legal character of recognition extricates the process of recognition from the arbitrariness of policy; its constitutive character liberates it from an equally disintegrating element of uncertainty and controversy' (Lauterpacht 1947, 76). Politics therefore becomes synonymous with national self-interest, expediency, and potential arbitrariness.[30] The key issue however is the meaning of politics in this latter context.

For many, the meaning of politics lies in issues of scarcity, competition for resources, constrained self-interest, arbitrariness, power, and such like. However, what is missing in this view is the point that politics is also an engagement with these basal facts. The view of politics as pure arbitrariness and self-interest thus narrows our understanding. There is one further argument worth noting: neither law nor morality can be lawfully or morally set in place in any human association. There cannot, for example, be a legal rule for setting up or maintaining the rule of law. Law, by definition, *requires* a political setting and the same is true for effective international law. Law is one of the modes through which politics engages with endemic plurality. Politics thus can provide the setting for the rule of law. It also provides the setting for an effective civil society.[31] This feature of politics also forms the groundwork for rights. Rights—including both legal and human rights—are always political. They are intrinsic to the situation in which politics becomes the *modus operandi* for mediating difference and plurality. Rights, including human rights, are generic recognized political goods, that is, 'third party institutional' arrangements, enabling the processes of mediation of difference.

In addition, because of the reasonableness of much disagreement and the contestable character of the concepts used in political argument, political judgements are most often indeterminate and contestable.[32] Differences in values entail that political judgements will always remain in part unresolved. Politics, as such, embodies therefore the implicit acknowledgement of indeterminacy. It is a non-algorithmic practice. Action and speech in the political realm are not thereby diminished. Political judgement is not just concerned with determinate judgements. It is more closely focused on what might be seen as reflective judgement, which is actuated in speech and action. Political judgement in this latter sense is concerned with the way 'we situate ourselves in the political world without relying upon explicit rules' (see Beiner 1983, 3, 111, 129–32).[33]

In political judgement—which is but one sphere of human judgement—we are essentially finding our way in this relational world of politics. Because of difference and plurality, there are often many possible judgemental standpoints that can be taken on events or courses of action. In judging politically we are always mindful of this diversity. Engaging with this diversity implies imagination, that is, envisaging the trajectories of differing value standpoints. In so doing, we are inevitably engaged in interpretation and a drawing upon our own life experiences. The richness, maturity, and depth of that life experience will have a deep effect on our capacity for making judgements.[34] Such political judgements will not give a 'right answer', but they will offer a more humane mature perspective on an event, more in tune with a *sensus communis*. In effect, this capacity is what makes a great statesman.

Politics is not therefore just about power, self-interest, and arbitrariness, as Lauterpacht intimated. Politics has its own internal sense of rightness, what might be termed political virtue, a rightness which is not appropriate for other domains of human experience. Political virtues are components necessary to deal with the inevitability of human conflict and the authoritative allocation of resources. Politics arises with the diverse tensions between humans. The normative components of politics will be variable and conditional upon circumstances; there are therefore no 'once and for all' formulae for politics.[35]

Politics therefore constitutes a specific type of public setting in which conflicts can be addressed. It functions in a setting where differences are mediated, ultimately, if successfully, into policy. In both this formal setting, as well as in all processes of adjudication, politics embodies an expectation of what Stuart Hampshire called 'hearing the other side' (*audi alteram partem*) (Hampshire 1999, 21–2).[36] This is a dimension of politics as an engagement with difference. It implies a habit of both balanced adversarial, as well as dialectical, engagement with difference and plurality. Politics thus denotes an approach to public affairs concerned with a regularization of deliberatively 'hearing the other side'. 'Hearing the other side' moves ultimately towards formalizing politics in rule-governed legal procedures (for practicality) and a crucial vessel for formalizing politics has been the civil state tradition.[37]

## Politics and law in a different key

Three further questions on the issue of politics need to be discussed. First, should politics be separated from law in both the international and domestic spheres? Second, what of those human associations which do not manifest politics (in the above sense), despite the fact that the United Nations recognizes such associations as states? Third, if a state or quasi-state intentionally abuses its own members (or the members of other associations) and in consequence offends, on a significant level, against human rights or international law norms, can it be said to have committed a crime?

On the first question, the critic might argue here that it is crucially important to keep the political sphere distinct from the legal, especially with regard to international law and human rights. A careful response to this query is contained in Martti Koskenniemi's work. Bluntly put, for Koskenniemi, both international law and human rights can be either considered to be a universal normative order, externally imposed upon states, or alternatively, something which has been extrapolated from actual state practices. In the former, international law stands outside state practices and subsists in a utopian moralized world; in the latter, it is something which simply reiterates existing concrete state practices. From the latter perspective, international law and human rights are just politics, simply an apology for sovereignty. From the former perspective, international law remains dreamily abstracted from reality. The more the autonomy of international law and rights from politics is stressed, the more utopian it becomes (Koskenniemi 1990, 9–10). Thus, whereas one perspective concentrates on concreteness and fails to maintain normativity, the other focuses on normativity to the exclusion of concreteness.[38] For Koskenniemi, the concreteness argument derives from the earlier-nineteenth-century doctrine of sovereignty, entailing the absolute liberty to legislate. Sovereignty is seen as externally imposed upon law.[39] Alternatively, if sovereignty is seen as subject to law—as in the recent 'responsibility to protect' debate—then the utopian normativity vision arises once again (see International Commission on Intervention and State Sovereignty 2001).[40]

For Koskenniemi, the bulk of international law and human rights debate has been a utopian struggle *against* politics. He notes that the rule of law, in international terms particularly, has been continuously pursued to the present day within the everyday activities of the United Nations. He describes this pursuit, *in toto*, as the 'liberal impulse to escape politics' (Koskenniemi 1990, 6). He infers that international society will not solve any hard issues by overtly agreed laws. Undoubtedly, a common legal rhetoric does exist among international lawyers and philosophers, but, as he comments, 'that rhetoric must, *for reasons internal to the ideal itself*, rely on essentially contested—political— principles to justify outcomes to international disputes' (Koskenniemi 1990, 7). Consequently, criticizing a state 'is not a matter of applying formally neutral rules', it rather 'depends on what one regards as politically right' (Koskenniemi 1990, 21). Abstract agreement on a legal rule can be gained, but when the rule is applied and interpreted it will immediately generate political judgement.

In one sense, the present argument concurs with Koskenniemi that international law and human rights are concerned with politics. Their separation is way overdone and the stress some lay on the autonomous character of law and human rights is a mistake. If international law and right do act as a limitation on states, it is a political limitation. Koskenniemi makes a valuable contribution here, particularly by insisting that international law and human rights have to be reconceived as a sophisticated form of political judgement, which takes full cognizance of divergence, diversity, and social conflict. I would also extend Koskenniemi's argument from international law to domestic state law.[41]

In summary, there is no clear immutable distinction between 'law' and 'politics'. A much better distinction would be between the 'ordinary normalities of domestic law' as against the 'extraordinary aspect of international law'. Further, law and politics are blended at both the domestic and international levels. What we think of as law, on the domestic state level, is habituated and institutionalized political judgement. Law is thus a formalized and regularized understanding of politics. It has been, in this domestic state sense, immensely useful (something that coincides with the development of the state form over the last two to three centuries and something which accelerated massively in nineteenth-century states) to train a corps of legal practitioners and regularize them into formalized political judgement, such that they perceive the world through determinate rules, which can be tested in courts and procedures. However, this should not allow us to philosophically and historically lose sight of the deep political substance of law. In the final analysis, the precision of law is a scholarly chimera, allowed for, maintained and stabilized by the evanescence of politics.

The above argument has parallels, on the domestic front, with Richard Bellamy's argument for political constitutionalism. The gist of his argument is that in any developed state reasonable disagreement about substantive issues is unavoidable. In essence, the political democratic process is envisaged as a more legitimate and coherent way to engage with this disagreement rather than legal constitutionalism. It embodies the most effective way of dealing with the 'circumstance of politics', where disagreement about the right and the good is unavoidable, but nonetheless collective decisions still have to be made. The rule of law is therefore seen to depend 'on the democratic self-rule of persons'. Keying into aspects of an older republican language, Bellamy argues that the most effectual way to avoid the dangers of political power and domination, is via democratic processes.[42] Those who focus, for Bellamy, simply on legal constitutionalism and legal resolutions to difference and plurality, miss what he calls the essentially ' "civilising activity" of politics itself' (quotations from Bellamy 2007, 80, 106).

One key problem in the domestic legal approach is that it tries to continuously 'depoliticize' the political sphere, something which directly parallels Koskenniemi's argument on the depoliticization of the international sphere (see Bellamy 2007, 147ff. ). The reason why politics has to be depoliticized (for its critics) is that it is assumed to denote self-interest and arbitrary power and these are part of the problem and not part of the solution. The same basic argument holds for all rights discourse. Many would therefore argue that rights would also need to be depoliticized to become helpful. However, under normal conditions of human cooperation 'disagreements about rights inform normal political debates no less than conflicts of interests. Therefore, a consensus on rights cannot be said to stand somehow outside politics.' Rights, as such, 'belong to the "circumstances of politics"' (Bellamy 2007, 25, 26). The same logic applies to human rights, which international lawyers and advocates of human rights frequently try to legalize or moralize as an explicit way of taking such issues outside the sphere of politics (see Bellamy 2007, 148ff.). This latter argument—in a neo-Kantian format—is alive and well, for example, in the arguments of Jürgen Habermas (see Habermas 2001).

Koskenniemi's and Bellamy's arguments strike me as a fruitful path to follow. The concept of politics is however the key to their success. What frequently hinders the development of this form of argument is the anomalous popularity of the idea that politics denotes self-interest, power, and conflict. It is often asserted but little defended. It also implies an unexpected adherence to the generic ideas of Carl Schmitt. Schmitt's 'state of exception' is largely where politics subsists (i.e. decisionism) (Schmitt 1996). The 'state of exception' stands for the arbitrariness, randomness, and unpredictability of politics. Any 'limit' is not a limitation on the state, but is rather a limitation on law (particularly international criminal law, although it also limits domestic law as well). Sovereignty, as the personification of the state of exception, decides on the limit, and this in turn invokes politics, which decides on the extralegal questions. Schmitt's 'state of exception' thus provides no room for legal judgement, except in the internal sphere of the territorial nation state; even there it is limited by sovereignty. Politics, per se, for Schmitt, provides a confined sphere of operation for law. It also provides no leeway for international law except in the more traditional pre-1945 sense of the term, that is as basically dealing with the customary interrelations between sovereign state entities.

Against Schmitt's monotonous and insipid notion of politics as implying antagonism, there is no reason not to see a subtle form of rightness implicit in political judgement. Politics does not exclusively equate with power, arbitrariness, and self-interest, although such ideas are not absent from politics. To equate politics though wholly with these ideas is, in point, a modernized and somewhat romanticized Augustinianism. Politics is a realm of plurality; it is also a realm of engagement with plurality. In this engagement a notion of 'rightness' in judgement, as distinct from legal or moral rightness, is invoked (see Koskenniemi 1990, 21). Political judgement, in this context, refuses to lay down 'determining rules or ready-made resolutions to future conflict'; it thus accepts that there are 'no determining legal standards' (see Koskenniemi 1990, 28). But this is not an argument either for inertia or an apology for state sovereignty. Koskenniemi interprets politics, in this latter sense, as a move away from the idea of a *Rechtstaat* towards a more flexible and contextually sensitive political condition.[43]

## States and quasi-states

However, this latter conclusion leads to a second key question: what of associations which claim recognition of statehood, via international law and the United Nations, but have little of what we might understand as politics and only a diminutive grasp of human rights? Are all current regimes or associations in, say, the United Nations, with the title 'state', really states in anything but name? The first thing to say here is that there are levels in which interactions between associations take place, in terms of, for example, foreign relations. A state in interacting with a regime—which militarily and practically dominates a territory and can thus be described as the dominant power—will engage in what can be termed the necessary pragmatics of diplomacy and foreign policy. A state will thus interact with such a grouping for various reasons—for the security of its own population or trade and so forth. Policy, power, trade, and pragmatism often prevail here. However, such pragmatism does not conceal—even from diplomats or foreign policy-makers—that they are often dealing with states only in name.[44]

Post-1945, and with the advent of decolonization, saw a large number of associations acquire formal recognition as states and membership of the

United Nations. However, many still have little sense of a consistent order, security, centralized administration, or rule of law structure. Diversity and conflict are often dealt with by bribery, direct violence, or unregulated power. The power and writ of the more dominant group does not necessarily even extend over the territory they claim. In this sense, they do not have a consistent population or territory. There is often more of a patchwork of diverse allegiances to clans or ethnic groups. Corruption and self-enrichment are usually the more secure currency to live by. In this scenario, there can thus be a regular uncertainty about the nature and consistency of authority and indeed the coherence of the public realm itself. This makes it difficult when entering into relations with other states. Government, power, and public offices are viewed as more the personal property of individuals, within a patrimonial elite. Although these general features do characterize a number of newer post-1945 associations, they do not as such qualify for the category of nation state, let alone a civil state. In fact, national unity is as much a myth here as statehood. They may have external recognition of sovereignty; internally they may have a formal written constitution and so forth, but they are only states by pure courtesy and customary interaction. As such these associations, which have been recognized as states in international law, are not states in anything but name and formality. Politics only exists in the crudest, most limited, and narrow of formats, that is, self-interest, power, uncertainty, and competition for resources. Some associations are aspirant state or almost-states, some are just collections of warring groups. Ideally, these should not be recognized as states: neither politics nor human rights subsist in them. It is, as indicated, mere politeness, pragmatism, trade, and security interests which govern this usage.

The above argument is not unfamiliar in contemporary political theory literature. The doyen of American liberalism John Rawls, in his *Law of Peoples*, proposed that only peoples who sustained human rights could actually be fully recognized as members of a society of peoples (which is similar to what I have called a comity of civil states). Rawls does indicate though that it is liberal regimes which form the core of recognized states. These form the ground to human freedom. It is worth noting here though that Rawls does not generally use the term 'state' in this context, preferring instead the term 'people'. In fact, the terms 'decent peoples' and 'liberal democratic peoples' are his customary terminology. 'People' here indicates 'the actors in the Society of Peoples, just as citizens are the actors in domestic society'. Such peoples for Rawls will have a 'reasonably just constitutional culture' (which he sees as institutional), will be united by 'common sympathies' (which he describes as cultural), and have, what Rawls calls a 'moral nature' (which he sees as implying a 'firm attachment to a political [moral] conception of right and justice') (quotations from Rawls 1999, 23). The term 'law of peoples' is basically a reformulation of a conventional group of doctrines derived from customary international law.[45]

Rawls does though allow for the possibility of incorporation of non-liberal peoples as participating members of an international society, but only insofar as they are sufficiently 'reasonable'. In this context, I would conceptualize such 'peoples' as 'aspirant states' or 'quasi-states'. For Rawls, the crucial question is how far 'liberal peoples are to tolerate non-liberal peoples' (Rawls 1999, 59). As long as a non-liberal reasonable society is not aggressive to its neighbours, tries to regulate itself internally by justice, consults its own citizen in some manner, and shows a basic respect for human rights, it can nonetheless be treated as an equal member of international society (see Rawls 1999, 5). The aim essentially is to discomfort right-violating associations. Admittedly, Rawls' notion of human rights in this international setting is fairly sparse and minimal, basically focused on

> the right to life (to the means of subsistence and security); to liberty (to freedom from slavery, serfdom, and forced occupation, and to a sufficient measure of liberty of conscience to ensure freedom of religion and thought); to property (personal property); and to formal equality as pressed by the rules of natural justice (that is, that similar cases be treated similarly).
>
> (Rawls 1999, 65)

There is no concern for social issues, poverty, or any broader distributive justice. Rawls sees no distributive justice arising from international human rights and the law of peoples.

Further for Rawls, there are also 'outlaw states'—although my own preference is to think of them as tortiously recognized states and thus states in name only. Outlaw states, or peoples for Rawls, are those which refuse to follow even the minimal conditions of the 'Law of Peoples'. Such outlaw regimes can indeed for Rawls become the subject for humanitarian intervention if they fail to acknowledge the law of peoples (Rawls 1999, 81). Unexpectedly, Rawls thinks of such interventionism as virtually pre-emptive, even against peoples who present no overt threat.[46] Rawls however does not specify the precise conditions which would enable one to identify or judge this situation. Much of the work done in Rawls' book is what he calls 'ideal theory'. In this context, he interprets the role of political philosophy as articulating 'the permanent conditions and real interests of a well-ordered society' (Rawls 1999, 97). In this sense, it is not clear how far ideal theory can provide guidance for actual non-ideal practice. However, the basic gist of Rawls' argument is clear and one that I would affirm, namely, that there is a meaningful distinction between states (where in my terms politics and human rights exist) and tortiously recognized quasi-states (where politics and human rights are either an aspiration or an irritant).

# Crimes of state

A third question arises here: if actions by states or quasi-states do infringe significantly on politics and thus violate the very substance of human rights, what sense can we make of the notion of state crime? The issue of state crime has, of course, a genealogy with a provenance from the mid- to late twentieth century. The domain in which this debate has largely taken off is in the sphere of international law. In one sense, international law is a prime disciplinary candidate for speaking about state crime. The very existence of international law is open to a broad ambit of interpretations (some interpretations being much less accommodating to the concept of state crime), but minimally it provides the possibility for the question of state crime to be raised, simply by positing some form of law which exceeds individual states.

Prior to 1945, as one scholar has noted, 'the only active subjects of international law were states' (Jørgensen 2000, 139). In this earlier era, the issue of state crime and responsibility was largely nugatory. Although dominating the nineteenth century, this older understanding was still reflected firmly in the early twentieth century, for example, in the principles of the Lotus Judgment of the 1920s. In this latter case, the Permanent Court of International Justice (*Lotus* Case, 7 September 1927) envisaged international law as solely governing the relation between states, with sovereignty taken as the central axiom; further, states were seen in this case to *make* international law.[47] Consequently international law, per se, could not be applied to a state unless it had expressly consented to it. This view underpinned a widely held unease with the concept of state crime, even to the present day. In fact, it would still be regarded with profound suspicion by many states.

The reasons for this unease have roots deep in our understanding of the concept and practice of specifically the European state over the last three centuries.[48] One core idea underpinning this disquiet is that a state cannot, by definition, commit a crime, since the sovereign state is the logical, and for many the legal, presupposition to the concept of crime. In this sense, crime simply cannot precede or transcend the state. Consequently, the idea of state crime is a self-contradiction. The temptation is therefore to steer clear of any suppositions of state crime and suggest that it is the *mens rea* of particular executive agencies, or individual officials, that have made misjudgements, have failed to follow rules, or have just misinterpreted rules. In addition, although it is extending this point too far at this stage, there is a strong juridical assumption that effectual law must imply definite legal remedies. Crime by a state, or alternatively human rights violations (to take a cognate example), require remedies. The question is: are there any? Crimes of state, or violations of human rights, might be regarded therefore as ineffectual simply because they have no actual consistently enforceable remedies, outside of war, military intervention, or the direct consent of the state at issue.

The above argument does not mean that the concept of state crime is meaningless, far from it. However, when the idea is commonly articulated it relies upon a fairly hard distinction between law and politics. Thus, one conventional, if quite optimistic response to the subject of state crime, insists that the distinction between politics and law must be maintained, not only on the domestic level, but more acutely, on the international level. Consequently, the response (in part) to the idea of state crime is raised within the forum of international criminal law. International criminal law, in effect, shows us the limits of lethal action by a state and makes the necessary legal judgments. This might be called the *Rechtstaat* solution. International criminal law is thus the *Rechtstaat* writ large. This argument presupposes that it is essential to maintain the rule of law at both the domestic and international levels and this entails keeping politics at arm's length. State crime then becomes a feasible option under basic rule of law principles.

State crime does have a fairly identifiable genealogy. Briefly, 1918, and much more significantly 1945, were crucial moments in thinking about state crime. Attention was focused largely—at these moments—on the idea of the criminal responsibility of persons or organizations representing the state. In some, slightly rarer, arguments it was the government or the state itself which was seen to be criminally responsible. The most decisive moment in this genealogy of state crime was unquestionably the Nuremberg trial. The conclusion of the 1939–45 war saw an Agreement for the Prosecution of the Major War Criminals of the European Axis and a Charter for an International Military tribunal, indicating three major categories of offence: crimes against peace, war crimes, and crimes against humanity.[49] The Nuremberg Charter was later used as a working model for attempts at formulating crimes of state particularly in the Rome Statute (1998). In all such cases, working as a state official or executive, in any capacity, was regarded as no exemption from criminal responsibility. It should be noted here that although the individual responsibility of state agents figured importantly after the Second World War, nonetheless the extent and range of both organizations, individuals, and groups, considered in the post-1945 trials, nonetheless gave rise to the idea that the state itself was, in large measure, still corporately responsible in some manner, insofar as it encompassed or incorporated these individuals and groups.[50] Post-1945, both individuals and states did become potential subjects for the imputation of responsibility in international law terms, particularly in terms of crimes against humanity, or crimes which affected the international community.

My argument here is that the post-1945 change of perception, concerning the nature of state crime, was largely a change in political judgement. In this sense, the Nuremberg trials represented a radical transformation of political judgement, in a more concrete form. The Nuremberg trials, like the Genocide Convention, were a political act and their long-term effects were and indeed remain fragile.[51] This argument is neither subscribing to a conventional critique, suggesting that the Nuremberg trials were victor's justice, nor to the view that there were distinct legal oddities and arbitrary dimensions to the trials.[52] In indicating that it was a political trial, it is not being argued that it was in any way wrong to consider that the regime in Germany (in 1945) had committed criminal acts.[53] There was, nonetheless, a deeply experimental aspect to the trials, although in the chaos of the immediate post-1945 world it was a reasonable moment to experiment (see Overy 2003, 28). In the more tempered reduced environment of the 1990s and 2000s this experimentation has, in smaller part, returned. The International Criminal Court of 2002 can thus be viewed as 'a direct descendant of the Nuremberg Military Tribunal, as were the European Convention on Human Rights signed in 1950 and the genocide convention' (Overy 2003, 29).

One immediate objection to the above argument is that it is surely vitally important to keep politics separate from law. The issue of state crime cannot be political since it makes the Nuremberg trials into a partisan subject, with little or no consistent grounding in legal rules. This is even more crucial in the international forum, where the accusation of political bias in international affairs is an ever-present impasse. As already argued, this whole argument is reliant upon a miniaturized and crude perception of politics. Politics is as much about the constitution of a public setting in which conflicts can be addressed. However, admittedly in international terms, the situation is much more complex and infinitely messier than the domestic sphere. International law is, at the present moment, an expectation of the habituation and formalization of politics at the international level.

When we therefore examine the Nuremberg trials, or alternatively if we try to identify what is implicit in the Rome Statute (1998), what we see in fact is extrapolations from the customary vernaculars of the civil state tradition and given that the civil state embodies politics, what we therefore see inferentially— at a deeper level—is the political character of state crime.[54] State crime is ultimately a transgression against political existence and a basic understanding of humanity. What state crime embodies therefore is a conscious intentional (*mens rea*) enterprise to rend the fabric of politics.[55] In this context, it would be true to say that international criminal law is parallel to the movement which created human rights post-1945. All such movements are political in character (see Broomhall 2004, 42).

Still, state crime as political does sound odd. Yet all crime, in my argument, can potentially be viewed as a falling away from politics, that is, a falling away from the conditions and substance of civil existence. Domestic crime is basically embroiled or immersed in the complexities and everydayness of habituated politics, which is regularized in legislation, lawyers' talk, and the processes of legal judgment and adjudication. The bulk of ordinary domestic crime is not intended to disrupt politics; it derives rather from facets of human fallibility and self-interest. Depending on its intensity, its ultimate effect is not necessarily to wholly disrupt politics, since politics itself is rooted in the acceptance of human fallibility (as well as the way to mediate this). Law is therefore regularized politics. Domestic criminal law might in this context be seen as shallow crime. State crime—which is distinct from international delicts—is potentially deep crime. Deep crime involves an intended profound destabilization of politics. Failure in a treaty obligation and genocide are both international wrongs, but they are distinct wrongs.[56] Internationally, state crime has a more confined sphere of operation, but its subject is more fundamental. It is concerned with issues which rip apart the fabric of politics, in a much deeper and more comprehensive manner.[57] Thus, Article 19 of the International Law Commission Draft Articles on State Responsibility argued that an international crime is 'An international wrongful act which results from the breach by a State of an obligation so essential for the protection of fundamental interests of the international community that its breach is recognised as a crime by the community as a whole and constitutes an international crime' (quoted in Pellet 1999, 427).[58]

# Conclusion: reconfiguring *jus cogens*

It is an unorthodox way to formulate this point, but the same argument (as outlined above) underpins the concept of *jus cogens*. *Jus cogens* is thus a profoundly political concept, which is telling us something fundamental about the character of both the civil state and the nature of humanity.[59] The origin of the term *jus cogens* derives from Article 53 of the 1969 Vienna Convention on the Law of Treaties, although it has been suggested that the idea can be found in Hugo Grotius' work.[60] *Jus cogens* conventionally refers to 'a peremptory norm ... accepted and recognised by the international community of States as a whole as a norm from which no derogation is permitted and which can be mollified only by a subsequent norm of general law having the same character' (Pellet 1999, 428; see also May 2005, 25). *Jus cogens* thus gives rise to obligations *erga omnes*, that is, obligations that appear within all—in my vocabulary—civil states.[61] Despite still being a contested issue—as one would expect given the odd prevalence of the sovereignty argument—such norms are often now taken to be binding on and within all states, although in practice the realization and acceptance of *jus cogens* remains subject to 'uncertainty and resistance' (see Broomhall 2004, 43).

Still, for many international lawyers, *jus cogens* norms constitute the clearest basis for the concept of international criminal law. As one scholar remarked, no one now seriously doubts that 'norms of *jus cogens* have a real specificity among international law rules' (Pellet 1999, 428). Such norms are though still thin and to a degree rare.[62] There are various ways in which these norms can be conceived: namely, as external normative imperatives, associative conditions of membership, or as the customary action of states.[63] My own supposition is that *jus cogens* norms are in essence speaking about the minimal customary conditions of politics within civil states; these also constitute the basic constituent elements of what it is to be human. An offence against *jus cogens* by a state can thus be conceived as an offence against politics and ultimately therefore an offence against our very humanity. This is what ultimately underpins the understanding of 'crimes against humanity'.

What advantage can be gained from seeing state crime in this manner? In my view, it begins to tackle a paradox in the legal position on state crime. Law has an odd continuing relation with the concept of sovereignty, both at the domestic and international levels. One can see why some lawyers would like to junk the term; it is in some ways the inconvenient truth about law. Domestically, sovereignty usually implies a supreme competence *within* a state. Thus, internally, sovereignty authorizes, recognizes, and legitimates law. Sovereignty decides the limit of law, as part of the state of exception. Externally—in the international realm—sovereignty implies a form of 'plenary competence' and 'the totality of international rights and duties' (Crawford 2006, 32). In this latter realm, sovereignty exists in a different but nonetheless still integral relation with law. International law is either legitimated (externally) by state sovereignty—as in the domestic sphere—or it is soft law, which still requires the decision of sovereignty. Some might wish for hard international law, but again what is the real obstacle here? The answer is straightforward. The reason why there is no hard international law is that there is no international sovereignty. Sovereignty is essentially the problem for law.[64] Even the idea that sovereignty can be contained by making international law internal to sovereignty still implies a decision. Thus, whichever way it is configured, law subsists with sovereignty domestically or internationally. One then asks the question: what is the problem here? The problem in a nutshell is politics. Sovereignty, as decisionism, implies the possibility of arbitrariness, inconsistency, and self-interested exercise of power, implicit in a predominant populist understanding of politics. That is to say, sovereignty implies politics as part of the 'state of exception'. One can see therefore law as both repelled by and intimately involved with politics, via the unpredictable vessel of sovereignty. Law therefore longs for the *Rechtstaat* in the midst of the *Realstaat*. In this scenario, the concept of state crime remains permanently in a paradoxical limbo.

The paradox for law therefore is that it is always subject to sovereignty both internally and externally.[65] In relegating politics to an external sovereign dimension, it unintentionally links it inextricably to arbitrary power. In consequence it creates a potential anarchic international realm. Thus, the refusal of law to accept its political substance creates the problem of arbitrary sovereign power, specifically in international terms.[66] In this sense, the demand to focus on law—autonomous from politics—makes law ultimately vanish into state sovereignty.

What therefore if we acknowledge that law is rooted in politics and further that politics is being given very short shrift if seen as pure arbitrariness and self-interest. Politics, in a richer understanding, engages with diverse self-interest and plurality. Further, if we accept the argument that the civil state tradition embodies the telos of politics in this richer sense, and this in turn is linked intimately with a prevalent understanding of our sense of humanity, then law can be reconceived as regularized politics, intimately tied to a prevalent sense of our very humanity. State crime—as political—then presupposes the judgement of rightness and civility implicit in politics, thus avoiding the irresponsibility implicit in the penumbra of the legal autonomy perspective. It is via this pathway that the desire for international law and human rights might be addressed, namely one which recognizes the rightness within politics, that is ultimately the desire to habituate politics on an international level.[67]

## ▢ NOTES

1. As Habermas puts it, we need to abandon any 'metaphysical assumptions of an individual who exists prior to all socialization and, as it were, comes into the world already equipped with innate rights' (Habermas 2001, 126).

2. At root, for the human person, 'existence as determinate being is in essence being for another' (Hegel 1971, §71). The same argument is also applied to the practice of the state. As Hegel (1971, §331, *Zusatz*) comments, 'A state is as little an actual individual without relation to other states as an individual [person] is actually a person without rapport with other persons.'

3. Thus to define an identity is both to articulate separateness (difference) and identity (premised on the recognition of others).

4. Hegel's ideas on recognition developed out of his early Jena writings, between 1802 and 1806, that is the *System of Ethical Life* and the *Realphilsophie* I and II. The latter were lectures delivered in the University of Jena between 1803 and 1806. None of these works were published in Hegel's lifetime; they were first published in Germany in 1913.

5. His use of Hegel's *Realphilosophie* writings is selective and tempered by his employment of G. H. Mead's and Winnicott's more empirical work.

6. 'I had set out to employ the young Hegel's model of recognition as the key to specifying the universal conditions under which human beings can form an identity; the underlying intention was basically to conceptualize the structures of mutual recognition analyzed by Hegel not merely as preconditions for self-consciousness but as practical conditions for the development of positive relation-to-self' (Honneth 2002, 500).

7. He suggests that each sphere of recognition will also embody its own specific standards of justice (see Honneth 2004, 361). In this sense, the notion of justice is intrinsically plural in character.

8. Rights in this setting are important constituents of recognition. Using the work of T. H. Marshall, Honneth in a predictable format views the gradual expansion of rights from civil to social claims, over the last few centuries, as part of a significant growth of social recognition (see Honneth 1996, ch. 5).

9. '[I]ndividuals can become members of society only by developing, via the experience of mutual recognition, an awareness of how rights and duties are reciprocally distributed in the context of particular tasks' (Honneth 2002, 501).

10. Every human subject is dependent on a 'context of social forms of interaction that are regulated by normative principles of mutual recognition; the absence of such recognition relations will be followed by experience of disrespect or humiliation that cannot be without damaging consequences for the single individual's identity formation' (Honneth 2004, 354).

11. That is 'to the extent that the demand for social recognition always possesses a validity overhang which ensures the mobilization of reasons and arguments that are difficult to reject, and hence in the long term brings about an increase in the quality of social integration' (Honneth 2004, 355).

12. This democratic reference is something I am directly sympathetic to, but do not develop, except in small part in chapter 8.

13. Civil rights are 'political rights universal within a given society. They are ways of acting, or ways of being treated, that are specifically recognized and affirmed in law for each and all of the citizens' (Martin 2003, 175).

14. The original constitutions of even the most developed of civil-minded states were 'in their beginnings, non-democratic and they contain many institutional essentials...that are not fully compatible with democratic institutions' (Martin 1993, 320). Consequently, as Martin (1993, 320) comments, 'the theoretic system I have sketched in this book explicates *one* important feature of the tendencies of *some* existing political societies'.

15. '[T]he status of being guided fitfully and only in part by the system of rights idea; none of them has become anything like a wholesale exemplification of that idea. Thus, though the idea of system of rights might be in fact a goal of some existing states...that idea is, right now, best understood as only a partial goal of any one of them' (Martin 1993, 320).

16. A state can formally be defined as a territorially based association whose affiliates are uniformly subject to a structure of laws; further, it embodies legislative procedures and civic administrative bodies that do not change significantly with alterations among the incumbents of municipal offices and in which lawfully regimented practices and rules are sustained for making such changes.

17. Despite what a host of commentators on nationalism will argue. For my own somewhat heterodox reading of nationalism, see Vincent (2002).

18. One might describe the state as a 'fictional reality', equivalent analogically, for example, to the institution of money, that is to say, a more or less universally accepted value which is fictional if concrete (see Runciman 2003, 33ff.).

19. Although some have seen elements of it in the work of Hugo Grotius.

20. Exactly how a state gains its territory is often regarded as an issue of fact rather than law. The ambiguity concerning the claim to territory is the assumption that the entity is a state in the first place—that is, the thing 'doing' the acquiring of territory. Factual effectiveness

and a capacity to wield power are not though the same as legal effectiveness. There is a difference between a mafia boss and a state executive acquiring territory.

21. '[T]he purely declaratory effect of recognition and the full internal and international existence of the State prior to recognition have on occasions been asserted both by the members of international commissions and by judges in municipal courts' (Lauterpacht 1947, 3).

22. In 1923, twenty-three nations of the Iroquois Indians brought before the League of Nations a complaint against the Canadian government and British Empire; they described themselves as a matter of fact as 'a State within meaning of Art 17 of the Covenant'. The Canadians argued conversely that they were legal subjects of the British Crown (Lauterpacht 1947, 49–50).

23. '[W]hen we assert that a State exists as a normal subject of international law by virtue of the fact of its existence, we must necessarily have in mind a State fulfilling the conditions of statehood as laid down in international law' (Lauterpacht 1947, 45).

24. Although it has nonetheless been pointed out that such constitutive recognition is less of a negotiating procedure than a determination of the facts (see Lauterpacht 1947, 58).

25. Treaties are often viewed in the context of formalizing recognition by some constitutive theories.

26. As such 'there is little substance in the assertion that a State commences its international existence with the concomitant rights and duties, as soon as it "exists". On the contrary, recognition, when given in the fulfilment of a legal duty as an act of application of international law, is a momentous, decisive and indispensible function of ascertaining and declaring the existence of the requisite elements of statehood' (Lauterpacht 1947, 51).

27. 'It is to be hoped that the political integration of the international community, which, in the long run, is the absolute condition of the full development of the potentialities of man and humanity in general, may, alongside other improvements, render possible the collectivization of the process of recognition as best in keeping with its nature and purpose' (Lauterpacht 1947, 78).

28. Martti Koskenniemi, for example, sees it as a middle way which remains 'question-begging' (Koskenniemi 1990, 17). For James Crawford, neither theory adequately accounts for the practices of current international law (see Crawford 2006, 5ff.).

29. '[W]hile the task of ascertaining the existence of conditions of statehood is essentially one of administration of international law, it is at the same time a political act fraught with political consequences involving the interests of the State called upon to grant recognition' (Lauterpacht 1947, 33).

30. The really objectionable element here is 'that recognition is seen to be "an arbitrary function of politics"' (Lauterpacht 1947, 62).

31. '[W]e need a political framework to regulate conduct.... Indeed, without political institutions and regulations, many otherwise private social relations... simply would not exist' (Bellamy 2007, 153).

32. Judgement, as such, is not something that can be avoided, it is ubiquitous in human life, underpinning all human experience. It is something we basically do 'when we seek to decide about a course of action' (Beiner 1983, 7).

33. There are no experts in politics, although there can be more maturity and statesmanship in political judgement (see e.g. Rawls 1999, 97).

34. In political judgement, we become open to 'the full human dimensions of the situation or the particulars being judged. Political judgment in the fullest sense confronts particulars in the light of the whole, the whole of what is meaningful and important to human beings' (Beiner 1983, 158). The gist of Beiner's study of political judgement is that in the final analysis, it needs both reflective distance (as argued by Kant and Arendt) as well as direct engagement and experience (as advocated by Gadamer and Aristotle).

35. It is important though to take note of the generic qualities of political actors and specifically a range of qualities needed in political conduct in government—the capacity for leadership, the ability to summon loyalty and trust, commitment, shrewdness, imagination, a sense of civil responsibility, and at times guile. Politics often works with human failings, vices, and fears. It regularly encounters the 'dirty hands' issue. Yet, it is not a means to something else. Politics is, in effect, a self-sufficient autonomous human practice and form of judgement which embodies potentially internal notions of right (see Philp 2007).

36. Hampshire gives this notion too legalistic a reading for my liking. I basically annex this terminology for what I would argue is crucial to politics.

37. Although politics becomes regularized in law, one should not forget the indeterminate and reflective root of law in politics. Law contains all the advantages and dangers of regularizing something which is ultimately unregularizable.

38. Koskenniemi also calls these the rule and policy approaches to international law.

39. He associates this view with the 1927 *Lotus* Case (Koskenniemi 1990, 14).

40. 'One style consists of preceding the law's substance with an analysis of the character of statehood and that of the international order—the "'political foundations". Another starts out by listing the sources of international law and lets the law's substance follow therefrom' (Koskenniemi 1990, 14).

41. His argument, almost by default, moves in this direction.

42. 'The only available heuristic is a political process that allows people to speak for themselves and to contest the proposals of others', that is, a democratic process (see Bellamy 2007, 66).

43. Koskenniemi suggests, in passing, that this whole scenario will also require lawyers—particularly international lawyers—to reform their whole self-image.

44. Some states are 'hodgepodge' and ramshackle. Thus, Rex Martin, for example, in his work on rights argues that he is not concerned with such entities (Martin 1993, 321).

45. Thus a concern for the self-determination of peoples, a basic respect for treaties, non-intervention in the internal affairs of peoples, norms regulating the conduct of war, the honouring of human rights, in certain contexts humanitarian intervention, and providing a frame for international organizations.

46. 'We must at some point face the question of interfering with outlaw states simply for their violation of human rights, even when these states are not dangerous and aggressive, but indeed quite weak' (Rawls 1999, 81, n. 26).

47. See *Lotus* Case (1927).

48. It would be truism to a large degree that 'the idea of states being criminally responsible for acts that violated international law had always been viewed with suspicion' (Jørgensen 2000, 139).

49. Crimes against peace (planning, preparing, initiating, or waging a war of aggression or a war in violation of international treaties, agreements or assurances or participating in a conspiracy for the accomplishment of the forgoing); war crimes (violations of laws or customs of war—e.g. ill-treatment of prisoners, killing hostages, etc.); crimes against humanity (murder, extermination, enslavement, deportation, inhumane acts against civilians on political, racial, or religious grounds).

50. 'It seemed more expedient to talk of individual criminal responsibility after the Second World War, although it would seem that, in the case of Germany, given the number of people tried as individual or members of criminal organizations, the entire state apparatus was in effect condemned' (Jørgensen 2000, 25).

51. 'The trials were without question a political act, agreed at the level of diplomacy, and motivated by political interests.... Yet the final outcome was less prejudiced and more self-evidently just than these objections might imply' (Overy 2003, 29).

52. For example, indictable charges only came about after a long period of legal wrangling, many did not even know that they were defendants for many months (see Overy 2003, 8).

53. Despite the fact that the German government was never branded a criminal organization, the idea of criminality of the whole state 'formed the basis of the trials' (Jørgensen 2000, 70).

54. Nuremberg was largely 'inspired by treaties, [and] the "customs and practices of states"' (Clapham 2003, 40).

55. The full significance of this argument can be supplemented by another argument, namely that it is in politics that we identify a deeply prevalent (but not uncontested) grasp of our very humanity.

56. In 1976, the International Law Commission decided to include in its Draft Articles on State Responsibility a distinction between normal international wrongful acts (delicts) and exceptional grave breaches (international crimes).

57. There are parallels here with the gist of the famous Barcelona Traction Case where a distinction is drawn between the obligation of states towards the international community as a whole, and those arising vis-à-vis another state in the field of diplomatic protection.

58. '[W]hen a state breaches an international obligation essential for the interests of the international community as a whole, it never acts by chance or unintentionally; therefore, the elements of intent and of fault, which are not necessarily present in other internationally wrongful acts, are part of the crimes, exactly as they are part of penal infractions in domestic law. Moreover, even without a judge, the reactions of the international community to a crime clearly include punitive aspects' (Pellet 1999, 434).

59. This would explain the *erga omnes* dimension.

60. UN Doc. A/CN.4/490/Add.1, para 48.

61. All *jus cogens* are *erga omnes*, although certain things are *erga omnes* but not necessarily peremptory norms.

62. For certain scholars, there are criteria for identifying such norms. They must be recognized by the international community as a whole; they need to be accepted as serious by all; they need to affect the conscience of humanity; they must be seen to offend against considerations of humanity; they will normally affect international peace and security;

they will also entail crimes of individual criminal responsibility under international law (see Jørgensen 2000, 161).

63. Larry May (2005, 29) argues that 'there are some principles that transcend national borders and achieve universal binding force'. He comments that 'all that matters is that there be a philosophical basis for universal or quasi-universal norms grounded in basic human rights, on which the norms of international law might rest. This is the basic insight of moral minimalism as I conceive it' (May 2005, 34). Thus, *jus cogens* norms are seen as 'providing a protection from the treatment by a State that would jeopardize the security of its subjects' (May 2005, 32). In a different mode, Thomas Franck sees certain deep rules underlying the whole idea of international criminal law; they form associative norms (rather than substantive norms) necessary for membership of the international community. They are not subject to the consent of states and form part of an 'ultimate canon' of preconditions to the very recognition of sovereignty (Franck 1993, 57–61).

64. Anthony Cassese sensed this conflict profoundly during his time as President of the International Criminal Tribunal for the Former Yugoslavia, arguing in retrospect that international law always remains the austere contrary to the potential irresponsibility of state sovereignty. He complained that even the 1998 Rome Statute has been still far too deferential to state sovereignty (see Broomhall 2004, 56–7). As H. G. Niemeyer commented in 1932, international law remains therefore 'an edifice built on a volcano—state sovereignty' (quoted in Broomhall 2004, 60).

65. If we take seriously the argument concerning the separation of law and politics, the problem is that this bypasses the ineffectiveness of international criminal law—even from the *Rechtstaat* perspective—compared to the effectiveness of sovereignty. It is still the case that much state crime goes unremarked and measures to address it often seem remarkably weak. However, more seriously, one key way in which this separation has been articulated—in both the above arguments—is via the use of the concept of sovereignty. Law is viewed as a self-contained system, which functions within a specific boundary; the boundary of law, as well as its core authorization, is in fact defined by sovereignty. Events beyond the boundary then relate to politics focused largely on the externalities of the state. Yet, paradoxically, it is the insistence of law on its autonomy from politics which generates the irresponsible and anarchic potential of sovereignty. This is simply because sovereignty defines the limits of law.

66. '[P]olitical constitutionalism tackles the Hobbes challenge at its source—the problem of the sovereign ruler....It is the political system that de-sovereigntises sovereign power' (Bellamy 2007, 57).

67. The idea is that sovereignty is not constituted in a vacuum but rather by 'recognition of the international community, which makes its recognition conditional on certain standards, has become increasingly accepted in the fields of international law and international relations....From this perspective, crimes under international law can be understood as a formal limit to a State's legitimate exercise of its sovereignty' (Broomhall 2004, 43).

# 8 Citizenship and Human Rights

The arguments of chapter 7 were focused on the idea that the fate of human rights has been tied closely to politics; this in turn was linked to facets of the state tradition. This argument was emphatically not providing any imprimatur on the state as such. In fact, as argued, the nation state—particularly since 1945—for both international law and human rights, has been the chief quandary. The problem here is not though so much the state, as the organic self-determining nation state as, in effect, the inheritor of the nineteenth- and early-twentieth-century racial state. Again, this is quite definitely not suggesting that the racial state is an involuntary concomitant of the nation state. The argument is rather that the nation state embodies the latency for genocide. This latency generated the initial human rights movement in the first instance. Nationalism, race, ethnicity, and group culture are the progeny of a certain particularizing ontological perspective on humanity, developed initially in the late eighteenth century and then transformed in the later nineteenth century through evolutionary theory. The echoes of this perspective reverberate to the present day and those who cultivate the language of culture, ethnicity, and nationality play with this unpredictable legacy, which can of course be innocuous much of the time. Overall, the state tradition has been both the problem and part of the solution. It contains both the substance of international law and human rights, as well as the object to which they are regularly applied. The argument concerning human rights was then linked to a theory of social recognition which was seen as central to both rights in general and human development in particular. Rights are not and can never be simply intrinsic justified claims. This latter idea is more focused on the mythical world of certain twentieth-century moral philosophers. Rights conversely only exist in the context of complex relational structures of social recognition; that recognition is tied to the nature of political association. It is also linked to the development of the human person and indeed humanity as such.

This final concluding chapter focuses on the conceptual links between the language of human rights and that of citizenship. The discussion will therefore track critically across the various accounts of citizenship in tandem with human rights debates. This tracking process will also invoke, briefly, parallel developments within understandings of democracy, freedom, and equality.

# Citizenship and human rights

Citizenship has gone through a series of phases of development, which accelerated within certain states during the twentieth century. The notion of citizenship itself has though a long genealogy in European thought. Very briefly, the term derives from the Latin *cives* and the Greek equivalent *polites*. In classical Greek thought it usually denoted the membership and identification with a city of one's birth, a collection of duties, an eligibility to participate in the adjudication processes of the city, particularly in larger cities such as Athens, and an inner capacity for rational virtue, entailing the internalization of communal norms. This older understanding of citizenship can be seen as a *civic* conception. The civic idea did not initially have a vocabulary of rights at its disposal. Aristotelian-influenced proponents of civic citizenship tended to speak more in terms of the duties of the citizen or what was due to the citizen. The assertion of the importance of citizens performing their civic duty was not therefore necessarily premised on any correlative right, rather what was due to and from the public good.

In a later republican format, particularly from the seventeenth and eighteenth centuries, civic citizenship, in addition to the above, focused on themes of self-discipline, public spirit and virtue, a conception of the common good, disquiet with private gain and self-interest, and a belief in a formal simplicity and piety of life. These themes were echoed in certain French republican ideas on citizenship in the era of the 1790s revolution. By this period, and later, civic-inclined exponents began to transform civic citizenship arguments into a vocabulary of rights. Such rights were usually conceptually tied to a substantive conception of the common good. The civic citizenship tradition also embodied a strong correlativity thesis. Rights were premised on the common good; they implied that the citizen had correlative duties to the common good. Citizenship also designated the consciousness of the ends of human life as embodied in the institutional forms of the public life. It was thus a disposition, where the individual developed to a level of self-consciousness and ethical awareness inclusive enough to be identified with the public sphere of the whole community.

# Civil citizenship and human rights

As distinct from the civic citizen, the *civil* citizen was a product of the era of embryonic liberal thought, which came to fruition in the nineteenth and twentieth centuries.[1] The civil citizen was understood as an independent agent with partially preformed desires and interests. The function of any public order was to protect and uphold these fundamental human interests.

These interests were often spoken of in terms of rights—natural or civil. Citizenship was thus conceived more negatively in terms of the legal protection of pre-existing rights to, for example, life, liberty, and property. The actual private concerns and interests of individuals were though distinct from the formal but minimal public ethos of citizenship—although at the same time the notion of the citizen still implied an internal private autonomy of the individual. For classical liberal theorists, throughout the nineteenth and twentieth centuries, although individuals may have lost some of the 'civic' benefits of close communal life, nonetheless, they had gained from the privacy, modern liberty, and new found prosperity of commercial liberal society.

In summary, civil citizenship was associated conventionally with classical liberalism, implying negative rights, that is, the protection of life, property, and liberty. The classical liberal view of citizenship favoured, in consequence, a more limited understanding of political rule, a framework of general laws, a clear separation between the public and private realms, and a very minimal publically orientated welfare. Classical liberal views on citizenship generally excluded any positive rights or entitlements to economic and social resources, as parts of any programme of collective good or social justice. Unencumbered economic markets, within this perspective, were the preferred mode of resource allocation. Essentially, this was a more procedural, minimal, constitutional, and rule of law-governed understanding of politics. The consequences of this for citizenship were that individuals were secured negative liberty and rights. They were largely both protected and left alone. The good citizen upheld the rule of law and equal negative liberty for all. This was the conventional liberal vision of the *Rechtstaat*.[2]

The nineteenth- and early-twentieth-century versions of civil citizenship did though clearly extend into democratic representation. Political rights to vote, or stand for office, *prima facie*, could be considered to be invoking older ideas of *civic* citizen participation. However, political rights to vote can, in this context, still be viewed as negative. As one writer noted, 'the occasional visit to the polling booth has seemed to many a pathetically inadequate definition of citizenship' (Heater 1990, 96). Some writers, such as Joseph Schumpeter, amongst many others, thus made a virtue of the negative apathetic citizen. Democratic citizenship could therefore be viewed as a negative protective idea. Participation was strictly constrained. The core intuition to grasp here is that political democratic citizenship can still be viewed as negative, purely protective, and in accord with a classical liberal understanding. In summary, citizenship in classical liberal thought is generally confined to a relatively narrow field. It is defined in terms of the constrained civil rights of persons, that is, protective civil rights to life and liberties and prevention of coercion. The citizen of liberal individualism could be described as a more 'minimal citizen', essentially being the mirror image of the more minimal procedural conception of the state.

When we move to the later twentieth century, significant developments took place in the understanding and practice of citizenship. The most significant of these was the controversial extension of rights and citizenship language in the post-1945 period. The fact that these contentious extensions took place post-1945 is not fortuitous, vis-à-vis the clear temporal parallel with human right developments. This extension of citizenship and rights language did not present any final resolution. In effect, what we see over the years from 1945 to the present day is an ongoing and unresolved debate about the nature of citizenship, rights, democracy, the state, and international law, which are part of the dialectic of the state tradition. The character of this debate over citizenship reflects a broader argument about politics and the state. In fact, the debate has in many ways intensified during this period. Consequently, on the domestic front, various models of citizenship have warred with each other, particularly from the 1980s to the present day.

Before discussing these developments, it is worth noting again that the idea of citizenship which was most familiar from the *Rechtstaat* tradition up to 1945 was that of civil citizenship. This conception implied definite individualistic rights. Rights expressed, ontologically, the separateness of individuals. They were claims asserted against other individuals, groups, or states—often under the rubric of justified claims.[3] As indicated, the more general of such rights were claims to life, liberty, speech, property, conscience, opinion, association, and so forth. Such rights correlated loosely with duties of forbearance or non-interference, usually with the proviso that such rights did not overtly injure or harm others. These rights did not, characteristically, demand extensive interventionary public action—except, for example, in the enforcement of duties to discharge one's debts or fulfil contracts. Such rights were usually perceived to be more negatively protective, implying passive, relatively costless duties. Such citizenship rights by the mid-nineteenth century included that of voting. This general understanding of citizenship is, to some extent, encapsulated in two of the categories of citizenship—civil and political—discussed by T. H. Marshall in his *locus classicus* account of citizenship, *Citizenship and Social Class* (1950). For Marshall, *civil* citizenship, which he saw developing from the eighteenth century, implied a comprehensive equality of rights to civil freedoms, which might broadly be called generic constitutional liberal freedoms. Political citizenship (meaning democratic suffrage rights), which developed for Marshall gradually over the nineteenth century, indicated the right to participate in the political process which determines the condition of one's life. Neither of these categories, as stressed earlier, necessarily caused any problems for classical liberal thought on citizenship.

The majority of these ideas—initially the civil conception and then by the early nineteenth century the political idea—were already, to a degree, familiar from earlier bills of rights. The French Declaration of the Rights of Man and of the Citizen (1789) and the United States Bill of Rights (1791) had already indicated that these more general civil rights of the citizen were *also* the rights of humanity.[4] The transposition from citizen to humanity seemed obvious to many proponents. If we delete the 'natural' and 'religious' dimensions, the first twenty-one articles of the 1948 Universal Declaration, as well as the European Convention for the Protection of Human rights and Fundamental Freedoms (1950), the American Convention on Human Rights (1969), amongst others, follow (at least in embryo) an analogous *Rechtstaat* pattern of conceptual presentation, namely that every human being has what are, in effect, the basic *civil* rights to life, freedom of thought and expression, to seek, receive, and impart information and ideas, freedom of peaceful assembly, and freedom of association with others. These rights also include the civil right not to be tortured or inhumanely treated, to have the right to fair trial, and not to be unjustly treated. We might call this general constellation of rights a *civil minimum*. The civil minimum would also include prohibitions against slavery, genocide, torture, prolonged arbitrary detention, and systematic racial discrimination. It is the minimum of what one would expect of citizenship within any state *qua* state, as well as what one would expect as a human being. Thus, transposed directly to the human rights sphere, these general civil rights have often been seen as having a more fundamental aspect to them. In fact, for some commentators, they form the foundational rung of a hierarchy of human rights (see Wellman 1999, 15). It is no surprise, in this sense, that what are often called first-generation human rights correspond quite directly to the basic rights of civil citizenship and thus what one expects of both the state and politics.[5]

This civil conception of citizenship and human rights also links directly to a very basic sense of what might be termed, for convenience, 'civil democracy'. For example, Article 23 of the American Convention, Protocol 1 Article 3 of the European Convention, and Article 21 of the 1948 Declaration include democratic citizen rights as basic human rights. Thus, for example, Article 21 of the 1948 Universal Declaration of Human Rights (UDHR) asserts that

> (1) Everyone has the right to take part in the government of his country, directly or through freely chosen representatives (2) Everyone has the right of equal access to public service in his country (3) The will of the people shall be the basis of the authority of government; this will shall be expressed in periodic and genuine elections which shall be by universal and equal suffrage and shall be held by secret vote or by equivalent free voting procedures.

Further, democracy, without civil human rights in general, would be largely unworkable, since the absence of freedom of speech, of association, free assembly, fair trial, and guaranteed physical security of the person, would make democratic participation a facade. This notion of *civil* (including therefore, in my usage, *political* citizenship rights) citizenship is further directly related to an understanding of civil liberty, that is, a basic conception of negative liberty, understood largely as a protection against intentional unjust coercion, interference, or cruelty to the person. It would further match up with a formal understanding of civil equality that is corresponding directly to the equal dignity and civil rights of all citizens. Again these are all correlated directly to the customary vernaculars of the civil state tradition.

## Social citizenship and human rights

The problematic category of both citizenship and rights, in the Marshall scheme, is the third concept, that is, *social* citizenship. This idea developed largely, in policy terms, post-1945. The social conception of citizenship was initially theorized in terms of civic duties, as well as a more expansive vision of rights. It thus keyed into some of the earlier ideas of civic citizenship. It implied a modicum of economic and social welfare and a share in the heritage of civilized political life, that is, the chance for all citizens to live according to certain prevailing standards of living. The idea of social citizenship had slowly developed in certain (but by no means all) developed states from the early twentieth century. In Britain, for example, it can be identified with ideas from the early 1900s around the 'new liberalism', 'liberal socialism', and 'social democratic' thinking, as implied in the work of, for example, L. T. Hobhouse, J. A. Hobson, William Beveridge, J. M. Keynes, and Marshall himself (see e.g. Simhony and Weinstein 2001). For one commentator, reformers such as Beveridge and Keynes particularly had a 'crucial place in defining the terms of the civic bargain that prevailed from 1945 to the 1970s' (Ignatieff 1995, 67). This bargain entailed guaranteed rights of protection or security against illness, old age, poverty, and unemployment, as well as opportunities for education. Social rights, largely financed out of general taxation, were provided for by the practice of social citizenship. Taxation and redistribution were essentially used to foster civic solidarity and a sense of a common good, connecting the private to the public realm.[6]

The ambiguity, at this point, concerns the 'duty' which the civic tradition had emphasized. Civic duty became largely institutionalized into the willingness to pay marginally higher levels of direct taxation. The civic component, in this scenario, began in fact to draw back subtly from some of its earlier ethical resources. Marshall clearly assumed though, in the post-1945 period, that a moral consensus, sense of community, and public-spiritedness existed in Britain. This assumption, in the immediate post-1945 world, was not far-fetched. It was part of exactly the same ethos that underpinned the developments of human rights in 1948. In the more globalized world of the 1970s and 1980s, this idea has had less purchase. The expected moral consensus, in the early 1950s, actually grounded the notion of social rights and social citizenship in an account of a common good. It also tempered aspects of the ontology of civil rights and provided the leitmotif for dutiful civic taxation and social justice; it was however seen by most proponents to complement rather than conflict with civil citizenship and civil rights, in the same way that social and economic human rights are often seen to complement civil human rights. However, the gradual thinning out of this consensus set the scene for debates over both citizenship and human rights in the 1980s and 1990s. It is also worth noting here that although ideas of social citizenship, particularly in the post-1945 era, developed in states such as Britain, France, Germany, New Zealand, Australia, and so forth, other states, such as the United States, still largely resisted it, until very recently. Again, if we examine responses to human rights on the same issues, that is, the debates over civil, social, and economic human rights, these theoretical divisions all slot into place. Thus, the fairly consistent critical opposition, from the United States, to social and economic human rights directly parallels their own civil state vernacular. Many US critics would still tend to see such social citizenship rights as social goals—possibly to aspire to—but not human rights as such. Thus, social rights as human rights would be a category mistake.

Consequently, the fact of theoretical and practical resistance to social rights and social citizenship, in the domestic frame, is not unexpected. The opposition to social citizenship rights carries over quite directly into human rights debates. In effect, in social human rights terms, we are speaking of Articles 22–26 of the UDHR and more substantially the International Covenant on Economic, Social, and Cultural Rights (ICESCR, 1966), particularly the substantive Articles 3–15 of the latter covenant. The European Social Charter (1961) also supplements the civil human rights of the European Convention for the Protection of Human Rights and Fundamental Freedoms (1950) with a substantial body of social and economic human rights. This concept of social human rights includes commitments to basic equality and non-discrimination for women, children, and minorities, access to employment opportunities, fair pay, safe and healthy working conditions, the right to form trade unions and bargain collectively, social security, an adequate standard of living (covering adequate food, clothing, and housing), health care, and education.[7] Some of these themes had been actively pursued in the International Labour Organization (ILO). The core intuition underpinning this move to social and economic human rights is that generic civil human rights are all very well, but if one is living in an insecure developing economy, subject to the vicissitudes of an unfettered free market, then basic economic and social (human) rights are at least as important as generic civil rights. It follows for many commentators and human rights practitioners that 'in a world rich in resources and the accumulations of human knowledge, everyone ought to be guaranteed the basic means for sustaining life, and that those denied these are victims of a fundamental injustice' (Beetham 2003, 119). The argument also maintains that human agency in order to function requires access to social rights concerning health, education, work, and so forth. Social human rights are, at least in intent, the domestic state rights of social citizenship writ large. As was observed in earlier chapters, this argument alone can generate deep irritation and consternation amongst some civil rights proponents in *both* the domestic and international setting.

Social citizenship and social rights arguments have further links with a particular understanding of democratic thinking. The argument is that democracy without social and economic rights would be a contradiction in terms: poverty, deprivation, lack of social and educational resources, or continuous unemployment, would make a mockery of any meaningful democracy. In this sense, genuine democracy would have to address a constellation of other social and economic concerns in order to function adequately. We might call this understanding—*social democracy*.[8] The assumption here is also one of a more participatory conception of democracy which moves (with varying degrees) beyond a basic representative protective conception. One modern form of this argument would be deliberative democracy, which has largely filled the vacuum left after the decline of older forms of participatory democracy. Participatory and many formulations of deliberative democracy also relate closely with a social rights and social citizenship argument. These arguments, in turn, are linked directly to the idea of a social minimum, entailing freedom from poverty and social deprivation. Such a social minimum again has direct parallels with the idea of a universal social minimum for humanity, as postulated in social human rights arguments, which try to address poverty and development. This argument also necessitates, by default, a conception of social equality, implying more substantive social guarantees of equality, in terms of income, education, social security, assistance in times of unemployment, health care, and the like. Again, this can also be related to a conception of social freedom. Freedom, in this latter sense, is concerned with socially enabled powers and opportunities for the individual citizens to realize their abilities in a richer and more satisfying manner and thus to be able to participate more fully in the life of a civil community. Although debates about social citizenship and social rights have come under severe pressure, particularly since the later 1980s, the generic ideas have certainly not gone away. In fact, unexpectedly, debates over social and economic human rights—particularly in relation to the vexed issue of world poverty—have if anything strengthened in certain domains of the human rights sphere (see e.g. Sen 1999; Pogge 2002; Vizard 2006).

It would be a truism to say that most of the controversial debates over human rights, up to the 1980s, focused on the relation between the civil and social understandings of human rights.[9] In one sense, this is again hardly surprising. The period, particularly from 1945 to the 1970s, was initially one of a moderate confidence, in many developed states, in the idea of the social welfare state (*Sozialstaat*). However, important qualifications need to be made here. First, although the idea of the social welfare state and social citizenship grew domestically in certain states during this period, yet its extension to the level of human rights was much patchier and thinner. The reasons for this are that the theoretical debates on the nature of social rights and social citizenship remained unresolved, not least in terms of how such social rights could be universally guaranteed. Many have argued that such guarantees are beyond the reach of many developing economies. Further, a vigorous domestic neo-liberal and neo-conservative opposition to social human rights has remained constant throughout this same time frame. Although these oppositional ideas were not dominant during the 1950s and 1960s, it was still a vociferous and articulate intellectual opposition. In addition, the impact internationally of both the cold war and the massive process of decolonization effectively muted and sidetracked much of the social rights and social citizenship debates. Further, the debate between civil and social human rights was often reconfigured—and profoundly distorted at points—as one between the cold war adversaries of liberalism and Marxism–Leninism, free market and authoritarian societies, or even between open and closed societies. Thus, the debate over social citizenship and social rights, both in the domestic state and in the realm of human rights, embodied overlapping awkward trajectories.

Yet by the 1980s and 1990s, two further dimensions appeared in debates on both citizenship and human rights. The first was a full-blown ideological neo-liberal resurgence of civil rights and civil citizenship argumentation, particularly from the 1980s, and second a largely unanticipated renaissance of nationalist and cultural argument. Much of this material is too well documented to dwell upon in any detailed manner. In short, the neo-liberal dimension led to a spirited revival of interest in all forms of classical liberalism and libertarianism—often under the guise of the odd incoherent amalgam of the 'new right' (see Vincent 2009, ch. 3). Each component of the neo-liberal new right structured its own negative restrictive vision of citizenship. All, whether it be Robert Nozick, Friedrich Hayek, or Milton Friedman, were enthusiastically orientated to the free market economy, the separation between public and private realms and rigorous limitations on the state. State intervention for purposes of social welfare was perceived to have failed during the 1945–70 period. The consensual post-war social welfare politics of planning, high taxation, public spending, bureaucratic growth, wages unrelated to productivity, and corporatism were all seen to be redundant trends. There was therefore no alternative to the free market, which had to be the final arbiter for virtually all social issues (including health and education)—whether in the international or domestic spheres.

Aspects of this classical liberal and libertarian ideological legacy have carried through to the present day, even among purported social democrats.[10] This has led in turn to a distinctly critical view of social human rights. For Hayek, for example, 'the time honoured political and civil rights…constitute essentially a demand that so far as the power of government extends it ought to be used justly'. Civil rights protected individuals. These for Hayek have simply been reproduced in the first twenty-one articles of the UDHR. However, the UDHR and later documents had added 'social and economic human rights'. For Hayek—in a very characteristic intellectual neo-liberal move—the UDHR was basically seen as 'an attempt to fuse the rights of the Western liberal tradition with the altogether different conception deriving from the Marxist Russian Revolution'. For Hayek, such social rights are dependent on a vision of society as a 'deliberately made organization'. They 'could not be made universal within a system of rules of just conduct based on the conception of individual responsibility, and so require that the whole of society be converted to a single organization, that is, made totalitarian in the fullest sense of the word' (all quotations from Hayek 1982, 102–4). Hayek (1982, 105) thus concludes that even 'the slightest amount of ordinary common sense ought to have told the authors of the [1948] document that what they decreed as universal rights were for the present and for any foreseeable future utterly impossible of achievement, and that solemnly to proclaim them as rights was to play an irresponsible game with the concept of "right" '. Conceptions of social human rights are thus seen to be the result of the besetting vice of rationalist constructivism in social philosophy, a cosy academic social-minded philosophy which has lost all sight of what constitutes a good society. The obsession with social justice, social rights, and social citizenship and the demand to address poverty through social engineering are all for Hayek part of the same corrupting ethos.

Hayek represents but one strand of a wide range of civil-based arguments and policies which developed from the 1980s, expressing deep misgivings about both social citizenship and social human rights. It is important though to underline the point—with regard to the Hayek criticisms—that he does *not* dismiss human rights. Conversely, first-generational civil rights are the only meaningful universalizable human rights. What we ought to advocate, for Hayek, in human rights and international law, is the classical liberal *Rechtstaat* writ large. What we see however in the social rights argument is the *Sozialstaat* writ large. In other words, what we can clearly observe in this conflict between civil and social conceptions of human rights is a debate within the state tradition itself and furthermore a deep disagreement concerning the reach of the political and the role of the social dimension.[11] In fact, the debate is not really at all one of international human rights set against domestic state rights, it is rather a deep and at times clamorous body of expectations of what is expected minimally of any state, wherever it appears.

# Cultural citizenship and human rights

Since the 1990s, debate has become a great deal more convoluted on human rights. The second dimension (mentioned earlier), which significantly affected the nature of human rights, was the post-1989 rebirth of nationalist, cultural, and identity arguments. This form of argument had its origins in late eighteenth and early nineteenth centuries. One deeply influential aspect of this rebirth focused on revivified nationalist argument, especially and unexpectedly within liberal theory and practice. Another important dimension of this argument in developed states was the rise of multiculturalism— although in the last few years it has begun to look more tarnished.

The idea of multiculturalism is more recent than nationalism. It made its first hesitant and quite minimal appearance in Australia, New Zealand, and Canada during the later 1970s, particularly with changes in immigration laws; indeed much of the initial theorizing about the idea arose particularly from Canadian and Australian academics. Although often discussed formally in the context of North American liberalism and communitarianism, it has also figured as a critical component within feminist, ethnic, postmodern, and postcolonial political theories. Nathan Glazer argues that multiculturalism is characteristically a North American concept, linked to a strong rights-based tradition with deep immigrant and racial divisions in society and consequently it is seen to have no real connection with European politics (Glazer 1999, 183–4). However, multiculturalism did begin to make a critical appearance in European debate during the 1990s. Some scholars thus still see the lifetime of *effectual* multicultural politics as comparatively short. For Glazer, it is a product (largely in educational circles) of the last twenty-five years. For Will Kymlicka, it has only been present since the early 1990s.[12] The fortuitous combination of globalizing forces and the mixing of populations, together with the renewed romanticized interest in ethnicity and culture, has underpinned a more general, if diffuse, interest in culture, nationality, and identity.

One effect of these developments has been, on the one hand, a more intense refocusing in many developed states on the *nation-state* compound. Not that this latter concept has ever really faded from public usage, far from it; however, from 1945 to the 1990s the 'nation' component of the 'nation-state' compound was often a verbal courtesy, rather than a substantive avowed ideological commitment (apart from the language of nascent decolonizing societies). By the 1990s, cultural and national obsessions had regenerated. There was now a rehabilitated interest in what might be called a *Kulturstaat* or, more significantly, a *Multikulturelle Staat*. Large amounts of intellectual space have been thus taken up with debates about ideas of Britishness, Englishness, Scottishness, ad nauseam. In this latter case, there is thus a persistent understanding of the human being, their identity, and substance, though culture—although the concept culture itself remains persistently obscure.[13]

This whole debate, during the 1990s and 2000s, has roots in the rich intellectualizations of the early nineteenth-century nation state, prior to the evolutionary upheavals of 1850s and 1860s. There is nothing fresh here. We are dealing with a reconstituted cultural artifice. Further, these theoretical preoccupations have quite logically given rise to the idea of a culturally defined citizen (although as mentioned this was an idea very familiar to late eighteenth-century thinkers such as Herder and Fichte). What is relatively novel in the 1990s—although again there are precursors in the political structures of the late nineteenth-century Habsburg Empire—is the concept of the *multicultural citizen*. The multicultural citizen is though (despite appearances) the offspring of the same body of argumentation. The multicultural citizen has been one of the most significant of recent developments in citizenship discourse. This latter idea of the citizen also has direct associations with the idea of *multicultural democracy*. What the latter means in practice is much more uncertain. There are, of course, strong antecedents in the diverse nationalist movements of the later nineteenth century for a close link between culture and democracy. For many scholars, to the present day, indeed a unified national culture is one crucial prerequisite for the development of democracy (see e.g. Miller 1994, 1995; Tamir 1993). Yet, multicultural democracy and citizenship are much more volatile categories, for the simple reason that there is nothing, or very little, which unifies such democracies or citizenships. Such categories are premised on acknowledged differences. However, we are not simply speaking of plurality and human difference. Cultural difference is uniquely different. It actually places a spiritual and moral importance on the distinctness of cultures. Such cultural differences are seen to require both respect and some degree of self-determination. In this context, a very different scenario is created. Such cultures then subsist not in dialogue, but simply side by side, like ships passing in the night. Adopting a felicitous phrase of Amartya Sen, this is a form of 'plural monoculturalism' (Sen 2006, 156). Multicultural democracy in this context then appears simply to be just re-presenting (not mediating) proportionally different cultural interests.

Deliberative democracy could, in this scenario, potentially encourage debates between these cultural groups, but given the ontological group focus, they would still tend to remain monocultural and incommensurable. Such monoculturalism would also be fostered and encouraged by, for example, faith schools. It also remains uncertain whether the concept and practice of deliberation actually gels with the ontological drive of multiculturalism, given that most deliberative theory assumes that there are background universal agreements which are required for the discourse to be activated. This idea of the multicultural citizen and democracy constitutes an intractable social issue, over which much ink has been spilt. Without entering into the detail of these arguments, my basic claim here is to stress that this whole argument has carried over semi-consciously into the sphere of human rights during the 1990s. We can thus see direct sequential parallels between the populist vernaculars of the *Kulturstaat* and *Multikulturelle Staat* and cultur-ally based human rights arguments. What human rights are doing in this context is addressing a *cultural minimum* for all human beings in any state. Such rights are thus purportedly implicit in the understanding of the state.

Thus, the key ideas concerning this cultural minimum setting can be directly sketched. The first argument is the importance of culture as a deter-minant of what a human being is. Cultural argument—partly because of the earlier nineteenth-century connections between national culture and the state—often views itself as correlated, in some manner, with a determinative political association such as the state. The conceptual device conventionally rolled out to explain this relation is self-determination. In a nutshell, culture as constitutive of humans requires concomitantly both respect (as the medium for individual identity) and the right of self-determination. Thus, the idea that one should be able to 'freely' practise one's culture, language, or religion can be inferred from the original constitutive ontological premise. The second idea—which is much more closely linked to multicultural theory—is that humans, as cultural beings, are *constituted* through groups and collective goods. It is therefore the group which nurtures and embodies the cultural identity. Nationalism has its own explicit monistic variant of this claim; the group in question here is the unitary nation. However, the same basic pattern of argument appears in multicultural theory; it is therefore the group culture which constitutes the person. However implicit in multicultural theory is the acknowledgment that multiple groups constitute a state. This latter scenario configures the intrinsic difference and potentially profound conflict with nationalism. Nationalism cannot easily accommodate, in theory or practice, such internal cultural difference. In this context, in many multicultural states, such groups are minorities within a state. The demand is then that, even if they are minorities, there must still be some mechanism for minority cultural groups to be accorded respect and some self-determination. This notion of group self-determination can however rapidly mutate, once again, directly back into standard nationalist claims. Thus, in a multicultural state where a minority group's demands for self-determination become stri-dent enough to lead to total secession, then the resulting seceding entity will usually be, at first blush, a new nation state and will often, in turn, become impatient with any internal cultural minorities within its own structure.

In the context of the above argument, human rights debates in the 1990s reflect and overlap with this same cultural fixation. Cultural and national ideas have thus been faithfully reflected in human rights documents. The UDHR was understandably more ambiguous on the issue of nationality and culture.[14] It does though include Article 15, 1, which speaks rather timidly of the human 'right of nationality', although again it is difficult to know precisely what this means. Article 27, 1 also includes the 'right freely to participate in the cultural life of the community', but it is difficult yet again to know what community is being referred to. The term 'nationality' dropped out in 1960s human right covenants, usually replaced by the anodyne word 'people'. Both the ICESCR and the International Covenant on Civil and Political Rights (ICCPR) begin very strangely with the same Article 1—'All peoples have the right of self-determination. By virtue of that right they freely determine their political status and freely pursue their economic, social and cultural development.'[15] As indicated, the concept 'nation' is studiously avoided, and 'peoples' and 'cultures' become prevalent. However, the gist of the words is parallel. Both 1966 conventions were of course written in the era of decolonization. Thus, the unreflective obsession with the self-determining nation or people was to a degree understandable. However, the upshot of both opening articles is paradoxically a human rights blessing upon the old idea of the nation state as a culturally distinct self-determining entity. In fact, the article appears to claim that there is a *collective human right* to self-determination by a nation or people. If one thinks back to the idea of human rights being largely created in 1948 to deal with the severe downside of the self-determining nation state, it does have a distinctly spooky feel to it.

It is no surprise that Article 1 of both 1966 conventions is potentially at odds with two other noteworthy human rights articles. First, as indicated, the human rights blessing on the self-determining nation state contrasts markedly with Article 1 of the UDHR, which states 'All human beings are born free and equal in dignity and rights. They are endowed with reason and conscience and should act towards one another in a spirit of brotherhood.' This latter article is clearly focusing on the human individual and civil human rights. It is worth noting again here that the key offender against this form of human right is the self-determining nation state. Second, Article 27 of the ICCPR (1966) states that 'In those States in which ethnic, religious or linguistic minorities exist, persons belonging to such minorities shall not be denied the right, in community with the other members of their group, to enjoy their own culture, to profess and practise their own religion, or to use their own language.' In this latter context, we have a human rights blessing being given to minority cultural groups (and indeed culture itself), and thus implicitly to a multicultural sensibility. The proviso here is that that it is 'persons' (belonging to cultural minorities) who are crucially important. This could be categorized as the liberal multicultural response to human rights. However, this latter article is potentially at odds with Article 1 of both the ICCPR and the ICESCR, insofar as many modernizing self-determining monistic nationalisms are, as a matter of empirical fact, violently, and occasionally genocidally, opposed to internal group difference or secession implications.

Such internal group cultural activity is also potentially ontologically at odds with the individualism of civil human rights which form the substance of the first twenty-one articles of the 1948 Declaration.[16]

In summary, since the 1990s, cultural human rights have taken a much higher profile in human rights discussion. The idea also reappears in parallel debates such as those over Asian values. They are usually configured as part of a blunt attack on the individualism of civil human rights perspectives—as part of a crude and caricatured understanding of purported Western cultural ideas. However, one key focus of the cultural human rights perspective has been the issue of both indigenous and minority groups. These are envisaged as forming the core identities (of their members), which ought to be respected. A number of conventions and declarations have focused on this cultural theme during the last few decades. The Declaration on the Rights of Persons Belonging to National or Ethnic, Religions and Linguistic Minorities was passed in the General Assembly in December 1992. The Council of Europe adopted a Framework Convention for the Protection of National Minorities in 1995. The ten years from 1995 to 2005 was also declared by the United Nations as the International Decade of the World's Indigenous Peoples. In September 2007, the General Assembly passed the Declaration on the Rights of Indigenous Peoples after many years of detailed discussion, although it is worth noting that the multicultural-inclined states (with indigenous peoples) of Australia, New Zealand, Canada, and the United States voted against it.

Some commentators have admittedly seen no problem with the advent of cultural argument, that is to say they see a natural continuity with civil and social human rights. The human rights of minority groups are thus viewed as part of a long-standing concern of the whole human rights movement. For example, as indicated, Article 27 of the ICCPR specifically argues that *persons* belonging to ethnic, religious, or linguistic minorities 'shall not be denied the right, in community with other members of their group, to enjoy their own culture'. The language is still tied here to individual civil human rights. However, if this was the whole case, why create so many separate conventions which explicitly mention culture, peoples, and groups? Something out of the ordinary is being envisaged here.

Other critics accordingly see the function of such conventions to enshrine the human rights of minorities, indigenous groups, and cultures, as distinct from (but often supportive of) other types of human rights. From the later 1990s, two forms of argument have populated the literature on cultural human rights. It is important to disentangle them to show their distinct trajectories, although they can often become confused. The first is *negative*, and its final view on the destiny of human rights remains wholly unclear. The gist of the argument is well known, namely that human identity is intrinsically connected with group culture, and group cultures are unique, autonomous, and self-determining entities. It follows therefore that group cultures require recognition and respect for their pre-existing identity. This, in turn, can lead to the negative inference that universal human rights are residues of a colonial monologic Western mentality which has been imposed on other cultures. Postcolonial theory would be one example of this latter type of argument.[17] However, this latter argument in effect re-articulates an older European nation-state argument from the nineteenth century, which asserts the prior cultural uniqueness, exclusivity, self-determination, and independence of a people or nation; this in turn legitimates resistance to all interferences or impositions of another nationality or culture.

A second argument embodies a much more *positive* claim, which is both rich and contentious, but will have to be dealt with very briefly. The core claim is that rights language should be viewed *through* cultures.[18] This is a variant on the argument already encountered in multicultural theorists such as Kymlicka. Human rights exist, but to become meaningful to different groups and cultures, they have to be filtered, in some manner, through the value substance of these diverse cultures. This argument, in turn, tends to undermine the claims of Western universalist theories of rights and morality and thus has overlaps with the more *negative* argument outlined above. Western human rights exponents who show deep commitments to universalism are consequently seen to be both ignorant of the deep cultural, religious, and philosophical resources of Asian cultures, and the Asian perceptions of the colonial legacy. Western human rights arguments, are still, to a degree, viewed as the progeny of ex-colonial Western states, their specific rights miraculously becoming universal 'human values' for humanity. In addition, critics argue that although this is an argument against a Western understandings of human rights (which often have an individualistic civil rights dimension), it is *not* an argument against human rights as such. Conversely, human rights are seen as saturated with cultural referents, aspirations, and values. It follows, for such critics, that Western human rights exponents fail to see their own culture (as encapsulating law, morality, and philosophy) as just *one* amongst many different world cultures.[19] This argument reasserts the familiar contention that human rights are cultural products, that cultures must take an absolute priority in human affairs, and that there is an assortment of cultures.

## Assessment on culture and human rights

One broad consequence of the above positive argument has been a surge of literature over the last few decades which attempts to relate human rights to, for example, Asian communitarian values, Confucianism, Islam, Buddhism, Christianity, and the like (see Langlois 2001). All these arguments are, again, simply manifestations of the same basic philosophical point outlined above, namely that humans are defined through the ontological filters of their cultures—religious or otherwise. This philosophical position, in itself, remains an ambitious but often ill-thought through idea, with multiple internal complexities which are often glossed over in much cultural argument.

My initial argument against this latter tendency would be to indicate that human rights are not privileges granted by any deity or higher moral law. To think otherwise is to completely fail to grasp the genealogy of human rights in the twentieth century. Further, they are not based upon any foundational moral or spiritual facts about humans. Islamic, Christian, and secularist scholars who try to relate human rights to foundational religious or moral systems are closer in their views to seventeenth-century natural law and natural right arguments than anything else. Such views are now largely an irrelevance. In the majority of such religious perspectives, rights do not really have much of a role to play (see Sharma 2005). This would include all the world religions to date. The religious claimants are often far more interested in spiritual duties than rights. Duties are usually the main driver of the religious argument. Rights become a courtesy add-on to satisfy modern sensibilities. Further, it is unlikely that many religious votaries could make an overwhelmingly strong case for the secular egalitarianism, pluralism, and incipient democratic tendencies implicit in much human rights argument.

To round off this section, two further arguments are constructed concerning the role of culture in human rights discourse: the first is multilayered but essentially refers back to arguments made earlier in this book concerning the state, nationalism, and politics. In a nutshell, aspects of the cultural debate which draw attention to the position of minority groups have an undeniable, if incomplete, utility.[20] However, what we see in the broader ambit of culturalist debates in the 1990s and 2000s is a subtle and sometimes half-conscious reconstitution of nineteenth-century arguments concerning the prioritizing of notions such as ethnicity, nationality, race, and culture. This is what underpins many of the more innocuous-looking arguments about minority or indigenous rights. It is this ontological underpinning which is of most concern. Basically, the cultural perspective creates a deep paradox for human rights.

The logic of the argument is as follows: the formation of nation states, in the nineteenth and twentieth centuries particularly, was both substantial and widespread. One central aspect of the way states formed in this period was via a linkage with the potent artifice of national culture. National culture was an invented singularity, which made nations exclusive and morally, legally, and politically prior to other values. Humans became identified wholly through a single national culture. This did not imply that the nation-state compound summarized the state tradition. Far from it, a distinction has been acknowledged, in the course of the argument, between the civil state and the nation state. Both are important facets of a European state tradition and they do clearly overlap in significant ways. The nation state though has been the dominant practice. In the organic understanding of the nation state, there has been an overwhelming concentration placed upon the idea of a singular culture and identity. This theme has remained strong where the people are regarded as taking part in government in some manner, that is, national democracy or national plebiscite. The link between nationalism and the state is thus strongly asserted in the organic conception.

One underlying implication of the consensual nation state is the idea of the purified singular community. On the surface, this might be innocuous and it undoubtedly has had some positive dimensions in terms of collective projects. However, when the nation, and more particularly race, were read through the lens of evolutionary biology in the later nineteenth and early twentieth centuries, new potencies were created. One of these potencies was implicit within the very singularity of the nation, culture, or race. This potency—as argued—carries the genetic code for genocide. Genocide is ultimately focused on defending or purifying a singular identity. Genocide is therefore linked intimately to the idea and practice of the organic nation state. Although it is implicit in most demands for cultural and racial uniformity, what the developed nation state embodies is the systematic *means* to achieve this uniformity. Genocide is thus a potential activity of a form of state. Quite literally, genocide, as distinct from other forms of mass killing, could not have existed without the organic nation state and, as importantly, it was directly related to the *conjunction* of nationality and race with the state, under certain circumstances. Genocide, as a potential, is thus an integral aspect of both modernity and the phenomenon of the nation state.

The significance of genocide—as a potency of the modern nation state—is that it acted as a catalyst for the human rights movement 1945–8. It was the *Kulturstaat*, or synonymous *Nationalstaat*, linked indissolubly to the potency and actuality of genocide, which created the momentum for the whole human rights movement. The Nuremberg trials contributed—if ambiguously and open-endedly—to a perception of the lethal danger implicit in this form of human association. A parallel logic has developed in international law post-1945. This is something that has been reinvigorated in the language of the International Criminal Court. The court is premised on a profound apprehension over the potential activities of officials and groups within current nation states. The concept of state crime has, in the last fifty years, thus made more leeway in international law circles.

The case of Germany in the 1940s is now taken as the symbolic salutary warning concerning the nation state. This process did not create any form of right-based universalism, such that natural law or cosmopolitan morality would rush into the vacuum in order to provide a justificatory rationale for human rights. Conversely, the substance and intellectual resources for human rights lay already in the customary vernaculars of the civil state tradition. All rights, and human rights in particular, imply relations between humans within a political association; they also require recognition within that political association. Human rights are essentially the rights of a citizen of a civil state writ large. Thus, no rights as such simply exist as justified externalized claims. What the civil state association implies is an ongoing fragile dialectic of human concerns. Politics, in the civil state tradition, provides no definitive resolution to an ongoing debate concerning minimal enabling requirements of citizenship.

Firstly, it is important to be clear that advanced nation states contain rich bodies of rights and indeed commitments to human rights. The problem here is embodied in the inherited code of national and cultural singularities (in my reading this would include the oblique progeny of nationalism, i.e. multiculturalism). This is a potency rather than a necessary actuality. In this case, the nation or singular culture *can*, in certain circumstances, parasitize on core components of the state structure to seek national or cultural uniformity. Such cultural singularity can be innocuous—even at times positive—but it also contains unpredictable costs. Through cultural uniformity, neighbours, groups, or regions, can band together for impressive projects of public works and mutual assistance. However, in other circumstances, the same neighbours, using the same latent cultural logic, can become genocidal fiends, capable of mass indiscriminate killing, sanctioned, and assisted by state powers.

However, even within the civil state tradition, which in my argument shows a relative indifference to cultural claims, there is a profound and unresolved issue which boils down to an unfinished argument between social citizenship (and social human rights), and civil citizenship (and civil human rights). It is neither an argument about the need for politics as such nor a denial of the need for states to embody the essentials of human rights as prerequisites for actually achieving our humanity. It is rather an argument about the nature of our humanity, that is, what it means to function as a human being via citizenship.

The core of the present human rights argument lies in this unresolved civil and social domain. However, as argued, there is also an ongoing complex relation between the nation state and the civil state, as part of an interwoven tradition. Culture, nationality, ethnicity, and race are important dimensions of this tradition, particularly from the nineteenth century; they have also had major implications for imperialism and colonialism. Yet the same basic terminology—concerning the unified self-determining sovereign *Kulturstaat* or *Nationalstaat*—was still being employed extensively in the new postcolonial states of the 1950s and 1960s. However, we must also grasp another aspect of this situation, namely, that this very same political vessel (the nation state), in the context of genocide, was the prime *object* to be addressed by human rights conventions and declarations. Thus, the paradox of cultural human rights in the 1990s is that—even in the context of speaking of minority or indigenous group rights or multicultural rights—the very same cultural logic and ontology are being invoked, as that of the late nineteenth- or early twentieth-century national or racial state. In fact, in the opening article of the ICCPR and ICESCR, in 1966, it is not even the minority group which is being invoked, it is rather the *self-same* self-determining nation state, which paradoxically is given a human rights imprimatur, although discreetly hidden under the weasel word 'people'. As perceived in 1948, this cultural logic still contains, in all essentials, the genetic code of genocide.[21]

My argument therefore is that cultural human rights—in the manner that they have been articulated—summon the same intrinsic logic as the nation state. This latency is the catalyst which actually gave rise to human right demands in 1948. This presents a deep paradox for the contemporary observer of human rights. On the one hand, the current situation is a testament to the subtle power and influence of the nation state and culturalist logic, such that it can permeate so pervasively into the core of debates about human rights. On the other hand, this should not surprise us too much since human rights themselves are intimately related to the customary vernaculars of the state tradition and citizenship. In many ways though there is a broader dialectic at work here, which embodies a struggle for the character of the state tradition. The tension between, on the one hand, civil and social rights as part of the civil state constellation, represents one pole of a debate. The other pole is embedded in cultural human rights, which find their *heimat* in the constellation of culturalist concerns surrounding the nation state. Human rights per se are consequently part of a deep and troubled struggle at the heart of contemporary political association.

My critical conclusion would be to try and make this argument about human rights more logically coherent. This would entail a reaffirmation of the civil and social human rights, as they have been configured in the civil state perspective, as the core of the human rights perspective. This in turn entails a rejection of cultural human rights arguments as they have been developed from the nation-state tradition. This would also entail deep scepticism concerning the whole concept of the *Kulturstaat* and *Multikulturelle Staat*.

The second key rounding-off argument, for this section, focuses on an important problem with cultural argument in general, namely that it rests upon a deep and persistent error concerning human identity, an error for which we have in the past—as a species—and will in the future pay a high price for, if we carry on fostering it. In my argument, this provides a further underpinning for the rejection of the cultural human right perspective. The culture argument fosters the view that human identity is singular.

The notion of cultural singularity has been promulgated by both critics and supporters alike. Samuel Huntingdon, as much as Osama bin Laden or Radovan Karadzic, all envisage the world as divided into singular discrete impervious cultural groups: religious, national, civilizational, or ethnic. Because of this skewed perception, the world is seen as a grouping of cultures—identified by various categories such as religion, nationality, civilization, or ethnicity. This same argument also gets a subtle but definite imprimatur from the multicultural mentality. Amartya Sen, commenting on this tendency, notes that culturalist thinking assumes 'that the people of the world can be uniquely categorized according to some *singular and overarching* system of partitioning'. This partitioning 'yields a "solitarist" approach to human identity, which sees human beings as members of exactly one group (in this case defined by civilization or religion, in contrast with earlier reliance on nationalities and classes)'. Sen notes that this solitarist approach is 'a good way of misunderstanding nearly everyone in the world'. For Sen, reflecting on the global violence of the last two decades, suggests that what is most disturbing in this culturalist and identitarian obsession is that 'The imposition of an allegedly unique identity is often a crucial component of the "martial art" of fomenting sectarian confrontation.' Thus, 'many of the conflicts and barbarities in the world are sustained through the illusion of a unique and choiceless identity'. Consequently, 'The uniquely partitioned world is much more divisive than the universe of plural and diverse categories that shape the world in which we live.' As Sen argues 'identity can . . . kill—and kill with abandon' (quotations from Sen 2006, xii–xv, 2). In this context, for many radical Islamists, for example, apostasy seems to matter far more than murder, violence, or barbarity. Terrorism, pogrom, genocide, community violence, and the like, frequently relate directly to the singularized identity of group culture. One might hazard the point here that the assertion of singular cultural identity and a potential for violence are regular bedfellows.

This does not mean that one should condemn such categories outright. Group culture can—as indicated earlier—be a positive contribution, in certain circumstances, to achieve collective goods. However, culture also functions in tandem with many other factors in civil society. It is never hermetic. No culture is ever unitary or homogeneous. Culture changes via interactions. It is not something which always needs conserving, simply because it is a culture. This argument bears upon Sen's critical opinion of multiculturalism and particularly multicultural education in faith schools, which in many ways fixes cultures into a social and educational inertia. He thus sees the policy of multiculturalism, and more particularly faith schools, as acutely damaging to the British state (Sen 2006, 118–19). Such policies artificially reconstruct Britain as a federation of narrow cultures: national and religious.[22]

Overall, singular cultural categories are flawed. The idea is an astonishingly rudimentary and historically imprudent way of thinking about humans. What follows from this is that culture should not be used as an exclusive or singularly important way of either talking about or demarcating human beings.[23] Humans are not just multiple across societies, but they are also multiple within their own lives and identities. Identities are always plural; we cross-cut many different commitments. The citizen may be a woman, working class, black, with a partial handicap, who is an ardent vegetarian, Buddhist, primary school teacher specializing in mathematics, who loves film noir, avidly supports Manchester United, and is a devotee of the music of Schoenberg and Jimi Hendrix. All these form aspects of a multifaceted human identity. If we pushed even deeper, on a psychoanalytic level, it is certain that the thickets constituting identity would grow even denser. Where then is the core identity?

What we call identity is a series of interpretive narratives which we bring together in terms of what we consider to be a concordance. An identity is a contingent concordance. There can be many such narratives running concurrently through a human life, all subject to temporal mutation. A human self is thus a process of multiple narratives, nothing more, nothing less. Probably the best life, in this context, is a narrative that is really worth telling to others. However, we should not confuse this narrative argument with some spurious championing of multiculturalism, or even some academically driven argument about liberal pluralism. What in fact is the case is human complexity and mutability at many levels. Humans tell different and often quite inconsistent stories about themselves during their lives. This is to be expected. Language places different restraints upon how the story is told, but different languages can be learnt and utilized. Culture is one facet of a larger opaque picture of human idiosyncrasies. It is one of those artifices of human narrative which we can occasionally fixate upon and build up into a rich social imaginary. It can also often be a treacherous and stifling narrative, if given singular or holistic attention. It follows that when culture is given a *primary* role in human association, it is more of a pollutant than a clarifier of categories such as human rights.

## LOYALTY AND HUMAN RIGHTS

There is one final conundrum to address here. For many, human rights, *prima facie*, seem to imply some form of commitment beyond the realm of the state. However, if human rights are integral to citizenship of the civil state, then how does this affect the practices of loyalty or patriotism? Essentially the argument of this book shows that it *is* possible to find a resolution to the relation between human rights and loyalty or even patriotism (of sorts) to a civil state. It is though a more limited or constrained loyalty than we might normally expect.

To briefly rehearse my argument again: human coexistence implies plurality and uncertainty. Politics is premised on this fact, but, at the same time, it also involves ways of mediating this uncertainty. A resonant institutional form in which politics mediates conflict is through the civil state. It follows that the civil state—invoking constitutionality and human rights as constituent parts—embodies the recognition of plurality and uncertainty. Human rights in this study are viewed as embedded recognized claims, derived from the customary constituents of states, constitutionality, and citizenship. Thus, a politicized understanding of right is employed. Human rights are meaningful and effective in the context of a specific kind of civil state association (or an agreement amongst and within civil states). Loyalty to a civil state is, in essence, loyalty to plurality and uncertainty. In this sense, loyalty implies a commitment to an ongoing uncertainty, critical hesitancy, and willingness to adjust. The character of a civil state tradition is thus necessarily open, self-questioning, and incomplete.

Consequently, any *substantive values* associated with loyalty or patriotism (and such values are continuously thrown up in debate in civil states) are always subject to uncertainty and criticism as part of a multiplicity of interests. The notion of *unpatriotic patriotism* or *disloyal loyalty* can be viewed as a commitment which '*refuses* or *resists* the very identifications on which citizens also depend' (Markell 2000, 54). To be loyal to politics and civil statehood, as plurality and uncertainty, is to be continuously and potentially unpatriotic or disloyal to the substantive loyalties that many might consider crucial. This disloyalty is though a deeper loyalty. It is intrinsically loyal to the constituent conditions of critical deliberation embedded in politics. To be loyal in this sense is to be committed to constitutionality and human rights which form the conditions of deliberation and mediation of conflict.

The commitment to a primary substantive loyalty, that is, to a singular sense of culture or nationality, is unquestionably a characteristic of the *Nationalstaat*. It also forms the fragmented body of substantive commitments within a *Multikulturelle Staat*. Loyalty and patriotism are therefore, in this reading, focused on a singular body of values and a particular identity. The question of critical argument and deliberation, in the context of the singularity of cultures, is intrinsically problematic. The cultural singularity argument—in the sense of multiple cultures—can undermine rational argumentation. Consequently, the argument is always threatening to tip over into relativism.

In order to avoid the charge of relativism, there could potentially be a positive utility in a more universalistic, virtually Kantian or Habermasian, approach to argument, something which bypasses the relativistic implications of cultural singularity. However, the problem with the Kantian or Habermasian approach to argument is the process of rational purification itself, which tries to resist all forms of conventionalism. As Paul Ricoeur comments, it then 'makes impossible the contextual mediation without which the ethics of communication loses its hold on reality'. What is needed is a sense of conventionalism which embodies commitment to rational critical argument. Ricoeur calls this an 'ethics of argumentation', which 'contributes to the impasse of a sterile opposition between universalism at least as procedural as that of Rawls and Dworkin and a "cultural" relativism that places itself outside the field of discussion'. In my reading, the 'ethics of argumentation' is another way of formulating the argument for disloyal loyalty, that is, a commitment to argue for argument, which is embedded within the citizenship and politics of a civil state. It is not providing the substantive content of argument. It is though maintaining the need, in certain contexts, for argument, practical reason, and critical judgement. In effect, it mediates between conventionalism and rational universalism. It allows us to take seriously the 'requirements of universalization in order to focus on the conditions for placing this requirement in context'. Instead of seeing a hard contrast between cultural conventions (and the context for citizens) and more universal argumentation, it substitutes 'a subtle dialectic between argumentation and conviction, which has no theoretical outcome but only the practical outcome of the arbitration of moral judgment' (all quotations from Ricoeur 1994, 287). This is the character of politics in a civil state.

What is necessary therefore is to see both the state and human motivations in a more multifaceted manner, as conventionally contingent products, which occasionally achieve a level of civility, where politics can exist. Politics is premised on diversity, conflict, and plurality, and a consequent recognition of the need to mediate this conflict through forms of deliberation, distribution, mediation, and negotiation. Some of these forms, such as law or democratic processes, are more concrete and formalized than others. Unpatriotic patriotism is a background loyalty to the fragility and uncertainty of politics, as well as an awareness of the wide range of human motivations. It is not a loyalty to any specific cultural or national object, it is rather an alertness to the immense complexity of human motivations and demands, as well as an acknowledgement of the substantively varied loyalties and demands of citizens within a polity. The civil state—where the comparative rarity of the politics exists—institutionalizes the procedures of civil mediation. The civil state is therefore envisaged as a formal procedural structure which engages with the condition of human plurality, that is, the inevitable range of interests and demands over resources which appears in the public sphere of politics. To be unpatriotically patriotic is a commitment to be sceptical of commitment, which is also seen as the ground to human freedom, understood as the sheer capacity to begin. Human rights enable and underpin this vision for humanity.

## Conclusion

The links between human rights and citizenship are envisaged as united by the expectation of what a state and politics should be. This expectation remains, in the civil state idea, unresolved between civil and social demands. There is a profound variance here which relates to how substantively we conceive our humanity and citizenship. It is also an argument about what precisely is required to flourish as a human being. Human rights are integral to this debate. This whole scenario invokes the issue of political existence. Humans are always relational creatures. We have to relate to other humans simply to exist. In fact, we only develop as human persons insofar as we are recognized by others. This recognition develops our sense of our own humanity and agency. In the family and friendship relations, this will usually have an intimate dimension. In the broader domain of social existence relating to others, and being recognized by others, invokes the possibility of politics. Politics is not something which necessarily exists in all human association. When it does exist—as a tried mode of activity—it is premised on human plurality, uncertainty, and competition, but it also focuses on ways to mediate this plurality—a plurality which incorporates cultures as one dimension of human diversity. Part of this mediating process is through critical deliberation. This is central to politics, citizenship, and human rights. The argument for the necessity of critical argument—which is central to politics—is the real object of loyalty within a civil state.

The relating process, implicit in politics, is mediated through the third-party institutional relations of rights and duties—civil and human. Rights are part of this relatively anonymous recognition process. The third-party institutional process of rights and recognition is realized most adequately within a civil state setting. The crucial right-medium through which this civil state setting functions is citizenship. Citizenship entails a form of recognition of the person as normatively valuable. This is the core of human rights. We realize our humanity through our recognition relations with other humans and more particularly via our citizenship of a civil state (a state which aspires to civil statehood). Further, we fully realize basic aspects of our humanity through being recognized as citizens of such a civil state, a state which is intrinsically jurally auto-limited. In this sense, human rights embody an ideal civil state vocabulary. Human rights can only fully develop where there exists a comity of aspirant civil states which recognize each other as states internationally, through their embodiment of human rights.

## ▢ NOTES

1. The origin of the terms civil and civic is open to debate. The civic/civil divide bears some conceptual parallels with the distinction, made by Benjamin Constant, after the French Revolution, between ancient and modern liberty (Constant 1988).

2. It was also a conception of citizenship which contained an inner logic of universality, a logic which drives a certain conception of human rights.

3. This idea of 'external justified claims' was underpinned, in part, by elements of the gene-alogy of civil citizenship and civil rights, which tended to see the human individual as prior in some way (actually or hypothetically) to society. Contract theory, natural rights, and elements of classical liberalism held this general ontology.

4. With the reservations that many, such as Kant, made as to who to include in the category humanity (see Vincent 1996).

5. Something that many North American commentators and politicians, amongst others, would still like to see as the core of human rights.

6. It is worth noting in passing that social citizenship arguments never really took off in the United States—welfare always has and still does imply a kind of stigma—thus public hospitals in the United States are usually always inferior to private (see Fraser and Gordon 1994, 90). However, there does seem now to be some movement on this issue in the Obama administration in the United States in 2010, although it remains uncertain.

7. These rights were made part of international law by treaties such as the European Social Charter. The ICESCR's list of rights includes non-discrimination and equality for women in the economic and social area (Articles 2 and 3), freedom to work and opportunities to work (Article 4), fair pay and decent conditions of work (Article 7), the right to form trade unions and to strike (Article 8), social security (Article 9), special protections for mothers and children (Article 10), the right to adequate food, clothing, and housing (Article 11), the right to basic health services (Article 12), the right to education (Article 13), and the right to participate in cultural life and scientific progress (Article 15).

8. I am not using social democracy intentionally in a specific ideological sense.

9. This did not mean that other issues were not present; women's human rights, discrim-ination, and the like, were still very much in the spotlight at points. I would still argue that the most consistent debates during this period did focus around the civil/social divide.

10. If, for example, there has been a lasting legacy of New Labour in Britain in 2010, it has been the, partly unintentional, strengthening and deepening of the foundations of a hege-monic neo-liberal ideology in public policy, in part encouraged and facilitated by a broader global dominance of the same doctrine. The central flaw in this perspective has been the credit and banking crisis (2008–10) which may well lead to the decline of the idea.

11. The same conflict is re-enacted in conflicts between more restrained notions of liberal democracy as against more developed conceptions of social democracy.

12. He does see though certain specific waves of argument affecting the debates (see Kymlicka essay in Joppke and Lukes 1999, 112–13).

13. The rough outline of the culture argument is that we are, as humans, constituted through a culture or nation and its values. We cannot therefore be prior in any way to our culture

or nation. We are culturally embedded creatures. This idea was reinforced during the 1990s by the popularity of communitarian arguments in moral and political theory.

14. The proximity of the Second World War and the violent culturalist and racial nationalisms of the 1920s and 1930s were too close in time.

15. The African Charter on Human and People's Right, Article 20, 1 includes: 'All peoples shall have the right to existence. They shall have the unquestionable and inalienable right to self-determination. They shall freely determine their political status and shall pursue their economic and social development according to the policy they have freely chosen.'

16. This unease can work a number of ways, if, for example, one considers Charles Taylor's and others' multicultural criticism of liberal universalism as distorting cultural autonomy, rights, and recognition (see Taylor essay in Gutman 1994).

17. The basic postcolonial argument is that power is embedded in texts and discourse, as well as in military force. Western colonialism therefore represented not just physical or political conquest, but also textual and linguistic domination. For this latter argument, what we then encounter in all Western human rights discourse is Western cultural parochialism in the disguise of universal human entitlements. The task for the postcolonial theorist is then to expose this. Where human rights finally stand in these arguments remains obscure.

18. As Abdullah A. An-Na'im argues, 'Like all normative systems, human rights regimes must necessarily be premised on a particular cultural framework' (see An-Na'im 1999, 147).

19. As Charles Taylor comments, 'An obstacle in the path to...mutual understanding comes from the inability of many Westerners to see their culture as one amongst many' (Taylor 1999, 143).

20. Politics and citizenship within a civil state imply a permanent recognition of different demands and interests.

21. An equivalent point arises with many of the obsessions of identity politics. Such demands embody the same understandings of humanity.

22. This whole enterprise miniaturizes human existence. Religion is now frequently used as one of these artificial cultural dividing lines and for Sen there is something quite bizarre, and deeply misguided, in making a child's identity focus wholly on religious or national culture. This culturalist view makes the further patently false, in fact crass, assumption that all nationalities or religions—Christian, Muslim, or Jewish—have exactly the same substance (see Sen 2006, 14). The solution that many now offer to problems with religious extremism is equally bizarre for Sen, namely, trying to get other more moderate elements of the religion to mediate with the extreme components; in an odd way this simply amplifies the narrowness of the whole enterprise.

23. This discussion will not though deal with an equally problematic issue, namely that the concept of culture itself remains totally opaque, despite its promiscuous usage in modern argumentation.

# Conclusion

Human rights have been interpreted in this book in a dissenting manner. The core arguments have been sceptical of the idea of any longevity to human rights, which is prior to the twentieth century. Human rights do have tentative family resemblance with the idea of natural rights, and inevitably to 'rights language' and the etymology of the word 'right'; but the idea of a specific substantive connection to natural rights is regarded with suspicion. There have undoubtedly been robust attempts to link human rights to natural law and natural rights, but the relation remains strained and tenuous. No doubt many will continue to try to forge the connection; however, it is something which is discarded in this book.

Human rights are interpreted in this study as arising initially out of a fortuitous combination of events and ideas. First, there was undoubtedly a natural rights perspective, but it all but collapsed in the nineteenth century. There are certain more standardized reasons adduced in the literature for this collapse. These are again, in the main, rejected. The reasons discussed for the collapse, put very briefly, were that the idea of natural right was effectively compressed between two dynamic forces: on the one hand, the singular development of nation states during the nineteenth century—particularly the spread of nationalism as a powerful normative idea. The latter doctrine located 'rights-talk' in the particularized sphere of statehood and nationality. This idea was again very effectively serviced within the burgeoning universities of Europe and elsewhere, within a broad range of academic disciplines. The disciplines discussed in this text were ecology and geography, although it could just as well have been history or even law. International law also developed significantly in the same period, and once again its main focus was on nation states and the relations between them. Any discussion of rights thus presupposed this predominantly state-orientated vocabulary. On the other hand, it was argued that a new and powerful language developed around the concept of nature itself, which was inherently changed by the growth and profound impact of evolutionary theory. This, in effect, made nonsense of the older uses of the term nature. The culmination of this process was the subtle combination of these two pressures in the form of the organic nation-state concept. This was the nation state that was given a biological imprimatur. What was particularly significant here was the manner in which the biologically orientated ideas of the nation and race concepts were gradually assimilated into a conception of statehood. The idea of the purified singular national culture—characterizing the state—became an important and pervasive motif, in this case enhanced through (what was understood at the time) quasi-scientific criteria.

Given this scenario the question arose as to why human rights appeared so forcibly post-1945. My answer here took up a more conventional response—relating it to the 1940's neologism of genocide—but then gave it a new twist. That is to say, it was argued that the powerful combination of empirical biological concerns, linked in with the idea of cultural and racial singularity of the nation state, contained the *latent* genetic coding for genocide. Genocide was consequently seen as embryonic in the modern nation state. This latency and then actuality of genocide formed the generative backdrop for the human rights movement in 1948.

There are many ways of speaking about human rights in the post-1948 setting. A more popular response, that many scholars develop, is to read human rights in terms of a moral justificatory terminology. That is to say, human rights are seen as intrinsic universal moral claims, external in some way to the processes of states, and thus potentially contributing to a more cosmopolitan culture of humanity. It is though worth recalling that the framers of the 1948 Declaration themselves never attempted any moral justification. In the present study, this moral path is rejected as philosophically superfluous. Another perspective is one which either sees human rights as soft law aspiring to hard law, or alternatively as a branch of international law which needs to be gradually accepted and assimilated into state law and then enforced globally. In fact, some would argue that we already have the rudiments of such a system in place. In other words, human rights are seen in terms of predominantly cosmopolitan jurisprudential concerns. The key task for human rights is therefore to enable international case law to be more broadly and universally acknowledged as the structure for regulating states. In this context, the hope is that judicial interpretations will gradually be assimilated to a more general conception of state conduct. Thus, the issue of human rights is seen in terms of a future legal agenda. The success or failure of human rights is all down in the end to broadening jurisdictions.

A third view loosely combines elements of the above, seeing them both as examples of a more general globalization process which has, in turn, shown the modern state as progressively transcended in all spheres—economic, legal, political, military, and so forth. Most problems, such as environmental pollution, international finance, global warming, international drug crime, disease control, money-laundering, and international terrorism, can—so the argument goes—no longer be addressed by the state. Human rights (from a different angle), like international law and international institutions, are thus seen as the inevitable consequence of a broader globalization process.

In my judgement, this whole globalization idea is way overdone, in fact it is now slightly passé. What has, or will be, achieved globally in economic, political, legal, environmental, legal, or related fields, will be done through the cooperation and deliberations of a comity of civil-inclined states. Little has changed in this matter. Without that agreement, and indeed this alone is hard enough to achieve, very little will be done.

The argument of this book rebuffs all the above interpretations. Conversely, the concept of politics takes on a major role in the argument. Politics is viewed as a complex and multidimensional concept and practice. At the most basic level, it is envisaged as something which is presupposed by the traditions of law and morality, in the sense that neither would exist *effectively* without it. Politics, in this latter sense, implies a certain form of ordering and maintenance of public existence. Further, politics is taken to refer to the acknowledgement of a plurality of interests, competitiveness over resources, and underlying uncertainty, which result from human association in any larger aggregations. What is taken though as further distinctive about politics, as a category, is that it entails the self-conscious skill which addresses, engages, and mediates this plurality. Not that it achieves satisfactory conclusions, but rather politics as a practice perceives it as necessary to engage with this plurality. One further implication of this notion of plurality is that, as a practice which is premised on differences, politics will often develop into something approximating to democracy. This argument however rejects any necessary link between democracy and nationalism. Nationalism is an artifice which gives an impression of cultural unity where none exists. In democracy, as a facet of politics, minimally there will be an acknowledgement of actual differences. Democracy is premised on plurality and has, as its *modus operandi*, the structures to mediate human plurality. Democracy is therefore *one* effective way in which politics mediates plurality.

Nothing is predictable or completely rule-governed in the political world. Dealing with multiple interests entails endemic uncertainty. Politics consequently involves a particular form of thinking which is distinct from highly determinative theoretical judgement. It rather calls upon a form of reflective judgement which is not guided by specific determinative rules, but conversely by practical decisions in specific circumstances. Political judgement is more of an art or skill which is learnt in practice and experience. In addressing plurality, politics utilizes various ways of concretely addressing differences in public affairs. Practical reasoning, in this context, involves a regularization of deliberatively 'hearing the other side', or imaginatively representing the other side. In this sense, politics intrinsically involves a form of public deliberation. Hearing the other side entails meeting momentarily in the middle point between two or more interests. The potential for fusing horizons is feasible, at this point, although not inevitable. Politics thus contains the possibility for understanding.

It might, however, be argued that not everyone has the capacity to use their reason or engage in public dialogue in this manner. Yet, as Amartya Sen reminds us,

> our ability to think clearly may, of course, vary with training and talent, but we can, as adult and competent human beings, question and begin to challenge what has been taught to us if we are given the opportunity to do so. While particular circumstances may not sometimes encourage a person to engage in such questioning, the ability to doubt and to question is not beyond our reach.
>
> (Sen 2006, 35)

Politics, in the present argument, regularizes such critical opportunities as part of its raison d'être. Not to have this opportunity is to be outside of politics and citizenship. Not to experience the possibility of politics in this sense is to be potentially dehumanized. To be denied politics is to be denied the right to have rights. The sad fact is that there are many associations in the world today—some laughably called states—who both live with and forcibly maintain this dehumanization.[1]

The use of public dialogue and reason in this plural context involves choices. Choice implies freedom. Freedom is integral to the use of practical reason and dialogue in politics. Freedom arises within politics as vital to the practical, non-determinative reason and judgement required for making choices. The freedom implicit in practical reason entails a capacity to begin or initiate in a public realm. Political reasoning as such has no end. It is an unfinished, fallibilist, public dialogue. The only crucial proviso to add here is that politics does seek, pragmatically, plateaus of regularization and standardization within certain practices, for example, law, democracy, and human rights. In this sense, the capacity to begin is necessarily more constrained in, for example, the sphere of law or democratic practice. Law regularizes politics for pragmatic purposes, although in the final analysis, it has no independence from its intricate political premise. Humans are creatures of habit; law regularizes the habitual dimension of civil existence. But despite its formalization as a discipline and its positivistic claims to autonomy, law is actually premised on politics and a particular conception of political association. The rule of law is clearly not founded *on* law.

It was argued that the fragile vessel which has predominantly carried and maintained politics, at a fairly consistent level of sophistication, over the last two centuries is the state tradition. A distinction was drawn however within the state tradition between the ideal characters of the nation state and the civil state. Both embody politics. However, the nation state (under which generic rubric I would also include the multicultural state) was seen to be engaged more exclusively with notions of culture, ethnicity, and nationality. These were seen to be of extraordinary importance for both the nation state and multicultural state, that is, as a way of seriously addressing human identity. The civil state—although embodying culture and nationality via politics, that is, as one amongst multiple human interests—nonetheless does not fixate upon such categories as of any singular importance. In fact, in this civil reading, 'cultural politics' or 'national politics' would be a *contradictio in adjecto*. It would imply one singular predictable monistic meaning for politics, a politics which is premised logically and intrinsically on the ineluctable and capricious fact of human diversity.

It was then argued that the state tradition, as embodying a commitment to politics, stands in a complex and paradoxical relation with the human rights tradition during the twentieth and twenty-first centuries. It embodies both the key problem for human rights and an important aspect of the resolution to that problem. I referred to this as the *state reflexivity syndrome*. In a nutshell, the generic category of the state is taken to be both the subject and object of human rights. Thus, the language of the prosecution of states (adjudicating human right violations), is one which has been derived from the customary legal and political resources of the defendant—that is, the same state tradition. However, there is also a customary state-based language which can justify both the infringement and denial of human rights. The state, in fact, figures here as one of the primary violators of human rights. Genocide, for example, is a state crime—something which has been viewed as latent in the practice of the nation state. However, paradoxically, there is also a state-based vernacular which is used to analyse, criticize, and ultimately to adjudicate on—via civil state proxies such as the International Criminal Court—the actions of the nation state. In this situation, it is the nation state which is identified as the more problematic object and the civil state provides the vernaculars of the prosecuting subject. The civil state tradition thus embodies a complex range of limitations contained within a pragmatic legal framework. One of the key facets of the civil state tradition (or the aspiration towards civil statehood) is the intrinsic dimension of jural auto-limitation. Such auto-limitation can though be either blunted or swamped if the idea of singular cultures or nationalities is allowed to overmaster politics.

The key argument developed at this point is therefore that what we understand by human rights is intrinsically part of the configuration of the civil state—understood politically. However, the distinction between these two dimensions of the state tradition (civil and nation state) should not be overdrawn. Rather than conceiving the state as either subject or object, a more nuanced dialectical relation was presented. What is still of key importance though in this dialectical relation is that we should try not to isolate human rights from broader debates about the state tradition. In reality, states are always mixed in their commitments; there is thus a nuanced overlap between the concerns of the nation state and civil state.

Another possible counter-argument to the idea that human rights are integral to the state tradition was then canvassed. This argument focused on the idea that human rights are externally valid claims. That is to say, the philosophical grounding for human rights must necessarily lie *outside* the state tradition altogether. That is the point of human rights for many. We have already encountered this argument as one of the key modes in the literature for tackling the whole question of human rights. This argument was rejected earlier in the book; however, one further argument was put forward against this, in chapter 7, focused on the role of recognition, not only for the development and character of the human person, but also for accounting for rights in general. The latter argument entails an explicit refutation of the universally valid claim argument. Whether in the form of a claim about God, autonomous secular reason or utility, such valid claim arguments are seen to be beside the point. They provide an abstracted philosophical rhetoric with little or no grounding in reality.

The more general issue concerning recognition was that a person, quite literally, cannot develop or grow in the absence of the ethico-legal-political setting. The human person requires both recognition and subtle mediations through the family, education, and neighbourhood up to the state. Without these subtle mediations and processes of recognition, the development of the person is negated or diminished. In this argument, therefore, rights are not external valid claims; they are rather relational accredited practices which involve recognition. This is though distinct from any solidarist, moral, or love-based recognition, which subsist in the family or friendship. Rights appear as a distinct *form* of recognition. All rights require recognition, including human rights. Having a human right involves a social relation which invokes a wider public trust, such that parties put their reliance upon a more anonymous institutional relational structure. This public fiduciary relation is not just a legal relation, it is also fundamentally political, since it links directly with the raison d'être of the civil state tradition. In fact, rights involve a specific conception of political relationships. The rights and implied public trust are maintained and respected within the institutional setting of the civil state. Consequently, human rights only make sense within the complex recognition processes of a civil state—or minimally within the aspiration towards civil statehood.

Initially, the discussion examined a multilevel account of recognition. It then turned to the grounding of human rights within the politics and recognition processes of the civil state. The character and recognition of the civil state in international law was then explored. The idea of recognition was thus seen to function in the international legal sphere. The argument offered here was more directly sympathetic to what is called the constitutive theory of recognition. That is to say the state is recognized by an international comity of states insofar as it fulfils certain established criteria of civil statehood. One of the stronger counter-arguments against the constitutive theory is that it invokes the unpredictability and arbitrariness of politics. Thus, existing states will follow their own self-interest in recognizing or not recognizing entities as states. This latter contention was countered by referring back to earlier arguments concerning the complex nature of politics, which should not be miniaturized into ideas of self-interest, power, and antagonism. The argument then broadened the thesis to suggest the importance of procedures through which politics mediates interests and conflicts, particularly in the fields of domestic and international law. The distinction that many have drawn between law and politics was treated sceptically. The idea of political rightness was then sketched. This was envisaged as a move away from the idea of a *Rechtstaat* and legal constitutionalism towards a more flexible and contextually sensitive political constitutionalism.

The discussion raised further doubts about whether many associations should really qualify, in anything but name, for the title state in international law. In this sense, the category of 'almost states' or 'quasi-states' was raised and compared with John Rawls' later work. If nation states do actually attempt to undermine politics, citizenship, and consequently destroy human rights, the argument was then constructed for the meaningful political use of state crime. Once a nation state has committed a crime in this sense, it is then up to the comity of civil-inclined states as to how to react. A link was then made with the doctrine of *jus cogens*, indicating at a fundamental level where a state had actually infringed against politics and had thus dehumanized its membership.

Finally, the discussion moved in the penultimate chapter to the analysis of where human rights debates have derived their substance from post-1945. Given that rights, including both legal and human rights, are in essence always political, they are therefore intrinsic to the situation in which politics becomes the *modus operandi* for mediating difference. Rights, including human rights, are generic public political goods, that is, recognized 'third-party institutional' arrangements enabling the processes of mediation of plurality, through various protective and enabling devices. In summary, the civil state embodies politics, which in turn contains the groundwork for both freedom and development of our humanity. In this setting, human rights become meaningful. The process of recognition continues here into the international sphere. Essentially a state is recognized *as a state qua state*, by both its citizens and other states, insofar as it embodies politics. If it embodies politics, it also contains a commitment to the self-realization of human beings via citizenship (and therefore a commitment to human rights).

The argument thus moved to the key vehicle through which the state tradition has conceived of humanity, that is, citizenship. The argument tracked through the various broad categories of citizenship in tandem with the basic accounts of human rights. The notional three-generational accounts of human rights—civil and political, social and economic, and cultural and minority group rights—were seen to directly overlap accounts of citizenship in the domestic state sphere. Thus, civil and political citizenship, social citizenship, and cultural citizenship are seen as the key groundwork for human rights debates. They are not just parallel to human rights. Human rights actually transubstantiate existing debates about the character of human political association. Human rights are therefore seen as intrinsic to the dialectic of the civil state. The fact that they are embodied in the civil state is part of its intrinsic constitutional jural auto-limitation.

Basically, if enough civil-inclined states form a comity, which signals the grounds on which a state ought or ought not to be recognized, then international law and human rights can become effectual. This is essentially exactly what happened in 1948. It is also largely what underpins the International Criminal Court and the human rights movement in general. However, if a critical mass of powerful nation states tries to undermine or refute these ideas, in say the next fifty years, then human rights will largely become nugatory or disappear. This will lead, once again, to the domination of the narrow normative singularities and horizons of the nation state, over those of the civil-inclined state. International law will remain in this scenario, but only at the superficial level that existed prior to 1945, that is, dealing largely with the formal relations between sovereign nation states. Despite all the recent Byzantine meanderings around international moral argumentation, cosmopolitan justice, developing international law, and globalization, this latter judgement is taken as a matter of empirical detail.

Two key problems were identified at this point. Even within the civil state setting, there is a deep conflict concerning the reach of the political, in terms of the debate between civil and social conceptions of citizenship and the civil and social conceptions of human rights. The debates about civil and social human rights are not just a reflection of a domestic state-based debate about constitutional, social, and civic rights. On the contrary, they are rather the continuous dialectic of the idea and practice of the state itself. The debates that have and continue to occur around the idea of poverty, development, and human rights, are in fact debates that exist at the core of civil states or civil-aspiring states. Such debates will, of course, be largely meaningless to quasi-states or tortiously recognized states, where politics hardly exist, except in the narrowest of senses. The solution to such debates about poverty, for example, is not to be addressed by isolating the sphere of human rights from the civil state sphere. The debate is largely to be won, lost, or delayed (more likely) within civil states themselves. At the present moment in time, it is difficult to have much optimism on this issue, particularly where states either emphasize their national or cultural particularism, or alternatively only stress the negative civil aspect of human rights.

This leads to the second key problem of culture and nationality. The discussion focused here on the ontology embedded in debates about cultural human rights, even where they appear in the apparently innocuous spheres of minority rights, or the rights of groups in a multicultural setting. The central argument was that these ideas represented a rebirth of late eighteenth- and early nineteenth-century arguments, underpinning the concept and practice of the nation state. In the last two decades, the key theories have tended to treat these arguments in a more romantic framework, echoing late eighteenth-century renditions. Worryingly, such theories lack acquaintance with the peculiar ideational genealogy of the nation state from the 1860s up to the 1930s. Culture is now seen as a largely anodyne, but nonetheless crucial factor of human identity. The philosophical premise remains largely unchanged, namely that human beings, their values, law, and moral beliefs are viewed and valorized through the filters of culture, race, ethnicity, and nationality. All these latter terms shift in and out of contemporary usage. In my argument, they all share a common philosophical ontology concerning the human self.

Culture, nationality, and race directly overlap, up to the 1940s, particularly in the context of the language of the nation state. The central paradox in this setting is that, in large part due to fortuitous historical events, the argumentation concerning the importance of culture and nationality became deeply embedded in human rights discussion. This was either a direct imprimatur on the self-determining nation state or a parallel blessing on the virtues of national subcultures, cultural minorities, or indigenous groups. The latter development 'took off' particularly in the 1990s and was echoed both in human rights conventions and in the multicultural languages and laws of certain states. My argument here was that this whole development constituted a basic conundrum. When human rights were established, the central catalyst was genocide. Simply stated, genocide was largely a crime of the nation state itself. In fact, the state crime involved here was directly linked to the attempt to establish or purify a singular racial or national culture. Culture and race are the key interwoven values which the state was meant to secure, defend, or purify. Consequently, it followed that the movement towards cultural human rights and cultural citizenship was a deeply retrograde step, in both state practice and human rights. This was not however an argument against culture, per se; it was rather an argument which relegated its existence, in value terms, to one amongst many human interests. It was and is not of singular importance. It is one of the areas of human interest within the complex sphere of politics. Politics was seen as necessary for freedom of choice and human self-realization. However, when culture or nationality was allowed to totally overmaster politics, then they became in turn profoundly unstable and unpredictable for human rights.

The argument at this point embodied a further critique of both culture and nationality as a ground for human identity and value. The main argument one sees in cultural claims is the ontological focus on a singular notion of identity. The counter-argument was that, in fact, human identity is multifaceted, inconsistent, and unpredictable.[2] Central to any and all politics is choice. This, in turn, implies practical reasoning. This reasoning, as argued, is not determinative, but reflective and non-algorithmic. There is no end or perfect resolution to political dialogue. Practical reason and politics address difference, whereas cultural solitarism will often try to overcome difference to establish uniformities.

Contrary to the above argument, many scholars have, of course, suggested that we are 'thrown' into cultures and thus have 'no choice'. This argument is rejected.[3] Politics, as such, implies multiplicity. Practical reason, as part of politics, engages with this multiplicity in dialogue, via such idioms as law and democracy. Freedom is integral to this process in politics. It follows that an approach which emphasizes the singular importance of culture acts as an intellectual barrier to politics and human freedom. It is in this setting that severe doubts about the whole enterprise of cultural human rights were raised. The most consistent position would therefore be to retain and refocus on the debate between civil and social human rights, as the core of the human rights debate, and then to jettison the whole package of cultural claims. The latter can clearly be dealt with via the first two categories of right. Further, despite their appearance as conduits of human rights, cultural rights are, in reality, often a stalking horse for those who oppose human rights and wish to return human communities to disciplined singular associations defined in narrow terms by apolitical or anti-political cultures. This is a retrograde step for humanity which we should cast aside.

This leads to the final point. Culture needs to be able to incorporate the element of 'criticizing cultures' (amongst other objects). In fact, it is essential that cultures do practise self-criticism, from a civil perspective. No cultures are sacrosanct. Citizens should be able to experiment with cultures and their substantive content. Limits to experimentation become just another issue of judgement. The argument refocused, at this point, on the idea of disloyal loyalty or unpatriotic patriotism as revealing the character of deliberation and practical judgement contained within the citizenship of a civil state. This stance views politics as plurality. It follows that a commitment to politics in a civil state is an equal commitment to plurality and the ways to mediate and deliberate. This mediation involves a loyalty to argument and critical deliberation as intrinsic to both citizenship and politics. This idea of citizenship and critical deliberation is needed desperately, since cultural ideas and narrow ideologies—as we can see time and time again from twentieth-century ideological experience—can so easily be imposed via the national state (*Nationalstaat*). It is in the critical deliberative consciousness of civil citizens, who can resist both fear and corruption, that the human spirit can find resilient sanctuary. The task is therefore to reconceive human rights in a political frame. It is this setting in which humans will flourish or fail.

## ☐ NOTES

1.  The question could arise here of humanitarian intervention. My reading of this is fairly straightforward. If a grouping or comity of civil-inclined states decide to intervene, for reasons relating to the gross abuse of citizens, then an intervention will happen. The moral dimension is one minor factor. The decision to intervene is a political judgement. There is no algorithm for humanitarian intervention. There are criteria on which a judgement can be made. These criteria will sometimes acquire a more systematic character, but they will always change according to circumstances. Further the state, as such, being a mixture of elements, can and will judge actions for mixed motives at times. Thus, accurately accounting for a humanitarian intervention will always be a difficult and contingent process.

2.  It is not a national or culturalist view of the self which underpins this study, but rather a narrative self, which often embodies contradiction and idiosyncrasy.

3.  As Sen (2006, 4) notes, it is critically important 'to see the role of choice in determining the cogency and relevance of particular identities which are inescapably diverse'.

# ☐ BIBLIOGRAPHY

Alexander, F. S. and Witte, J. J. (eds) (1988) *The Weightier Matters of the Law: Essays on Law and Religion* (Atlanta, GA, Scholars Press).

Almond, B. (1993) 'Rights' in Peter Singer (ed) *A Companion to Ethics* (Oxford, Blackwell).

An-Na'im, Abdullah A. (1999) 'The Cultural Mediation of Human Rights: The Al-Arqam Case in Malaysia' in Bauer and Bell (eds) *The East Asian Challenge for Human Rights*.

Anglo, S. (2002) *Chinese Thought and Human Rights: A Cross-Cultural Inquiry* (Cambridge, Cambridge University Press).

Archard, D. (2000) 'Nationalism and Political Theory' in O'Sullivan (ed) *Political Theory in Transition*.

Arendt, H. (1958) *The Human Condition* (Chicago, IL and London, Chicago University Press).

——(1963) *On Revolution* (London, Faber and Faber).

——(1966) *The Origins of Totalitarianism* (New York, Harcourt and Brace).

——(1968) 'What Is Freedom?' in Arendt *Between Past and Future* (Middlesex, Penguin Books).

——(1992) *Eichmann in Jerusalem: A Report on the Banality of Evil* (Middlesex, Penguin Books).

Armstrong, A. H. and Markus, R. A. (1964) *Christian Faith and Greek Philosophy* (London, Darton, Longman and Todd).

Avineri, S. and De-Shalit, A. (eds) (1992) *Communitarianism and Individualism* (Oxford, Clarendon Press).

Baehr, Peter R. (2001) *Human Rights: Universality in Practice* (London, Palgrave).

Baker, A. R. H. and Biger, G. (1992) *Ideology and Landscape in Historical Perspective* (Cambridge, Cambridge University Press).

Ball, T., Farr, J., and Hanson, R. L. (eds) (1989) *Political Innovation and Conceptual Change* (Cambridge, Cambridge University Press).

Barker, E. (1927) *National Character and the Factors in Its Formation*, 4th edition 1947 (London, Methuen).

Barry, B. (2001) *Culture and Equality* (Cambridge, Polity).

Bartov, O. (2003) 'Seeking the Roots of Modern Genocide: On the Macro- and Microhistory of Mass Murder' in Gellately and Kiernan (eds) *The Specter of Genocide*.

Bauer, J. R. and Bell, D. (eds) (1999) *The East Asian Challenge for Human Rights* (Cambridge, Cambridge University Press).

Bauman, Z. (2002) 'Modernity and the Holocaust' in Hinton (ed) *Genocide*.

Beetham, D. (2003) *Democracy and Human Rights* (Cambridge, Polity).

Beiner, R. (1983) *Political Judgment* (London, Methuen).

——(ed) (1995) *Theorising Nationalism* (New York, State University of New York Press).

Bellamy, R. (2007) *Political Constitutionalism* (Cambridge, Cambridge University Press).

Bentham, J. (1970) *Introduction to the Principles of Morals and Legislation* (London, Methuen).

—— (2002) 'Anarchical Fallacies' in Waldron (ed) *Nonsense Upon Stilts.*

Benton, T. (1993) *Natural Relations: Ecology, Animal Rights and Social Justice* (London, Verso).

Berger, S., Donovan, M., and Passmore, K. (eds) (1999) *Writing National Histories* (London, Routledge).

Billig, M. (1995) *Banal Nationalism* (London, Sage).

Bloom, A. (1980) 'The Study of Texts' in M. Richter (ed) *Political Theory and Political Education* (Princeton, NJ, Princeton University Press).

—— (1987) *The Closing of the American Mind* (London, Penguin Books).

Blouet, B. W. (1987) *Halford Mackinder: A Biography* (College Station, TX, Texas A&M University).

Bluntschli, J. K. (1895) *The Theory of the State* (Kitchener, Ontario, Batoche Books).

Bobbio, N. (1996) *The Age of Rights* (Cambridge, Polity Press).

Boucher, D. (2009) *The Limits of Ethics in International Relations: Natural Law, Natural Rights and Human Rights in Transition* (Oxford, Oxford University Press).

Bowen, J. R. (2002) 'The Myth of Global Ethnic Conflict' in Hinton (ed) *Genocide.*

Bradley, F. H. (1962) *Ethical Studies* (Oxford, Clarendon Press).

Bramwell, A. (1989) *Ecology in the Twentieth Century* (London and New Haven, CT, Yale University Press).

Brett, Annabel S. (1997) *Liberty, Right and Nature: Individual Rights in Later Scholastic Thought* (Cambridge, Cambridge University Press).

Broomhall, B. (2004) *International Justice and the International Criminal Court: Between Sovereignty and the Rule of Law* (Oxford, Oxford University Press).

Brownlie, I. (1973) *Principles of Public International Law*, 2nd edition (Oxford, Clarendon Press).

Brundtland, G. (ed) (1987) *Our Common Future* (Oxford, Oxford University Press).

Burrow, J. W. (1966) *Evolution and Society: A Study in Victorian Social Theory* (Cambridge, Cambridge University Press).

Canovan, M. (1996) *Nationalism and Political Theory* (Cheltenham, Edward Elgar).

Castiglione, D. and Hampsher-Monk, I. (eds) (2001) *The History of Political Thought in National Context* (Cambridge, Cambridge University Press).

Chalk, F. and Jonassohn, K. (1990) *The History and Sociology of Genocide* (New Haven, CT, Yale University Press).

Chappell, T. D. J. (1995) *Understanding Human Goods* (Edinburgh, Edinburgh University Press).

Charney, I. (ed) (1999) *The Encyclopaedia of Genocide*, 2 volumes (Santa Barbara, CA, Denver, CO, and Oxford, ABC-CLIO).

Clapham, A. (2003) 'Issues of Complexity, Complicity and Complementarity from the Nuremberg Trials to the Dawn of the New International Criminal Court', in Sands (ed) *From Nuremberg to the Hague.*

Clark, R. W. (1984) *The Survival of Charles Darwin: A Biography of a Man and an Idea* (New York, Random House).

Constant, B. (1988) 'The Liberty of the Ancients Compared with that of the Moderns' in Constant, *Political Writings*, translated by B. Fontana (Cambridge, Cambridge University Press).

Cornish, P. J. (1996) 'Spanish Thomism and the American Indians: Vitoria and Las Casas on the Toleration of Cultural Difference' in Nederman and Laursen (eds) *Difference and Dissent*.

Cornu, G. (ed) (1996) *Vocabularie Juridique*, 6th edition (Paris, Presses Universitaires de France).

Craig, M. (1998) *Cultural Geography* (London and New York, Routledge).

Cranston, M. (1973) *What Are Human Rights?* (London, Bodley Head).

Crawford, J. (2006) *The Creation of State in International Law*, 2nd edition (Oxford, Clarendon Press).

Crospey, J. and Strauss, L. (ed) (1987) *History of Political Philosophy* (Chicago, IL, Chicago University Press).

D'Entrèves, A. P. (1977) *Natural Law*, 2nd edition (London, Hutchinson).

Dagger, R. (1989) 'Rights' in Ball, Farr, and Hanson (eds) *Political Innovation and Conceptual Change*.

Darby, D. (2009) *Rights Race and Recognition* (Cambridge, Cambridge University Press).

Darwin, C. (1958) *The Autobiography of Charles Darwin* (London, Collins).

——(1985) *On the Origin of Species by Means of Natural Selection: Or the Preservation of Favoured Races in the Struggle for Life* (London, Penguin Classics).

Davidson, S. (1993) *Human Rights* (Maidenhead, Open University Press).

Dickinson, R. E. (1969) *The Makers of Modern Geography* (London, Routledge and Kegan Paul).

Dietal, C. (1983) *Dictionary of Legal, Commercial and Political Terms* (New York, Matthew Binder and Con Inc).

Donnelly, J. (2002) *Universal Human Rights in Theory and Practice*, 2nd edition (New York, Cornell University Press).

Dworkin, R. (1977) *Taking Rights Seriously* (London, Duckworth).

——(1986) *Law's Empire* (London, Fontana).

Etzioni, A. (1997) *The New Golden Rule: Community and Morality in a Democratic Society* (London, Profile Books).

Fein, H. (2002) 'Genocide: A sociological perspective' in Hinton (ed) *Genocide*.

Feinberg, J. (1980) 'The Nature and Value of Rights' in Feinberg, *Rights, Justice and the Bounds of Liberty: Essays in Social Philosophy* (Princeton, NJ, Princeton University Press).

Ferry, L. and Renaut, A. (1992) *Political Philosophy 3: From the Rights of Man to the Republican Idea* (Chicago, IL, University of Chicago Press).

Fine, R. (2007) *Cosmopolitanism* (London, Routledge).

Finkelkraut, A. (2001) *In the Name of Humanity* (New York, Columbia University Press).

Finnis, J. (1980) *Natural Law and Natural Rights* (Oxford, Clarendon Press).

Flathman, R. E. (1976) *The Practice of Rights* (Cambridge, Cambridge University Press).

Franck, T. (1993) *Fairness in the International Legal and Institutional System* (Oxford, Oxford University Press).

Fraser, N. and Gordon, L. (1994) 'Civil Citizenship Against Social Citizenship? On the Ideology of Contract-Versus-Charity' in Steenbergen (ed) *The Condition of Citizenship*.

Freeden, M. (2005) 'What Should the "Political" in Political Theory Explore?' *Journal of Political Philosophy*, 13(2).

Freeman, M. (2002) *Human Rights* (Cambridge, Polity).

French, P. A. (1984) *Collective and Corporate Responsibility* (New York, Columbia University Press).

Gellately, R. and Kiernan, B. (eds) (2003) *The Specter of Genocide: Mass Murder in Historical Perspective* (Cambridge, Cambridge University Press).

Geuss, R. (2001) *History and Illusion in Politics* (Cambridge, Cambridge University Press).

Gewirth, A. (1978) *Reason and Morality* (Chicago, IL, Chicago University Press).

Glacken, C. (1967) *Traces on the Rhodian Shore* (Berkeley, CA, University of California Press).

Glass, B., Temkin, O., and Strauss, W. (eds) (1968) *Foreunners of Darwin 1845–1859* (Baltimore, MD, Johns Hopkins Press).

Glazer, N. (1999) 'What Can Europe Learn from North America? in Joppke and Lukes (eds) *Multicultural Questions*.

Glendon, M. A. (1991) *Rights Talk: The Impoverishment of Political Discourse* (New York, Free Press).

——(2001) *A World Made New: Eleanor Roosevelt and the Universal Declaration of Rights* (New York, Random House).

Golding, M. (1990) 'The Significance of Rights' *Philosophical Topics*, 18 (1).

Gray, C. S. (1996) 'The Debate on Geopolitics. The Continued Primacy of Geography' *Orbis*, Spring, 40.

Griffin, J. (2008) *On Human Rights* (Oxford, Oxford University Press).

Grisez, G. (1983) *The Way of the Lord Jesus,* Volume I: *Christian Moral Principles* (Chicago, IL, Franciscan Herald Press).

Gubernau, M. (1996) *Nationalisms: The Nation-State and Nationalism in the Twentieth Century* (Cambridge, Polity).

Gutman, A. (ed) (1994) *Multiculturalism: Examining the Politics of Recognition* (Princeton, NJ, Princeton University Press).

Haakonssen, K. (1985) 'Hugo Grotius and the History of Political Thought' in *Political Theory*, 13(2).

——(1991) 'From Natural Law to the Rights of Man: A European Perspective on American Debates' in Lacey and Haakonssen (eds) *The Culture of Rights*.

——(1996) *Natural Law and Moral Philosophy: From Grotius to the Scottish Enlightenment* (Cambridge, Cambridge University Press).

Habermas, J. (1998) *The Philosophical Discourse of Modernity* (Cambridge, Polity).

——(2001) 'Remarks on Legitimation through Human Rights' in Habermas, *The Postnational Constellation: Political Essays* (Cambridge, Polity).

Haddock, B. and Sutch, P. (eds) (2003) *Multiculturism, Identity and Rights* (London, Routledge).

Haeckel, E. (1917) 'Charles Darwin as an Anthropologist' in E. Haeckel, J. A. Thomson, and A. Weismann (eds) *Evolution in Modern Thought* (New York, Boni and Liverwight Inc).

——(1929) *The Riddle of the Universe* (London, Watts and Co.).

Hampshire, S. (1999) *Justice as Conflict* (London, Duckworth).

Hannaford, I. (1996) *Race: The History of an Idea* (Baltimore, MD, Johns Hopkins Press).

Hart, H. L. A. (1955) 'Are There Any Natural Rights' *Philosophical Review*, 64.

—— (1983) 'Bentham on Legal Rights' in Hart, *Essays on Bentham* (Oxford, Clarendon Press).

Hayek, F. A. (1982) *Law, Legislation and Liberty* (London, Routledge).

Heater, D. (1990) *Citizenship: The Civic Ideal in World History, Politics and Education* (London, Longman).

Hegel, G. W. F. (1971) *The Philosophy of Right* (Oxford, Oxford University Press).

Herbert, Gary B. (2002) *The Philosophical History of Rights* (New Brunswick, NJ and London, Transaction Publishers).

Hinton, A. L. (ed) (2002) *Genocide: An Anthropological Reader* (Oxford, Blackwell).

Hirst, P. (2000) 'Globalization, the Nation-state and Political Theory' in O'Sullivan (ed) *Political Theory in Transition*.

Hobbes, T. (1968) *Leviathan* (Middlesex, Penguin Books).

Hohfeld, W. (1946) *Fundamental Legal Conceptions as Applied in Judicial Reasoning* (New Haven, CT, Yale University Press).

Honneth, A. (1996) *The Struggle for Recognition: The Moral Grammar of Social Conflicts* (Cambridge, MA, MIT Press).

—— (2002) 'Grounding Recognition: A Rejoinder to Critical Questions' *Inquiry*, 45(4).

—— (2004) 'Recognition and Justice: Outline of a Plural Theory of Justice' *Acta Sociologica*, 47(4).

Horkheimer, M. (1972) *Critical Theory* (New York, Seabury Press).

—— (1996) 'Reason Against Itself: Some Remarks on Enlightenment' in Schmidt (ed) *What Is Enlightenment?*

Hueck, I. J. (2001) 'The Discipline of the History of International Law—New trends and Methods on the History of International Law' *Journal of the History of International Law*, 3.

Hull, I. V. (2003) 'Military Culture and the Production of "Final Solutions" in the Colonies: The Example of Wilhelminian Germany' in Gellately and Kiernan (eds) *The Specter of Genocide.*

Hume, D. (1966) *Hume on Religion* (London, Collins).

Hunt, L. (2007) *Inventing Human Rights: A History* (New York, W.W. Norton & Co).

Ignatieff, M. (1995) 'The Myth of Citizenship' in Beiner (ed) *Theorizing Citizenship.*

—— (2003) *Human Rights as Politics and Idolatry*, edited by Amy Gutman (Princeton, NJ, Princeton University Press).

Ingram, A. (1994) *The Political Theory of Rights* (Oxford, Clarendon Press).

International Commission on Intervention and State Sovereignty (2001) *Responsibility to Protect: Report of the International Commission on Intervention and State Sovereignty* (Ottawa, International Development Research Centre).

Ivison, D., Patton, P., and Sanders, W. (eds) (2000) *Political Theory the Rights of Indigenous Peoples* (Cambridge, Cambridge University Press).

Jackson-Preece, J. (2003) 'Human Rights and Cultural Pluralism' in Lyons and Mayall (eds) *International Human Rights.*

Jellinek, G. (1901) *The Declaration of the Rights of Man and of Citizens: A Contribution to Modern Constitutional History* (New York, Henry Holt and Company).

Jenning, R. and Watts, A. (eds) (2008) *Oppenheim's International Law*, 9th edition (Oxford, Oxford University Press).

Jhering, R. von (1915) *The Struggle for Law* (Chicago, IL, Callaghan and Company).

Jones, P. (1994) *Rights* (London, Macmillan).

Joppke, C. and Lukes, S. (eds) (1999) *Multicultural Questions* (Oxford, Oxford University Press).

Jørgensen, N. H. B. (2000) *The Responsibility of States for International Crimes* (Oxford, Oxford University Press).

Kamenka, E. and Tay, A. (eds) (1978) *Human Rights* (London, Arnold).

Kant, I. (1965) *The Metaphysical Elements of Justice*, Part 1 of the *Metaphysics of Morals*, translated by John Ladd (New York, Bobb-Merrill).

Kiernan, B. (1996) *The Pol Pot Regime: Race, Power and Genocide Under the Khmer Rouge 1975–1979* (New Haven, CT, Yale University Press).

Kohn, H. (1945) *The Idea of Nationalism: A Study in Its Origins and Background* (New York, Macmillan).

Koskenniemi, M. (1990) 'The Politics of International Law' *European Journal of International Law*, 1(1).

—— (2001) *The Gentle Civilizer of Nations: The Rise and Fall of International Law* (Cambridge, Cambridge University Press).

—— (2006) *From Apology to Utopia: The Structure of International Legal Argument* (Cambridge, Cambridge University Press).

Kramer, M. H. (1998) 'Rights Without Trimmings' in Kramer, Simmonds, and Steiner (eds) *A Debate Over Rights*.

—— Simmonds, N. E., and Steiner, H. (eds) (1998) *A Debate Over Rights: Philosophical Enquiries* (Oxford, Clarendon Press).

Kuper, L.(1981) *Genocide: Its Political Use in the Twentieth Century* (New Haven, CT, Yale University Press).

—— (2002) 'Genocide: Its Political Use in the Twentieth Century' in Hinton (ed) *Genocide*.

Kymlicka, W. (1991) *Liberalism, Community and Culture* (Oxford, Clarendon Press).

—— (ed) (1995) *The Rights of Minority Cultures* (Oxford, Clarendon Press).

—— (1999) 'Comments on Shacher and Spinner-Halev: An Update from the Multicultural Wars' in Joppke and Lukes (eds) *Multicultural Questions*.

Lacey, M. J. and Haakonssen, K. (eds) (1991) *The Culture of Rights* (Cambridge, Cambridge University Press).

Langlois, A. (2001) *The Politics of Justice and Human Rights: Southeast Asia and Universality Theory* (Cambridge, Cambridge University Press).

Las Casas, B. de (1971) *In Defense of the Indians* (DeKalb, IL, Northern Illinois University Press).

—— (1992) *The Devastation of the Indies: A Brief Account* (Baltimore, MD, Johns Hopkins Press).

Lauterpacht, H. (1947) *Recognition in International Law* (Cambridge, Cambridge University Press).

—— (1950) *International Law and Human Rights* (London, Stevens).

Lemkin, R. (1944) *Axis Rule in Occupied Europe* (Washington, DC, Carnegie Endowment for International Peace).

—— (2002) 'Genocide' in Hinton (ed) *Genocide*.

Lenoir, T. (1980) 'Kant, Blumenbach, and Vital Materialism in German Biology' *Isis*, 71 (256).

Locke, J. (1965) *Two Treatise of Government*, edited by Peter Laslett (New York, Mentor Books).

——(1969) *An Essay of Human Understanding*, 5th edition (London, Collins).

*Lotus*, The Case of the S.S. (1927) Judgment no. 9, Permanent Court of International Justice, Ser. A, No. 10 – http://www.worldcourts.com/pcij/eng/decisions/1927.09.07_lotus/

Lovejoy, A. O. (1968) 'The Argument for Organic Evolution before the Origin of Species 1830– 1858' in Glass, Temkin, and Strauss (eds) *Forerunners of Darwin*.

Lowenthal, D. (1985) *The Past Is a Foreign Country* (Cambridge, Cambridge University Press).

Lyons, D. (1969) 'Rights, Claimants, and Beneficiaries' *American Philosophical Quarterly*, 6(3).

Lyons, G. M. and Mayall, J. (eds) (2003) *International Human Rights in the 21st Century: Protecting the Rights of Groups* (Lanham, MD, Boulder, CO, New York and Oxford, Rowman and Littlefield Publishers Inc).

McCloskey, H. J. (1965) 'Rights' *Philosophical Quarterly*, 15(59).

——(1976) 'Rights – Some Conceptual Issues' *Australasian Journal of Philosophy*, 54.

MacCormick, N. (1982) *Legal Rights and Social Democracy: Essays in Legal and Political Philosophy* (Oxford, Clarendon Press).

McGrade, A. S. (1974) *The Political Thought of William of Ockham* (Cambridge, Cambridge University Press).

——(1980) 'Ockham and the Birth of Individual Rights' in P. Lineham and B. Tierney (eds) *Authority and Power: Studies in Medieval Law and Thought Presented to Walter Ullman on His Seventieth Birthday* (Cambridge, Cambridge University Press).

MacIntyre, A. (1981) *After Virtue* (London, Duckworth).

——(1990) *Three Rival Versions of Moral Enquiry* (London, Duckworth).

Mackie, J. L. (1998) 'Can There Be a Rights-Based Moral Theory?' in J. Rachels (ed) *Ethical Theory*.

McKim, R. and McMahan, J. (eds) (1997) *The Morality of Nationalism* (Oxford, Oxford University Press).

Margalit, G. and Raz, J. (1995) 'National Self-Determination' in Kymlicka (ed) *The Rights of Minority Cultures*.

Maritain, J. (1944) *The Rights of Man and Natural Law* (London, Geoffrey Bless).

Markell, P. (2000) 'Making Affect Safe for Democracy? On "Constitutional Patriotism"' *Political Theory*, 28(1).

Marshall, T. H. (1950) *Citizenship and Social Class* (Cambridge, Cambridge University Press).

Martin, R. (1993) *A System of Rights* (Oxford, Clarendon Press).

——(2003) 'Rights and Human Rights' in Haddock and Sutch (eds) *Multiculturism, Identity and Rights*.

Marx, K. (1972) *Early Texts* (Oxford, Blackwell).

Mauss, M. (1985) 'A Category of the Human Mind: The Notion of Person: The Notion of Self' in M. Carruthers, S. Collins, and L. Steven (eds) *The Category of the Person* (Cambridge, Cambridge University Press).

May, L. (2005) *Crimes Against Humanity: A Normative Account* (Cambridge, Cambridge University Press).

Mayr, E. (1991) *One Long Argument: Charles Darwin and the Genesis of Modern Evolutionary Thought* (Middlesex, Penguin Books).

Meinig, D. W. (1979) *The Interpretation of Ordinary Landscapes* (Oxford, Oxford University Press).

Melden, A. I. (ed) (1970) *Human Rights* (Belmont, CA, Wadsworth Publishing House).

Meyer, H. C.(1955) *MittelEuropa in German Thought and Action 1815–1945* (The Hague, Martinus Nijhoff).

Michelman, F. (1996) 'Parsing "A Right to Have Rights"' *Constellations*, 3(2).

Midgley, M. (1985) *Evolution as Religion: Strange Hopes and Stranger Fears* (New York and London, Methuen).

Mill, J. S. (1962) *Utilitarianism, Liberty and Representative Government* (London, Dent).

Miller, D. (1994) 'The Nation-State: A Modest Defense' in C. Brown (ed) *Political Restructuring in Europe* (London, Routledge).

——(1995) *On Nationality* (Oxford, Clarendon Press).

Milne, A. J. M. (1986) *Human Rights and Human Diversity: As Essay in the Philosophy of Human Rights* (New York, State University of New York Press).

Moore, J. (1979) *The Post-Darwinian Controversies: A Study of the Protestant Struggle to Come to Terms With Darwin in Great Britain and America 1870–1900* (Cambridge, Cambridge University Press).

Morsink, J. (2000) *The Universal Declaration of Human Rights* (Philadelphia, PA, University of Pennsylvania University Press).

Mulhall, S. and Swift, S. (1996) *Liberals and Communitarians* (Oxford, Blackwell).

Nash, R. (2001) *Wilderness and the American Mind* (New Haven, CT, Yale University Press).

Nederman, C. J. and Laursen, J. C. (eds) (1996) *Difference and Dissent: Theories of Toleration in Medieval and Early Modern Europe* (New York, Rowman and Littlefield).

Nickel, J. W. (1987) *Making Sense of Human Rights: Philosophical Reflections on the Universal Declaration of Human Rights* (London and Berkeley, CA, University of California Press).

Nozick, R. (1974) *Anarchy, State and Utopia* (Oxford, Blackwell).

O'Sullivan, N. (ed) (2000) *Political Theory in Transition* (London, Routledge).

Oakeshott, M. (1975) *On Human Conduct* (Oxford, Clarendon Press).

——(1991) *Rationalism in Politics and Other Essays* (Indianapolis, IN, Liberty Press).

Orend, B. (2002) *Human Rights: Concepts and Context* (Toronto, Broadview Press).

Overy, R. (2003) 'The Nuremberg Trials: International Law in the Making' in Sands (ed) *From Nuremberg to the Hague*.

Pagden, A. (1986) *The Fall of Natural Man* (Cambridge, Cambridge University Press).

——(ed) (1987) *The Languages of Political Theory in Early Modern Europe* (Cambridge, Cambridge University Press).

——(2003) 'Human Rights, Natural Rights, and Europe's Imperial Legacy' *Political Theory*, 31(2).

Paley, W. (1802) *Natural Theology or Evidences of the Existence and Attributes of the Deity* (London, J. Faulder).

Pellet, A. (1999) 'Can a State Commit a Crime? Definitely, Yes!' *European Journal of International Law*, 10(2).

Philp, M. (2007) *Political Conduct* (Cambridge, MA, Harvard University Press).

Pogge, T. (2002) *World Poverty and Human Rights* (Cambridge, Polity).

Rachels, J. (1991) *Created from Animals: The Moral Implications of Darwinism* (Oxford, Oxford University Press).

——(ed) (1998) *Ethical Theory* (Oxford, Oxford University Press).

Ratzel, F. (1896) *History of Mankind* (London, Macmillan and Co).

——(1996) 'The Territorial Growth of State' in J. Agnew, D. N. Livingstone, and A. Rogers (eds) *Human Geography: An Essential Anthology* (Oxford, Blackwell).

Rawls, J. (1999) *Law of Peoples* (Cambridge, MA, Harvard University Press).

Ricoeur, P. (1994) *Oneself as Another* (Chicago, IL, Chicago University Press).

——(2000) *The Just* (Chicago, IL, Chicago University Press).

Ritchie, D. G. (1952) *Natural Rights: A Criticism of Some Political and Ethical Conceptions* (London, George Allen and Unwin, originally published in 1894).

Ross, W. D. (1930) *The Right and the Good* (Oxford, Oxford University Press).

Rothbard, M. (1978) *For a New Liberty: The Libertarian Manifesto* (New York, Macmillan).

Rubinstein, N. (1987) 'The History of the Word *Politicus* in Early Modern Europe' in Pagden (ed) *The Languages of Political Theory*.

Runciman, D. (2003) 'The Concept of the State: the Sovereignty of a Fiction' in Strath and Skinner (eds) *States and Citizens*.

Salter, M. (1999) 'Neo-Fascist Legal Theory on Trial: An Interpretation of Carl Schmitt's Defense at Nuremberg from the Perspective of Franz Neumann's Critical Theory of Law' *Res Publica*, 5(2).

Sands, P. (ed) *From Nuremberg to the Hague: The Future of International Criminal Justice* (Cambridge, Cambridge University Press).

Sarat, A. and Kearns, T. R. (eds) (2001) *Human Rights Concept, Contests, Contingencies* (Ann Arbor, MI, University of Michigan Press).

Sauer, C. (1929) 'The Morphology of Landscape' in Sauer (ed) *The University of California Publications in Geography* (1919–28), 2(2).

——(1962) *Land and Life: A Selection From the Writings of Carl Sauer*, edited by J. Leighley (London and Berkeley, CA, University of California Press).

Sawyers, R. (ed) (1982) *The Concise German Dictionary* (London, Harrap).

Schapiro, I. (1986) *The Evolution of Rights in Liberal Theory* (Cambridge, Cambridge University Press).

Schmidt, J. (ed) (1996) *What Is Enlightenment? Eighteenth Century Answers and Twentieth Century Questions* (Berkeley, CA and London, University of California Press).

Schmitt, C. (1996) *The Idea of the Political* (Chicago, IL, Chicago University Press).

Scruton, R. (1990) 'In Defense of the Nation' in Scruton, *The Philosopher on Dover Beach* (London, Carcanet Press).

——(1999) 'First Person Plural' in Beiner (ed) *Theorizing Nationalism*.

Sellars, K. (2002) *The Rise and Rise of Human Rights* (Phoenix Mill, UK, Sutton Publishing).

Semelin, J. (2003) 'Analysis of a Mass Crime: Ethnic Cleansing in the Former Yugoslavia, 1991–1999' in Gellately and Kiernan (eds) *The Specter of Genocide*.

Semple, E. C. (1911) *Influences of Geographic Environment: On the Basis of Ratzel's System of Anthropo-Geography* (New York, Henry Holt and Co, reprinted in 1947).

Sen, A. (1999) *Development as Freedom* (Oxford, Oxford University Press).

——(2006) *Identity and Violence: The Illusion of Destiny* (London, Penguin).

Sharma, A. (2005) *Hinduism and Human Rights* (New Delhi, Oxford University Press).

Shue, H. (1980) *Basic Rights: Subsistence, Affluence and US Foreign Policy* (Princeton, NJ, Princeton University Press).

Simhony, A. and Weinstein, D. (eds) (2001) *The New Liberalism: Reconciling Liberty and Community* (Cambridge, Cambridge University Press).

Simmonds, N. E. (1998) 'Rights at the Cutting Edge' in Kramer, Simmonds, and Steiner (eds) *A Debate Over Rights*.

Smith, A. (1971) *Theories of Nationalism* (London and New York, Torchbook Library).

—— (1991) *National Identity* (London, Penguin).

Smith, R. K. M. (2003) *Textbook on International Human Rights* (Oxford, Oxford University Press).

Soffer, R. (1994) *Discipline and Power: The University and the Making of an English Elite 1870–1930* (Stanford, Stanford University Press).

Spinoza, B. de (1951) *A Theologico-Political Treatise, A Political Treatise* (New York, Dover Publications).

Steenbergen, B. van (ed) (1994) *The Condition of Citizenship* (London, Sage Publications).

Steiner, H. (1998) 'Working Rights' in Kramer, Simmonds, and Steiner (eds) *A Debate Over Rights*.

Strath, B. and Skinner, Q. (eds) *States and Citizens: History, Theory and Prospects* (Cambridge, Cambridge University Press).

Strauss, L. (1952) *The Political Philosophy of Hobbes: Its Basis and Its Genesis* (Chicago, IL, Chicago University Press).

—— (1953) *Natural Right and History* (Chicago, IL, Chicago University Press).

—— (1977) *City of Man* (Chicago, IL, Chicago University Press).

Tamir, Y. (1993) *Liberal Nationalism* (Princeton, NJ, Princeton University Press).

Taylor, C. (1989) *Sources of the Self: The Making of Modern Identity* (Cambridge, Cambridge University Press).

—— (1994) 'The Politics of Recognition' in Gutman (ed) *Multiculturalism*.

—— (1999) 'Conditions of an Unforced Consensus on Human Rights' in Bauer and Bell (eds) *The East Asian Challenge for Human Rights*.

—— (2004) *Modern Social Imaginaries* (Durham, NC, and London, Duke University Press).

Taylor, K. (1998) 'From Physical Determinism to Cultural Construct: Shifting Discourses in Reading Landscape as History and Ideology' in J. Willis, P. Goad, and A. Hutson (eds) *Firm(ness) Commodity DE-light?: Questioning the Canons: Proceedings of the Fifteenth Annual Conference of the Society of Architectural Historians, Australia and New Zealand* (Melbourne, University of Melbourne Press).

Tierney, B. (1983) 'Tuck on Rights: Some Medieval Problems' *History of Political Thought*, 4(3).

—— (1988) 'Villey, Ockham and the Origin of Individual Rights' in Alexander and Witte (eds) *The Weightier Matters of the Law*.

—— (1997) *The Idea of Natural Rights: Studies on Natural Rights, Natural Law and Church Law 1150–1625* (Emory University Studies in Law and Religion, Atlanta, GA, Scholars Press).

Tomuschat, C. (2003) *Human Rights: Between Idealism and Realism* (Oxford, Oxford University Press).

Tuck, R. (1979) *Natural Rights Theories* (Cambridge, Cambridge University Press).

—— (1987) 'The "Modern" Theory of Natural Law' in Pagden (ed) *The Languages of Political Theory*.

Uekert, B. K. (1995) *Rivers of Blood: A Comparative Study of Government Massacre* (Westport, CT, Greenwood Publishing Group).

UNESCO (1949) *Human Rights: Comments and Interpretations. A Symposium edited by UNESCO* (New York, UNESCO).

Villey, M. (1961) "Abrége du droit natural classique' *Archives de philosophie du droit*, 6.

—— (1962) *Leçons d'Histoire de la Philosophie du Droit* (Paris, Dalloz).

—— (1964) 'La genése du droit subjectif chez Guillaume d'Occam' *Archives de philosophie de droit*, 9.

Vincent, A. (1987) *Theories of State* (Oxford, Blackwell).

—— (1989) 'Can Groups Be Persons' *Review of Metaphysics*, 42(4).

—— (1996) 'Kant's Humanity' *Political Theory Newsletter*, 7(2).

—— (2002) *Nationalism and Particularity* (Cambridge, Cambridge University Press).

—— (2004) *The Nature of Political Theory* (Oxford, Oxford University Press).

—— (2009) *Modern Political Ideologies*, 3rd edition (Oxford, Wiley-Blackwell).

Vincent, R. J. (1986) *Human Rights and International Relations* (Cambridge, Cambridge University Press).

Vizard, P. (2006) *Poverty and Human Rights: Sen's 'Capability Perspective' Explored* (Oxford, Oxford University Press).

Waldron, J. (1993) *Liberal Rights: Collected Papers 1981–1991* (Cambridge, Cambridge University Press).

—— (ed) (2002) *Nonsense Upon Stilts: Bentham, Burke and Marx on the Rights of Man* (London, Routledge).

Wanklyn, H. (1961) *Friedrich Ratzel: A Biographical Memoir and Bibliography* (Cambridge, Cambridge University Press).

Weber, M. (1970) 'Politics as a Vocation' in H. H. Gerth and C. Wright Mills (eds) *From Max Weber: Essays in Sociology* (London, Routledge and Kegan Paul).

Weitz, E. D. (2003*a*) *A Century of Genocide: Utopias of Race and Nation* (Princeton, NJ, Princeton University Press).

—— (2003*b*) 'The Modernity of Genocides: War, Race, and Revolution in the Twentieth Century' in Gellately and Kiernan (eds) *The Specter of Genocide*.

Wellman, C.(1975) 'Upholding Legal Rights' *Ethics*, 86(1).

—— (1999) *The Proliferation of Rights* (London and New York, Westview Press).

Wendt, A. (2004) 'The State as Person in International Theory' *Review of International Studies*, 30(2).

White, A. R. (1985) *Rights* (Oxford, Clarendon Press).

Wight, C. (2004) 'State Agency: Social Action Without Human Activity?' *Review of International Studies*, 30(2).

Wilks, M. (1963) *The Problem of Sovereignty in the Later Middle Ages* (Cambridge, Cambridge University Press).

Young-Bruehl, E. (1982) *Hannah Arendt: For Love of the World* (New Haven, CT, Yale University Press).

# □ INDEX